Hollywood

Warts 'N' All

Volume 1

by

Alan Royle

Hollywood

Warts 'N' All

Volume 1

An anthology of scandal, trivia and anecdotes about the first one hundred years of American cinema. For more than a decade the author has gleaned thousands of items from hundreds of films, biographies and movie publications in general, focusing on the bizarre, the scandalous and the controversial aspects of Tinseltown and, in particular, the private and public lives of the stars themselves. As the title implies, it is a no-holds-barred portrait of an industry notorious for its promiscuity, eccentricities and outrageous behavior.

In these pages the reader will find tales of 'the casting couch', racial discrimination, criminal activity, drug and alcohol abuse, shady deals and cover-ups. Myths and legends are exposed and war records examined. Accidental deaths, suicides and murders are scrutinized as well as censorship wrangles, ruined careers and sexual preferences.

On the set clashes, feuds and insults, romances and affairs, marriages and divorces are all depicted as they happened. Editing and continuity gaffs, humorous exchanges, mishaps and technical problems, tricks of the trade and casting anomalies are also featured. For movies based on actual events, the author has drawn comparisons between Hollywood's, quite often, ludicrous interpretations and historical fact.

Over five hundred films are featured alphabetically, from *A Bill of Divorcement* to *Zulu*, from the industry's humble beginnings in 1905 to the present day. This book is for movie buffs intrigued by the unusual and seamier side of the business, for those more interested in what makes their idols tick than in their actual performances on the screen.

Alan Royle

Royle Publishing

Melbourne Australia

Introduction

When we were kids back in the early fifties, before the advent of television in Western Australia, the cinema was the best place to learn about the outside world, about values and about right and wrong. Every Friday night or Saturday morning we absorbed it all and believed it all. Heroic fanfares for the US cavalry and menacing drums for the Indians told us, unequivocally, that the only good Indian was a dead Indian. We watched America single-handedly win the war a hundred times. And we believed it all. Such was the influence of the movies on the average Aussie kid in the decade after World War ll.

Now, we know differently. For the most part, the cavalry were anything but heroes, and Amerindians got a raw deal and are probably still getting it. And if any nation can lay claim to winning the war it should probably be Russia since ninety-three out of every hundred Germans who died in that conflict did so on Russian soil. But in those halcyon days John Wayne, Roy Rogers, Gary Cooper and Audie Murphy were our idols. Between them they managed to save the frontier or the world at least once a week, twice if you counted Saturday matinees.

'Coops' was our first movie hero, but he had some stiff competition. Roy Rogers was King of the Cowboys and we even liked The Durango Kid, although none of us could figure out just what the hell a 'Durango' was. Of course, life wasn't all westerns and war. We loved Jerry Lewis and couldn't stand Dean Martin because he always brought the fun to a screeching halt by singing one of his tuneless love songs to some girl who had no right to be in the picture in the first place. Audie Murphy was cool because he was about our size and even more baby-faced than we were. Let's face it, if Audie could become a movie star so could we. We thought the Three Stooges were hilarious and Laurel and Hardy were boring. When you're under ten you like your comedy up-front and obvious. The only female we could barely tolerate was Roy's wife Dale Evans because she could ride a horse.

The stars always seemed larger than life then, so much better than we mere mortals. But were they? Odd rumors began circulating at school that Rock Hudson, for instance, preferred boys to girls. Ridiculous. Someone said Errol Flynn preyed upon teenagers. Others said Coops was as thick as a brick, and Audie a gun freak who ran with gangsters. The most disturbing rumor of all accused John Wayne of avoiding fighting in the war. Well, we weren't buying *that* one for a minute. We were very young, you see.

As more and more tales surfaced, however, it gradually dawned on us that these people we idolized might not be perfect after all. With that in mind, I began to read whatever I could about the industry and its people, to find out for myself what was fact and what was fiction. For decades I devoured hundreds of biographies, authorized and unauthorized, fan magazines, annuals, critiques and reviews. In short, any book I could find on films and film stars. And, of course, I watched a truckload of movies. And that brings me to this volume.

Here you will find the distilled product of all that paraphernalia I digested over three decades. If I read something that surprised me or roused my curiosity I put it into a temporary file. There it remained until I had uncovered at least *two* corroborating, reliable sources to support it. Then I moved it into the 'facts substantiated' file, from which I drew the data for this and my second book, *Movies Based on True Stories* (2015).

Hollywood Warts 'n' All contains anecdotes going as far back as 1905. You will read about production problems and censorship, devious producers and directors, behind the scenes studio conniving, dubious and contrived publicity, outlandish salaries and 'perks', and so on. But above all the focus is on the movie stars themselves, their private lives, the scandals, gossip, war records and more. Everything I discovered about the business and its people that might interest the average movie buff is contained within the pages of this book. Movie stars pay a hefty price for their celebrity status. Being rich and famous sounds great, but living their lives in the public eye is the price they pay for all that glamour and glory. It must be very difficult to exist like that, when every look or word is captured, analyzed and regurgitated in the tabloids, more often than not from a viewpoint that is anything but compassionate or understanding.

I have chosen to present the information in the form of an alphabetical list of movies, rather than as a list of the stars themselves. When the reader sits down to watch a film, he or she can quickly glance through to see if there is any data on the picture in question. I have used the titles to introduce anecdotes about the players in that movie, as well as any tales related to the production itself. I have also taken the liberty of including the occasional personal comment here and there. No doubt, it will quickly become apparent to the reader that I am no theatre critic and know next to nothing about the technical side of filmmaking. I plead guilty on both counts. This work is not about the techniques of filmmaking. Neither is it about acting or directing. It is about the people involved in these processes. I am old-fashioned when it comes to movies and their purpose. I prefer to be enchanted, thrilled, saddened or amazed, than have some political or social message pounded into my brain. Neither do I relish being served up a 'kitchen sink' portion of reality. There is enough of that outside the theatre. And I especially do not want to be splattered with blood, drowned in violence or buried in expletives. All these exist in abundance outside as well. Having said that, I make no apologies for the use of expletives in this volume, albeit only in the context of direct quotes. Most movie stars, for reasons known only to them, seem to find it fashionable to use the same group of adjectives as a matter of course, and have done so since the industry began. The only difference between today's stars and those of yesteryear is that, now, they get to use them on-screen as well as off.

In this book I have tried to remain as objective as possible, but it is a 'warts and all' account of life in Hollywood, so I have spared no one from the truth. For the most part I have let their own words and deeds, their own recollections, depict them as they really are, multifarious personalities in an extraordinary business unlike any other. We need our heroes to be fallible, if for no other reason than to enable us to live with our own deficiencies, our own limitations. This book will illustrate that nothing and nobody is perfect, least of all those imbued with the aura of perfection.

At the end of this book you will find lists of all those performers who have died from other than natural causes. Considering we are dealing with a peaceable industry here and not espionage or formula one racing, the lists are surprisingly long. On a less morbid note, I have also thrown in my fifty personal favorite movies of all time. (The wonderful thing about writing a book is you can do things like that if you want to). I always enjoy reading other writers' 'favorites' lists, just so I can compare them with mine. You might care to do the same. Theatre critics can simply skip that bit. *Citizen Kane*, for instance, does not rate with me, so there goes my credibility in the eyes of the 'experts'. Nevertheless, these are the films I most enjoy because they *entertain* me the most. And after all, that is why most of us go to the cinema in the first place.

Alan Royle

Contents

Bachelor Party (1984)
Backfire (1987)
Bad & the Beautiful, The (1952)
Basic Instinct (1992)
Batman (1989)
Battle Cry (1955)
Battle Hymn (1957)
Bear, The (1984)
Best Years of our Lives, The (1946)
Beau Geste (1939)
Becket (1964)
Beetle Juice (1988)
'Bend Of The River' (1952)
Ben-Hur (1925)
Ben-Hur (1959)
Berserk (1967)
B.F.'s Daughter (1948)
Beverly Hills Ninja (1997)
The Bible – In the Beginning (1966)
The Big Steal (1949)
The Big Trail (1930)
Billy Budd (1962)
Birth of a Nation, The (1915)
Bitter Tea of General Yen, The (1933)
Blackboard Jungle (1955)
Blade Runner (1982)
Blue Angel, The (1930)
Blue Dahlia, The (1946)
Blue Hawaii (1961)
Blues Brothers, The (1980)
Bonnie & Clyde (1967)
Born Free (1966)
Born Yesterday (1950)
Boston Strangler, The (1968)
Boy on a Dolphin (1957)
Bridge on the River Kwai, The (1957)
Buck Privates (1941)
Bugsy (1991)
Bus Stop (1956)
Butch Cassidy & the Sundance Kid (1969)
Butterfield 8 (1960)
Cabaret (1972)
Cactus Flower (1969)
Caddyshack (1980)

Calamity Jane (1953)
California Split (1974)
California Suite (1978)
Call of the Wild (1935)
Camelot (1967)
Camille (1936)
Cannon for Cordoba (1970)
Can't Stop the Music (1986)
Captain Blood (1935)
Captain Newman MD (1963)
Captains Courageous (1937)
Carmen Jones (1954)
Carpetbaggers, The (1964)
Carry on Cleo (1965)
Carry on Doctor (1967)
Casablanca (1942)
Cat Ballou (1965)
Champion (1949)
Charade (1963)
Charge of the Light Brigade, The (1935)
Chariots of Fire (1981)
Charlie Chan at the Olympics (1937)
Chicago (2002)
China Syndrome, The (1979)
Chinatown (1974)
Citizen Kane (1941)
City Lights (1931)
Cleopatra (1963)
Colditz Story, The (1955)
Comancheros, The (1961)
Coming Home (1978)
Conqueror, The (1956)
Coogan's Bluff (1968)
Counterfeit Traitor, The (1961)
Country Girl, The (1954)
Court Jester, The (1956)
Court Martial of Billy Mitchell, The (1955)
Crow, The (1994)
Cruel Sea, The (1953)
Crusades, The (1935)
Cry Baby Killer, The (1958)
Curse of the Pink Panther (1983)
Cutthroat Island (1995)
Daddy's Gone A-Hunting (1969)

Dam Busters, The (1954)
Dances with Wolves (1990)
Dangerous Liaisons (1988)
Dangerous When Wet (1953)
Dark Victory (1939)
Dawn Patrol, The (1938)
Dead Calm (1989)
Death Takes a Holiday (1934)
Defiant Ones, The (1958)
Desperately Seeking Susan (1985)
Destination Tokyo (1943)
Destry Rides Again (1939)
Dial 'M' for Murder (1954)
Die Hard (1988)
Dirty Dancing (1987)
Doctor Zhivago (1965)
Dodge City (1939)
Double Indemnity (1944)
Down Argentine Way (1940)
Down Periscope (1996)
Driving Miss Daisy (1989)
Dr. Kildare's Crisis (1940)
Dr No (1962)
Duck Soup (1933)
Duel in the Sun (1946)
Dumbo (1941)
East of Eden (1955)
East of Java (1935)
East of Sumatra (1953)
East Side, West Side (1949)
Easy Rider (1969)
Ecstasy (1932)
Edge of Darkness (1943)
Egyptian, The (1954)
El Dorado (1967)
Enigma: Crack the Code (2001)
Erin Brockovich (2000)
Escape from Fort Bravo (1953)
ET – The Extra-Terrestrial (1982)
Exorcist, The (1973)
Far Country, The (1954)
Farewell, My Concubine (1993)
Farmer's Daughter, The (1947)
Fastest Guitar Alive, The (1968)

Ferris Bueller's Day Off (1986)
55 Days at Peking (1963)
Firehouse (1987)
First Blood (1982)
Five Fingers (1952)
Flaming Star (1960)
Flesh and the Devil (1926)
Flight of the Phoenix, The (1965)
Flintstones, The (1994)
Flying Down to Rio (1933)
Foreign Correspondent (1940)
Forever Amber (1947)
Fort Apache (1948)
48 Hours (1982)
For Whom the Bell Tolls (1943)
Four Feathers, The (1939)
Four Jills in a Jeep (1944)
4 Weddings & a Funeral (1993)
Francis Goes to West Point (1952)
From Here to Eternity (1953)
From Russia with Love (1963)
Full Monty, The (1997)
Funny Girl (1968)
Furies, The (1950)
Gallipoli (1981)
Game of Death (1978)
Gangs of New York (2002)
Gaslight (1944)
Genevieve (1953)
Genghis Khan (1965)
Gentlemen Prefer Blondes (1953)
Get Shorty (1995)
Ghost (1990)
Giant (1956)
G I Blues (1960)
Gilda (1946)
Girl Interrupted (1999)
Girl in the Red Velvet Swing, The (1955)
Gladiator (2000)
Godfather, The (1972)
Godfather Pt III, The (1990)
Going My Way (1944)
Golden Earrings (1947)
Goldfinger (1964)

Gone with the Wind (1939)
Good News (1947)
Grease (1978)
Grapes of Wrath, The (1940)
Great Escape, The (1963)
Green Dolphin Street (1947)
Greystoke: The Legend of Tarzan, Lord of the Apes (1984)
Guess Who's Coming to Dinner? (1967)
Gunfight at the OK Corral (1957)
Guns of Navarone, The (1961)
Guys and Dolls (1955)
Harry & Tonto (1974)
Harry Potter & the Chamber of Secrets (2002)
Heaven Knows, Mr. Allison (1957)
Heaven's Gate (1980)
Hello Dolly (1969)
Here We Go Round the Mulberry Bush (1967)
Hey, Let's Twist (1961)
High Noon (1952)
High Society (1956)
Hook (1992)
Hop-along-Cassidy (1935)
Horse Feathers (1932)
Horse Soldiers, The (1959)
Houdini (1953)
House of Cards (1968)
How the West Was Won (1962)
How to Marry a Millionaire (1953)
Hurricane, The (1937)
I am a Fugitive from a Chain Gang (1932)
I Claudius (1937)
Imitation of Life (1959)
Indiana Jones & the Last Crusade (1989)
In Old Chicago (1938)
In the Name of the Father (1993)
Intolerance (1916)
In Which We Serve (1942)
Irma La Douce (1963)
Isadora (1969)
Island in the Sun (1957)
It Happened at the World's Fair (1963)
It Happened One Night (1934)
It's a Mad, Mad, Mad, Mad World (1963)
It's a Pleasure (1945)

Ivanhoe (1952)
I Wanted Wings (1941)
Jailhouse Rock (1957)
Jaws (1975)
Jaws – the Revenge (1987)
Jazz Singer, The (1927)
Jeremiah Johnson (1972)
Jesse James (1939)
Jezebel (1938)
John & Yoko: A Love Story (1985)
Johnny Belinda (1948)
Johnny Eager (1941)
Johnny Guitar (1954)
Joy in the Morning (1965)
Jurassic Park (1993)
Karate Kid, The (1984)
Kind Hearts & Coronets (1949)
King Kong (1933)
King of Kings, The (1927)
King's Row (1942)
Krakatoa: East of Java (1968)
Kramer vs Kramer (1979)
Krays, The (1990)
Kremlin Letter, The (1970)
Ladies' Man, The (1961)
Lady and the Tramp (1955)
Lady Sings the Blues (1972)
Land of the Pharaohs, The (1955)
Lassie Come Home (1943)
Last of the Mohicans, The (1992)
Laura (1944)
Lavender Hill Mob, The (1952)
Lawrence of Arabia (1962)
Libeled Lady (1936)
Lifeboat (1944)
Life of Brian (1979)
Lili (1953)
Limelight (1952)
Lion King, The (1994)
Lipstick (1976)
Little Big Man (1970)
Little Miss Marker (1934)
Little Women (1933)
Lives of a Bengal Lancer (1934)

Lodger, The (1925)
Lolita (1962)
Longest Day, The (1962)
Long Gray Line, The (1955)
Long, Long Trailer, The (1954)
Lost Weekend, The (1945)
Lost World, The (1960)
Love Affair (1994)
Love at First Bite (1979)
Love Happy (1950)
Love is a Many Splendored Thing (1955)
Lovely to Look at (1952)
Loving You (1957)
Love Me Tender (1956)
Ma & Pa Kettle (1949)
Madness of King George, The (1994)
Magnificent Obsession (1954)
Magnificent Seven, The (1960)
Magnum Force (1973)
Male and Female (1919)
Maltese Falcon, The (1941)
Mame (1974)
Man Bait (1926)
Manhattan Melodrama (1934)
Man Who Loved Cat Dancing, The (1973)
Man Who Shot Liberty Valence, The (1962)
Man Who Would be King, The (1975)
Man with the Golden Arm, The (1955)
Man with the Golden Gun, The (1974)
Marathon Man (1976)
Marnie (1964)
Mary Poppins (1964)
Maytime (1937)
McLintock! (1963)
Mexican Spitfire (1939)
Mildred Pierce (1945)
Million Dollar Mermaid (1952)
Mogambo (1953)
Money for Nothing (1993)
Monster's Ball (2001)
Moon-Spinners, The (1964)
Moonstruck (1987)
Mortal Storm, The (1940)
Mrs. Miniver (1942)

Mr. Smith Goes to Washington (1939)
Mummy, The (1999)
Murder by Death (1976)
Murders in the Rue Morgue (1932)
Mutiny on the Bounty (1935)
My Best Friend's Wedding (1997)
My Cousin Vinny (1992)
My Fair Lady (1964)
My Forbidden Past (1951)
My Geisha (1962)
My Man Godfrey (1936)
My Own Private Idaho (1991)
Myra Breckinridge (1970)
Nanook of the North (1921)
National Velvet (1944)
Neptune's Daughter (1949)
Network (1976)
Never-ending Story II: The Next Chapter (1990)
Niagara (1953)
Night and Day (1946)
Night of the Hunter, The (1955)
Night Shift (1982)
Noah's Ark (1929)
None but the Brave (1964)
North by Northwest (1959)
North to Alaska (1960)
Not as a Stranger (1955)
Nothing but Trouble (1991)
Ocean's Eleven (1960)
Oh, God! (1977)
One-Eyed Jacks (1961)
One Flew Over the Cuckoo's Nest (1975)
One Hundred Men and a Girl (1937)
On Golden Pond (1981)
On Her Majesty's Secret Service (1969)
Only the Valiant (1951)
On the Beach (1959)
On the Waterfront (1954)
'OUR GANG' Series of shorts (1930s and 40s)
Paint Your Wagon (1969)
Paleface, The (1948)
Pandora's Box (1928)
Papillon (1973)
Paradise Garden (1917)

Parent Trap, The (1961)
Party, The (1968)
Patton (1970)
Peg 'O' My Heart (1932)
Perfect (1985)
Pete Smith Presents (1935 – 1950s)
Peyton Place (1957)
Picnic at Hanging Rock (1975)
Places in the Heart (1984)
Plank, The (1967)
Pocketful of Miracles (1961)
Poltergeist (1982)
Postman Always Rings Twice, The (1981)
Pretty Woman (1990)
Pride and Prejudice (1940)
Pride of the Yankees, The (1942)
Professionals, The (1966)
Psycho (1960)
Pt 109 (1963)
Public Enemy, The (1931)
Pulp Fiction (1994)
Quiet Man, The (1952)
Quo Vadis? (1925)
Raiders of the Lost Ark (1981)
Raintree County (1957)
Random Harvest (1942)
Rasputin & the Empress (1932)
Raw Wind in Eden (1958)
Reach For the Sky (1956)
Rear Window (1954)
Rebecca (1940)
Rebel Without a Cause (1955)
Red Dust (1932)
Red River (1948)
Reluctant Debutante, The (1958)
Remember My Name (1978)
Riders of the Purple Sage (1925)
Riders of the Whistling Pines (1949)
Right Stuff, The (1983)
Rio Bravo (1959)
River of no Return (1954)
Road to Singapore (1940)
Rock! Rock! Rock! (1956)
Rocky (1976)

Romancing the Stone (1984)
Roman Holiday (1953)
Romeo & Juliet (1936)
Romeo Must Die (2000)
Romper Stomper (1992)
Rope (1948)
Rose, The (1979)
Ruthless People (1986)
Ryan's Daughter (1970)
Saboteur (1942)
Sabrina (1954)
Sailor Beware (1951)
Saint, The (1997)
Salome (1918)
Salome (1923)
Samson and Delilah (1949)
Sanders of the River (1935)
Sands of Iwo Jima (1949)
San Francisco (1936)
Saratoga Trunk (1945)
Save the Tiger (1973)
Scalp Hunters, The (1968)
Scaramouche (1952)
Scared Stiff (1953)
Schindler's List (1993)
Seabiscuit (2004)
Searchers, The (1956)
Send Me No Flowers (1964)
Sense & Sensibility (1995)
Serenade (1956)
Sergeant York (1941)
7th Heaven (1927)
Seven Year Itch, The (1955)
Sextette (1978)
Sgt. Bilko (1996)
Shampoo (1975)
Shane (1953)
Sheik, The (1921)
She Loves Me Not (1934)
Sheriff of Fractured Jaw, The (1959)
Shining, The (1980)
Ship of Fools (1965)
Showboat (1951)
Sincerely Yours (1955)

Since You Went Away (1944)
Singin' in the Rain (1952)
Six Days, Seven Nights (1998)
Smokey & the Bandit (1977)
Snow White & the 7 Dwarfs (1937)
Somebody Up There Likes Me (1956)
Some Like it Hot (1959)
Something's Got to Give (1962)
Song of Old Wyoming (1945)
Son of Ali Baba (1952)
Son of Captain Blood, The (1962)
Son of Lassie (1945)
Son of the Sheik (1926)
Sons of the Pioneers (1942)
Sound of Music, The (1965)
South Pacific (1958)
Spartacus (1960)
Spice World (1997)
Stalag 17 (1953)
Stand by Me (1986)
Star! (1968)
Star 80 (1983)
Star Trek: The Motion Picture (1979)
Star Wars (1977)
St Elmo's Fire (1985)
Stormy Weather (1943)
Story of G I Joe, The (1945)
Sunset Boulevard (1950)
Sun Valley Serenade (1941)
Superman, the Movie (1978)
Support Your Local Sheriff (1969)
Swarm, The (1978)
Sweet Smell of Success (1957)
Swiss Family Robinson (1960)
Take Me Out to the Ball Game (1949)
Taming of the Shrew, The (1929)
Tap Roots (1948)
Tarzan Movies (1932-42)
Taxi Driver (1976)
Teacher's Pet (1958)
Ten Commandments, The (1956)
Terminator 2: Judgment Day (1991)
Terms of Endearment (1983)
Tess (1979)

That Forsyte Woman (1949)
Thelma & Louise (1991)
They Died With Their Boots On (1941)
They Shoot Horses, Don't They? (1969)
They Were Expendable (1945)
They Won't Forget (1937)
Thirteen Women (1932)
This is the Army (1943)
Those Magnificent Men in Their Flying Machines (1965)
Three Coins in the Fountain (1954)
Three Men and a Baby (1987)
Tillie and Gus (1933)
Tillie's Punctured Romance (1914)
Toast of New York, The (1937)
To Catch a Thief (1955)
To Have and Have Not (1944)
To Hell and Back (1955)
Tom Jones (1963)
Top Gun (1986)
Track of Thunder (1968)
Treasure Island (1950)
Trip to Bountiful, The (1985)
Trouble With Harry, The (1955)
Truth About Cats & Dogs, The (1996)
True Grit (1969)
Twilight Zone – the Movie (1982)
Two-Faced Woman (1941)
Unconquered (1947)
Underwater (1955)
Untouchables, The (1987)
U. S. Marshals (1998)
Valley of the Dolls (1967)
Virginia City (1940)
Wake up and Dream (1934)
War and Peace (1956)
War of the Worlds (2005)
Waterloo Bridge (1940)
Way Down East (1920)
Westerner, The (1940)
West of Cimarron (1942)
West Side Story (1961)
When Harry Met Sally...(1989)
Where the Boys Are (1963)
Wild in the Country (1961)

APPENDIX

SELECTED BIBLIOGRAPHY

ABOUT THE AUTHOR

The Films & Stars

A Bill of Divorcement (1932)

Katharine Hepburn made her debut in this film alongside screen icon John Barrymore. As he was prone to do with his leading ladies, the lecherous Barrymore exposed himself to her at the first opportunity. Hepburn treated the incident with the contempt it deserved and made no secret of her loathing for the legendary star. Clark Gable, aware he had tried the same thing on his wife Carole Lombard some years earlier, also detested him.

John Barrymore (1882-1942)

Known relationships:

Astor, Mary
Bankhead, Tallulah
Eagels, Jeanne
Hopper, Hedda
Lombard, Carole
Nesbit, Evelyn

Married:

Dolores Costello
Blanche Oelrichs & 2 others.

Barrymore was in San Francisco and lucky to survive when the great earthquake struck in 1905.

In 1920 he invited Mary Astor's mother to have tea on his porch while he seduced the fourteen year-old Mary in his living room. He had few qualms about indulging in under-aged sexual liaisons, possibly because of his own experiences as a youth. His stepmother seduced him when he was fifteen. A monumental egotist, he once proclaimed, 'my only regret in the theatre is that I could never sit out front and watch me'.

Tales of his outrageous conduct are legendary. One day, a hopelessly drunk Barrymore staggered into a ladies toilet and was confronted by a frosty-faced matron who ordered him out. 'This is for women!' she sternly informed him. With considerable flourish the nefarious actor whipped out his penis, waved it at her and roared, 'and so, madam, is this!'

On another occasion an obviously needy woman arrived at the stage door and offered him sex if he would agree to help her out. After accommodating the destitute young lady he magnanimously handed her free tickets to his show. When the desperate woman rejected them, explaining she needed bread, not theatre tickets, he callously told her, 'madam, you want bread – go fuck a baker!'

A hopeless alcoholic, he once went on an extended cruise in an attempt to dry out, but wound up drinking anything and everything he could lay his hands on that contained even a semblance of alcohol. This included mouthwash, perfume, kerosene and Spirit of Camphor. In his final years on the stage he often staggered, hopelessly drunk, through his performances oblivious to catcalls from disgruntled patrons.

During one production he brought gasps from the audience when he halted in mid-sentence and relieved himself in a flowerpot!

His second wife was actress turned author Blanche Oelrichs, a rather bizarre individual who called herself Michael Strange and preferred to dress in men's clothing. The last of his marriages was to a girl who interviewed him for a high school magazine. She was not yet twenty when they eventually tied the knot. By then Barrymore was a ravaged fifty-four year-old who looked much older.

Even in death 'the Great Profile' as he was once known, got to perform one last time. His good friend Errol Flynn arrived home to find the dead actor propped up in a chair in his living room, cigar in hand and clutching a drink. Flynn took one look and bolted from the house. Director Raoul Walsh and a few of his cronies had stolen Barrymore's corpse from the morgue for one final party, or so the story goes. Walsh had told his butler, 'Alex, Mr. Barrymore didn't die. He's drunk. Help me carry him into the house'. Errol refused to be a part of the unsavory proceedings so Walsh reluctantly took the corpse back to the morgue. Blake Edwards used the incident for a scene in his 1981 film *S.O.B.*

Barrymore's son John Drew was a drug addict who sold his father's prize gun collection to support his habit. Later still, in need of somewhere to sleep, he sold his parents' love letters. Current star Drew Barrymore is his daughter.

Katharine Hepburn (1907-2003)

Known relationships with women:

Colbert, Claudette
Garbo, Greta
Harding, Laura
Holliday, Judy
Landi, Elissa
Loring, Jane
Page, Bettie
Steele, Suzanne

Known relationships with men:

Anderson, Eddie 'Rochester'
Cotten, Joseph
Fairbanks Jr, Douglas
Farrow, John
Ford, John
Hayward, Leland
Hughes, Howard
Mackenna, Kenneth
McCrea, Joel
Ryan, Robert
Stewart, James
Tracy, Spencer

If we chose to believe Hollywood ballyhoo, Spencer Tracy was the love of her life, but that depends on what is meant by 'love'. They were certainly great friends for 25 years, but did that friendship include intimacy? Maybe not. During her long life Kate dropped scores of hints about her sexuality in interview after interview, yet she remained a sexual anomaly until the day she died. It has since been shown that of her many, many lovers, few were males. Her revisionist biographer, William J Mann, went as far as to say she 'tried sex once, but didn't like it', so it is entirely possible she refrained from the act pretty much altogether.

Throughout their 25 years of friendship she and Tracy never once lived together. She had her place and he lived with his wife or in hotel rooms when on one of his many drunken binges. Even when they dined together, Kate would later leave with one of her girlfriends. 'I wouldn't give you 10 men for any one woman', she said. 'All men are poops'. It is no surprise, therefore, to discover that all her boyfriends were bisexual, including Howard Hughes, director John Ford, and Tracy. Tracy was rumored to turn tricks for male clients at gay director George Cukor's mansion from time to time. Other close friends of Kate's included Cukor and Cary Grant. She met Hughes through their mutual 'friend' Grant.

Kate went out with a lot of male stars and directors, but how many of them slept with her is total conjecture. She was with Douglas Fairbanks Junior for a while, but left him in 1930 for a four-year romance with her agent Leland Hayward. She was with Hughes from 1935 to 1938, had a three month fling with Jimmy Stewart (1938-9), and (believe it or not), enjoyed a 'relationship' with black comedian Eddie 'Rochester' Anderson from 1932 to 1935. What kind of relationship that was is anyone's guess. Throughout her life she only ever lived with women or lived alone. Never with a man.

Close friend Margaret Sullavan referred to her once as, 'that dikey bitch'. 'The most completely honest woman I've ever met', said Cary Grant of Kate, although his interpretation of the concept of 'honesty' was decidedly different from mine I might say. Others found her much less impressive. At RKO Studios her peers referred to her as 'Katharine of Arrogance'. Lucille

Ball commented dryly, 'she wasn't really standoffish. She ignored everybody equally'. Her ability as an actress has also been questioned. Renowned wit Dorothy Parker commented on her performance in *The Lake*: 'She runs the gamut of emotions from A to B'. Thirty-five years later Kate described the comment as 'extremely accurate and funny'. 'Cold sober, I find myself fascinating', said Kate somewhat revealingly. 'I'm a legend because I've survived over a long period of time and still seem to be master of my fate, whereas Garbo has always been a mysterious sailboat who disappeared over the horizon the moment she felt she couldn't cope'. Hepburn also made an interesting assessment of her profession. 'Acting is the most minor of gifts', she said. 'After all, Shirley Temple could do it when she was four'.

Adventures of Don Juan (1948)

Errol Flynn (1909-1959)

Known relationships with women:

Bankhead, Tallulah
Bennett, Joan
Bishop, Julie
Christian, Linda
De Carlo, Yvonne
De Havilland, Olivia
Del Rio, Dolores
Dietrich, Marlene
Domergue, Faith
Duke, Doris

Ekberg, Anita
Garson, Greer
Hayworth, Rita
Hill, Virginia
Hutton, Barbara
Lake, Veronica
Lamarr, Hedy
Landis, Carole
Lupino, Ida
Methot, Mayo
Peron, Eva
Sheridan, Ann
Turner, Lana
Vanderbilt, Gloria
Velez, Lupe
Winters, Shelley

Known relationships with men:

Alexander, Ross
Diaz, Appolonia
Goulding, Edmund
Hughes, Howard
Lundigan, William
Mead, William
Niven, David
Power, Tyrone

Married:

Lili Damita
Nora Eddington
Patrice Wymore

In the final scene of this film, the pretty young woman in the carriage who asks Don Juan for directions is Nora Eddington. She was Errol Flynn's real life wife at the time, and their marriage was unconventional to say the least. She had insisted they marry after Errol allegedly raped her while he was high on cocaine. Pregnant at seventeen (and a devout Catholic), she refused to abort the child, so he reluctantly tied the knot. The last thing he needed was another paternity issue, having just avoided prison on a charge of statutory rape involving two under-age girls. He and Nora stayed together for a few years with Flynn *permitting* her to live in a separate wing of his home, as long as she did not interfere in his sex life in any way.

Errol kept two prostitutes on the set of this film for its duration, their sole purpose being to fellate him during breaks and at the end of the day's shooting. He boasted to his cronies how he would 'just lie there reading the trade papers while they worked on me'. By the time he made *Adventures of Don Juan* his drug taking was completely out of control, although he refused to admit it. 'I'll shoot up with anything', he said, 'and I know I'll never become addicted because I do it only for fun'. Just a couple of years earlier he had contemplated suicide, sitting up for two full days and nights with a loaded revolver in his hand, drinking himself into a stupor, but he could not go through with it. His so-called friends Bruce Cabot and Freddie McEvoy saw him with the gun during that time, but made no move to stop him.

Off-screen, actor Robert Douglas and Flynn became fast friends. At Errol's mansion they would reputedly watch lesbians in action while masturbating each other. As he readily admitted to anyone who would listen, he enjoyed all kinds of sex with all kinds of partners. Nothing was considered to be out of bounds or beneath his dignity. Douglas, too, was avidly interested in Errol's collection of pornographic films, especially those involving men and women performing with animals.

Adventures of Robin Hood, the (1938)

The studio's first choice to play Robin Hood in this film was James Cagney, believe it or not, but he withdrew over a dispute about money. And we are all truly grateful. Robert Donat was next but he was too ill to accept. Douglas Fairbanks Junior was also approached. 'I felt that it would be sacrilege to copy my father's kind of silent picture action', he said, when he too declined.

The picture was shot entirely in southern California, which may surprise some people. In fact, David Niven, who was wanted for the role of Will Scarlet, was unavailable because he was off holidaying - *in Britain*. The site chosen as Sherwood Forest was Bidwell Park in Chico, California, famous for containing the world's largest living oak tree, the Sir Joseph Hooker, a 92 foot giant with a branch-spread of 149 feet and a trunk that measured 28 feet in circumference. Just why it was considered necessary to attach hanging vines to it and other trees in the movie is a mystery, as they are not normally found in England anyway. By the way, the palomino horse ridden by Olivia De Havilland later became Roy Rogers' steed Trigger. Stuntmen were paid $150 per shot if they agreed to have arrows fired into them by expert bowman Howard Hill.

British character actor, chubby-faced Herbert Mundin, plays Much the Miller. Tragically, in less than twelve months of completing the picture he would die in a car crash at the age of forty.

Olivia De Havilland (1916 -)

Known relationships:

Aherne, Brian
Brent, George
Feldman, Charles
Hughes, Howard
Huston, John
Meredith, Burgess
Stewart, James
Stover, Frederick
Tone, Franchot
Tracy, Spencer

Aherne would later marry Olivia's sister Joan Fontaine. I have not included Errol Flynn in her 'Known relationships' because she has steadfastly refused to acknowledge her co-star of all those films as being one of her intimates, even though she said many times that she had a crush on him back in the thirties and forties. Were they ever lovers? Who knows?

Clearly a much tougher lady than she appeared on screen, it was De Havilland who took on the studios' dictatorial rules regarding breaches of contract and secured a Supreme Court ruling in her favor. Until then, studios deliberately gave actors assignments they knew would be rejected, enabling them to impose lengthy extensions to their contracts as punishment. Some performers found their seven-year contracts extended to as long as fifteen years because of this process. De Havilland changed all that and consequently incurred the wrath of the studios for the rest of her career.

The rivalry between Olivia and her sister Joan Fontaine was very real and appears to have been instigated and continued by Olivia, the older of the two siblings. Since childhood the outgoing, vibrant Olivia bullied and demeaned the more reserved and unsure Joan. Olivia was first to gain an acting contract and first to become a star, but Joan married first, had a child first and *unforgivably* won an Oscar first. She also died first – in 2013, aged 96. Olivia (as of May 2015) is still battling on.

Her first big break came in 1934 in the much-publicized Max Reinhardt production of *The Dream* at the Hollywood Bowl. It was without doubt the event of the season. She was involved initially as an 'understudy to an understudy' for the part of Hermia. Gloria Stuart (the same Gloria Stuart who would be nominated for *Titanic* 64 years later) was all set to play Hermia when both she and her understudy were called away to appear in movies.

This left the door ajar for Olivia. She went on and was instantly recognized as a real talent by Hal Wallis of Warner Brothers who signed her up at once. Stuart caught her first performance as Hermia and went back stage to offer congratulations. She claims Olivia turned her back on her and the two women did not speak to each other again for twenty years. Bette Davis had already been selected to play Hermia in the movie, but she was having one of her fights with the studio, so lady luck smiled again and, again, the part went to Olivia.

Flynn was born in Hobart, Tasmania in 1909. His mother Marelle Young was directly descended from a midshipman aboard *HMS Bounty* named Richmond Young. Hollywood would typically claim Errol was descended from Fletcher Christian but that was not so. His father was a marine biologist, happy to pursue his vocation while Marelle led the high life with a string of wealthy lovers in Paris. Errol never forgave her for it. The man who literally had hundreds of affairs in his own lifetime could not condone any semblance of such behavior in his mother.

At seventeen Errol joined the Constabulary in New Guinea, but was soon dismissed because of his scandalous affairs with several married women.

He then tried his hand at gold prospecting in the interior, and when that failed, he 'black birded' for a slaving outfit. It was during these operations he shot and killed a native while his party was under attack. Charged with murder, he was released partly on the grounds of self-defense, but primarily because the victim's body could not be produced.

While in New Guinea he contracted malaria and also suffered his first bout of gonorrhea. Malaria and a touch of tuberculosis would later keep him out of World War Two. While still in New Guinea he landed an acting job with an Australian crew making *In the Wake of the Bounty* in 1933. Errol's performance was very ordinary and he was paid just six pounds for his three weeks on the film.

It was around this time that he became friends with a rather shady German of dubious political persuasion. Stories of Errol being a Nazi stem from this, but appear completely groundless. The FBI investigated him at length and found nothing solid. In fact, the head of British Intelligence, William Stephenson, dismissed the claims as well, as did Errol's ex-wife Nora Eddington. She maintained he thoroughly detested Nazis, although he genuinely thought they would probably win the war.

But back to the 1930s. Irving Asher, the director of the British division of Warner Brothers, met Errol in London and was impressed by his looks.

He signed the young Australian to a contract without even checking to see if he could act or not, then booked him passage to America to try out for the movies. While crossing the Atlantic Errol introduced himself to film star Lily Damita, a bi-sexual fireball he would later marry. She was eight years his senior, but subtracted them on the wedding certificate, making both parties twenty-six years old at the time of the union.

She was a resident of the notorious Garden of Alla, a three and a half acre complex on Sunset Boulevard founded by the exotic Crimean-born artiste Alla Nazimova.

The Garden was a hotbed of lesbian activity and home to the 'Sewing Circle', a euphemism for the Hollywood lesbian fraternity. It was here Flynn first met David Niven, another recent arrival in the movie colony. The two men became close friends. Marlene Dietrich told writer David Bret she was sure they were lovers as well. 'Carole Lombard was a very good friend of mine', said Dietrich, 'who spent much of her time with these twilight boys.

One morning, when she went over to Niven's place, she found him in bed with Errol Flynn. They maintained they were not gay in the conventional sense, but just fooling around for fun. None of us thought it such a big deal, though. Lots of actors slept with each other if there were no women around'. Considering this was wartime, it is stretching credulity to the limit to have us believe there was a shortage of available women. Those young men who never made it into uniform must have felt like they were rabbits in a carrot patch.

Besides, we are talking about movie stars Flynn and Niven here. A shortage of women was a problem they never encountered, war or no war.

Lombard was the undisputed doyenne of the lavender set, and believed the two men shared many male lovers at Niven's apartment, among them actor William Lundigan. Errol was certainly intimate with the young star, but there is no evidence that Niven was. When he was sober Flynn confided in Lombard that Lundigan was as good in bed 'as any woman he had ever been with'.

With several of his anti-Semitic pals Flynn formed a carousing group dubbed 'the Olympiads'.

Alan Hale Senior and Patrick Knowles were regulars, while John Barrymore, W C Fields, Bruce Cabot and assorted writers dropped in from time to time. Edward G Robinson was refused admission because he was Jewish. Errol's known anti-Semitism has often been misinterpreted as pro-Nazism.

He once philosophized on his attitude to women in general. 'From the time I began to have women on the assembly-line basis, I discovered that the only thing you need, want, or should have, is the absolutely physical. No mind at all.

A woman's *mind* will get in the way'.

His home was installed with secret two-way mirrors to enable him and his cronies to observe the bedroom and bathroom antics of his invited guests. They were usually well known Hollywood couples. He would often hire a large group of prostitutes to entertain his single male guests. His own personal favorite arrangement was to have sex with a very young girl while observing two men copulating via his two-way mirrors.

The house was also furnished with lounge chairs from which erect rubber penises sprung as unwary victims sat in them. To open his liquor cabinet it was necessary for someone (preferably a female guest) to squeeze the testicles of a china bull that adorned it.

Errol once estimated he spent between 12,000 and 14,000 nights of his life indulging in sexual activities of some kind or other. Reliable sources number a four-year affair with Argentina's Evita Peron as one of his exploits. He also regularly visited his Acapulco beach boy lover Apollonia Diaz.

It was far less dangerous, he said, to pursue under-age boys and girls in Mexico than risk exposure chasing them in

Hollywood. Before arriving at that conclusion, however, he often indulged in the highly risky practice of picking up young girls at Hollywood high schools and taking them back to his home for sex.

Apart from his well-publicized trial for the statutory rape of two teenage girls aboard his yacht during the Second World War, he was also charged with 'libidinous behavior' with a seventeen year-old girl in Monaco a few years later.

He wriggled out of both charges. He met Nora Eddington when she was serving behind a counter selling chewing gum and cigarettes in the lobby of City Hall *during his trial for statutory rape*. He arranged to see her during the trial, although he was careful to treat her with kid gloves until its outcome was decided. After all, she was the daughter of a captain in the Los Angeles County Sheriff's office! When nineteen year-old Nora refused to sleep with him he filled himself with cocaine and alcohol and summarily raped her. She was a devout Catholic and would not abort the resultant pregnancy, so he reluctantly agreed to marry her.

Friends aboard his yacht the *Sirocco* were awarded silver lapel pins depicting an erect penis and testicles and emblazoned with the letters 'FFF'. The initials stood for 'Flynn's Flying Fuckers'. The yacht was the scene of regular sex contests as he and his buddies seduced the numerous young women brought aboard. On one notorious occasion he invited the cast and crew of a film he was making to a 'feast' aboard *Sirocco*. Such an invitation coming from Flynn usually meant an orgy, so his guests were greatly surprised to find no women when they arrived. At a signal from their host, however, a number of girls hidden under the large banquet table undid the men's flies and fellated them.

Incidentally, the tall tale that Errol was possessed of an outrageously huge penis is not true. Earl

Conrad, his biographer, described it as in no way special or out of the ordinary, and he saw it many times as did any friend of the actor. Errol was always walking about naked (especially around the pool) and cared nothing about it. Over the years he became addicted to morphine and suffered regularly from gonorrhea, brittle bones and piles. On the set he would suck on oranges injected with vodka, a trick taught him by actress Ann Sheridan. He put cocaine in his water bottle and used an eyedropper to insert it in his sinuses. He was also known to put a pinch of cocaine on the end of his penis as an aphrodisiac.

When he married Patrice Wymore, the bride was doubtless unaware that *all four* of her bridesmaids had slept with the groom while they were extras on one of his movies *Adventures of Captain Fabian*. Even in his final years he remained obsessed with sex. Spending his time in Jamaica, he would arrange for a half a dozen or more prostitutes to be presented each day at noon for his inspection. He would then select one or more for a brief twenty-minute interlude. Generally they were very young, sometimes only thirteen or fourteen years old. His 'secretary' at that time was a thirteen year-old girl named Dhondi whom he would also service each day.

In the marketplace he would pay young girls to lift their tops and reveal their breasts to him, and then offer those he fancied extra money to come to his bed.

In those final years creditors came after him from all directions as he sunk farther into debt. None of this overly bothered him until Bruce Cabot, the man he once described as 'my brother in all but name', sued him for $17,000 salary owing on a Flynn-produced movie he had worked in. Cabot, who had dined with Flynn just hours before, also threatened to expose details of Errol's sex-life to the media unless he was paid. 'I could have killed the bastard!' said Errol. 'I *should* have killed him".

But in the end he rang Cabot and forgave him, as was often his way.

When Errol died in Toronto, Canada, he was with Beverly Aadland, a girl of fifteen who had been his lover for more than a year. His body was so ravaged by alcohol and drugs it resembled that of a man of sixty-five or seventy years of age. It is believed he intended to marry the girl as soon as she came of age. Her parents attempted to sue his estate for $5 million dollars, claiming the actor had corrupted their daughter - but there was nothing left to get. He had spent nearly everything. Six bottles of whiskey went into his coffin with him. When a reporter once asked him what he would like written on his tombstone the typical but unpublished reply was, 'If it moved, Flynn fucked it!'

African Queen, The (1951)

Although this film was made on location in the Congo, the classic scene where Humphrey Bogart drags the boat through the reeds was shot in a huge water tank at Pinewood Studios in London. Robert Morley who plays Hepburn's brother never even left England during the entire shoot. All his scenes were completed in the London studio. In some long shots you can detect an unconvincing stand-in waddling about in his place.

Bogart did not think much of Katharine Hepburn as a person. 'How affected can you get in the middle of Africa?' he complained. 'Katharine Hepburn used to say everything was 'divine'. The god-dam stinking natives were 'divine'. Oh, what a divine native, she would say.

Oh, what a divine pile of manure'.

Hollywood gatecrasher and conman Sam Spiegel produced *The African Queen*. To avoid having to pay several outstanding debts he used the name S P Eagle, which appears in the credits. When he wrote a letter to Darryl Zanuck, asking if he would be interested in distributing the picture he even signed it, 'S P Eagle'. Zanuck responded in the negative, signing his reply, 'Z. A. Nuck'.

For most of his career Bogart made fun of the Oscars – until he won one himself for this picture. During a heated debate about acting with Richard Burton, he suddenly got up and stormed out of his lounge-room. A moment later he returned and thumped down his Oscar on the table and growled, 'you were saying...?

Agony & the Ecstasy, The (1965)

Historically, the casting of one of the leads in this movie leaves a lot to be desired. The real Michelangelo was a homosexual dwarf, yet he is portrayed by, of all people, the statuesque and utterly heterosexual Charlton Heston. Truman Capote would have been the perfect choice, but then, who's going to pay good money to watch him in anything?

A Guy Named Joe (1943)

Spencer Tracy (1900-1967)

Known relationships with women:

Bennett, Joan
Bergman, Ingrid
Crawford, Joan
Davis, Nancy
De Havilland, Olivia
Fontaine, Joan
Goddard, Paulette
Hepburn, Katharine
Kelly, Grace
Lamarr, Hedy
Landis, Carole
Loy, Myrna
Luce, Claire
Tierney, Gene
Young, Loretta

Known relationships with men:

Derek, John

Tracy was a sour alcoholic much of the time with an eye for the ladies, although away from the public eye he was known to be bi-sexual, as mentioned previously here. During love scenes in this film with Irene Dunne he would whisper graphic details in her ear of his intentions, should he ever get her alone. The prim and proper Miss Dunne threatened to walk off the picture unless he desisted. After Van Johnson was badly disfigured in a car crash during the production, L B Mayer agreed to put the picture on hold until he recovered, but only if Tracy would lay off his leading lady. Tracy deigned to put Johnson's needs before his own and the problem was resolved. The picture made Van a star. Incidentally, Keenan Wynne, who was reputedly Johnson's lover, received superficial injuries in the same crash.

A Hard Day's Night (1964)

George Harrison's future wife Patti Boyd has a miniscule role here. She is the girl who sits next to Paul McCartney on the train and sings on 'I Should Have Known Better'. She and George married in 1966. Two years after they divorced in 1977 she wed rock guitarist Eric Clapton. Look for young Phil Collins (wearing spectacles) in the audience at the television theatre.

The Beatles' manager Brian Epstein made a staggering blunder when he signed a deal with an American firm named Seltaeb ('Beatles' backwards) in the year this picture was released.

He naively handed over 90% of all profits from the group's merchandising! On receipt of the first royalty cheque for $9,700, he complained to Saltaeb's manager, 'I suppose I owe you 90% of this?' The man quietly advised him that the company had already taken its cut of $87,300! The deal would cost the Beatles about fifty million pounds in lost revenue.

Wilfrid Brambell achieved fame as the dirty old man in the British TV series *Steptoe & Son*. In 1955 he divorced his wife after she became pregnant to his lodger.

Just before he made *A Hard Day's Night* he received a conditional discharge from a magistrate for 'importuning for immoral purposes' in a men's toilet in London. From 1969 until his death he lived with his Chinese boyfriend Yussof Saman to whom he left the bulk of his estate.

Air Force (1943)

Tom Neal once smashed Franchot Tone's nose to a bloody pulp in a fight over their lover, actress Barbara Payton. She would later star in the 1951 Gregory Peck film *Only the Valiant*. Tone was in the hospital for weeks and married Payton on his release. Following their divorce a few months later she moved back in with Neal! The bad press greatly affected both their careers, Payton eventually drifting into prostitution when roles dried up.

In 1965, Neal was charged with murdering his third wife Gail Evatt. He claimed (rather lamely) that his gun accidentally discharged during a quarrel. To everyone's surprise, considering his violent reputation, the jury bought his story and he was convicted of the lesser crime of involuntary manslaughter. He served six years in prison, was released in 1972, and died eight months later.

Alamo, The (1960)

John Wayne's choice of English actor Laurence Harvey to play Colonel Travis was considered to be almost blasphemous by most Texans. To overcome their protests, he had Governor Price of Texas make Harvey an honorary citizen of the state before filming began. As a sweetener he gave Price's brother the most important task of doing the voice-over at the start of the film. His amateurish performance sets the picture's standards from the outset.

Wayne and Laurence Harvey were cut from vastly different cloth. While observing Harvey walking along one of the parapets Wayne roared out to him, 'Jesus Christ, can't you at least *walk* like a man?' Harvey, aware of Wayne's real name, leaned over and sarcastically enquired, 'speaking to me Marion?

Character actor Chill Wills was nominated for an Oscar for *The Alamo* (for reasons known only to God and the Academy) and nauseated everybody (especially the rest of the cast and crew) when he took out trade advertisements promoting his performance. These included a picture of the cast captioned: 'We of *The Alamo* cast are praying harder than the real Texans prayed for their lives in the Alamo, for Chill Wills to win the supporting Oscar'. Another of his publicity man's efforts listed *every* Academy member's name alongside a picture of Wills that read: 'Win, lose or draw, you're still my cousins and I love you all'. Ad nausea.

Groucho Marx responded with an advertisement of his own: 'Dear Mr. Wills: I am delighted to be your cousin, but I'm voting for Sal Mineo'. Wayne's insinuations that anyone not voting for his picture was 'Un-American', combined with Wills' obnoxious fawning, soon had wags in Tinsel Town crying 'Forget the Alamo'. Not surprisingly, neither the picture nor Wills won. Good.

Alfie (1966)

Michael Caine was rejected for the stage version of *Alfie* because 'he wasn't right for it'.

Incidentally, the song 'What's It All About, Alfie?' was not written for the film. It was added in later when Cher's version was included in the soundtrack for its American release. Later still, Cilla Black and Dionne Warwick recorded the tune as well. Millicent Martin, the girl Alfie seduces in the front seat of a Mini, sings it on the film's soundtrack. Gillian Vaughan, the girl he seduces in the *back* seat of another vehicle, was the wife of singer/compere Des O'Connor at that time.

Vivien Merchant plays the middle-aged woman taken to the backyard abortionist by Alfie.

Her marriage to playwright Harold Pinter (*The Birthday Party, The Caretaker*) collapsed in 1975 when he took up with Lady Antonia Fraser, the wife of a Tory MP. The break-up sent Vivien spiraling into alcoholic depression. She even sought to join the notorious suicide group 'Exit' but was refused membership because,' she had too much to live for'. In 1982 she died from chronic alcoholism at fifty-three, still unable to accept the loss of her husband to another woman.

Ali Baba & the Forty Thieves (1944)

Maria Montez was a native of the Dominican Republic and stars opposite Jon Hall in this 'actioner' made during the war. She never rose above 'B' pictures but managed to reach the periphery of the big time by wedding Jean-Pierre Aumont when his star was on the rise in 1943. 'When I look at myself, I am so beautiful I scream with joy', the mightily impressed actress would exclaim to anyone silly enough to listen. She went to great lengths to maintain that beauty, which was considerable even to others, and regularly took scalding hot baths to shed weight. In 1951 she took one too many, suffered a heart attack, and drowned. She was thirty-three.

Alien (1979)

The original ending to this film was supposed to have the alien bite off Ripley's head and then send a message back to earth using her voice. Fox executives thought such a finale was a little on the dark side so it was rejected.

The shorthaired female crewmember crunched by the Alien was Veronica Cartwright, the older sister of *The Sound of Music's* Angela Cartwright. Actually, Veronica was supposed to play the lead until the producers switched to newcomer Sigourney Weaver at the last moment. Cartwright made *Goin' South* with Jack Nicholson in 1977, and was soon involved with him off screen. She was considered to be as good a 'party animal' as Jack. No small achievement in itself.

The two enjoyed periodical flings, even though he was heavily involved with Anjelica Huston at the time. Veronica later described him as an amazing lover. 'Funny, charming, and capable of maintaining an erection for hours on end', she enthused to friends. A decade further down the track she gained the small role of Felicia Alden in *The Witches of Eastwick*, another Nicholson vehicle, and intermittently frolicked with him again whenever they got the urge, still gushing to anyone who would listen about her appreciation of his 'undiminished staying power' in bed. Maybe, the script didn't lie. Maybe, Jack truly was a 'horny little devil'.

All About Eve (1950)

It was only because Jeanne Crain became pregnant that Anne Baxter was thrown into her Oscar-winning role as Eve Harrington. Barbara Stanwyck had first dibs on the Margo Channing role but declined it, probably because playing an aging star struck a little too close to home. Claudette Colbert said 'yes' but then hurt her back and withdrew. Gertrude Lawrence also agreed to play Margo but was released when she insisted the drunken scene featuring her character be removed from the script. That left Bette Davis in the plum role.

Hollywood Warts 'N' All

Celeste Holm made several observations about her co-stars in *All About Eve*. Davis and Gary Merrill fell in love right away, she said, and sat apart from the rest of the cast throughout the shoot sniggering and smirking like a couple of schoolchildren harboring a secret. George Sanders never spoke to anyone at all unless compelled to do so.

Marilyn Monroe, who was embarking upon her career, was an hour late for the first of her two scenes and took twenty-five takes to get it right. 'She was terribly shy', said Holm,

'In fact, she was scared to death...' Marilyn, in fact, was *always* late on this and every other set she was ever on. 'She was not very talented', said Holm years later, 'and she had a strange delivery, which was something she'd learned from a bad coach (Natasha Lytess). So, I was not that impressed with her, and in fact none of us were'.

Davis disliked Holm the moment the affable, classy actress wished her a 'cheery good morning' on the set. 'Oh shit, good manners', snarled Bette. Celeste did not speak to her again – ever.

Zsa Zsa Gabor said she observed four different men from the film crew go into Monroe's suite for sex on one evening alone.

Zsa Zsa was married to George Sanders at the time and was a regular visitor to the set. George later told his wife of *his* arrival at Marilyn's apartment one evening during filming. She greeted him clad in nothing but a fur coat, which she promptly opened to him. 'Who am I, darling, not to make love to a woman like that?' he asked.

Merrill recalled how he felt 'an almost uncontrollable lust' when he first met Davis.

'I walked around with an erection for three days', he proudly proclaimed. The couple later married, fought like cat and dog and inevitably divorced. While Bette was carrying on with Merrill her estranged husband sent her an affectionate note professing his undying love, and offering to do whatever was needed to save their marriage. She read the letter out loud at her birthday party on the set, saying it was 'the funniest thing'. No one laughed.

Bette Davis (1908-1989)

Known relationships:

Brent, George
Foulk, Robert
Henreid, Paul
Hughes, Howard
Litvak, Anatole
Mercer, Johnny
Roland, Gilbert
Sherman, Vincent
Tone, Franchot
Wyler, William
Young, Gig

Married:

Gary Merrill & 3 others

In 1930 a studio executive was sent to the train station to welcome her to Hollywood. He returned empty-handed, reporting that 'no one faintly like an actress got off the train'. Studio mogul Carl Laemmle was even less complimentary in his appraisal of bug-eyed Bette. 'She has as much sex appeal as Slim Summerville', he wailed. Summerville was a lanky, skinny, hook-nosed, hayseed comedian of the era who resembled a cross between a scarecrow and a praying mantis.

She was only 5'2" tall.

Her first screen test sent Samuel Goldwyn into fits. 'Who did this to me? She's a dog!' he ranted. Bette ran screaming from the projection room. In time, however, as her popularity and power grew the little scrapper became known as 'the fourth Warner Brother' because of her feisty nature.

Her feud with Joan Crawford stemmed from Bette's affair with Joan's lover at the time Franchot Tone. It was only a brief fling and took place when they made *Dangerous* together in 1935. 'That coarse little thing doesn't stand a chance with Franchot', sneered Joan. Just to make doubly sure of it she married him.

Not that this worried Bette in the slightest. The love of her life was director William Wyler.

One of her husbands, Arthur Farnsworth, died of an aneurysm in 1943, almost certainly brought on when he struck his head on a railway platform after Bette pushed him during an argument. Years later she admitted as much to intimates.

Jack Carson recalled asking a marine why all the servicemen clustered around

Davis at the Hollywood Canteen during the war. 'I hear she screws like a mink', the man replied. It was true. Bette seduced scores of serviceman she picked up at the canteen.

Ava Gardner recalled her first meeting with the by then legendary star. Spotting her in a hotel in Madrid, Ava walked up to the famous actress and introduced herself. 'Miss Davis, I'm Ava Gardner and I'm a great fan of yours'.

Bette gave her a cursory glance and said, 'Of course you are, my dear. Of course you are', then swept on. 'Now *that's* a star', exclaimed the star struck Ava.

Michael Curtiz, in his inimitable way, referred to Bette as, 'a no good, sexless son of a bitch'. Carl Laemmle could only say, 'I can't imagine anyone giving her a tumble'.

Barbara Stanwyck called her 'an egotistical little bitch'. Bankhead threatened to 'tear every hair out of her moustache'. 'That dame is too uptight', observed Humphrey Bogart. 'What she needs is a good screw from a man who knows how to do it'. John Mills starred opposite her in *Murder with Mirrors* in 1985. 'I was never so scared in my life', he recalled. 'And I was in the war!'

Miriam Hopkins also detested her, although their notorious feud was played up for publicity purposes. 'She was like a greedy little girl at a party table who just had to sample every other woman's cupcakes', whined Hopkins.

One of the cupcakes Bette was sampling at the time was Miriam's husband Anatole Litvak.

Like Crawford, Bette suffered the ignominy of seeing her daughter pen a critical book about her life.

Apparently, the young woman gave her mother the option of equaling the $150,000 publishing fee she had been promised, or else watch the book go into publication. Bette slammed the door in her face.

In 1983 the aging icon suffered several strokes following mastectomy surgery. Even in her sixties she continued to use an on-going stream of young men for sex. They were mostly homosexuals, many of whom she would ask to marry her after three or four dates. She hated to be alone.

George Sanders (1906-1972)

Known relationships:

Ates, Nejla
Bankhead, Tallulah
Chanel, Lorraine
Del Rio, Dolores
Dell, Claudia
Duke, Doris
Lamarr, Hedy
Monroe, Marilyn
Paget, Debra
Raymond, Paula

Married:

Benita Hume
Magda Gabor
Zsa Zsa Gabor & 1 other

George was born in Russia shortly before his parents escaped the Bolshevik Revolution and settled in England in 1917. Actor Tom Conway was his real life brother. In 1937 George told friends if he lived to be sixty-five he would take his own life. He would keep his word.

Openly pro-Fascist at the commencement of World War Two, he confided to Douglas Fairbanks Junior, 'I couldn't care less if Hitler took everything'. Referring to the Nazis as 'reformists', he wrote in his diary that America should befriend them and thus gain 'a ring-side seat for ourselves in the New World they create'.

He agreed with Errol Flynn that neither would lift a finger to stop the Germans. After Pearl Harbor, however, George became decidedly more pro-American in his outlook. He even wrote to President Roosevelt suggesting he create a fast moving infantry division equipped with roller-skates! He also proposed the invention of a bomb that emitted an 'all clear' signal as it plummeted earthwards, designed to catch unwary civilians as they emerged from air-raid shelters. Not surprisingly, neither hair-brained scheme was adopted.

Ironically, the man who played the utterly nerveless theatre critic

Addison de Witt in *All About Eve* was reduced to tears when he won an Oscar for his performance. 'I can't help it', he said in his acceptance speech, 'this has un-nerved me'. During his life he had four wives and seven psychiatrists. True to his statement of 1937, when he turned sixty-five George topped himself. His suicide note read, 'Dear world: I am leaving because I am bored. I am leaving you with your worries in this sweet cesspool'.

Barbara Bates has a small part as the young starlet who ingratiates herself to Baxter at the end of the picture. After such a promising start to her career she struggled to get roles and eventually left Hollywood to find work as a dental assistant.

Harry Cohn of Columbia did offer her a contract before she left, but only if she would divorce her husband immediately! Understandably, she refused to do so. A few nights later dirty Harry called her at home in the middle of the night and invited her to spend the weekend with him aboard his yacht. 'Don't bring that midget husband of yours', he added. Bates hung up on him. Later, when a reporter asked Harry why he had not signed the promising young actress for his new production *Born Yesterday*, he lied and said, 'I missed signing her by minutes – dammit!' In 1969, beset with personal problems, Barbara drove to her mother's home and committed suicide with carbon monoxide in the old lady's garage. It was not her first attempt, but this time she got it right.

All Quiet on the Western Front (1930)

This picture was banned in Germany for being anti-German. In Poland it suffered the same fate for being pro-German! When it first appeared in German cinemas, Nazi thugs disrupted screenings by releasing snakes, rats and stink bombs in the aisles. Its anti-war, anti-nationalism theme infuriated Hitler whose determination to make Germany the dominant power in Europe was founded on extreme nationalism and the need to achieve that aim through military action. The last thing he wanted was a wave of pacifism sweeping his Third Reich.

When director Lewis Milestone was told to inject an uplifting ending into his rather bleak World War One epic, the exasperated director wrote back to studio executives, 'I've got your happy ending. We'll let the Germans win the war'.

Eric Maria Remarque wrote the famous novel on which the film is based. He would go on to marry Paulette Goddard and embark upon scores of Hollywood affairs. During the Second World War his sister was be-headed by the Nazis for uttering subversive remarks about the regime. Another sister was sent a bill from the Gestapo for 495 marks to cover the cost of the execution.

Lew Ayres (1908-1996)

Known relationships:

Dru, Joanne
Gaynor, Janet
Gray, Coleen
Harlow, Jean
Knox, Mona
Larsen, Christine
Maritza, Sari
Paige, Janis
Patrick, Dorothy
Rodriguez, Estelita
Thurston, Carol
Totter, Audrey
Valentine, Nancy

Wyman, Jane

Married:

Ginger Rogers
Lola Lane & 1 other

Ayres was a devout Quaker who refused to serve as a combatant in World War Two. Instead, he enlisted in the Medical Corps and served with distinction under fire on three Pacific island beachheads during the conflict. He turned over all his pay to the American Red Cross. Among his peers, only Hedda Hopper and Jane Wyman publicly stood up for him, Hopper describing Ayres in her column as 'one of the finest characters in Hollywood'.

The publicity surrounding his refusal to bear arms reached the ears of Louis B Mayer who was infuriated. 'Lew Ayres has some kind of phobia about killing people', he raged and then took steps to wreck the actor's career.

John Garfield also complained about Lew's reluctance to commit legalized murder. 'Lew made us want to show the world that he doesn't represent Hollywood', he sniffed. Garfield was classified as 4F because of a heart murmur and was, himself, often harassed about not being in uniform. He did, in fact, suffer a heart attack during the conflict, a precursor of the one that would kill him at thirty-nine.

Ayres described his marriage to Ginger Rogers as doomed from the start. 'Ginger Rogers was married to her career', he said, 'and to that mother of hers. I often felt like an interloper'. There was scarcely a soul in Hollywood who had a kind word to say about Ginger's domineering, pushy mother.

All the President's Men (1976)

The guard who reports the Watergate break-in in the film is the same man who discovered the real break-in on June 17, 1972. It is still possible to purchase a souvenir bottle of 'Watergate Whiskey' from the store in the Watergate complex.

The actual room where the burglars' lookout was situated also still exists across the street at the Howard Johnson Motor Lodge. It can be booked at a special fee if you specifically request that particular room.

The true identity of 'Deep Throat' was revealed in 2005. He was W Mark Felt, second in command at the FBI.

Plans to shoot the *Washington Post* scenes in the paper's actual newsroom had to be scrubbed because employees kept looking at the camera during filming.

Some even disappeared into restrooms, applied make-up and attempted to 'act' in the background.

Take note of when Robert Redford gets a phone-caller's name mixed up. It was a genuine error on his part, but since he stays in character the mistake seems understandable so it was left in the final print.

Jason Robards picked up an Oscar here for portraying the *Washington Post* editor Ben Bradlee. During the Second

World War Jason served as a navy radioman and saw action in thirteen major engagements. He was in Pearl Harbor on December 8, 1941, the day after the Japanese attack and was later torpedoed *twice*, once while aboard the USS *North Hampton* off Guadalcanal, and again off Formosa aboard the USS *Honolulu*.

Amadeus (1984)

When *Amadeus* won the Best Picture Oscar, Sir Laurence Olivier was the presenter at the Academy Awards ceremony. He loftily tossed away the script he was supposed to follow and said, 'I trust I won't do too badly'. Upon opening the envelope he then proceeded to announce the first name he saw as the winner. He was actually looking at the *nominations* listed, which was in alphabetical order. Fortunately for him the actual winner *Amadeus* was at the top of the list.

A Man Called Horse (1970)

For the excruciating Sundance ritual actor Richard Harris wore a fake chest created by brilliant make-up artist John Chambers. Two years earlier it was Chambers who devised the astonishing humanoid-ape make-up for *Planet of the Apes*.

American Graffiti (1973)

American Graffiti cost just $750,000 to make and grossed $55 million. Harrison Ford was working as a carpenter in Hollywood when George Lucas offered him the role of the youth in the cowboy hat, eager to challenge the town drag champion to a race. The pay was only $485 a week for this low budget film. 'I can earn more than that as a carpenter', complained Ford before reluctantly accepting the job. His career, of course, would go on to earn him millions.

'Wolfman Jack', the DJ in *American Graffiti*, was certainly *not* a national celebrity back in the fifties. In fact, he was barely known outside a very small area. The movie transformed his image into that of a major icon of the early Rock & Roll days.

Mackenzie Phillips is the young actress who plays the spunky pre-teen picked up by Paul LeMat's character. Her stepmother is the Mamas and Papas icon Michelle Phillips, and her father was John Phillips the leader of the group. Dad taught her how to roll marijuana joints when she was ten, and then went one better by injecting her with liquid cocaine at seventeen. 'To any normal, decent person reading this, that probably sounds horrific', she understates, 'but dad didn't know any better. To him it was all part of being cool, being a 1960s dude'. Rubbish. Apparently, it was also cool for him to allegedly give her to aging rocker Mick Jagger one evening while dear old dad was in an adjoining bedroom. 'I have been waiting for this since you were ten years old', Mick told the eighteen year-old before bedding her. In time she overcame her cocaine addiction, eventually going on to star as the mother in the Disney TV series *So Weird*.

Americanization of Emily, The (1964)

Judy Carne was the 'sock it to me' girl on *Rowan & Martin's Laugh-In* series on sixties TV. Any hopes of her tiny role in this film generating a decent movie career were soon dashed by her descent into drug abuse. Carne began by experimenting with marijuana and mescaline in the sixties, before graduating to heroin in the seventies. Affairs with Vidal Sassoon, Steve McQueen, Anthony Newley, Warren Beatty and racing car champion Stirling Moss came and went. So, too, did her love affair with a woman she identified only as Ashley. She then moved on to ill-fated TV star Peter Duel, who committed suicide at the height of his popularity in the western series *Alias Smith and Jones*. In 1963 she wed Burt Reynolds, but they divorced three years later amid nasty accusations from both sides. He said he tired of her drug abuse and low-life friends. She claimed he beat her. Today, by all accounts, 76 year-old Judy is single.

A Midsummer Night's Dream (1935)

Fourteen year-old Mickey Rooney plays Puck here. He broke his leg tobogganing while the movie was in production, so he performed in some scenes aboard a tricycle, cleverly camouflaged behind bushes and trees. Mickey started out in vaudeville as a cigar-smoking midget. By 1940 he was number one at the box-office.

An Affair to Remember (1957)

Cary Grant (1904-1986)

Known relationships with men:

Hughes, Howard
Orry-Kelly
Scott, Randolph

Known relationships with women:

Brian, Mary
Brooks, Phyllis
Cummins, Peggy
Donaldson, Maureen
Early, Margaret
Furness, Betty
Hawks, Slim
Kelly, Grace
Kovack, Nancy
Landis, Carole
Loren, Sophia
Lupino, Ida
McLeod, Janet
Selznick, Irene
Smith, Queenie
Totter, Audrey
Vickers, Yvette

Married:

Barbara Harris
Barbara Hutton
Betsy Drake
Dyan Cannon
Virginia Cherrill

As soon as shooting on this picture was completed Cary commenced a three-year treatment involving a series of weekly injections of the new experimental drug LSD. Although he was by far the most famous user of the yet to be banned drug, he was not alone as a guinea pig. Jack

Nicholson, Rita Moreno and Andre Previn also took a crack at it. Grant later claimed the LSD sessions helped him come to terms with his hang-ups and fears, in particular his life-long dread of knives. He never attempted to explain the fear or the cure.

Apparently, these treatments suddenly made him acutely aware of his mortality and the need to have a child to carry on his name. With that in mind he married the much younger Dyan Cannon, who bore him a daughter. They later divorced after a bitter custody trial, the little girl going with her mother.

Then in 1968 he met a Brazilian beauty named Luisa Flynn, a woman in her early thirties and the mother of an extraordinarily beautiful little boy. The aging star took the stunning woman aside at a function and offered her a million dollars to have his baby. She declined his kind offer.

Grant and cowboy star Randolph Scott were lovers for decades, and Cary's first marriage to actress Virginia Cherrill failed to alter that fact. When his new wife realized she was to share her marital home with both men she threatened to walk out unless Cary moved with her to another location. To her disgust, randy Randy immediately purchased the house next door! When the marriage inevitably collapsed Cary and Randy moved back in together.

Studio executives would arrange for women to be present as 'blinds' at Hollywood parties attended by the two men who invariably arrived together. The women were required to exit the parties in the company of either of the two actors before going their own way, just in case there were media people present. When questions arose about their living together, the studio said they were saving on rent! Nobody bought that for a moment, as both stars were earning a mint and their rent was negligible. Grant was a much bigger star than Scott, but the studio protected both men's reputations equally, because if one's career went down the drain they both would.

In 1940, after repeatedly dodging calls for him to return to Britain and enlist to fight the Nazis, Cary applied for US citizenship. By the time it was granted, in June 1942, America itself was in the war and he was eligible for the draft there instead. Less than a month after wedding Woolworth's heiress Barbara Hutton he enlisted in the armed forces and was ordered to report to the induction center. He never showed up, yet nobody in the government ever said anything about it. Three months later his 1A fitness rating was changed to 1H by the Selective Service. It seems (from FBI manuscripts) that J Edgar Hoover had a special 'arrangement' with the actor. In return for keeping quiet about Cary's homosexuality, the FBI director had him spy on Hutton's correspondence and business transactions. Her ex-husband, Count Reventlow, was being held by the Nazis in Denmark and being pressured by them to extract as much of Barbara's $150 million from her as he could in exchange for his freedom. It is even possible Grant married her under FBI instructions in order to keep tabs on her fortune. The couple divorced in 1945 shortly after Reventlow was suddenly released by the Nazis and flown to New York.

Cary *hated* being asked for his autograph, yet throughout his long career he made a considerable amount of money from giving it. He insisted on charging 25 cents a pop (increased to 50 cents by 1960), even to children, insisting the money was being put aside and donated to charity. That was simply not true. He pocketed the lot.

Because they shared the same initials, he and Clark Gable called each other every December 26th and exchanged any unwanted monogrammed gifts they had received. Cary's tightness with money was legendary. Director Billy Wilder liked him as a person but said he was one of the stingiest people he had ever met. 'He had a room full of gold cigarette-lighters', said Wilder. 'He would get one and just toss it in the room - his own gold stockpile'. Carole Lombard once appraised his long relationship with Scott, 'their friendship is perfect. Randy pays the bills and Cary mails them'. Melvyn Douglas also had a low opinion of him albeit for an altogether different reason. 'Cary Grant didn't give a damn about anyone but himself', he said. 'Myrna Loy and I tried to get him to join the stars who were speaking out against the political witch-hunts. He refused to say anything or sign anything, didn't even wish us good luck...'

Anatomy of a Murder (1959)

This movie caused an uproar because several words appeared in the script that the censors and some of the public considered offensive. These included 'penetration', 'slut', 'bitch', 'rape', 'sperm', 'contraceptive' and, (horror of horrors), 'panties'! Jimmy Stewart's own father deemed it a 'dirty picture' and took out a local newspaper advertisement asking people not to see it!

George C Scott's loss to Hugh Griffith in the race for Best Supporting Actor seems to have soured him on the Academy Awards from that moment onwards. Until then he had made no public statements regarding the Oscars one way or another. Admittedly, he was probably entitled to feel aggrieved. Hugh Griffith probably won because he was swept up in the absurd *Ben-Hur* euphoria. His performance was anything but special. Scott, however, took it personally and vowed never again to have anything to do with the Academy Awards. He was further disillusioned in 1961 when his performance in *The Hustler* lost out to George Chakiris in *West Side Story,* an undeserving winner if there ever was one.

Anchors Aweigh (1945)

Dancer Gene Kelly greatly upset cartoonists Hanna and Barbera when he accepted *all* the accolades for the sequence in *Anchors Aweigh* where he dances with the animated Jerry Mouse. In a lengthy speech he completely neglected to mention the cartoonists and their astonishing achievement, content instead to concentrate on his own exertions and difficulties performing in the sequence.

Actually, Mickey Mouse was supposed to be his dancing partner, but Disney refused to have his biggest star appear in an MGM movie.

Judy Garland always suspected Kelly had a homosexual relationship with her husband Vincente Minnelli. The allegedly bisexual dancer wed for the third and last time in 1990 when he was seventy-seven years old. His bride was thirty-six.

Angel and the Badman, The (1946)

The lovely Gail Russell stars opposite John Wayne in this western. She was an alcoholic who died from cirrhosis of the liver before she was forty. Director Joseph Losey recalled her standard response when called upon to play a difficult scene. 'Get me a drink...' she would cry. 'She was deathly frightened of acting', he said.

She was married for a while to Guy Madison and her lovers allegedly included Wayne, former child star Freddie Bartholomew and William Holden. It is believed her treatment at the hands of sadistic womanizer John Farrow ultimately drove her into the arms of actress Dorothy Shay in her final years.

A Night at the Opera (1935)

The 'foreign' language Groucho spouts in this picture is actually English played backwards on the audio track.

Coming from a very poor background in New York City, the Marx Brothers were pushed into show business by their mother. Chico took piano lessons, and to save the family money he passed the knowledge on to Harpo who taught himself to play the harp. Groucho began as a boy singer when he was eleven. Because their movies were all shot in black and white, not many fans knew that Harpo's wig was red, not blonde. In the early days he was part of a harmony act called the Four Nightingales. He said he was so scared making his stage debut he wet his pants. 'There are three things that my brother Chico is always on', Groucho once said, 'a phone, a horse or a broad'. Because his piano teacher could only play with his right hand and faked the left, Chico became an expert one-handed piano player.

A Night to Remember (1958)

Several survivors of the actual sinking of the *Titanic* visited the set while this terrific picture was being made. The lucky stuffed pig used in the film is the one Edith Russell had with her aboard the ill-fated vessel on that April night in 1912.

Another real life survivor (from second class) named Lawrence Beesley attempted to enter the set and (this time) symbolically 'go down with the ship'. He was prevented from participating because he was not an actor and would be contravening union rules if he appeared in the picture.

The opening footage of the launching of *Titanic* is actually a shot of the Cunard liner *Queen Elizabeth* being launched in 1938.

No footage exists of *Titanic's* launching.

Character actor George Rose plays the baker who survives the sinking by getting drunk on whiskey, thus temporarily insulating his body against the freezing waters of the Atlantic. In 1988, while on a trip to the Dominican Republic, George was murdered by his adopted son, the young man's birth father, and two others. Michael Goodliffe portrays Andrews the builder of the Titanic who went down with the ship. In 1976 he leapt to his death from the upper floor of a hospital.

Keep your eye on a female guest in the scene at the captain's dinner table aboard *Titanic*. As she sprinkles salt on her meal the top accidentally falls off the saltcellar and dumps the contents on her meal. After the briefest of pauses she stoically continues as if nothing has happened.

Animal Crackers (1930)

Although he made a lot of money on Broadway over the previous decade or so, Groucho was completely wiped out by the Great Depression. Chico simply gambled everything away. On one occasion he wrote a cheque for a gaming debt but advised the recipient not to cash it until noon the next day. When it bounced anyway the man confronted him. 'What time did you cash it? Chico asked. 'Five minutes past twelve', the man replied. Chico slowly shook his head. 'Too late', he said.

When his long-suffering wife caught him in an uncompromising position with one of his many show girl lovers, Chico lamely explained. 'I wasn't kissing her, I was just whispering in her mouth'.

Anne of Green Gables (1919)

The director of this silent film was the mysterious fifty year-old William Desmond Taylor. In 1922 he was found dead on his Hollywood living room floor. He had been shot in the back. His murder has never officially been solved, although director Charles Vidor's investigation decades later suggested the probable killer was a disgruntled lover named Charlotte Shelby, the mother of the star of this film, Mary Miles Minter.

Taylor's black manservant (and lover) Henry Peavy discovered the body and raised the alarm. A bizarre sequence of events then unfolded. Instead of ringing the police, his actress neighbor Edna Purviance called her pal, major star Mabel Normand, who was the deceased's current girlfriend. Well, *one* of them anyway.

Mabel did not call the police either. She rang the General Manager of Famous Players Lasky Studio, Charles Eyton. He then called Paramount head Adolph Zukor, who in turn rang Miss Minter. She, too, was one of the dead man's squeezes. Minter was not at home, so her mother, Charlotte Shelby, *another* of Taylor's lovers, contacted her by phone soon afterwards. None of these people bothered to inform the police until they were good and ready to.

When the authorities did finally arrive on the crime scene they found it being trampled underfoot by no fewer than four persons. Zukor was burning papers in the fireplace, Normand was frantically searching for letters she had written to the deceased, Eyton was bundling illegal bootleg whiskey into sacks, and leaning against a wall surveying the scene was Edna Purviance.

Mabel's letters were soon found inside one of the dead man's boots. Also impounded were pornographic photos of him with five well-known actresses. Money quickly changed hands, so their identities were never revealed. Among those interviewed by police, however, was Mary Pickford, but no official reason was ever given regarding her connection to the case.

Peavy admitted taking the snapshots, at his former employer's behest, of Taylor in explicit poses with the actresses. The dead man, it later emerged, had been blackmailing them for some time prior to his death. It was also said that actress Zelda Crosby, yet another of his conquests, had committed suicide under his threat of blackmail when he terminated *their* affair months before.

A love letter from the twenty-two year-old Miss Minter was found along with a collection of women's panties, believed to be trophies of his conquests. A negligee monogrammed 'M' and obviously belonging to Mary was also unearthed.

Since Normand was the last person known to have visited Taylor the evening before his murder, suspicion initially fell on her, but she soon produced an alibi and was quickly exonerated. Charlotte Shelby, on the other hand, had been observed practicing with her personal .38 pistol a few days before the shooting. Taylor had been shot with a .38 yet, inexplicably, she was permitted to leave for Europe at the height of the investigation! Decades later Vidor would name her as the probable killer, claiming she lost the plot when she found out her boyfriend was also seducing her daughter, the gorgeous but not too bright Miss Minter.

At Taylor's funeral service what was left of Mary's career went down the drain when she kissed the corpse full on the lips, before declaring to the mourners that the dead man had just whispered his undying love for her as she leant over him. Good one, Mary.

By 1981 the 79 year-old grossly overweight Minter had been living for decades as a total recluse. She was found in her Santa Monica kitchen that year, beaten, gagged and left for dead by intruders. She managed to live on for another two years. Her mother, the probable murderer, had already passed away in 1957.

Mabel Normand began in movies at the age of thirteen, following an interesting interview (given her age) with Mack Sennett in his offices. Even he was taken aback when in response to his instruction, 'let's see your knees, honey', she hoisted her skirt all the way up and spun around buck-naked! Not one to look a gift horse in the mouth, he hired her on the spot.

By 1923 her career started to wane after she was cited as co-respondent in a divorce case. It got the staggers altogether when her chauffeur was found standing over the body of Hollywood millionaire Cortland S Dines and clutching Mabel's pistol in his hand! At the Taylor inquest her addiction to cocaine and booze emerged (the coke addiction having come from her fondness for cocaine peanuts, a popular confection of the 1920s), and this proved to be the last straw for her public. Mabel retired from the industry. She died from tuberculosis at the age of thirty-five, her last words were said to have been about her long dead lover: 'I wonder who killed Bill?'

A Patch of Blue (1965)

At eighteen years of age Elizabeth Hartman was nominated for her role as Selina D'Arcey in *A Patch of Blue*. In 1987 at the age of forty-five she died after falling from a fifth story apartment, an apparent suicide.

A Perfect Murder (1998)

This is a remake of the 1954 Hitchcock thriller *Dial 'M' For Murder* that starred Grace Kelly and Ray Milland. Most times re-makes are not as good as the original, but not so in this case. This version is faster-paced and incorporates a couple of twists that place it above the original, in my opinion. Of course, we don't have Grace to look at, but you can't have everything. The paintings you see on display in Viggo Mortenson's apartment, by the way, are works by the actor himself.

Gwyneth Paltrow was uneasy about playing intimate scenes with Michael Douglas. He had been a friend of the family since she was a child and like an uncle to her. Paltrow's mother, incidentally, is actress Blythe Danner who played Thomas Jefferson's wife in the 1972 musical *1776*.

Alan Royle

A Place in the Sun (1951)

Elizabeth Taylor first met Montgomery Clift on the set of *A Place in the Sun*. She was completely smitten by him, refusing to accept he was bisexual and unable (or unwilling) to physically return her affections. She repeatedly proposed marriage, but he always changed the subject. He often handed on her passionate letters (usually unopened) to his male lovers, and told friend Ashton Greathouse how he had tried to seduce Liz but 'couldn't get it up'. Years later he succeeded in seducing her, but the experience did nothing for him and frustrated Liz. The two remained close platonic friends until his death.

All his adult life he struggled with his sexuality and indulged in drug taking in an endeavor to block it out. The result of all this was a lowering of his self-esteem that increased as the years went by. When he was rejected for war service (because he suffered from chronic diarrhea, of all things), his self- respect suffered a further blow, especially since the reason for his unfit classification could scarcely be made public. His final years saw him hanging out in seedy bars where transvestites, gay bikers and butch lesbians would stretch him out on tables and crawl all over him when he was drunk.

One of his lovers was Jack Larsen the actor who played Jimmy Olsen in the TV series *The Adventures of Superman*. Another was Sal Mineo. Marlon Brando and Clift had an intimate 'encounter'.

April Love (1957)

Many people still believe Pat Boone refused to kiss Shirley Jones in this picture because it was against his religion to do so. Actually, the director asked him late one afternoon if he would shoot a kissing scene before wrapping for the day. Boone said he should check with his wife first, but if she agreed he would shoot it first thing next morning. Mrs. Boone gave it the OK, but by then the media was saying he had refused to kiss Shirley on religious grounds. If he then went through with the scene after all the publicity, he believed would appear a hypocrite, so the shot was cancelled.

Incidentally, he claims to be the great, great, great grandson of legendary frontiersman Daniel Boone. Richard Boone of *Have Gun, Will Travel* fame said he, too, was descended from the Kentucky woodsman.

Around the World in 80 Days (1956)

At the end of his career Ronald Coleman agreed to play a cameo role in Mike Todd's *Around the World in 80 Days*. When a reporter asked him if it was true he was receiving a Cadillac as payment for just one day's work, the veteran actor tartly replied, 'No, for a *lifetime's* work. Trevor Howard had written into all his contracts, a guarantee that he would not be called to a movie set on any day that England was playing in a Test Cricket Match.

Mike Todd's first wife died under anesthetic (reportedly from shock) after cutting the tendons in her wrist with a kitchen knife during an argument with her husband. A rumor persisted that Todd had bribed the anesthetist, but it was never substantiated. He broke the nose of his second wife, actress Joan Blondell, during one of their numerous domestics. He also managed to clean her out financially before giving her the 'heave-ho'.

After becoming engaged to actress Evelyn Keyes he took back the $50,000 ring on the pretext it needed altering. He then presented it to Elizabeth Taylor as her engagement ring and announced to the press it had cost him $200,000. On their wedding night he brought his pal Eddie Fisher into the bedroom to show him Liz lying semi-naked in a short see-through nightgown. Eddie wrote he could see 'everything' and that Liz seemed to enjoy his appraisal. No wonder Eddie considered Todd his best friend!

Todd died when his private plane, 'the Lucky Liz', crashed after encountering icing problems, closely followed by a mountain. Liz had bronchitis at the time otherwise she, too, would have been aboard. Her husband had just spent several thousands of dollars on the aircraft's bedroom, but only a few hundred on de-icing equipment. The extra 2,000 pounds weight in the bedroom fatally overloaded the aircraft.

The Motion Picture Academy threatened a lawsuit if his son's plan to erect a nine-foot high replica of the Oscar statuette at his gravesite went ahead. The project was cancelled. In 1977 his coffin was stolen from the Chicago Cemetery but recovered three days later. Police think thieves incorrectly believed he was buried wearing a valuable diamond ring.

Arsenic and Old Lace (1944)

This picture was completed in 1941 but not released until three years later. A contractual agreement guaranteed that the stage play in New York would run its full course before the movie could make an appearance. This suited the star Cary Grant because he hated the thing and his performance in it. The legendary gay Edward Everett Horton features here. He may be remembered for his role as Roaring Chicken in the TV comedy series *F Troop*.

Arthur (1980)

Lawrence Tierney was the real life brother of actor Scott Brady, and plays Arthur's future father-in-law in this film. Tierney was an alcoholic and a brawler who was arrested sixteen times for contrary behavior before he turned forty. In 1973 he was stabbed outside a New York City bar as he was getting into his car, but survived the attack. By 1974 he was reduced to driving a horse-drawn carriage in Central Park, just to pay his rent. A year after that he was drinking with a young woman when she fell to her death from her fourth floor apartment in Manhattan. Authorities ruled her death a probable suicide, but no-one really knows what happened for certain.

A Star is Born (1954)

Columnist Hedda Hopper used one of her many contacts to discover how Judy Garland lost by just seven votes to Grace Kelly for the Best Actress Oscar in 1955. 'You know where those seven votes were, don't you?' said Hedda. 'They belonged to those bastards in the front office at MGM'. Hopper believed MGM held a grudge against the singer since ditching her four years earlier, and she was probably right. Groucho Marx sent Judy a telegram that simply read: 'This is the biggest robbery since Brink's'.

Away All Boats (1956)

George Nader has second billing in *Away All Boats*. For years he insisted his friendship with Rock Hudson was purely platonic, even after Rock reputedly left the bulk of his estate to him when he died. In Hudson's final days Nader was living with the stricken actor's secretary Mark Miller.

George revealed in his later years how every new edition of *Confidential* magazine had both he and Hudson on tenterhooks, their stomachs churning, wondering if they were about to be exposed. Telephone calls between the two actors required a system of code words in case of eavesdroppers. 'Is he musical', for example, was the code for asking if a new acquaintance was gay. Unable to reach the top rung in Hollywood, Nader went to the continent where he became number one at the box-office in Germany for several years, portraying spies until the genre fizzled. He then returned to the United States and lived in retirement off his considerable European earnings.

A Yank at Oxford (1938)

Robert Taylor (1911-1969)

Known relationships:

Bruce, Virginia
Darnell, Linda
De Carlo, Yvonne
Garbo, Greta
Gardner, Ava
Grey, Virginia
Parker, Eleanor
Parker, Jean
Tcherina, Ludmilla
Turner, Lana

Married:

Barbara Stanwyck & 1 other

Rumors persisted for decades that Taylor was bisexual, but there is no real evidence of this because both he and his wife, Barbara Stanwyck, guarded their sexuality very closely indeed. Their marriage was said to be 'lavender' and studio-backed, and it almost certainly was. Whether the studio's aim was to protect Barbara, Bob or both of them, is open to conjecture.

Taylor was quite a timid man in his early days in Hollywood and did whatever the studio told him to do. That included marrying Barbara Stanwyck. It was, therefore, with some trepidation he went to see LB Mayer about a salary rise. Mayer, who was quite possibly a better actor than half those he employed, went into his usual routine, recounting how he had nurtured the actor, trained and encouraged him through thick and thin and so on. Finally, he draped a paternal arm over Taylor's shoulder and ushered him towards the door. 'If God had blessed me with a son', he said,

'I can think of nobody I'd rather have wanted than a son exactly like you'. When asked later if he had gotten his raise, Taylor replied, 'No, but I gained a father!'

Bob's 'friendship' with MGM worker Ralph Corser enraged Stanwyck. Convinced the two men were intimate, she would call out when Corser rang their home, 'Hey, Bob. Your wife wants to talk to you'. The marriage ultimately collapsed, partly through Taylor's inability to become aroused by his wife. His second union was with Ursula Thiess who apparently did arouse him now and then. 'At least I can get it up with her', he told Stanwyck. His stepdaughter from this marriage was arrested for murder in Munich in 1963 and would suicide six years later.

The Motion Picture Alliance for the Preservation of American Ideals was an organization formed around the time of the communist witch-hunts in the USA. Its aim was to sniff out any 'commie-Jews', as its members liked to put it, and bar them from the motion picture industry. Stanwyck and Taylor were foundation members. John Wayne became President. Other rednecks only too willing to beat the drum included Clark Gable, Gary Cooper, Ward Bond, Charles Coburn, Adolph Menjou, Irene Dunne, Hedda Hopper, Ginger Rogers and Walt Disney.

Stanwyck and Taylor were hypocrites. Their careers always came first and they were soon working with writers and directors whom they had helped to blacklist, the only difference being these people were now working under pseudonyms and for a fraction of their worth. MGM added insult to injury years later by christening its screenwriters' workplace the Robert Taylor Building. In 1990, many years after Taylor's death, fifty screenwriters successfully petitioned to have the structure's name changed to the George Cukor Building. Taylor's anti-Semitism and his betrayal of so many of their brethren, they argued, were reasons enough to warrant the change.

Babe (1995)

In the USA pork sales slumped by 20% following this film's release. The makers insisted the forty-eight female pigs that played Babe were not to be slaughtered once filming was completed. They were sent to a breeding farm instead. It was necessary to use so many animals because baby pigs have an inconvenient habit of growing up too fast. An animatronic double was also used.

Bachelor Party (1984)

Angela Aames plays the voluptuous Miss Klupner in this film. In 1988 she was found dead at the age of thirty-two from a heart problem. It was probably induced by her habit of regularly popping diet pills to maintain her figure.

Backfire (1987)

Dean Paul Martin was the son of singer Dean and was once wed to actress Olivia Hussey. Dino, as he was known, was a very good tennis-player who made it to Wimbledon one year, only to be eliminated in an early round by the legendary Australian Ken Rosewall. He was also one third of a sixties pop group, called Dino, Desi & Billy, that scored with a couple of minor hits. In the same year that he appeared in *Backfire* he was killed, when the Phantom jet he was piloting crashed into a mountain. His father never fully recovered from his loss.

Bad & the Beautiful, The (1952)

Unhappy with the tilt of her upper lip, Gloria Grahame stuffed cotton wool along her gum line to straighten it out. The innovation made it difficult for her to speak and partners in kissing scenes often ended up with a mouth full of soggy cotton.

She married director Nicholas Ray when she was twenty-eight, but that came crashing down when he caught her fast-tracking his thirteen year-old son Anthony's education in the ways of the flesh. A few years after she and Nick divorced, she married Tony.

Basic Instinct (1992)

Writer Joe Ezterhas claims Sharon Stone's notorious leg-crossing scene was no accidental piece of camera-work. According to him it was scripted, with make-up and hair styling spending considerable time between the lady's legs preparing for the shot. Miss Stone, on the other hand, vehemently denies she had any idea director Paul Verhoeven was filming up her dress in the scene. She also claims to have slapped his face when she saw the rushes. He denies that happened at all. Well, *somebody's* telling whoppers. When we consider the fact that Sharon was involved in relationships with both Ezsterhas and Verhoeven, it becomes even more confusing about who is and isn't telling the truth. Come to think of it, who the Hell cares anyway?

Gay protesters were up in arms over the killer being depicted as a gay woman. On location sites they threw paint, blew car horns and shouted obscenities to disrupt shooting. Ezsterhas bowed to the pressure and made 'politically correct' changes to the script. 'Now we know this man has no principles', huffed Stone's co-star Michael Douglas as he banked his $15 million fee. Members and supporters of Queer Nation protested at the film's opening, wearing T-Shirts that read: 'CATHERINE DID IT!' intent on scuttling the thriller's so-called surprise ending. About five hundred protesters also demonstrated outside the Oscars the following year.

Sharon Stone spent much of her school years in a class for children of high intelligence. A former Miss Pennsylvania, she has a reported IQ of 154 - one point higher than that of actress Geena Davis – if you can believe those kinds of stories. After *Basic Instinct* put Sharon in the superstar bracket, she refused the lead opposite Clint Eastwood in his film *In the Line of Fire*. He was not a big enough star anymore, she is reported to have said. I am more inclined to believe the part itself was not big enough.

Most pundits agree she probably had an affair with President Bill Clinton. The assumption gained added credence one evening at a function honoring the President. As he made his way around the room greeting people and shaking hands with well-wishers, Sharon remained seated and merely tossed a casual, 'Hi Bill', over her shoulder as he passed her table.

Her agent's partner William Skryzniarz has been quoted as saying, 'When Sharon wants someone she rents a hotel room and tells him exactly where and when to turn up. She makes it clear it's a one-time opportunity, take it or leave it. She's made the move on some major names'.

Batman (1989)

Michael Keaton does not really have the physique he displays in this movie. Body armor (complete with built in muscles) created the impression of a muscular, well-proportioned body. The thirty-seven year old actor had to be bolted into it on the set each day. Batman fans were incensed when he was chosen to play their hero, by the way. His real name, incidentally, is Michael Douglas. Kirk's son, of course, had first dibs on the name so Keaton had to come up with something else.

Jack Nicholson received (after adding together his fee, merchandising and percentage of the gross) a cool $60 million for his portrayal of The Joker. The picture raked in an extra $750 million from merchandising alone! Today he is the highest paid 'character' actor ever.

If you have wondered why he was not nominated for an Oscar for this picture, part of the reason is this: Academy members did not know whether to group him in the Best Actor or Best Supporting Actor category, so votes were split between the two. Consequently, he ended up receiving insufficient numbers to make the final five in either one! Whether he could have defeated Daniel Day-Lewis's *My Left Foot* for Best Actor, or Denzel Washington's *Glory* for Best Supporting Actor is problematic. But he certainly stole this picture.

Jack Nicholson (1937 -)

Known relationships:

Anspach, Susan
Basinet, Cynthia
Bergen, Candice
Bernay, Lynette
Broussard, Rebecca
Carter, Georgianna
Cartwright, Veronica
Flynn Boyle, Lara
Hamilton, Paula
Hollman, Winnie
Huston, Anjelica
Machu, Mimi
Mayo-Chandler, Karen
Phillips, Michelle
Richman, Tracy
Smith, Amber
Van Ravenstein, Apollonia
Ward, Rachel
Zouzou

Nicholson's upbringing was strange even by Hollywood standards. Until he read the story in *Time* magazine, he was unaware the woman he believed was his sister was, in fact, his mother. Therefore, the woman he had always thought was his mother was actually his grandmother! Singer Bobby Darin faced an identical situation. 'I get high about four times a week' Jack once told an interviewer. 'I think that's average for an American'. In a *Rolling Stone* interview in 1984 he elaborated. 'I've said, forever, that I smoke marijuana. I missed no acting classes during 12 years. I haven't missed a day's work from illness in 30 years. I'll put my medical charts, my sanity charts up against anybody'

'There are two ways up the ladder', he told *Time* in 1974, 'hand over hand or scratching and clawing. It's sure been tough on my nails'. Life is a little easier on the nails these days. By Hollywood standards he lives in a modest $500,000 home, but his art collection is estimated to be worth around $150 million! Part of his collection is a plate of shredded money. 'It creates more interest than any other art in the room', he says.

In 1994 his forty-eight year-old half-sister Pamela Liddicoat was shot to death after partaking in a sexual threesome with her girlfriend and a white water-rafting guide at the man's mountain cabin. The girlfriend and the guide were convicted and imprisoned for her murder.

Kim Basinger once revealed that before her marriage to Alec Baldwin she 'tried out' all her male co-stars and rated them on performance in her diary. Recording artists Prince and Eminem are numbered among her conquests. Fans were surprised to see her involved with the diminutive Prince who is both five years younger and five inches shorter than the blonde bombshell.

After mentioning matter-of-factly to an interviewer of how she learned about oral sex in the fields around her hometown, Kim's exasperated father sent her a package containing a tennis ball and some adhesive tape. It was accompanied by a note that read 'When you give an interview and the feeling of being outrageous is present, please place this ball in your mouth and then tape your mouth shut. If you are still able to say 'oral sex' after doing this then you are hopeless'.

On the set of *The Marrying Man* she and Baldwin were reputedly detested by nearly everyone.

Their temper tantrums, tardiness, demands and arguments with producers made the shoot a particularly unpleasant one. The picture bombed anyway. After their divorce in 2002, Basinger found it necessary to hire a bodyguard to deter her ex-husband from attempting to rekindle the flame. Interviewer Jonathan van Meter once described her as, 'the most self-indulgent, dumb, irritating person I have ever met'. On the other hand, Russell Crowe had the greatest admiration for her when they made *L A Confidential* together. So, who do we believe?

Battle Cry (1955)

'George Cukor gave me my big break in this business,' said Aldo Ray. 'I knew somebody important like him could really help me, so I let him take his pleasure, and it didn't compromise me in the least. Everyone knew he was homosexual. It was no secret'.

Aldo was a Navy frogman during World War Two and a county constable after the war. In 1979, down on his luck, he accepted a role in a hard-core porno flick entitled *Sweet Savage*, although he did not strip or take part in any of the sexual activity.

Tab Hunter's career looked set to take off like a rocket until he was arrested at an all-male pajama party and rumors questioning his sexuality started to surface. Consequently, he quietly faded from view, re-appearing in the eighties when he featured in two of John Waters' trashy flicks *Polyester* and *Lust in the Dust* acting alongside the transvestite Divine.

During the Second World War James Whitmore saw action on Saipan, Tinian and the Mariana Islands, during which time he received a battlefield commission to the rank of Lieutenant.

Battle Hymn (1957)

Robert Mitchum was all set to play the true-life role of the minister turned fighter pilot Colonel Dean Hess. Then Hess himself vetoed the idea. 'I cannot possibly allow a man who has been jailed for taking drugs to play me on the screen', he bleated. Mitchum had just been busted for smoking a reefer – the naughty boy. The role went instead to Rock Hudson. Like most people outside the industry the good Colonel had no idea of the interesting skeletons inhabiting Rock's closet. As it happened, Colonel Hess turned out to be a lying publicity seeker himself (for details, see *Movies Based on True Stories*, my second book).

Bear, The (1984)

Jon-Erik Hexum's career was just beginning to take off following his performance in this Gary Busey vehicle when it was tragically cut short. In 1984, on the set of a TV series called *Cover Up*, he died in bizarre circumstances after picking up a .44 Magnum revolver containing a blank cartridge, light-heartedly putting it to his head and pulling the trigger. The blank had enough power from such close range to drive a piece of his skull into his brain. The young actor died six days later at the age of twenty-seven. He indulged in a brief romance with Joan Collins at the height of his short career.

Best Years of our Lives, The (1946)

Harold Russell was a disabled war veteran who lost both his hands in a grenade explosion. After appearing in this film he was nominated for an Oscar for Best Supporting Actor. On the night of the Academy Awards he was presented with a statuette 'for bringing hope and courage to his fellow veterans'. The award was made *before* the Best Supporting Oscar was announced, the Academy not expecting him to win. When he *did* win he found himself the recipient of two statuettes for the one performance. In 1992 he became the first winner to sell his award, which he did to raise money for his wife's medical expenses. The highest bid was for $60,500.

Steve Cochran also features in this film. He died at forty-seven in 1965 aboard his boat while taking an all-girl crew on an ocean trip. It is thought he perished from an acute infectious edema, which is an accumulation of fluid on the lungs. The girls, one of whom was only fourteen years old, were panic-stricken and dehydrated by the time the Guatemala Coast Guard picked them up. They had been sailing in circles off the coast for twelve days with Cochran's decomposing corpse on board all that time.

Not everyone was happy with the verdict of 'death by natural causes'. Friend Merle Oberon attempted to have the police launch a fuller investigation but got nowhere. Before he departed Acapulco Cochran had, according to some sources, been displaying all the symptoms of someone who had been poisoned.

Beau Geste (1939)

Brian Donlevy was as nasty on the set as he was on the screen. Director William Wellman (himself a former French legionnaire, by the way) said of him 'I've never seen a guy who could get everybody to dislike him as he could'.

Ray Milland became thoroughly exasperated by Donlevy and deliberately struck him in an un-padded area of his body during a fencing sequence. The blow drew blood and Donlevy fainted. The crew to a man applauded.

Albert Dekker portrays the bullet-headed leader of the mutineers. His bizarre death in 1968 is something of a mystery. The man's body was found kneeling in his bathtub, a hyper-dermic needle stuck in each arm and a hangman's noose knotted around his neck. The other end was looped over the shower curtain rod above him. A scarf was wrapped around his eyes and a rubber ball-bit clamped in his mouth with its metal chains tied firmly behind his head. His wrists were handcuffed, leather belts were fastened around his body and he was clad in a lady's negligee!

The closeted gay actor was believed to have indulged in the sexual practice of auto-erotic asphyxia, a technique requiring the participant to be partially strangled, the resultant cutting off of blood to the brain apparently bringing about a heightened orgasm. As there was no sign of forced entry to his home or of any kind of struggle, authorities concluded a lover had engaged in the practice with him and something had gone terribly wrong.

Friends of the actor disputed that scenario and suspected foul play, primarily because an amount of $70,000, a tape recorder and photographic equipment were missing from his home.

In the 1920s Ray Milland was a sentry outside Buckingham Palace during his stint as a Royal Guardsman.

He was prevented from joining a combat unit in World War Two, however, after accidentally lopping off part of his thumb with a circular saw. In the latter days of the war he trained as a civilian pilot and was sent to the Solomon Islands where he managed to contract dengue fever.

Although he gravely endangered his marriage by conducting an affair with Grace Kelly when they made *Dial 'M' For Murder* together, his wife forgave him and the couple remained together for 54 years.

Becket (1964)

In the London stage production of *Becket*, O'Toole and Richard Burton were eager to play both leading characters, so they agreed to swap roles each night. Consequently, many patrons saw the show twice to catch both versions.

O'Toole claims he was raised as a girl until he was twelve years old. His slight lisp is the legacy of a school rugby match in which part of his tongue was sliced off in a scrimmage.

Sir John Gielgud was nominated in this for his portrayal of the King of France. In 1953 he received a knighthood from the Queen of England, but a few months after that he was arrested for 'importuning' in a public toilet and seriously contemplated suicide. The story was kept under wraps.

When he died in 1996 he was still a bachelor, having lived for many years with his partner Martin Hensler. Sir John won an Oscar for his portrayal of Dudley Moore's butler in *Arthur*.

Beetle Juice (1988)

Winona Ryder (1971 -)

Known relationships:

Beck
Damon, Matt
Depp, Johnny
Duritz, Adam
Hahn, Scott Mackinlay
Lowe, Rob
Pirner, David
Rubin, Henry Alex
Slater, Christian
Soper, Blake

Winona was named for her hometown of Winona, Minnesota. Her surname was borrowed from sixties rock singer Mitch Ryder. At school she wore male clothing and her hair short. She was even beaten up once by other children who thought she was a gay boy!

Raised by hippie parents, self-proclaimed 'intellectuals' who chose to live in a teepee in an electricity-free commune in Mendocino, California, Winona and her family traveled about in a psychedelic bus named Veronica! Her godfather was the sixties counter-culture twit Timothy Leary, the man who gave the world the ultimate slice of useless advice: 'Turn on, tune in, drop out'.

Her father sold books exclusively dealing with the drug experience, while Mum was a 'video artist' (whatever that is). Together they wrote *Shaman Woman, Mainline Lady: Women's Writings on the Drug Experience*, no doubt a thrilling tome. 'It's great', says Winona. 'It's about famous women...who used opium or whatever while they were creating their masterpieces. It goes all the way up to Patti Smith'. Wow!

Like the Phoenix tribe, the Ryders gave their kids weird names: Sunyata, Jubal and Yuri (after the Russian cosmonaut). 'Whenever I've had choices to make', Winona gushed in an interview, 'I've known how to make them...it's a wonderful thing to know'.

Presumably inspired, she rushed off and chose 'a $525 black leather Dolce and Gabbana purse with metal eyelets and leather fringe' - but neglected to pay for it. Later, she chose a further $4,000 worth of jewelry from Sachs in New York, and didn't bother to pay for that either.

When she was eventually busted for shoplifting, the arresting police officer emptied her handbag and, lo and behold, found it crammed with Demerol, Endocet, Vicoprofen and Vicodin, all supplied to her by the 'Doctor to the Stars' Jules Lusman. Twenty other doctors had filled thirty-seven more prescriptions for her between 1996 and 1998. Lusman had his license revoked and Winona, as invariably happens with high profile stars, had all drug charges against her dropped. It comes as no surprise to learn she is a close friend of fellow oddball and drug enthusiast Courtney Love.

The stealing charge, however, was proceeded with. She copped 480 hours community service, three years' probation, and a $10,000 fine for thieving from Sachs Fifth Avenue. Mark Jacobs, the company whose clothes she stole, then made a mockery of the sentence by offering her a modelling contract to display their wares! The judge in her trial would not admit testimony regarding three previous charges of theft, two in New York City in 2000 and 2001, and another in Beverly Hills in 2001.

Apparently, evidence that the accused thief has a record of thieving is not pertinent – or something.

She apparently dates a *lot* of musicians (according to the tabloids and her best buddy, the illustrious Miss Love). 'In rock', Courtney said, 'you are nothing until you've slept with Wynona Ryder and had a feud with me'. With friends like Courtney who needs enemies?

'Bend Of The River' (1952)

Stepin Fetchit was the black actor who made a fortune playing stupid, lazy and cowardly 'darkies', much to the understandable disgust of his fellow African-Americans. Born Lincoln Perry, he possibly adopted his stage name from a racehorse that won him a wad of money as a youth. Either that, or he simply held on to the name of his burlesque act that featured *two* black comedians known as 'Step and Fetchit'.

At the peak of his acting success Perry owned sixteen cars and employed a similar number of Chinese servants in his mansion. In fact, he became the first millionaire black actor. By 1947 he had squandered every cent of the estimated $2 million earned over his career. In 1960 further tragedy struck when his son killed three people on the Pennsylvania Turnpike and then committed suicide.

It is difficult to determine the legacy left by this man. His depiction of a black man being lazy, stupid and subservient to whites, stereotyped African-Americans for a generation, convincing many white cinema-goers that his character typified the race. Consequently, for decades African-Americans detested him, yet in 1976 the NAACP did a complete about face and gave him a 'Special Image Award' for his pioneering movie career that opened the door for black actors. Go figure. Perry passed away in 1985.

Ben-Hur (1925)

Francis X Bushman, who portrays Messala in this silent version, played the big movie star to the hilt in real life. He cruised about in a twenty-three feet long Marmon limousine with his name *embroidered* down its side. He smoked eight inch long lavender cigarettes and kept *three hundred* Great Danes on his California estate. Five of them generally accompanied him wherever he went. At his peak he was raking in around a million dollars a year in an era when far too many poor souls were surviving on the smell of an oily rag.

Bushman's decision to divorce his first wife and marry Beverley Bayne turned out to be a disastrous career move. His fans had no idea he was a family man with five children until the divorce proceedings hit the newsstands. They were OK with the divorce as such, but livid about his duplicity regarding his marital status. Suddenly, his pictures stopped making money. Exit one movie star.

Just when things could not possibly get any bleaker – they did. His entire fortune vanished overnight in the Stock Market Crash of 1929. By 1931 he was a nonentity and flat broke. In desperation he even tried to auction himself to the highest female bidder, on the proviso the winner would keep him in the style to which he had become accustomed. There were no takers. He died in 1978 in complete obscurity.

May McAvoy began as an extra in 1916 and progressed to play opposite Ramon Novarro in this silent classic, earning $3,500 a week for her trouble. In a cruel twist of fate she would receive a paltry $100 a week as an extra in the 1959 remake. 'After all', she said philosophically, 'it is 20 years since I retired, and that's 1,000 years in Hollywood'. Her career began teetering in 1923 when she backed out of Cecil B DeMille's *Adam's Rib* after refusing to appear in the scantiest of costumes. But it was the advent of sound that really put paid to her star status.

Novarro plays the title role and was the real life cousin of actress Dolores Del Rio. In 1968 he was bludgeoned to death in his New York apartment and robbed of $45, all his assailants could find. The old actor was a homosexual who paid rent boys to come to his lodgings for sex. Over the final six months of his life at least 140 of these boys had serviced him.

The two who murdered the old actor may have mistakenly believed he kept a fortune hidden on the premises, although both denied this later. After brutally torturing him to learn its whereabouts they became frustrated and suffocated him to death by ramming a statue down his throat. The implement was a present from his long ago lover Rudolph Valentino, reputedly an erect penis posed for by Valentino himself. As the old man lay dying one of his killers rang a girlfriend and casually described what was transpiring to her over the phone. She at once called the police and both men were arrested.

Novarro's killers were two brothers, Paul and Tom Ferguson. Each received a life sentence, yet both were released within eight years. While on parole, Tom Ferguson raped a fifty-four year old woman and was sent back inside. Soon afterwards his brother too was re-incarcerated for another rape, but eventually would commit suicide by cutting his own throat, quite possibly the only useful thing he ever did in his wretched life; not that it did poor old Ramon any good.

Ben-Hur (1959)

In this version starring Charlton Heston, second unit director Yakima Canutt was supervising filming of the chariot race when his youngest son Joe, who was doubling for Heston, was thrown from his chariot after it collided with wreckage on the racetrack. The resultant shot of Joe flying out of the chariot, hanging on and somehow remaining aboard, was exciting enough to cause the script to be altered to include it in the final cut.

The Roman soldier run over near the center island and the charioteer who gets run down after being flung from his chariot were actually articulated and weighted dummies, designed to 'react' as a human would under those circumstances.

At the risk of sounding 'picky', nine chariots start the race, six of them crash – and *four* finish. You might also notice that on the formation lap each chariot has only three horses, but during the actual race they have four. That is because nine chariots abreast, drawn by 36 horses, would not fit across the track.

Berserk (1967)

At the age of sixty-three Joan Crawford went to England to make *Berserk*. Young producer Herman Cohen told of the aging actress displaying her remarkable figure to him in her dressing room. 'Not bad, huh?' she asked, as she stood before him completely naked. Cohen muttered something about being surprised and very impressed with her body. Then he beat a hasty retreat.

Diana Dors was born with the unfortunate name of Diana Fluck. 'I had to change it', she joked, 'in case the 'L' blue off a marquis in a high wind'.

Her first husband Dennis Hamilton died of tertiary syphilis in 1959, but not before he had defrauded Diana of all her earnings. He once put paid to Diana's affair with Bob Monkhouse by threatening to slit the man's eyeballs with a razor! Her second venture down the aisle was with British comedian Richard Dawson who was a regular in the cast of

TV's *Hogan's Heroes* and later a successful stand-up comic in Las Vegas.

Husband number three was actor Alan Lake. His chief claim to notoriety was his involvement in a bar room brawl in 1970 that saw his good friend pop singer 'Leapy' Lee Graham ('Little Arrows') sentenced to three years for knifing the hotel's landlord. Lake got eighteen months for 'handing him the knife'. A few months after Diana succumbed to cancer he put a shotgun in his mouth and pulled the trigger.

Diana had limited talent, so she played up to her tabloid image of a sex kitten by holding 'adult' parties at her home. It was her choice of husbands that proved to be her Achilles' heel. All three were 'lowlifes', unscrupulous, greedy men who used her fame for their own ends. Maybe, just maybe, her two year romance with Rod Steiger (1956-7) may have made a difference, had it endured?

B.F.'s Daughter (1948)

Barbara Stanwyck fumed when co-star Van Heflin attempted to up-stage her by rolling a silver dollar back and forth across his fingers while she was delivering a lengthy piece of dialogue. When it came his turn to deliver a monologue he stopped dead as several of the crew burst out laughing. Looking behind him he saw Barbara slowly pulling her dress over her head. 'What are you doing?' he asked. 'Showing them a trick a helluva lot more interesting than yours' she replied.

Beverly Hills Ninja (1997)

Twenty-one stone comedian Chris Farley died following a day of drugs and booze while entertaining a hooker in his apartment in Chicago. After hiring the woman for $2,000, he was unable to get aroused because he was too drunk. She waited for four hours and was about to walk out when he suddenly collapsed.

As he lay dying, Farley pleaded with her not to leave him. She left anyway, but not before taking time to snap a photograph of the stricken actor. Although his corpse contained traces of morphine, cocaine, heroin, marijuana and Prozac, as well as an enormous amount of alcohol, it was his great weight and the narrowing of three coronary arteries that caused his death.

The Bible – In the Beginning (1966)

John Huston only played the role of God here because Charlie Chaplin wisely refused it!

While driving on Sunset Boulevard on September 25, 1933, Huston knocked down and killed a dancer named Tosca Roulien. L B Mayer shelled out $400,000 to keep it quiet, while the culprit left for an indeterminate stay in England. Mayer would perform similar services for others over the years to protect his investments.

The Big Steal (1949)

Robert Mitchum was awaiting sentencing on a narcotics charge when Howard Hughes chose Jane Greer to star opposite him in *The Big Steal*. She had somehow slipped through sleazy Howard's net a couple of years before, so he was mightily displeased with her, and determined to make her pay. When Hughes purchased RKO, he made it clear that her contract would remain intact, but he would *never* put her in a picture unless she divorced her husband and went with him! By 1949, however, he was in a quandary. Unsure how the public would react to Mitchum's conviction, he did not wish to risk one of his top actresses working alongside Bob, for fear she might damage her career by association. So he chose Greer. She had no career to lose, not having worked since he took over the studio.

The upshot of all this was that Bob did sixty days at a minimum-security farm; the picture was completed and movie fans forgave him for getting caught puffing on a reefer; and Jane's career was off and running again. And Hughes never did get her into his bed.

The Big Trail (1930)

This was John Wayne's first major opportunity to become a star but, unfortunately for him, the picture was made just as the Great Depression arrived in America. To make matters even worse, the picture was shot in the new 70mm format, which meant distribution was restricted to theatres able to afford installation of the equipment necessary to screen it. In 1930 there were just two venues capable of showing the picture.

A vastly inferior 35mm print was hurriedly rushed out for general distribution, but it flopped badly when no fewer than than *4,000 theatres* closed their doors through financial difficulty. Studios were also feeling the pinch and laid off hundreds of personnel, keeping only established proven stars on their books. Wayne, not yet one of these, found himself back in one and two reel 'B' pictures on Poverty Row. It would be a further nine years before he finally made it with the release of *Stagecoach* in 1939.

Billy Budd (1962)

Ronald Lewis was a Welsh actor who played opposite Peter Finch in *Robbery under Arms* in 1957 as well as appearing in a minor role in this wonderful drama about the British Navy in Napoleonic times. In 1980 Lewis declared bankruptcy and two years later took his own life with sleeping pills.

Birth of a Nation, The (1915)

This film's depiction of the Ku Klux Klan as knights' errant for the white race rightly caused a furor among conservatives in America, yet director D W Griffith could see nothing wrong with his epic. 'We spent over $250,000 the first six months, combating stupid persecution brought against the picture by ill-minded censors and politicians who were playing for the Negro vote', he complained.

It is quite possible the Klan might never have re-emerged from its post-Civil War beginnings if not for this picture. Its chivalrous portrayal of Klansmen as heroic defenders of Americanism, coupled with President Woodrow Wilson's avowed admiration for the film, lent the organization a semblance of respectability that trebled its numbers in the 1920s.

Wilson described the film as 'like writing history with lightning', adding, 'my only regret is that it is all so terribly true'.

At the Atlanta premiere, 25,000 Klansmen marched and rode in a procession! Only one black actor was hired in the cast, by the way. Every other African-American part was filled by a white actor, or extra, masquerading in 'black face'.

The epic was supposedly based on Thomas Nixon's novel *The Clansman,* but Griffith bought the rights to the book simply to give his film the prestige of having an authentic literary basis. It bore so little resemblance to the novel that Nixon complained to Griffith after viewing it, 'this isn't my book at all'.

The disgruntled author was supposed to be paid $10,000 for the rights, but Griffith had only given him $2,500 before running out of money. So, he talked Nixon into reluctantly settling for 25% of the film's profits in lieu of the balance. The movie was a smash hit and the novelist's share ran to a whopping $750,000!

On the set, as in all of his films, Griffith insisted on no flirting and no swearing. People were not even permitted to address each other by their Christian names. It was all Mr.

This, Miss That... Despite this Victorian approach, however, tales still abounded about DW and his off-screen penchant for young girls – *very* young girls.

In his youth, future director Raoul Walsh rode as a cowboy with cattle herds in Mexico. He also did some filming and negotiating with Pancho Villa during the Mexican Revolution. He plays the role of John Wilkes Booth in *The Birth of a Nation*.

Donald Crisp portrays General Grant. On completion of the picture he went off to Russia to spy for Britain in the First World War.

Wallace Reid plays Jeff the fighting blacksmith, a role that projected him to the front ranks of Hollywood stars. Before long he was a matinee idol, virile, handsome and personable. Unbeknown to the public he also suffered from an addiction to morphine that would kill him at thirty-one.

A doctor prescribed the drug to combat severe pain in his back, the legacy of an accidental injury incurred while performing a movie stunt. At that time the addictive side effects of the drug were unknown. As his addiction worsened the studio pushed him into more and more films, rather than rest him and treat the problem.

By the time he attempted to cure himself it was too late. In 1923 he contracted influenza at a sanitarium and died.

In that same year his mother rushed out a thin biography of her son that turned into a best seller. His widow, actress Dorothy Davenport, also cashed in. Changing her professional name to Mrs. Wallace Reid, she produced an exploitive feature on drug addiction entitled *Human Wreckage* that did quite well.

Mitchell Leisen wrote, 'Wallace Reid was the stud of the studio, and whenever DeMille had a new sweet thing under contract, he sent Wally over to 'make her a woman' as they said in those days'.

Louis B Mayer made a small fortune when he acquired the distribution rights to *The Birth of a Nation*. Aware the real money lay in producing, he stole actress Anita Stewart away from Vitagraph Pictures in 1918 by offering a deal that included a position on his company's board of directors for her non-talented husband Rudy Cameron. Then he signed Hedda Hopper as a character actress and the foursome headed for California.

The land he purchased, soon to become MGM, was half studio and half zoo, hence the roaring lion company trademark. Unable to get Charlie Chaplin, he signed the comedian's sixteen year-old bride, Mildred Harris, for the publicity value.

Mayer chased starlets whenever he got the chance, which was often. His wife spent most of her time in a sanitarium, leaving him free to indulge himself with the scores of young hopefuls provided by his bootlegger friend Frank Orsatti. He also had a private tunnel constructed under the sound stages that wended its way to selected dressing rooms.

Yet for all that he was quite a prude – in public, anyway. On hearing of Charlie Chaplin's impregnation of juvenile actress Mildred Harris, he confronted the comedian in a highly fashionable restaurant, called him 'a filthy pervert' and knocked him down.

During the thirties he proudly displayed an autographed portrait of Benito Mussolini over his desk.

It was Mayer who set up the 'Look-alike Brothel', where visiting VIPs could satisfy their sexual fantasies by bedding starlets made up to look like Harlow, Garbo, Lombard and others. The phony Garbo, for instance, would sweep down the stairs and exclaim, 'Dahlings, I *never* vant to be alone!' She charged $250 a night.

Jeanette MacDonald slept with LB to advance her career. He became insanely jealous of her love for Nelson Eddy and would have ended Eddy's career there and then had it not been for the phenomenal popularity of the MacDonald-Eddy musicals. Business always took precedence over everything else.

Ann Miller was also his lover and he genuinely hoped to marry her. She refused him because he insisted on her giving up her career if they tied the knot.

After falling from a horse and injuring himself in 1949, LB was informed that Frank Sinatra had quipped, 'he didn't fall off a horse. He fell off Ginny Simms'.

Simms was Mayer's mistress at the time. Sinatra's contract was immediately torn up and he never worked for the studio again.

His brother Jerry held an executive position, but nobody knew what (if anything) his function was at the studio. Irving Brecher finally it figured out. 'Jerry has a very important job and he has to have that big corner office', he explained. 'He's supposed to watch Washington Boulevard and warn everybody to evacuate the studio if icebergs are spotted coming down the street'.

By 1938 Mayer was the highest paid man in America, earning $1,400,000 annually plus stocks and bonuses from the company. Studio executive B P Schulberg dubbed him 'Tsar of all the Rushes'.

Bitter Tea of General Yen, The (1933)

The anticipated box-office problem of having a Caucasian woman infatuated by an Oriental man was addressed by casting Swedish actor Nils Asther in the role of General Yen. The producers figured white audiences would be more likely to accept a European *impersonating* an Oriental in the love scenes than they would a real Chinese. They were wrong.

Even though Yen only kisses the girl's *hand,* the outcry was loud and long. In racist Australia, for example, the *Truth* tabloid became hysterical over the depiction of a 'loathsome Chinese bandit pawing and mauling a white woman'. The paper got even more hysterical when Australian censors passed the film intact.

Blackboard Jungle (1955)

Sidney Poitier was 28 and Vic Morrow 26 when they played two of Glenn Ford's high school students in this film. Even Jamie Farr, the future Corporal Klinger in TV's *M.A.S.H.* series, billed as Jameel Farrah, was 21.

Blade Runner (1982)

The set of *Blade Runner* was not a happy one, because director Ridley Scott fought with nearly everyone. Before long t-shirts began circulating relating to the long ago Will Rogers comment: 'I never met a man I didn't like'. The *Blade Runner* t-shirts read: 'Will Rogers never met Ridley Scott'.

Blue Angel, The (1930)

Emil Jannings' bisexuality and his frequenting of Berlin ambisexual clubs was tolerated by the Nazis because of his movie popularity and his willingness to star in the propaganda vehicles thought up by Herr Goebbels.

His Oscar for this film had a particularly embarrassing tinge to it. You see, the canine hero Rin Tin Tin actually received more votes than he did, but the Academy could not bring itself to give out its Best Actor Award to a dish-licker.

Blue Dahlia, The (1946)

Veronica Lake always personally opened her fan mail because, quite often, admirers would enclose a coin to cover costs of a hoped for reply from the star. She would extract any such coins, toss them in a jar and throw the letters away. Any letters not containing a coin were discarded unopened.

She was one of the most difficult stars to control on the set, as well as being notorious for her habit of taking stagehands back to her home for orgies. She also had a *lot* of one-night stands with her fellow actors and various other celebrities; JFK, Aristotle Onassis, Porfirio Rubirosa, among them.

By 1950, the career of this cantankerous and voracious actress was over. Once she did away with her silly peek-a-boo hairstyle, the face revealed was found to be quite plain. By 1960 she was working as a barmaid at the Martha Washington Hotel for Women in Manhattan and living in obscurity. A few years later she was arrested for drunkenness. It was the ravages of alcohol that finished her in 1973 at the age of fifty-four.

Blue Hawaii (1961)

Jenny Maxwell plays Ellie Corbett in this. While taking a walk outside her Beverly Hills home in 1981, she and her husband were shot to death by persons unknown.

Elvis Presley (1935-1977)

Known relationships:

Alden, Ginger
Ann-Margret
Bova, Joyce
Case, Kathleen,
Connors, Carol

Craig, Yvonne
Dors, Diana
Jackson, Wanda
Juanico, June
Leigh, Barbara
Lime, Yvonne
Locke, Dixie
Moreno, Rita
Ryan, Sheila
Satana, Tura
Shepherd, Cybill
Sinatra, Nancy
Thompson, Linda
Westmoreland, Kathy
Wood, Anita
Wood, Natalie

Of course, you may add hundreds of brief 'encounters', perhaps even thousands of them. There is also a *very* strong school of thought that is certain Elvis had more than a platonic relationship with actor Nick Adams, and that Colonel Tom Parker was well aware of it and approved. Parker, who was forever chasing the almighty dollar, was always fearful of his meal-ticket impregnating some young thing and being sued for millions. With Adams, needless to say, that was not about to happen. Then again, surely exposure of Elvis as anything but straight would do much more damage.

It is generally believed Ed Sullivan only showed Elvis from the waist upwards when he appeared on his variety program in the late fifties. Well, that is not entirely true. Elvis did three Sullivan shows and Ed only bowed to pressure from the censors to restrict shots to the singer's upper torso in the third and last show. The first two were not restricted.

Cybill Shepherd's first invitation to Presley's Graceland home was an eye-opener. She was amazed when he spent $40,000 flying his entourage to Denver to pick up a certain kind of sandwich he was partial to! Their affair was, shall we say, transitory. She quickly discovered she was just a 'fill-in', called upon only when his current girlfriend Miss Tennessee Linda Thompson was out of town.

He had almost any woman he wanted and Cybill was just one of many, even though she was living with director Peter Bogdanovich at the time. Not that seemed to bother her or Elvis too much. In her tacky nightclub routine years later she openly discussed the King's refusal to indulge in mutual oral sex with her - until she ultimately changed his mind. Clearly, she felt her audiences needed her to share that with them.

Elvis seduced hundreds of girls and women before, during and after his marriage to Priscilla Beaulieu in 1967. He met her when she was only fourteen years old and he was in West Germany doing his National Service stint. Nearly eight years later, after she turned twenty-one, the thirty-two year old megastar married her.

He found time to race married British sex symbol Diana Dors across the Mexican border for a weekend of passion in 1956. In the same year he bedded Natalie Wood, but they were complete opposites and the romance quickly faded. 'He didn't drink. He didn't swear. He didn't even smoke!'

complained the street-wise Natalie who did all those things in spades.

His affair with Nancy Sinatra was lengthy and must have been known to his wife, yet the two women appeared to get along quite well. At the height of the affair in 1968, when *Speedway* was being shot, Priscilla gave birth to Lisa-Marie while Nancy organized and hosted the baby shower!

In Hollywood Elvis moved into the mansion formerly owned by Prince Aly Khan and Rita Hayworth and began to seriously party with his bodyguards and friends. Each night the house would be filled with attractive young women selected by Presley to strict specifications. They had to be no taller than 5'2", weigh no more than 110 pounds, and be as young as was legal, and certainly no older than eighteen. He also required girls not too far removed from the condition of virginity and preferably dressed in white. He would take the 'pick of the litter' to his master bedroom, leaving the remainder to be enjoyed by his henchmen. Often he was content to merely watch the rest of the group strip down to their panties and wrestle. With the help of some of these co-operative young things he would make his own private videos of their bedroom frolics.

Fifty percent of every dollar he earned went to his manager Colonel Tom Parker. Another 10% went to the William Morris Agency. Of the remaining 40%, the Internal Revenue taxed Elvis in the 75% bracket, leaving the singer with between 10 and 15% of everything he earned. It is estimated he accumulated about $4 billion dollars during his career, yet on his death his bank balance showed just $2,790,799 once his will was settled.

Parker vetoed any plans 'the King' envisioned of touring overseas. The 'Colonel', you see, was born Andreas Cornelius van Kujik in Holland, but left there in 1929 and illegally entered the USA where he changed his name to Tom Parker. The 'colonel' is a bogus title. Fearful his illegal status would be discovered if he applied for a passport, he refused to let his meal-ticket leave the US on tour, with or without him.

In 1976, in a disgraceful deal, he sold the rights to Presley's entire catalogue of songs to RCA Records for a paltry $6 million, half of which he pocketed himself. Parker never bothered to read scripts submitted to his client. 'Just send me a million dollars, never mind the script', he said, 'and Elvis will do the picture'. No wonder Presley's movies were garbage.

In a 1979 *Playboy* interview Marlon Brando was asked his opinion of the now legendary singer. 'Elvis Presley...bloated, over the hill, adolescent entertainer', sneered the bloated, over the hill and adolescent actor, 'suddenly drawing people to Las Vegas has nothing to do with excellence, just myth', he added. Evidently, there weren't a lot of mirrors at Marlon's place.

Bing Crosby said of Presley, 'He never contributed a damn thing to music...he was successful ... hard to account for. Oh, he sings well enough, I suppose'. Maybe Bing thought everybody should croon like him.

Elvis acquired his drug habit while serving in the army in Germany. Troops were often plied with Benzedrine to keep them going when on maneuvers. By 1970 the drug-soaked singer could not control his intake. Around that time President Richard Nixon laughably appointed him an 'honorary narcotics agent'. Just what that position entailed is anyone's guess, but if it had anything to do with Elvis setting an example for the youth of America it was a pretty ordinary choice.

By now Elvis was so messed up with drugs he found it difficult to have actual intercourse with a woman, so he delved further into voyeurism.

Three or four chorus girls performing lesbian activities on each other was said to be his favorite form of viewing, all of which he recorded for posterity on his video cameras. It's a wonder Nixon didn't appoint him 'honorary pornography agent' as well.

Towards the end of his life Presley's bodily functions were so disrupted by his drug addiction that his bodyguards were required to wrap him in diapers every day. He had an enlarged colon and a liver infection and was either swallowing or injecting as many as thirteen different drugs into his system daily.

At 2 pm on the day he died, his current girlfriend awoke to find him lying in a fetal position in the toilet. He had bitten down on his tongue, necessitating medics knocking out two of his front teeth to enable breathing tubes to be inserted down his throat. All their efforts were in vain and he was pronounced dead at 3.30 pm. His doctor had prescribed an astonishing 5,300 pills and vials for him over the seven months prior to his death!

On the day of his death the ever-vigilant Parker moved quickly. He contacted the singer's father and negotiated a new contract that virtually maintained the status quo. Many of Presley's relatives were appalled when the good colonel attended the funeral wearing a bright blue shirt, no tie, and a baseball cap! The funeral service itself was chaotic. Two young girls in the crowd were run over by a car and killed.

An attempt was also made to steal the corpse. One of Presley's uncles Bobby Mann sold a picture of his nephew in his coffin to the *National Enquirer,* reportedly for $78,000. The photo is almost certainly a fake. The 'corpse' seemed to be too young and too slim to be the Elvis of that time. Still, it's the thought that counts.

Although ex-wife Priscilla collected $2 million and hefty monthly payments, she was not mentioned at all in the will. He never forgave her affair with karate instructor Mike Stone, even though Elvis himself was unfaithful to her almost on a nightly basis. All his estate went to daughter Lisa-Marie, his father, and his grandmother. In the first three years following his death his estate earned more money than he had in his entire career!

Blues Brothers, The (1980)

Two months before he died from a drug overdose in 1982, John Belushi gave this interview to *Rolling Stone* magazine:

'I don't do more drugs than any other schmuck out there in the public. And uh…I liked doing it. I'm just noticed more than anyone else'.

After doing different drugs all day, he threw a party at his residence on the eve of his death. Robin Williams arrived, but left quickly when he observed Belushi drifting in and out of consciousness. Robert De Niro snorted a few lines of coke, then he also left.

Cathy Smith, a former back-up singer and girlfriend of Gordon Lightfoot, gave Belushi another speedball and went to bed. He was found dead next morning. Smith was later convicted of administering a lethal injection. Dan Aykroyd, his co-star in *The Blues Brothers*, led the funeral parade clad in black leather and jeans atop his Harley Davison.

It is very difficult to feel sorry for smart, gifted people who die because of gross stupidity. Belushi, River Phoenix, Whitney Houston – the list goes on. They had it all and pissed it away through drugs. Don't trip over your ears gang. Donkeys.

Bonnie & Clyde (1967)

Jack Nicholson seemed set to play the part of C W Moss until studio executives came to the odd conclusion that he and Beatty looked too much alike and might cause confusion for the audience!

Quirky actor Michael J Pollard was once involved with rocker Janis Joplin. What a pity they never had a child. It would have been something to see.

Three of the banks raided in the film were the actual banks hit by Bonnie and Clyde during their crime spree of 1934. Situated at Pilot Point, Red Oak and Venus, they have remained unchanged since their closure back in the Depression days. Over the course of their four-year crime spree the gang killed thirteen people.

Warren Beatty (1937 -)

Known Relationships:

Adjani, Isabelle
Alt, Carol
Bergen, Candice
Buell, Bebe
Cardinale, Claudia
Carne, Judy
Caron, Leslie
Cher
Chi, Greta
Christie, Julie
Chung, Connie
Collins, Joan
Dickinson, Janice
Dunaway, Faye
Eggar, Samantha
Ekland, Britt
Haddon, Dayle
Harris, Barbara
Hawn, Goldie
Hayward, Brooke
Heatherton, Joey
Hemingway, Margaux

Hershey, Barbara
Hyser, Joyce
Jackson, Kate
Keaton, Diane
Knudsen, Bitten
Ladd, Diane
MacPherson, Elle
Madonna
Minty, Barbara
Mitchell, Joni
Nelkin, Stacey
Phillips, Michelle
Plisetskaya, Maya
Prowse, Juliet
Ross, Diana
Seymour, Stephanie
Simon, Carly
Stevens, Stella
Sukarno, Dewi
Tyler Moore, Mary
Ullmann, Liv
Van Doren, Mamie
Von Furstenberg, Diane
Welch, Raquel
Wood, Natalie

Married:

Annette Bening

If we add in his 'one-offs' this list would probably extend for another ten pages. Beatty, Howard Hughes and Errol Flynn probably had more women than the rest of Hollywood's male population combined. All the above ladies lasted past night one, which is something I suppose. Then, along came Annette Bening and 'bingo', his roaming days were over. Maybe...

Alan Royle

The younger brother of actress Shirley MacLaine, Beatty once worked as a rat-catcher for the National Theatre in Washington to make ends meet. Actually, he was really a rat *watcher*, so to speak. After an actor was bitten, Equity insisted someone be stationed in the alley outside the theatre to ensure no more rats made it into the building. Beatty got the job. Just after that he scored a regular supporting role in the TV sit-com *The Many Loves of Dobie Gillis* playing the snobbish Milton Armitage.'He has always fallen in love with girls who have just won or been nominated for an Academy Award', observed former girlfriend Leslie Caron.

She then went on to list Natalie Wood, Julie Christie, Diane Keaton and herself in that category. In 1991 he fell for and married Annette Bening shortly after her Oscar nomination for *The Grifters*.

Joan Collins said he would have sex with her three or four times daily and take phone calls at the same time. He also bedded Cher, reputedly when she was only fifteen. 'He was technically good, but I felt nothing', was her expert assessment. His sister Shirley says, 'sex is the most important thing in his life. It's his hobby, you could say'. Bruce Dern commented, 'Jack Nicholson and Beatty have contests about it'. If sex were an Olympic event, the man would clean up.

One day at Chasen's Restaurant, during what Natalie Wood thought was the height of their romance, he told her he was going to the bathroom, but failed to return to their table. He had done a runner with a voluptuous hatcheck girl.

Natalie incinerated all his clothes when she found out. Interestingly, when she accompanied him to the Oscars following his debut in *Splendor in the Grass*, his future wife, Annette Bening, was just three years old.

Born Free (1966)

Austrian-born Joy Adamson, the woman who raised the lion cubs in real life, made a nuisance of herself on the set of *Born Free* when she attempted to interfere with most aspects of the movie. In the end the director lost patience and banned her from the set altogether. Virginia McKenna who plays her in the film said it was pitiful to see the lady crawling about on a nearby hill with a pair of binoculars trying to see what was going on. Incidentally, all the lions used in the film had to be shipped into Kenya from California. Kenyan law forbids the use of its wildlife in motion pictures.

Real life husband and wife team Bill Travers and Virginia McKenna formed Zoo Check following their involvement with the lions of *Born Free*. It is a charity that has since evolved into The Born Free Foundation for the preservation and care of African wildlife. Travers served in the Gurkhas for some time and spent six years in the east, India in particular, before turning to the acting profession to earn a living. He spoke both Gurkhali and Urdu.

Alan Royle

Born Yesterday (1950)

It is not generally known, but Marilyn Monroe unsuccessfully auditioned for the lead role in this picture. 'Those who saw it thought it was excellent', recalled Garson Kanin, 'but Harry Cohn, the head of the studio, did not trouble to take the six steps from his desk to the projection room to look at her'. Marilyn had already rejected Cohn's advances prior to the audition, so he chose not to renew her contract.

Kanin originally wrote the play for Jean Arthur, but when she withdrew from the Broadway production the film role went to Judy Holliday and it made her a star.

When she was twenty Judy lost her virginity to Yetta Cohn, a female employee of the New York Police Department. A year later, so Judy claimed, she was raped by actor John Buckmaster the son of British screen legend Gladys Cooper.

She began in the show business industry as a switchboard operator backstage with Orson Welles' Mercury Theatre. Her normal voice, incidentally, was quite soft and devoid of any trace of her New York origins.

Although she won an Oscar for her inimitable portrayal of the dizzy blonde in *Born Yesterday*, she was actually a very intelligent woman with an IQ of 172. When called to appear before the House for Un-American Activities during the McCarthy free-for-all she purposefully adopted her famous dizzy blonde persona and was quickly dismissed.

Boston Strangler, The (1968)

'They gave me away as a prize once', Curtis told the *Sunday Express* in 1965. "A 'Win Tony Curtis for the Weekend' competition. The woman who won was disappointed. She'd hoped for second prize, a new stove".

In 1998, at the age of seventy-two, he responded to questions about his young girlfriends by saying, 'Can you imagine me with a woman old enough to be my wife? Forget it. My girlfriend is 25 years old'. The following year he wed a twenty-eight year-old lingerie model named Jill Vanden Berg.

Boy on a Dolphin (1957)

The diminutive Alan Ladd was a former US Diving Champion before embarking on an acting career. Just 5'5" tall he was often required to stand on a box or ramp when performing alongside taller leading ladies. At other times the ladies were asked to stand in a specially cut trench, an indignity Sophia Loren refused outright to submit to when the two stars made *Boy on a Dolphin*.

A year or so before his death Ladd was mysteriously shot and wounded on his premises. The media was told he had surprised an intruder and accidentally shot himself. Most people in the know suspected it was really a failed suicide attempt by the disturbed actor. In 1964 he died from an overdose and the coroner's verdict again suggested an accident. I guess if you're a lousy shot then pills are the way to go.

Bridge on the River Kwai, The (1957)

Laurence Olivier angered the usually sedate Alec Guinness during the 1930s, when he told friends that John Gielgud was Alec's lover. 'Not that he could not have been', remarked Guinness, (who was gay anyway), 'But, in fact, he was not'. Olivier himself was gay right down to his toenails, so why he was trying to 'out' poor Alec is a mystery.

It seems a pity that so extraordinary an actor as Guinness will probably be recalled by the majority of the movie-going public as Obi-Wan in *Star Wars*, and not for any one of a hundred marvelous portrayals, on both stage and screen, throughout a long and illustrious career.

When Japan attacked Pearl Harbor in 1941, Sessue Hayakawa was living with a woman in Paris, where he was more than happy to remain for the duration. When asked how he explained his six -year absence to his wife on his return to Japan at war's end, he simply replied, 'She would not dare ask'. His portrayal of the Japanese commandant in this film was his definitive role.

Buck Privates (1941)

This was Bud Abbott and Lou Costello's second picture, and it was a phenomenal success, grossing over $10 million and becoming Universal's most successful feature to that time. During World War Two the Japanese used to show the 'drill routine' sequence to demonstrate to their armed forces how stupid American soldiers were. In retrospect that seems only fair. There must have been *a thousand* Hollywood productions that depicted Japanese *and* Germans as complete morons.

In his early years Lou Costello (that's the little fat one) was a prizefighter and a stuntman. He also worked as a carpenter at MGM and Warner Bros. Even more surprisingly, he doubled at times for the stunningly beautiful Dolores Del Rio in some of her scenes!

At the height of the 'Reds scare' in the fifties he became obsessed about communists taking over the movie industry, so he took petitions around the studios asking people to sign them, stating whether or not they were members of the Communist Party.

Abbott was an epileptic who occasionally suffered an attack while performing on stage. At such times Costello would thump him in the stomach in an attempt to quell the attacks. Audiences, unaware of his condition, would always laugh and applaud, convinced it was part of the act.

In 1942, at the height of their popularity, the comedy duo reached number one at the box office. As a publicity stunt they insured themselves for $100,000 with Lloyds of London, in case someone died from laughter during one of their films. A year later Costello's infant son was accidentally drowned and the comedian unfairly blamed his wife for the tragedy. Friends said his whole personality changed from that day onwards.

In 1946 the Hitching Post Cinema in Beverly Hills showed only westerns, and the famed comedy duo were regular patrons. They would bring in their gambling cronies to bet on the number of white horses that might appear during the course of the movie.

Both men also had a penchant for pornographic movies and dealt with mobsters and prostitutes on a regular basis. Consequently, they were under constant FBI surveillance for over a decade, which says a lot about J Edgar Hoover. The man who obdurately denied there was any such thing as organized crime in America, squandered the taxpayers' money detailing agents to shadow harmless little Louie Costello.

Bugsy (1991)

In the film, Bugsy meets Virginia Hill on the set of a movie and they fall in love. In reality she was a bagwoman for the New York mob, sent out to California to keep an eye on Siegel whose antics were gaining too much publicity for their liking. She had been intimate with scores of gangsters, among them Joe Adonis, Frank Costello and Frank Nitti and knew Siegel from his days in New York. Her Hollywood lovers included Anthony Quinn and drummer Gene Krupa among many others.

That Bugsy became infatuated with her there is no doubt. Whether or not she was spiriting Syndicate funds away in a Swiss bank is still argued, but Luciano, Lansky and Co lost patience with her boyfriend and assassinated him anyway. Hill died years later in Switzerland, her body found in a forest under suspicious circumstances.

Siegel did not stand in the desert and have an epiphany about Vegas as the film would have us believe. The Flamingo Casino was built by the founder/editor of the *Hollywood Reporter*, William

Wilkerson, who *did* come up with the idea while standing in the desert waiting for a tow-truck to pick him up. The name 'Flamingo' came from his love of exotic birds and not from Bugsy's nickname for Hill. In fact, she was not even in Vegas at the time. She was in Paris on mob business. Later, after the casino was built, Siegel invested mob money in it when Wilkerson got into debt. The gangster's troubles started from there.

Siegel was a New York gangster sent out to Hollywood to organize mob involvement in the burgeoning movie industry. While there, he made about a half a million a year for his associates by shaking down the studios with threats of strike action and labor withdrawal if his demands were not met. He also ran drugs, gambling and prostitution.

He refused to allow African-American performers to reside at his establishment, forcing them to stay in the run-down Vegas shantytown. When black superstar Lena Horne told him she would not work at the Flamingo under that arrangement he reluctantly let her stay in a cabana. But the bigoted gangster insisted on the maids burning her linen every day after she had slept on it.

One evening at Romanoff's restaurant he was introduced to Darryl Zanuck and his wife. Mrs. Zanuck, a most direct woman, said to him, 'I understand that you and your cronies kill people'. He smiled and gave his now legendary reply: 'But Mrs. Zanuck, we only kill each other'.

Many Hollywood celebrities enjoyed his company, among them Cary Grant, Gary Cooper and Al Jolsen. They found it exciting to mingle with the dangerous gunman. Several sources claim Norma Jean Baker (who would, of course, become Marilyn Monroe) had a brief fling with him in her early days. So too did Wendie Barry and Marie (the Body) McDonald.

Dean Martin worked in the pit dealing blackjack for Bugsy on the disastrous opening night of the Flamingo Casino on December 26, 1946. By then its construction had gone millions over budget, partly because of Siegel's obsession with perfection and detail. For instance, his own phobia about hygiene caused him to insist on every toilet in the complex having its own separate sewerage line. Three of his Hollywood pals attended that first night - George Raft, Charles Coburn and George Sanders. In 1947 the mob tired of him wasting their money so they shot him to pieces as he sat in his living room. Police found one of his eyes stuck to the door!

Bus Stop (1956)

This picture saw the debuts of Don Murray and Hope Lange who, later that year, became husband and wife. They divorced in 1961. Director Joshua Logan only agreed to do the film after Lee Strasberg assured him that, in his opinion, Marilyn Monroe was one of the two most talented actors he had ever coached (the other being Marlon Brando). At the film's completion Logan said, 'I finally realized that I had a chance of working with the greatest artist I'd ever worked with in my life, and it was Marilyn Monroe. I couldn't believe it'. Neither can anyone else.

Butch Cassidy & the Sundance Kid (1969)

Butch Cassidy's aged real-life sister, Lula Parker Betenson, actually visited the set during shooting. 'Hi, I'm Butch', said Paul Newman on being introduced to her. 'Hi, I'm your sister', she replied. She would later agree to 'endorse' the film for a small fee.

The bicycle-riding scene was originally cut to the Simon and Garfunkel tune 'Mrs. Robinson', but the studio then asked Burt Bacharach to write something else for it. 'Raindrops Keep Falling on My Head' was the result and it was substituted in the final cut.

Ted Cassidy, who played Lurch in TV's *The Addams Family*, has a bit here as one of the Wild Bunch. When he died, at forty-six, his wife interred his ashes in the backyard of their home. Then she changed domicile and left him behind. So, some unsuspecting tenant has 'Lurch' residing in his or her back yard to this day.

Butterfield 8 (1960)

'LIZ DYING!' blazed the headlines in Los Angeles on the very day Academy members were mailed their Oscar ballot papers. Elizabeth Taylor was the lady in question and she was duly nominated for Best Actress for this film - and won. 'I lost to a tracheotomy', complained unsuccessful nominee Shirley MacLaine. And she was probably right.

Liz had married singer Eddie Fisher the year before, the public convinced she had *stolen* him off everyone's favorite little Hollywood sweetheart, Debbie Reynolds, so neither Liz nor Eddie was exactly 'flavor of the month'. But then, suddenly, Liz lands at death's door and the very ordinary *Butterfield 8* grows an extra leg. The movie-going public is nothing if not fickle.

Liz moved heaven and Earth to get Eddie into *Butterfield 8*, to kick-start a movie career for him. The guy was a seriously good singer, but he could not act to save himself. He also had a drug problem at the time, so the producers wouldn't touch him with a barge pole. A couple of years later she did manage to coerce 20th Century Fox into paying him $1,500 a week while she was making *Cleopatra*. The studio agreed, secretly telling Fisher it was his task to get his wife to the set on time and to keep her off the booze. That was the extent of his duties.

His name actually appears in the credits as a stage manager in *All About Eve*, but his performance must have ended up on the cutting room floor where it probably belonged. If we can believe his autobiography, Eddie's performance in the bedroom was decidedly better. During his affair with model Renata Boeck, he exalted in print over his ability to climax nine times the first night, eight times the following night, and seven more the night after that! Well, if it helped to sell his book...

Cabaret (1972)

Liza Minnelli, of course, is the daughter of Judy Garland and director Vincente Minnelli. She made her movie debut at the age of three in the final scene of her parents' picture *In the Good Old Summertime*. Marlene Dietrich was her godmother in real life. As a child Liza was doted upon by her father to the extent that on one occasion she persuaded him to drive 100 miles out of his way so she could change her dress for a party. She was four years old at the time.

Her affair with Peter Sellers ended abruptly when she stole up behind him at a dinner and playfully snatched his toupee from his head. He was extremely vain and did not like it known he was almost bald. Liza got the boot.

While performing at Chequers Nightclub in Sydney, Australia in June 1968, she was visited in her dressing room by the then Prime Minister of Australia John Gray Gorton, who brought along a bottle of champagne for the occasion. The couple remained alone behind the locked door for an inordinate length of time, sparking rumors she and the PM had been intimate. Both, naturally enough, denied any involvement.

Her grandfather was gay, as were her father and her husband, Peter Allen. Her mother was bi-sexual. Allen was an Australian who scored with the hit songs 'I go To Rio' and 'I Still Call Australia Home'. He and Liza reputedly did not even spend their wedding night together because he was elsewhere having sex with a male friend. Later he would complicate things even further by sleeping with one of her mother's gay husbands Mark Herron. Allen died from AIDS in 1992.

Cactus Flower (1969)

Goldie Hawn won an Oscar for this, her first big role. For those who might think success came easily for the dizzy blonde who rocketed to prominence in TV's *Laugh-In* series, the following may be of interest. She began ballet and tap lessons at three. At sixteen she played Juliet in the Virginia Stage Company's production of *Romeo and Juliet*. Two years later she started a dancing school in her hometown.

Next, she worked in the chorus line of *Can-Can* at the New York World's Fair followed by stints in road companies of *Kiss Me Kate* and *Guys and Dolls*. After that she was in the chorus line in Puerto Rica for a while, a go-go dancer back in New York and then a choreographer in Los Angeles. From there she danced on TV's *The Andy Griffiths Show*, after which she gained an audition for *Laugh-In*. Only then did her career finally take off at the age of twenty-four. Stardom is rarely a walk in the park in Tinsel town.

Caddyshack (1980)

Chevy Chase's stepmother was heir to the Folger coffee fortune. He started out as a writer for *Mad* magazine in the 1960s. Since hitting the big time he has had to overcome drug problems stemming from work-related back injuries that were later enhanced by his inability to cope with the failure of his movie career.

In 1980 Cary Grant filed a $10 million lawsuit against him after Chase publicly referred to the ageing star as, 'a great physical comic, and I understand he was a homo – what a gal!' For obvious reasons Cary did not follow through on the suit. Too many people knew the truth.

Calamity Jane (1953)

Dick Wesson was good as the dance hall comedian Frances Fryer masquerading as Adelaide Adams in this Doris Day musical. Three weeks before his sixtieth birthday he put a gun to his head and pulled the trigger.

California Split (1974)

Ethel Merman's ex-daughter-in-law Barbara Colby features in this film in the small role of a receptionist, but she was a TV comedienne on the rise, with a sitcom called *Phyllis* just beginning. In July 1975 the thirty-six year old actress was shot to death as she left a yoga class with her boyfriend. He also died from his wounds. There was no robbery involved and police put the crime down to a random, senseless shooting. The murders were never solved.

California Suite (1978)

Dana Plato plays Jenny in this, but is probably best known for her role as Kimberley Drummond in TV's

Different Strokes. She was also a lesbian who became heavily involved in drugs after the series folded. By the 1990s she was performing in porno films, usually in lesbian situations, and dabbling in prostitution on the side, often being assaulted by her 'Johns'. At thirty-five she ended her life with an overdose of the painkiller Loritab. Her fiancée at the time reputedly offered to sell pictures of her dead body on the Internet, together with what he claimed were tapes of her 'dying breaths'! As human beings go, it is difficult to imagine one getting much lower than that.

Call of the Wild (1935)

Loretta Young (1913-2000)

Known relationships:

Asher, Irving
Boyer, Charles
Columbo, Russ
Cortez, Ricardo
Gable, Clark
Greene, Richard
Hughes, Howard
Lawford, Peter
Mankiewicz, Joseph L.
Morris, Wayne
Niven, David
Power, Tyrone
Ratoff, Gregory
Roland, Gilbert
Romero, Cesar
Stewart, James
Talbot, Lyle
Tracy, Spencer
Wellman, William

Married:

Grant Withers & 2 others

Actress Sally Blane was Loretta Young's real life sister. Loretta was not much of an actress, even though she picked up an Oscar in 1947 for *The Farmer's Daughter*. New York Times critic Bosley Crowther wrote of her thespian shortcomings before that in 1944, saying, 'Whatever it was that this actress never had, she still hasn't got it'.

Loretta was not a popular woman. Many of her peers were disgusted by her 'holier than thou' attitude. Marlene Dietrich said of her, 'Every time she sins she builds a church'. Virginia Field was quoted as saying, 'She was and is the only actress I really dislike. She was sickeningly sweet, a pure phony'. Because of her Puritan façade and her 'tough as nails' underneath persona she became known in the industry as 'Attila the Nun'.

For all her piety and prim and proper attitude to others, Loretta's romantic past stamps her as a hypocrite of the first order. At seventeen she eloped with actor Grant Withers but the union was over inside a year. Two years later she had a lengthy affair with the married Spencer Tracy, a liaison she ultimately ended on the advice of her priest. Tracy was shattered.

The following year, 1934, she became pregnant to another married man. This time it was Clark Gable on the set of *Call of the Wild*. 'I thought you knew how to take care of yourself', was his response when she broke the news to him. He then took a powder and high-tailed it for engagements in New York City.

Her Catholicism vetoed any thought of an abortion, so Loretta had the baby in secret, sent it to the St. Elizabeth's Infant Hospital in San Francisco for a few months, and then arranged to *adopt* her own daughter! When she wired Gable with news of the birth he flushed the cable down the toilet. Nobody could ever say Clark wasn't consistent. By then she was married to a man named Lewis who generously agreed to the adoption. The girl was baptized Judy by a congenial priest who agreed to substitute false parental names on the documents. Maybe the Lord spoke to him and told him to give Loretta a break.

Papers commented that Judy 'had the biggest ears ever seen on a baby'. Loretta later had them fixed by cosmetic surgery. Home movies released to the public prior to the operation always showed the child either wearing a bonnet or with her hair covering her ears. Loretta kept little Judy in the dark about Gable. It was not until the girl married that she learned the truth from her husband on her wedding night. Nearly everyone in the industry knew except her.

In an interview with writer Gregory Speck nearly fifty years later, Young had this to say: 'Yes, I've heard all those fifty year-old rumors about Clark and me and our romance during the making of *The Call of the Wild* in 1935. They were rumors then, they're rumors now, and they'll always be rumors...as a person he was just a delight, but I didn't see him too much socially'.

Just before dying of ovarian cancer in 2000 she at last acknowledged the long dead Gable as Judy's father in her biography entitled *Forever Young*. It had only taken this gilt-edged hypocrite sixty-five years to do so.

Camelot (1967)

Critic John Simon described this laborious musical thus: 'The film is the Platonic idea of boredom, roughly comparable to reading a three-volume novel in a language of which you know only the alphabet'. And he was right.

Vanessa Redgrave who plays Guinevere, and Franco Nero who plays Lancelot, fell in love while making this film. She subsequently became pregnant, bore him a son, and married him – in 2006!

She was repeatedly unsuccessful in her bids to gain a seat in the British Parliament as a candidate for the Workers Revolutionary Party, a group advocating the destruction of capitalism and the abolishment of the monarchy. She also led Ban-the-Bomb rallies, Anti-Vietnam War marches, and spoke publicly in support of both the IRA and the PLO. One actor who openly scoffed at her Marxist position was Robert Duvall. 'Some Trotskyite', he sneered. 'She travels by Rolls Royce'. In 1971 the Nixon administration blacklisted her from attending the Oscars because of her political stance over the Vietnam War.

The same lady, it should be acknowledged, has established a home in London for disadvantaged children as well as a nursery in one of the city's poorer neighborhoods. 'I choose all my roles very carefully', said Vanessa, 'so that when my career is finished I will have covered all our recent history of oppression'.

Natasha and Joely Richardson are her daughters by her former husband director Tony Richardson. She divorced him in 1967 after naming French actress Jeanne Moreau as co-respondent. Tony later died from AIDS in 1991. Novelist Anthony Burgess commented after his demise, 'Tony Richardson was a terrible person. Not because he had AIDS, nor because he was bi-sexual, not because he was hypocritical about it. Because he was a terrible person. Not a terrible director, just a terrible human being'. Richardson won a directing Oscar in 1963 for *Tom Jones*.

Camille (1936)

At the film's premiere Greta Garbo turned up (reluctantly), wearing pajamas underneath her coat, waved to her fans and then walked through the front door and straight out the back one without bothering to watch the picture. She only agreed to appear as a mark of respect for Irving Thalberg who died shortly before the picture's release. It was a monumental effort from a woman notorious for doing *nothing* for anyone except herself.

Greta Garbo (1905-1990)

Known relationships with women:

Bankhead, Tallulah
Brooks, Louise
Colbert, Claudette

D'Orsay, Fifi
De Acosta, Mercedes
De Rothschild, Olga
Dietrich, Marlene
Gaynor, Janet
Holiday, Billie
Hutchinson, Josephine
Munson, Ona
Pollak, Mimi
Tashman, Lilyan
Viertel, Salka

Known relationships with men:

Addams, Charles
Asther, Nils
Beaton, Cecil
Brent, George
Feldman, Charles
Gilbert, John
Guilaroff, Sydney
Hauser, Gaylord
Hayward, Leland
Kennedy, Joseph P.
Mamoulian, Rouben
Onassis, Aristotle
Roland, Gilbert
Romero, Cesar
Stiller, Mauritz
Stokowski, Leopold
Weissmuller, Johnny

At the age of thirteen Garbo was seduced in a tent in the family's backyard by her older, prettier sister, Alva. A little later she had her first heterosexual union with a local boy in the same tent. Incidentally, Garbo always said she wanted to be *let* alone. She did not want to *be* alone. The lady craved privacy not solitude.

Alan Royle

This legend of the silver screen became an American movie star virtually by default. When her mentor director Mauritz Stiller was signed by MGM, he insisted she should also be signed, or there would be no deal. Mayer put her on $250 a week with the parting comment to Stiller, 'and tell her that in America we don't like fat women'. Garbo thereafter referred to Mayer as 'that gross pig'.

She could be extremely irritating. A knock on her dressing-room door would most likely earn an angry 'not in!' from the grumpy actress. An invitation to dinner next Wednesday night might elicit, 'how do I know I will be hungry next Wednesday night?' She would walk straight past people she knew without speaking, but if *they* did not speak she would quickly mutter 'Hullo', just to make them feel guilty. And then she would walk on.

Her label as 'the woman of mystery' was cooked up by MGM to keep her from conducting interviews in which she invariably offended someone, or made some outlandish observation or statement that damaged her image. Personally, she cared little about adverse publicity at the height of her career, probably because she encountered so little of it.

When gay director F W Furneau died in a car crash while being fellated by his fourteen year-old Filipino chauffeur, the only movie personage brave enough to attend his funeral was Garbo.

Louise Brooks spent one night with her and described the screen goddess as 'a completely masculine dyke', but also 'a charming lover'. Brooks was certain Garbo's affair with John Gilbert was publicized to cover up her lesbian proclivities. Writer Anita Loos interpreted the Gilbert-Garbo affair differently. 'She spread her legs like most actresses who wanted to get ahead', she said with disdain.

Garbo moved in with Gilbert for a while and enjoyed entertaining his friends by playing tennis and swimming naked in his pool. The guests who all wore bathing costumes tried not to gawk at her nakedness.

Once, an MGM tour group was astonished to behold her perched on a high chair, stark naked and trying on a hat! Neighbors were known to complain about her naked romps with health guru Gaylord Hauser in his backyard. There is just no pleasing some people.

Although essentially a lesbian, she still had many affairs with men and was once diagnosed with gonorrhea following a brief holiday with director Rouben Mamoulian. Polish poet Antoni Gronowicz was bemused with her ritual for warding off pregnancy. Just prior to actual coitus she would suddenly leap out of bed, perform a series of aerobic exercises, chant an obscure Scandinavian peasant song and then hop back into the sack again raring to go.

Ina Claire said Garbo once made an unsuccessful pass at her. When Claire followed her to the bathroom she was surprised to find the Swedish actress had left the toilet seat up. Author Barry Paris believed Greta had an affair with the aging, dowdy, lesbian Marie Dressler when they worked together on *Anna Christie*.

Her housekeeper for many years described the actress as mean and penny-pinching. Given just $100 a month to purchase food, the woman was compelled to shop at cheap wholesale outlets to make the money last. Even then, Garbo complained that $100 was too much to spend on a month's food, so she reduced the budget to just $80. Every cent had to be accounted for. Soap and shampoo were considered luxuries and she seldom purchased them. Yet all this time she was earning a staggering $25,000 a week when the average movie extra, for instance, took home (and got by on) just $10 a week.

Her interest in magazines (provided they carried stories about her) was a life-long obsession. She would order copies of every movie publication, read each one over and over while circling articles about herself that she felt were flattering, and then mail them off each week to her mother in Sweden.

She did not retire at the peak of her popularity simply because she became bored with stardom. There was more to it than that. Surprisingly, her final film was a major critical and financial flop, but more importantly, World War Two erupted and her European fan base evaporated overnight. Her pictures rarely made money in America anyway, yet she was number one at the box-office in nearly every European country before the war. When that market dried up she became a liability. Aware the writing was on the wall she accepted $250,000 from MGM to terminate her contract ahead of time.

During the war she steadfastly refused to sell war bonds, participate in USO tours, or even help out at the Hollywood Canteen. One evening, as she and Orson Welles were leaving a restaurant, she accidentally collided with a one-legged soldier. When the man asked for her autograph she coldly refused him. Welles was appalled.

Soon after this incident she did manage to do her bit for the boys in uniform. Well, one of them anyway. After running across actor Gilbert Roland who had just enlisted, she accompanied him to his home and had sex with him, and then gave him her panties as a memento. Months later when he came back to town on leave he tried to renew her acquaintance, but she refused to answer his calls.

Some sources claim she was acknowledged as having identified several prominent Stockholm Nazis during the war. She was even credited with carrying messages for British Intelligence on visits to her native Sweden. There is no verification of this, however, and such activity attributed to such a private and self-centered individual seems totally out of character.

By the 1950s she had become so utterly selfish and unsociable that most of her Hollywood acquaintances avoided her, often hiding in their homes when spying the aging, short-tempered actress walking up their driveways. She still managed the occasional conquest, however, as Frank Sinatra's valet George Jacobs recalled. He was given the task of looking after Garbo, Marlene Dietrich and Hal Wallis's sister Minna for a couple of days at one of Frank's homes. Garbo and Marlene swam naked in the pool, he wrote, and lay nude on the chaise, kissing and fondling while an obviously jealous Minna studied every move they made.

To everyone's surprise Garbo lived with the very gay Cecil Beaton for a few months in her final years. When he made the fatal error of publicly claiming they were lovers she threw him out. She still loathed any measure of publicity, as he must have known.

Beaton, incidentally, also laid claim in his autobiography to having had an affair with none other than Gary Cooper! Like author Truman Capote, he often made outlandish statements simply to gain attention during career lulls. However, if we can believe Clara Bow and Anderson Lawler's own brother, Coops lived with Anderson several times and was definitely intimate with him. In fact, at a party one evening, Cooper's current lover, the outrageous Lupe Velez, undone his flies and, in front of a hundred people, sniffed 'for Anderson Lawler's cologne', or so she said.

Garbo's final appearance in a movie was in the tacky sex flick *Adam and Yves* made in 1974. She was depicted as herself walking down a New York street. The makers of the film neither paid her nor asked for her consent. By then she was a total recluse and had no intention of returning into the public eye by suing anybody, so she let the matter drop.

She lived out her last days in New York City and died in 1990 from pneumonia, leaving an estate valued at $32 million. Among her assets were two Renoirs worth $19 million. Her body was cremated and nobody seems to want to say where her ashes are located. A recluse to the end.

Cannon for Cordoba (1970)

Pete Duel was a highly promising television star of the sixties. He played Sally Field's brother-in-law in the *Gidget* series and starred alongside Ben Murphy in the popular western series *Alias Smith & Jones*. For a time he was romantically involved with Judy Carne of *Laugh In* fame.

Apparently, he became disgruntled with the direction his movie career was taking, having only appeared in a couple of small roles, one of which was the film above, and he didn't much care for his performances in his TV series either. He was also struggling with alcohol and substance abuse. On 31 December 1971 he shot himself, his naked body found lying beneath the Christmas tree in his living room. He was 31.

Can't Stop the Music (1986)

This monstrosity was released after the disco boom had ceased to be fashionable. It was a movie searching in vain for an audience that no longer existed. To make matters worse it was decided to allot the homosexual Village People *girlfriends*, a move that instantly alienated their gay following. 'You don't spend $20 million on a minority movie', said the producer in defense of the decision. The only country in which the picture was a success was in Australia where it briefly set new box-office records.

The Village People's single *Y.M.C.A.* was the biggest selling record worldwide of the entire seventies, and the group was still popular 'down under', well after it had waned elsewhere. As an Australian, I wish to state *categorically* that I in no way contributed to the picture's success in this country! I do admit to watching the first ten minutes of it on Foxtel recently, entirely out of curiosity. I am expecting my Victoria Cross in the mail any day now for doing so. It was only ten minutes, but I earned it. God, what an *awful* movie.

Captain Blood (1935)

Captain Blood was Errol Flynn's first major role. It made millions for Warner Brothers, yet he was initially paid only $150 a week for his performance in it. Because of the asthma that would shortly kill him, Robert Donat had to give up the lead roles in both *Captain Blood* and *The Adventures of Robin Hood*. Errol landed both parts and became an instant star. That much was clear even before *Captain Blood* had completed shooting. Errol realized it too and demanded a pay increase from $150 to $750 a week or he would refuse to finish the picture. Jack Warner had no choice but to comply. The two men would feud for decades.

Errol's new found fame also put paid to his marriage to Lili Damita.'Now that he has become famous, he won't want me anymore', Lili cried, and she was right. They soon separated. Lili, who was bi-sexual, was the Hollywood star of caricature, and would often attend parties accompanied by a tame leopard on a leash, which was probably all a bit too much, even for Errol.

He tried everything to win over his leading lady, Olivia de Havilland, but was unsuccessful. Years later she admitted to having a crush on him, but had shrewdly determined that any relationship with the rampant Flynn might ultimately destroy her. On screen she came across as sweet and innocent, but in reality Olivia had a stubborn streak that in time would stand the whole studio system on its head. She would bring about much needed changes in the system, changes that would have far reaching consequences.

Errol did succeed in bedding another member of the cast, however; the young Ross Alexander who plays Jeremy Pitt. Director Michael Curtiz detested Alexander because he could not tolerate homosexuals. It was common knowledge that the young actor had carried on a relationship with Rod la Roque on Broadway, and it was equally obvious he and Flynn enjoyed a similar liaison. 'Those two are just another couple of no good son-of-a-bitch faggots', Curtiz told the rest of the cast. Two years after *Captain Blood* was released Alexander shot himself during a fit of depression over gambling debts.

Lionel Atwill plays Olivia's uncle, Colonel Bishop, in the picture. He was married to Louise Cromwell, the former wife of General Douglas MacArthur and a direct descendant of Oliver Cromwell. Lionel was notorious in Hollywood for hosting the best orgies in town. Guests at these parties were required to show proof they were VD-free before gaining admittance to his home.

At a signal from him, and to the strains of 'The Blue Danube', revelers were ordered to strip naked for the orgy to begin. Only the wearing of jewelry was permitted. All this came to a sudden halt after the Christmas bash of 1940. Directors Joseph von Sternberg and Eddie Goulding, as well as actor Victor Jory were among the twenty-six guests who enjoyed the porno films and orgy that evening. Unfortunately for Atwill, a sixteen year-old girl named Sylvia was also taking an active part. She later told her parents of having sex with producer Eugene Frencke during the evening. Consequently, Atwill (not Frencke) was arrested and charged. The ensuing press coverage ruined his career. Von Sternberg, Goulding, Jory et al were bigger fish in the Hollywood pond, so they were never publicly associated with the scandal.

South African-born Basil Rathbone plays the 'heavy' opposite Flynn. A hero of World War One (he was decorated with the Military Cross), he was also a fencing expert in real life and disliked the airy-fairy movie style swordplay he was ordered to employ on the screen. For that matter, Curtiz himself once represented Hungary as a fencer in the 1912 Olympics.

He too was disparaging of movie swordplay but realized it was a necessary evil. Proper fencing was simply too fast and too subtle for movie audiences and it lacked flair and drama. Rathbone also took male lovers from time to time but he could not cotton to Flynn at all. In time they eventually got along but the friendship was strained at best. Dorothy Parker once described Basil as 'two profiles pasted together'.

Captain Newman MD (1963)

Although his marriage to starlet Sandra Dee is common knowledge, Darin's long romance with singer Connie Francis is probably less known. The couple's feelings for each other were strong enough for him to propose marriage, but Connie's father was against it for reasons unknown.

In 1961 Bobby purchased a car for $150,000, a feature of which was a paint job consisting of thirty coats containing crushed diamond dust! He died from heart problems in 1973 at the age of thirty-seven. There was no funeral and, as per his instructions, his body was donated for research to the UCLA.

Captains Courageous (1937)

Spencer Tracy's Oscar for *Captains Courageous* was incorrectly engraved to 'Dick Tracy'.

Lionel Barrymore, who plays the skipper of the trawler, suffered terribly from arthritis in his later years. Some sources claim he was wheelchair-bound because of a fall. Others say it was because he suffered from syphilis. Either way, Louis B Mayer procured for him $400 worth of cocaine *per day* to help ease the pain when it was at its worst.

Freddie Bartholomew plays the snobbish boy picked up by the fishing trawler. By 1938 he had amassed over a million dollars in his short film career. It all disappeared when his guardian aunt and his parents fought out no fewer than twenty-seven highly expensive legal battles over the money. A judge eventually awarded 10% of Freddie's earnings to his parents, 10% to his Aunt Millie who had raised him and a further 5% to his sisters! Nobody seemed to know why.

Some bean counter at MGM's marketing department thought Irving Thalberg's funeral would provide a good opportunity to publicize Freddie's latest movie. With that in mind they sent the boy along to the service dressed in his black velvet *Little Lord Fauntleroy* outfit!

Carmen Jones (1954)

Despite having a mellifluous voice, Harry Belafonte does not sing in this film. All his songs are dubbed, would you believe?

In 1968 he found himself at the center of a controversy after appearing on an NBC TV special hosted by British songstress Petula Clark. When Miss Clark gently touched his arm during a duet, it was the first time two people of different color had affectionately come in contact with each other on American television. The Plymouth Car Company got very nervous over the 'incident', and the resultant furor (especially in the Deep South) highlighted the bigotry existent at that time in the US media.

In 1953, Dorothy Dandridge and Peter Lawford had a lengthy affair, which they agreed to end before it endangered their careers.

Otto Preminger, who directed *Carmen Jones*, used his position of authority to seduce Dandridge by telling her sex with him would make her 'bloom' before the cameras. Their affair was lengthy but doomed. He made it very clear he would never divorce his wife to marry a black actress.

In the early 1960s Dorothy lost everything after investing in some 'get rich quick' oil schemes. In 1965, at the age of forty-one, she killed herself with Tofranil anti-depressant tablets. The once much sought after actress was found to have just $2.14 in her bank account at the time of her death.

This was Diahann Carroll's screen debut. She and Sidney Poitier were married to others throughout most of their five-year romance, before Diahann broke it off a month or so after they announced their engagement. A few years later she and Britain's David Frost became involved and were together for a few years, but that relationship didn't go the distance either. Incidentally, Frost died aboard MS *Queen Elizabeth* at sea, between England and Portugal, in 2013.

Carpetbaggers, The (1964)

Alan Ladd was fifty years old when he made this film, but looked sixty if he was a day. When the script calls for him to tell Carroll Baker that he is *forty-three*, she has to respond with the line, 'You look thirty'. The lady should have been given an Oscar, just for managing to keep a straight face as she said it.

Howard Hughes (1905-1976)

Known relationships with men:

Buetel, Jack
Cromwell, Richard

Flynn, Errol
Grant, Cary
Power, Tyrone
Scott, Randolph

Known relationships with women:

Adoree, Renee
Astor, Mary
Bankhead, Tallulah
Bennett, Constance
Blondell, Joan
Brooks, Phyllis
Bruce, Virginia
Carroll, Georgia
Carroll, Nancy
Cawford, Joan
Chapman, Marguerite
Charisse, Cyd
Churchill, Marguerite
Clarke, Mae
Cummins, Peggy
Dahl, Arlene
Darnell, Linda
Davis, Bette
De Carlo, Yvonne
De Havilland, Olivia
Domergue, Faith
Dove, Billie
Ekberg, Anita
Emerson, Faye
Fontaine, Joan
Frazier, Brenda
Freeman, Mona
Furness, Betty
Gabor, Zsa Zsa
Gardner, Ava
Gaynor, Mitzi
Gilbert, Helen
Goddard, Paulette

Grayson, Kathryn
Greer, Jane
Griffith, Corinne
Harlow, Jean
Hayward, Susan
Hepburn, Katharine
Hutton, Barbara
Knudsen, Peggy
Lake, Veronica
Lansing, Joi
Lombard, Carole
Lupino, Ida
Mayo, Virginia
Miller, Ann
Moore, Terry
Negri, Pola
Oberon, Merle
Paget, Debra
Payton, Barbara
Rogers, Ginger
Shearer, Norma
Sheehan, Pat
Sheridan, Margaret
Stanwyck, Barbara
Sweet, Blanche
Tierney, Gene
Turner, Lana
Van Doren, Mamie
Vanderbilt, Gloria
Winters, Shelley
Young, Loretta

Married:

Jean Peters & 1 other

This movie is *very* loosely based on Howard Hughes' rise to prominence, especially his takeover of RKO Pictures and his creation of Jean Harlow as a screen goddess.

In July 1936, Hughes was charged with negligent homicide over the death of a man in an auto accident, but the charges were soon quietly dropped.

In 1938 he designed and built a superb airplane and then flew it around the world in a record ninety-one hours. The Japanese were impressed enough to steal the plans and build the excellent Zero fighter plane from them.

He nearly always managed to bed the women he fancied, usually by making them a monetary offer they could not refuse. His pursuit of actress Billie Dove was typical. After she continually turned him down (because she was still a married woman), he offered her husband, director Irvin Willat, $325,000 to divorce her, an enormous sum back in the 1920s. Willat accepted, the divorce went through and Hughes at once seduced her. Then he just as quickly lost interest in the flighty Miss Dove (please forgive the pun) and ditched her.

His biographer said he preferred inter-mammary intercourse and fellatio, rather than full or conventional intercourse, and was a thoughtless and inconsiderate lover who only bothered to satisfy himself. Since he mostly bedded women he paid for, either in cash or expensive gifts, it could be argued he was entitled to indulge himself in whatever manner he pleased, since they were more or less glorified prostitutes.

Carry on Cleo (1965)

Charles Hawtrey, the weedy bespectacled member of the *Carry On* gang, was an alcoholic homosexual who liked to pick up sailors in bars for sex. He was so universally disliked (both by his peers and his family) that not one of his family or acquaintances was close enough to him to know his actual birth date. When he died only nine people attended the funeral.

Barbara Windsor recalled him chasing after champion footballer George Best at a publicity event in Manchester. After being fired from the 'Carry On' films over a billing dispute he moved to the seaside town of Deal where he made a nuisance of himself propositioning young men in the local pubs.

He had always drank to excess, but in his final years he descended into alcoholism. In 1984, the local fire brigade was called to rescue him from his home when it went up in flames. A news photographer snapped the seventy year-old comedian completely naked, minus even his toupee.

The story gained momentum that his bedmate, a young man some sources stated was just sixteen, was also saved from the conflagration. For several weeks local louts made life unbearable for the aged Hawtrey. A virtual prisoner in his new lodgings he was compelled to send a taxi to do his shopping for him.

In 1988, he collapsed in a drunken state outside a pub and accidentally broke his leg in the process. His drinking excesses had so harmed his body it became necessary to amputate both his legs in order to save his life. This he refused to permit, and he passed away soon afterwards.

Kenneth Williams, too, was gay, but it did not stop him proposing marriage to Joan Sims. She promptly turned him down. A formidable raconteur and radio panelist he died from a drug overdose at sixty-two.

Sid James was born in Natal, South Africa and always considered himself a Springbok, not an Englishman. He claimed he had sex and a bottle of whiskey every day of his adult life until his death at sixty-three. One of his many lovers was Barbara Windsor, the actress with the enormous bust who was a regular in the *Carry On* films.

Off screen Joan Sims was a shy recluse who was lonely all her life. She said she only ever received one proposal of marriage and that was from her gay 'Carry On' co-star Williams. 'I will give you a child if you want one', he magnanimously offered, 'but after that we wouldn't be sleeping together'. His proposal was scarcely the stuff of romantic legend. He also promised her: 'I would be frightfully amusing company and we would throw the most wonderful parties'. No wonder she turned him down.

Carry on Doctor (1967)

Frankie Howerd was another unabashed homosexual gracing the ranks of British comedians of the sixties. At a show business dinner in 1966, attended by fellow funnyman Tommy Cooper, the room was packed with people keen to see Howerd in person. 'Well, there's one thing you can say for Frankie', a colleague said to Cooper, 'He certainly puts bums on seats. The laconic Tommy replied, 'Yes, safest place for them'.

Casablanca (1942)

On completion of the film it was decided to remove the song *As Time Goes By* from the final print because music director Max Steiner did not agree with building his score around an old Tin Pan Alley tune. Ingrid Bergman in the meantime had gone off to make *For Whom the Bell Tolls*, and her hair had been cropped short for that role. Even with her donning a wig, convincing re-shoots of the 'Play it Sam' sequence didn't look right, so the song was reluctantly left in. It is now considered to be one of the great movie love songs of all time.

Remembered for his haunting rendition of *As Time Goes By* is Dooley Wilson. He was actually a drummer and not a piano player.

The Marx Brothers were all set to release *A Night in Casablanca* when Warner Brothers threatened to take legal action against them, claiming the use of 'Casablanca' in the title was cashing in on their hit film. Groucho responded by threatening to sue the studio for using the word 'brothers' in its studio title, arguing that the Marx Brothers had been around longer than the Warner Brothers. It now appears Groucho kept up the battle of words as a promotional stunt for his movie. But it was fun while it lasted.

Hal Wallis and Jack Warner feuded non-stop. When Wallis won the Best Picture Oscar for producing *Casablanca*, Warner, as head of the studio, raced to the stage ahead of him and accepted the award. 'The entire Warner family was blocking me', recalled Wallis ruefully. 'I had no alternative but to sit down again, humiliated and furious'. He left the studio two years later.

A poll of extras (they were allowed to vote in those days) indicated that only 25% of them had seen the 'limited release' of *The Song of Bernadette* due to the high ticket prices, while nearly all had seen *Casablanca*. It has since been suggested this was the reason for the Bogart picture outscoring the Jennifer Jones outing in the race for Best Picture. Surely not. *Casablanca* is an infinitely better movie and deserved to win.

When Michael Curtiz won the Oscar for *Casablanca* his acceptance speech was a classic. 'So many times I have a speech ready, but no dice. Always a bride's maid, never a mother', he said wistfully.

The final scene at the airport is faked. The airplane in the background is a model and the personnel in overalls bustling around it are all midgets.

Conrad Veidt was the gay actor who plays the Nazi officer Major Strasser. He died from a heart attack in the same year the picture was released. On loan as a contract player from MGM, he was being paid $5,000 a week, more than anyone else in the picture, including the two stars. Ironically, he was once forced to flee Germany in 1929, so he loathed all Nazis.

After Bogart's wife Mayo Methot threatened to kill him over an imagined affair she thought he was having with Bergman, the producers of *Casablanca* were compelled to insure his life for $100,000 in case she carried out her threat before the picture was completed. Three months after he married Lauren Bacall he recommenced his long-running affair with Verita Thompson, a liaison that lasted throughout the final fifteen years of his life.

Peter Lorre had a brief but memorable part in the film playing the sleazy thief and killer Ugarte. When Bela Lugosi died and was about to be buried as per his request in his full Dracula costume, it was Lorre who quietly suggested to Vincent Price as they gazed upon their friend's corpse in its open casket, 'maybe we should drive a stake through his heart to make sure'.

Lorre's daughter very nearly became a victim of the 'Hillside Stranglers'. They chatted to her on a street corner with the intention of picking her up and murdering her, but decided against it when she mentioned who her father was. Apparently, they were fans.

Cat Ballou (1965)

Lee Marvin's acceptance speech for the Best Actor Oscar for *Cat Ballou* began with, 'I think half of this belongs to a horse somewhere out in the valley'. Perhaps the horse merited a *nomination*, but Marvin was hilarious as the drunken gunfighter Kid Shalleen.

J C Flippen plays the crooked sheriff in *Cat Ballou*. While making the film he noticed a sore developing on his leg. After treating it with some home remedies he realized he had a serious problem. Doctors informed him that it had turned gangrenous and he would have to make a choice – lose his leg or lose his life. He was in unbearable pain anyway, so the operation was performed and his leg amputated. He died during an operation seven years later at 71.

When former lover Michelle Triola took Marvin to court in what became the very first palimony case, evidence of his drinking problem surfaced that included an incident in which he once held a young woman out of a Las Vegas hotel window by her feet! The drinking problem would remain with him all his life, a possible legacy of his horrendous war experiences. In his later years he slept with an axe under the mattress and a loaded .45 on the table next to his bed.

He really had a terrible time of it in World War Two. As a US Marine he stormed a number of Pacific beachheads before he was out of his teens. While fighting on Saipan his company was decimated by Japanese suicide attacks that left just six survivors out of 247 marines. Severely wounded, Marvin was one of the six who were repatriated back to the USA. It was the second time he had suffered grave injuries and narrowly escaped death. When he died in 1987 his ashes were interred in Arlington National Cemetery under a simple US Marine headstone that reads: Lee Marvin, PFC US Marine Corps, 1924-1987.

If you ever take note of him handling a gun you will observe he invariably sticks his little finger out as if he is taking tea with the Queen. He does it here, in *The Man Who Shot Liberty Valence* and in *The Comancheros*, just to name three of his pictures. Despite his little mannerisms he had a genuine screen presence and a powerful voice that demanded to be heard. He was one of the all-time consistent scene-stealers in cinema history.

Brooke Hayward, when reminiscing about her early days at Vassar with Jane Fonda, recalled, 'Jane had a reputation for being easy'. She was also strong-willed and utterly shameless. On one occasion, after being chastised for refusing to wear the traditional white gloves and pearls to the daily Tea Party, she stormed off to her room, only to return a few minutes later wearing the gloves and pearls - and nothing else!

After denouncing former husband Roger Vadim for his 'sexual exploitation of women' she had to withstand a savage counter-attack from the Frenchman. When he brought other women to their bed, he said, 'she seemed to understand and, as always, went all out – *all the way*'. Actress Jennifer Lee claimed she managed to evade the Vadims, but doubts whether fellow actress Patti D'Arbanville did.

Another of Jane's husbands Tom Hayden was part of the original Chicago Seven of 1968, a high-profile group of anti-Vietnam War protesters. Fonda herself became known as 'Hanoi Jane' after her trip to North Vietnam in 1972 and her anti-war statements. In 1988, she publicly apologized for some of her comments during the war, in particular for the anti-American views she broadcast over Radio Hanoi, and for insisting that American POWs were being treated 'with care and respect'. Her naïve and offensive stance greatly incensed Vietnam veterans, especially after she called them 'hypocrites and liars'.

Married for a time to billionaire Ted Turner, she divorced him after becoming a born again Christian. 'She just came home and said I've become a Christian. That's a pretty big change for your wife of many years to tell you. That's a shock', he explained. It must have *really* been a shock for Ted, he being the man who publicly described Christianity as 'a religion for losers' and strongly advocated the removal of adultery from the Ten Commandments.

Champion (1949)

Upon watching Kirk Douglas's performance in this film, Joan Crawford cabled him an invitation to dine with her. He accepted, so they went to a restaurant and then to her place. 'The front door closed and she slipped out of her dress in the hallway', he recalled. They made love on the floor after which she took him upstairs to meet her children who were strapped into their beds. 'It was so professional, clinical, lacking in warmth, like the sex we just had' he shuddered. 'I got out fast'.

This was standard procedure for Crawford. Scores of her lovers described the exact same scene. She would walk in her front door and instantly strip naked, then lay on her foyer rug. Her date was expected to strip on the spot and service her there and then. And if he hesitated he was shown the door. There were no second chances.

Charade (1963)

Edited just weeks after JFK had been killed, the final print of *Charade* had the word 'assassinate' over-dubbed with the word 'eliminate'.

Cary Grant was sixty years old when he made this film, yet the script required him to take a shower in one scene. Concerned about displaying his ageing body, he convinced the director that the sequence would be funnier if he took his shower fully clothed. Pretty smart of him. It proved to be a highlight of the picture.

Ex-wife, Dyan Cannon, told of his attitude towards the Oscars as he watched the ceremonies unfold on TV each year. 'He was so emotionally involved that he jumped up and down on the bed abusing the nominees he feared might win. Now *that* is the proper spirit', she recalled.

Charge of the Light Brigade, The (1935)

When director Michael Curtiz called for rider-less horses with the immortal words, 'bring on the empty horses', co-stars Errol Flynn and David Niven fell about laughing. Incensed, he screamed at them, 'You lousy bums. You and your stinking language! You think I know fuck nothing. Well, I tell you – I know fuck *all!*' Both men dissolved into hysterics. Curtiz regularly butchered the English language as he ordered extras to 'go stand about in huddles', or to 'stop standing in bundles'.

Like C Aubrey Smith, Nigel Bruce was a first class cricketer in England. Eleven machine gun bullets in his left leg at Cambrai during the First World War soon put an end to that.

Chariots of Fire (1981)

This movie was financed by Mohammed El Fayed, the father of Dodi Fayed who would later die in the car crash that claimed the life of his girlfriend Princess Diana. Another of Dodi's reputed lovers was actress Winona Ryder.

Gay actor Ian Charleson, who plays Eric Liddell, died from AIDS in 1990. The gentleman playing the captain of the Cambridge University athletics team is former Test cricketer Derek Pringle.

Brad Davis was the star of *Midnight Express,* but he is also remembered as the American sprinter Jackson Scholz, the runner who gives a note of encouragement to Eric Liddell before his Olympic event. The bi-sexual Davis descended into drug and alcohol abuse and died from AIDS after using a dirty needle in 1971. He was only forty. He was scathing of the Hollywood duplicity that held fund-raisers and charities in the fight against AIDS, yet refused work to anyone even *suspected* of being HIV-Positive. He had managed to keep his condition secret until a doctor inadvertently disclosed it.

Charlie Chan at the Olympics (1937)

Warner Oland, the man who plays oriental sleuth Charlie Chan, was not Chinese but *Swedish*. He never wore make-up for the role, but simply combed his eyebrows up, his moustache down, grew a goatee and squinted.

Allan 'Rocky' Lane appears in this picture. Decades later he would provide the voice for TV's *Mister Ed*.

Chicago (2002)

While eight months pregnant with her second child, Catherine Zeta-Jones performed a strenuous song and dance number from *Chicago* at the 2003 Oscars. An ambulance stood by in case her water broke during a particularly high note or difficult move. Catherine already had a decent grounding in musicals long before she made it as a big Hollywood star, so the extra dimension required for this role was not something she had to learn from scratch. Renee Zellweger, on the other hand, had no musical background at all, yet almost steals the show.

Charlize Theron had already secured the role of Roxie Hart before a change of directors saw her lose it to Renee. Whoopi Goldberg missed out on the Mama Morton role which went to Queen Latifah whose real name is Dana Owens. She first achieved prominence as a rapper.

Michael Douglas admits he set out to win Catherine after seeing her in *The Mask of Zorro*. And who could blame him? He met her in Cannes and then sent roses to the Scottish location where she was filming *Entrapment* with Sean

Connery. In 1999 the tabloids were full of topless shots of her taken with a long lens as she and Douglas relaxed at home on their lawn. The pictures have since found their way onto over 1,200 US websites.

Following unsubstantiated accusations that both he and his wife Crawford were gay, an outraged Richard Gere took out the following full-page, $100,000 ad in *The Times* just prior to their separation: 'We are heterosexual and monogamous and take our commitment to each other very seriously'. Well, the separation made nonsense of the last bit and consequently caused some pundits to question the validity of the first half of the statement as well.

China Syndrome, The (1979)

This somewhat over-rated picture about a nuclear accident was sinking into obscurity when an extraordinary coincidence catapulted it into the limelight. Just two weeks after its release a nuclear accident really did happen at Three Mile Island, Harrisburg, Pennsylvania. By an even greater coincidence there was a line in *The China Syndrome* suggesting just such a mishap 'could render an area the size of Pennsylvania uninhabitable'. A promoters' dreams made.

Chinatown (1974)

Roman Polanski's opinion of Faye Dunaway was not all that great. 'A gigantic pain in the ass...she demonstrated certifiable proof of insanity', he said after directing her in *Chinatown*.

Ali MacGraw was originally supposed to play the female lead. Her husband was producer Robert Evans and it was his film to cast, but when Ali ran off with Steve McQueen while they were making the appropriately named *The Getaway* together, Evans replaced her with the volatile Miss Dunaway.

Polanski plays the hoodlum who slices Jack Nicholson's nose with a flick knife. The blade he used had a hinge that only went one way. Had he turned it the wrong way it really would have slit Nicholson's nose open.

In 1977, the charming Mr. Polanski was convicted of unlawful sexual intercourse with thirteen year-old Samantha Geimer at the home of Jack Nicholson and Anjelica Houston (they were both away at the time). He had taken the girl there on the pretext of doing a photo shoot. The official police report charged him on six counts: Furnishing Quaaludes to a minor, child molesting; unlawful intercourse, rape by use of drugs, oral copulation and sodomy. Inexplicably, these were later reduced to a single charge of unlawful sexual intercourse. He was convicted and the judge was about to slap him with a 50-year sentence when Polanski fled to France where he has remained ever since.

Whereas most of the movie world was appalled by his conduct, several friends and acquaintances publicly supported him. Producer Robert Evans, for instance, wrote to the judge highlighting Polanski's ordeal during the war. 'If ever a person is deserving of compassion, I think it is Roman', he gushed.

Mia Farrow also wrote the judge, calling Polanski 'a brave and brilliant man'. Producer Howard Koch was even more nauseating, describing him as 'a man of tremendous integrity', adding somewhat alarmingly: 'I'm sure the situation he finds himself in now is one of those things that could happen to any of us'. Uh-huh. Polanski once told an interviewer, 'normal love isn't interesting. I assure you that it is incredibly boring'. Evidently.

The unfortunate Miss Geimer later married and moved to Hawaii and bore three children. 'I would love to see him resolve it, the sooner the better', she said in 2003, 'My God, he knew I was just a child. He behaved like a coward and I'll never forget that'. If 'resolving it' means she hopes Polanski is sorry and has learned the errors of his ways, then she seems doomed to disappointment.

In his autobiography entitled *Roman* he describes how he bedded fifteen year-old Nastassja Kinski on the first night they met. That was two years *after* the rape scenario. Once again he claims he thought the girl was much older. Does the man *ever* bother to find out beforehand?

In 2003, while still residing in Europe, he won an Oscar for *The Pianist*. The Academy members at the 75th Awards night gave the absent director a standing ovation! No doubt he was gratified to learn of Harrison Ford's offer to deliver his statuette to him in person. Perhaps Kenneth Tynan summed up Polanski best when he described him as, 'the four-foot Pole you wouldn't touch with a ten-foot pole'.

Citizen Kane (1941)

Citizen Kane is a thinly disguised interpretation of the relationship between newspaper tycoon William Randolph Hearst and his actress mistress Marion Davies. Hearst certainly believed so anyway, and went to great lengths to have the picture destroyed before it could see the light of day.

His Cosmopolitan Pictures Company was affiliated with Louis B Mayer's MGM at that time, so when Mayer offered RKO, who made the picture, $805,000 to destroy the master print and all copies, he was clearly acting on orders from Hearst. RKO chief George Schaefer rejected the offer and released the picture.

It has been argued by those in the know that Hearst was particularly incensed over the use of the word 'Rosebud' in the film. According to actress Louise Brooks, a confidante of Davies, Rosebud was the tycoon's pet name for Marion's clitoris, a fact Brooks had previously made known to Herman Mankiewicz, the writer of the screenplay for *Citizen Kane*.

The only Oscar that Orson Welles ever won was for the screenplay of this film. He and Mankiewicz were deemed to be joint writers, yet that might not have been the case. Herman dictated the script to his nurse, 'from the first paragraph to the last', she later said. 'Welles didn't write (or dictate) one line of the shooting script of *Citizen Kane*'. Many sources dispute this, however, as the claim is based entirely on hearsay. At the 1941 Academy Awards, the film was booed each time one of its nine nominations was announced.

Look for the unknown Alan Ladd as a reporter smoking a pipe at the end of the picture. The pianist playing the music in the 'El Rancho' is the yet to be famous Nat King Cole.

After being wrongly accused in print by Hedda Hopper of having an affair with teenage star Deanna Durbin, Joseph Cotten caught up with the columnist at a Hollywood party. To the delight and astonishment of guests he walked up to the lady and booted her in the backside sending her sprawling. Walter Wanger and studio president Danny O'Shea carried him on their shoulders to the bar and toasted him in champagne. The next day his home was filled with flowers and telegrams from well-wishers who had always wanted to kick Hedda's backside themselves, but lacked the courage. He pasted the telegrams on his bathroom walls.

Cotten made an interesting comment on the movies in 1977. 'Orson Welles lists *Citizen Kane* as his best film', he said. 'Alfred Hitchcock opts for *Shadow of a Doubt* as his best, and Sir Carol Reed chose *The Third Man*. I'm in all of them'.

Orson Welles (1915-1985)

Known relationships:

Calvet, Corinne
Del Rio, Dolores
Dietrich, Marlene
Fitzgerald, Geraldine
Garbo, Greta

Garland, Judy
Holiday, Billie
Horne, Lena
Kitt, Eartha
Kodar, Oja
Leigh, Vivien
Lollobrigida, Gina
Padovani, Lea
Pampanini, Silvana
Remar, Lynn
Tcherina, Ludmilla
Valentine, Nancy
Vampira
Zorina, Vera

Married:

Rita Hayworth & 2 others

Welles became an overnight sensation with his Mercury Theatre presentation of *The War of the Worlds* on American radio in October 1938. Before the program even went to air CBS insisted upon 28 changes to the script because they felt it was too realistic. They were soon to be proven right. At 8pm the show began with the usual introduction telling the audience it was about to hear a presentation of HG Wells' classic sci-fi tale. The studio orchestra played a little Tchaikovsky and a weather report was issued followed by some dance music – and then the fun began.

A sudden news flash and a 'live' cross to a Professor Pierson (played by Welles himself) told of a series of gas emissions observed on the surface of the planet Mars. Additional dance music was broadcast until it was again interrupted by another 'live' cross, this time to a field near

Grover's Mill outside Trenton, New Jersey, where it was reported a strange cylinder had crashed to earth. A clearly agitated reporter described creatures emerging from the cylinder and killing people. Then the line went dead. This would come to be known as 'the moment that panicked America'.

Listeners who tuned in late to the broadcast believed the world really was under attack by aliens from Mars. Panic broke out across much of the nation, especially in the Trenton area. Whole families packed up and fled to the country. One man came home to find his wife about to take poison rather than risk capture by the invaders. Vigilante groups were formed to fight the Martians. Several listeners suffered heart attacks.

Meanwhile, Welles had no idea all this was happening, until the switchboard at CBS lit up with hundreds of calls from terrified listeners requesting more information. At the conclusion of the show he made an announcement to the effect that the program was simply his group's contribution to Halloween. They were merely saying 'Boo!' to America.

Orson avoided any writs, but CBS had to settle out of court in numerous instances with listeners who had suffered mentally or physically from the broadcast. Oddly enough, children were not fooled by the show at all. They instantly recognized Orson's voice because he played their hero 'The Shadow' on radio every week.

The incident made him a household name and he was soon inundated with offers from Hollywood. His first project there would be *Citizen Kane* and another controversy would erupt. He was suddenly one of the most famous men in America. Dorothy Parker was introduced to him. 'It's like meeting God without dying', she dryly commented.

In 2003, his Oscar for the screenplay of *Citizen Kane* looked set to fetch in excess of a quarter of a million pounds sterling at auction. That was until the Academy invoked its right to buy back the statuette for 60p!

City Lights (1931)

Virginia Cherrill, who would one day wed Cary Grant, plays the flower girl in Chaplin's 1931 classic *City Lights*. Chaplin is said to have made her do the scene 300 times until he was satisfied with her performance. Apparently, he was livid because she had refused his advances, although in fairness to Charlie she was nearly twenty at the time and probably far too old for his tastes anyway.

Charlie Chaplin (1889-1977)

Known relationships:

Bankhead, Tallulah
Barry, Joan
Bradford, Virginia
Brooks, Louise
Davies, Marion
Del Rio, Dolores
Dunn, Josephine
Falkenburg, Jinx
Hale, Georgia
Holmquist, Sigrid
Kelly, Hetty

La Marr, Barbara
Lamarr, Hedy
Landis, Carole
Lee, Lila
Maritza, Sara
Minter, Mary Miles
Negri, Pola
Normand, Mabel
Purviance, Edna
Velez, Lupe
West, Rebecca
Windsor, Claire

Married:

Paulette Goddard & 3 others

His little tramp character was deliberately devised as a complete contradiction, trousers too large, vest too small, boots too large and hat too small. All of these items he borrowed from his peers. The trousers, for example, once belonged to Fatty Arbuckle. By 1916, Mutual Pictures was paying Chaplin the astonishing sum of $670,000 a year to act for them. No shrinking violet, he once commented: 'I am known in parts of the world by people who have never heard of Jesus Christ'.

In 1918, when he was twenty-nine, he married sixteen year-old Mildred Harris. Before long she filed for divorce citing cruelty, so Chaplin charged her with infidelity, but refused to name the other party. All Hollywood knew the co-respondent was lesbian actress Alla Nazimova. Still sixteen and pregnant with Chaplin's baby, Mildred had moved into the 'Garden of Allah', Nazimova's residence and a hotbed of lesbian activity.

In 1924 he again married, this time to sixteen year-old Lita Grey who was already pregnant to him. He silenced her complaints over his sexual demands by telling her, 'I'm a stallion and you better get used to it'. He had met Lita when she was fourteen (her name then was Lolita McMurray) and ravaged her several times before they tied the knot. At their divorce hearing she accused him of making her perform 'abnormal, against nature, perverted, degenerate and indecent acts' before and during their marriage.

In private, she threatened to name five major actresses he had slept with during their union, unless he settled out of court. It is quite feasible that Lita's mother may have planned the entire romance in order to get her hands on some of Charlie's $16 million. The eventual settlement was for either $65,000 or $625,000, depending on which source you believe.

Another lover, Joan Barry, twice broke into his home, and on one of those occasions threatened him with a loaded pistol. When he ended their affair she brought a paternity suit against him, but it was soon proved the child was not Chaplin's at all. Billionaire Paul Getty paid Barry's legal fees for reasons never fully explained. Nevertheless, the jury found *against* Charlie and he was ordered to pay alimony.

Millionaire, man-hungry Peggy Joyce Hopkins wasted no time in getting to the point when she first met him. 'Is it true what all the girls say', she asked straight out, 'that you're

hung like a horse?' If another of his wives Paulette Goddard
is to be believed, he was. 'Charlie takes everything out of me',
she told a close friend when asked about the size of his
equipment. The gentleman himself often referred to his
penis as 'the eighth wonder of the world'. Another lover,
Edna Purviance, never made a film after 1926, yet Chaplin
kept her on full salary until her death thirty-two years later!
Nobody seems to know why.

His need to wed very young girls, as evidenced by the
following, was a lifelong obsession:

First marriage: 1918 – Charlie 29 Mildred Harris 16.

Second marriage: 1924 – Charlie 35 Lita Grey 16.

Third marriage: 1936 – Charlie 47 Paulette Goddard 19.

Fourth marriage: 1943 – Charlie 55 Oona O'Neill 17.

In 1931 a group of Japanese militants plotted to
assassinate Chaplin during his visit to Tokyo. Unaware he
was English born and not an American, they hoped his death
would bring about a declaration of war from America on the
Empire of Japan.

The House on Un-American Activities Committee went
after him during the McCarthy witch-hunts, citing two of his
films as 'anti-capitalist'. He was aboard ship in 1952, on his
way to London, when told he was barred from returning to
America indefinitely.

While accepting an honorary Oscar in 1972, the eighty-three year old legend beamed, 'You're all sweet, wonderful people'. Later, he told friends, 'I hated them all'.

Somebody stole his coffin from its resting place in 1977. It turned up in a field sixteen days later with Charlie still in it.

Cleopatra (1963)

20TH Century Fox decided in 1958 to remake *Cleopatra* using a budget of between one and three million dollars. After the first seven and a half minutes of screen time was shot in England in 1962 at a cost of seven million dollars, the brilliant decision was reached that the budget might need revising. After several more revisions the picture would ultimately cost a whopping $31 million to complete.

The fallout from the disastrous drain on its resources caused Fox to sell off 262 acres of its studio lot for a paltry $55 million. The acreage situated in the most valuable urban district on the planet is today worth fifty times its selling price. Fox retained a mere 73 acres of its property, although the discovery of oil on the premises proved to be an unexpected bonus. Ironically, in the long run the film actually showed a profit of about $5 million but that would not be for decades.

In 1963 Fox wanted Susan Hayward to play the title role even though she was then forty-five years old. She wisely declined it. Joanne Woodward, hot off her success with *The Three Faces of Eve,* was also a possibility. Joan Collins, too, was thought of as a candidate for the Queen of the Nile. Even the bust-less Audrey Hepburn was considered by Billy Wilder to portray the great sex siren of history.

Marilyn Monroe vigorously pursued the role through her Fox 'contact' studio mogul Spyros Skouras, actually going to the trouble of having photographs taken of herself in Cleopatra costume. The photos made their way into *Life* magazine, but Marilyn did not make her way into the picture. Perhaps, if she had, she might still be alive today. She stayed in America and started work on *Something's Gotta Give,* and died before she could complete it. In the end, of course, Liz Taylor became Cleopatra.

Peter Finch was signed to play Caesar and Stephen Boyd, having just hit it big with *Ben-Hur,* was to play Anthony. Delays eventually saw both actors withdraw to fulfil other contractual obligations. When Richard Burton replaced Boyd as Antony he remarked to friends, 'I've got to don my breastplate once more, to play opposite Miss Tits'.

It was while shooting the earliest scenes in London that Taylor contracted what one physician diagnosed as meningitis, followed by influenza and then pneumonia. In a critical condition (her heart actually stopped five times), she was saved by a tracheotomy.

If we can believe husband Eddie Fisher's version of events, however, Liz's scrape with death was due more to her being 'addicted to every pill on the market' than on anything else. One doctor told him her respiratory failure was the result of depressant drugs. 'She was eating Demerol like candy' said Fisher. He was also injecting her with morphine, sometimes twice a night. This, combined with her binge drinking and heavy smoking, resulted in an acute fever that may or may not have been meningitis. She may simply have overdosed.

Nevertheless, on 10 March 1961, doctors in London announced her 'very rare recovery', and five weeks later she was personally on hand at the Oscars in Santa Monica to pick up her statuette for *Butterfield 8*. Academy historian Anthony Holden wrote: 'Liz Taylor in 1960 remains the only example of someone voted an Oscar because the electorate thought she was at death's door – and then recovering in time to collect it'. Soon after the awards she delivered a phony, melodramatic reconstruction of her dice with death at a dinner put on by the LA Medical Fund. The speech had been ghostwritten by Joe Mankiewicz, and was not one of his best works.

After returning to the set of *Cleopatra* (now being filmed in Italy) she became embroiled in a passionate affair with her new co-star Richard Burton. In February 1962, following one of their countless fights, she overdosed on Seconals and *again* nearly died. Fox announced she had eaten bad oysters. Four months later a stomach pump was again needed to save her life when she *again* overdosed.

Richard Burton (1925-1984)

Known relationships:

Bell, Jeannie
Bloom, Clair
Bujold, Genevieve

Delon, Nathalie
Gabor, Zsa Zsa
Gardner, Ava
Heatherton, Joey
Leigh, Vivien
Lyon, Sue
McBain, Diane
Olivier, Laurence
Princess Elizabeth of Yugoslavia
Roberts, Rachel
Simmons, Jean
Strasberg, Susan
Turner, Lana

Married:

Elizabeth Taylor (twice) & 3 others

Burton would often get very drunk and bore everybody senseless with endless recitals of Shakespeare, Dylan Thomas and others, for hours on end. While he did so it was impossible for anyone to engage him in any kind of conversation. Libby Purvis wrote of him: 'the rudest man I ever met, and unattractive – pock-marked as an Easter Island statue'.

In his first twelve months in Hollywood his womanizing was said to have destroyed nine marriages. Stewart Granger once considered him to be a good friend, but that ended when he realized the incorrigible Welshman had been seducing his wife, Jean Simmons, while a guest in their home. Granger confronted his 'friend' and demanded an explanation. 'Why do you fuck the wife of one of your best friends?' he insisted on knowing. All Burton could offer was some feeble excuse about 'being drunk at the time'. 'Let's face it', said Granger later. 'Burton was a prick. He was a clever actor, but a shit, an absolute shit'.

He threw a backstage party on Broadway for the cast of *Camelot,* during which he bragged he would have Liz on her knees giving him oral sex within days of his arrival in Italy to begin his new role as Antony. Then, after seducing her for the first time, he appeared on the set of *Cleopatra* the next morning and announced he had 'nailed' her in the back seat of her hired Cadillac. 'I am worth a million dollars more today than I was yesterday', he boasted.

Liz, on the other hand, was completely smitten by her new lover. Friends noted she immediately stopped carrying about the mangled wedding ring retrieved from the charred remains of her former husband Mike Todd, something she had adamantly refused to do for her current husband Fisher.

A media circus erupted over the affair and it astounded Burton. 'I've had affairs before', he grossly under-stated, 'but how was I to know she was so fucking famous?' In a 1963 *Playboy* interview he condescendingly described Liz as, '... a pretty girl but she has a double chin and an over-developed chest. And she's rather short in the leg. So I can hardly describe her as the most beautiful creature I've ever seen'.

Fisher wrote how he and Burton drank brandy together for six hours one evening while discussing the Welsh actor's budding romance with Liz. 'You don't need her anymore', said Burton. 'You're a star already. I'm not, not yet. But she's going to make me one. I'm going to use her, that no talent Hollywood nothing'.

Not surprisingly, given both were alcoholics, Richard and Liz fought like cat and dog while they were together. But they always made up either by indulging in a bedroom romp or by Burton buying her an expensive gift – or both. Having already given her the Krupp diamond, he went one better in 1969 and paid $1.1 million for the Cartier diamond which the couple promptly re-named the Taylor-Burton. Liz wore it on a necklace to Princess Grace's fortieth birthday bash - flanked by two machine-gun toting guards, would you believe? Not long afterwards Sir John Gielgud found it lying on a sink at the Chalet Ariel. Liz had removed it to wash her hands and forgotten to put it back on!

Burton raised eyebrows during an interview with *People* magazine when he suggested, 'perhaps most men are latent homosexuals and we cover it with drink. I was once a homo, but it didn't work'. Laurence Olivier and he were lovers who married prominent, beautiful women rather than live together as a gay couple and risk ruining their careers. Before that, it is believed Burton had male lovers while serving in the RAF during World War Two.

Burton's short-lived affair with Susan Strasberg, conducted while they appeared together in a Broadway stage play, was nothing if not energetic. The noise levels of their lovemaking emanating from Miss Strasberg's dressing room caused members of the cast to complain to the manager!

By 1974 Burton's body was so run down it required a complete blood transfusion to keep him alive. The procedure prolonged his life by ten years but his kidneys eventually failed completely and he was dead at fifty-nine.

Colditz Story, The (1955)

Richard Wattis plays the part of Richard Gordon in this World War Two escape story. Diarist Colin Clark wrote of the flaming homosexual Wattis, 'all he wanted to do was pick up some gorgeous hunk of man'. Eric Portman who plays Colonel Richmond was also gay.

Comancheros, The (1961)

John Wayne often said he could not afford to join the services during the war because the studio would have sued him for every penny he ever earned if he broke contract. That is simply not true. Amid the patriotic fervor of the time, *no* studio penalized its stars for joining up. Such an action would have had dire consequences at the box-office and was just not worth it. Even Gable had no problems with his studio when he enlisted and he was the biggest star on the planet.

As for the Duke's other excuses for not enlisting; that he was too old and had a family to support, these do not stand up to close scrutiny either. Gable, Robert Montgomery, Spencer Tracy, Ronald Reagan and Tyrone Power to name a few, were his age or older. They, and many other Hollywood recruits, had families, but still did their bit.

When Wayne was re-classified as 1-A, fit for duty, he still managed to have his studio run interference for him. His friend Paul Fix remembered him saying one time, 'I better go do some touring. I feel the draft breathing down my neck'. There seems little doubt either he or his studio pulled strings to keep him out of the draft.

After so many years in obscurity he had no intention of surrendering his new found stardom or interrupting his career by going off to war. His greatest blunder in this regard, however, came years later when he publicly called on other generations to fight in the Korean and Vietnam conflicts, accusing those who refused to do so as 'soft' and unpatriotic. His obvious hypocrisy angered many.

War service aside, he certainly had his detractors amongst his peers over other issues. Melvyn Douglas said of him, 'John Wayne and his drinking buddy Ward Bond went around wrecking careers with their gung-ho willingness to blacklist anyone who politically disagreed with them during the 1950s'. Ralph Bellamy was equally scathing, 'He certainly doesn't publicize it now, but in the 1950s John Wayne was one of the biggest Hollywood supporters, financially, of the Ku Klux Klan'.

Coming Home (1978)

Jon Voight can thank Jane Fonda for his Oscar for *Coming Home*. United Artists offered her a million dollars *not* to sign him for the role of the crippled war veteran, because they felt he did not have enough box-office clout. Fonda refused, arguing that it was her production and she would cast whom she wanted.

It is common knowledge that he is the father of actress Angelina Jolie, but not quite as well known is that his brother, whose professional name is Chip Taylor, wrote the monster 60s hit song *Wild Thing* for the Troggs.

Conqueror, The (1956)

An indication of imminent cinema disaster should have been evident in John Wayne's comments regarding his interpretation of the Genghis Khan character. 'The way the screenplay reads this is a cowboy picture', said the Duke, 'and that's how I'm going to play Genghis Khan. I see him as a gunfighter'. Hm.

Despite the woeful casting of the world's most recognizable cowboy as a Mongolian warlord, the major problem with the film was its truly awful script. Howard Hughes was told that Oscar Millard was an expert on Genghis Khan, so he hired him as screenwriter. Millard later recalled how he spent thirty minutes trying to find Genghis Khan in an encyclopedia *because he could not spell it*. The resultant script was both banal and ludicrous, a kind of archaic western dialogue impossible to utter with any degree of seriousness.

The movie was shot in St George, Utah, across the border from the Nevada nuclear test sites at Yucca Flats. The infamous 'Dirty Harry' atomic bomb had been detonated there only a year before and a sudden wind change had blown contaminated dust into St George before filming even began. The radiation-laden dust falling on St George saturated the town, coating everything with a grey ash that discolored clothing, killed livestock and burnt unprotected skin. Ten subsequent tests added to the contamination in the town.

Not only did the film crew stay on location in the contaminated area for several weeks, but they also transported sixty tons of the contaminated sand back to Hollywood to stage indoor shots for completion of some unfinished scenes. An extraordinary number of the cast and crew succumbed to cancer-related sicknesses over the ensuing decades. By 1985 the count stood at ninety-one cancer sufferers out of the 220 professionals on the set, forty-six of whom were terminal cases. Over that period half the population of St George also contracted some form of cancer.

Wayne, Dick Powell and Agnes Moorehead died from lung cancer, Susan Hayward from brain cancer, and Pedro Armendariz suicided while riddled with lymph cancer. Lee Van Cleef, Jeanne Gearson, art director Carroll Clark and make-up chief Web Overlander also fell to the disease in one form or another. Wayne, of course, may simply have contracted lung cancer from his habit of consuming a hundred high tar cigarettes daily, although a combination of both factors is probable.

Coogan's Bluff (1968)

David Janssen and Clint Eastwood became friends while in the services together in the Korean War. Another friend of

Clint's was Eric Fleming, his cohort from the TV series *Rawhide* who played trail boss Gil Favor. Fleming was drowned while filming on location in Peru in 1966. The forty-one year-old actor's remains were not recovered from the piranha-infested river for six days.

At the start of their movie careers Eastwood and Burt Reynolds were both fired from Universal on the same day; Clint being told his Adam's apple stood out too far to be a film star. Burt was simply informed that he had no talent. Later, at the height of Clint's spaghetti westerns fame, there was an Italian actor cashing in on his name by calling himself Clint Westwood.

In a 1974 *Playboy* interview Clint made the following perceptive assessment of the fairer sex: 'Women tend to be smarter than men in a lot of areas. You see a lot of terribly intelligent men with dumb women, but you never see terribly intelligent women with dumb guys'. In 1996, after long-time partner Sondra Locke charged him with sabotaging her directing career, he settled with her out of court for $5 million. Evidently, Sondra was not too dumb either.

Counterfeit Traitor, The (1961)

Klaus Kinski was the father of beautiful actress Nastassja, and plays a dying refugee in this film. In real life Mr. Kinski was not a nice man. Introduced to sex by his sister Inge, he bragged of seducing very young girls (some as young as thirteen) for most of his life. He also claimed to have bedded 'at least fifty virgin lesbians', evidently considering that to be quite an achievement. Not long before he died he spent a stretch of ninety days in a lunatic asylum.

Country Girl, The (1954)

1953 was a busy year for Grace Kelly, and not just on the screen. She had a number of full on romances, beginning with William Holden on *The Bridges at Toko-Ri,* and then with Ray Milland when they made *Dial 'M' For Murder.* Then came *The Country Girl* with Holden and Bing Crosby. Before long she was intimate with old Bing as well, while at the same time getting the occasional service from both Jean-Pierre Aumont and Oleg Cassini.

After refusing Bing's overtures of marriage (he was already hitched to Dixie Lee), she again took up with Holden when the picture wrapped. And all this time she was carrying a torch for Milland who had dumped her after his wife had issued him with an ultimatum. By all accounts 'butter wouldn't melt in her mouth' Grace spent much of 1953 horizontally.

In that same year she took Holden home to meet her parents, but he received a cold reception, more than likely because he, too, was a married man. He was also a nasty drunk. Not to be thwarted, she then took Cassini home and announced to her folks she wished to marry *him.*

That idea was also vetoed by her father, who considered Oleg to be 'a worm', a wop' and 'a dago', and told him so to his face. Cassini was a notorious womanizer to boot. Hedda Hopper could not understand what Grace saw in him. 'It must be his moustache', she wrote. In response, Cassini fired off a cable to Hedda that read: 'I'll shave off mine if you shave off yours'. Eventually, he drifted off the scene (for a while, anyway), as Grace found bigger fish to fry.

Over the next twelve months she took on Spencer Tracy (briefly) and then David Niven (not so briefly). Cassini was both irate and gob-smacked when Grace suddenly rang him to *ask his permission* to go out again with Crosby. He was even more confused when she asked him if he would give his blessing to her dating *Frank Sinatra*. He indignantly refused, so she nailed Frank anyway. Oleg bowed out at last, belatedly convinced she was possibly a little too flighty to ever *really* become a one-man woman. Then Aumont introduced her to Prince Rainier of Monaco.

The Royal marriage nearly did not take place. Grace's mother ran a ten-part series in American newspapers headlined: MY DAUGHTER GRACE KELLY: HER LIFE AND ROMANCES. If Rainier ever thought his future bride was a virgin, that notion should have been dispelled by the series once and for all. He *must* have had his suspicions. After all, he had people working for him whose job it was to screen potential brides and lovers. If you are wondering why the name of Cary Grant has not yet been mentioned, it is because her affair with him did not get started until the seventies. It lasted, on and off, for six or seven years.

Court Jester, The (1956)

Elsa Lanchester did not much care for Danny Kaye. 'In person he wasn't the least bit funny. Rather, he was egotistical and one of those comedians who secretly envy dramatic actors. Add to that his ever-present and unpleasant wife, and his being as they say in the closet, and he was no picnic to work with'. Gay actor/designer William Haines said of him, 'I think that he's the most repressed innate homosexual I ever met', yet Eve Arden considered him the love of her life.

In 1983, he and wife Sylvia threatened their daughter with disinheritance if she ever wrote a book about the family's dirty laundry. She wisely chose not to. Many people still believe Kaye died from AIDS. His doctor insisted the cause of death was hepatitis. Mildred Natwick was a bird-like character actress who graced scores of films. A lesbian, she never married.

Court Martial of Billy Mitchell, The (1955)

Elizabeth Montgomery starred as Samantha in TV's *Bewitched* series. For that matter, she also played Serena in the series, even though the credits always listed the bogus name of Pandora Sparks. When her co-star in *Bewitched*, Dick Sargent, came out as a gay, she courageously supported him by agreeing to be Grand Marshall of the Los Angeles Gay Parade.

Crow, The (1994)

Brandon Lee never lived to see this picture's completion. One day while on the set, he was struck and killed by a bullet, fired from a gun everyone thought was unloaded. In the fatal scene, fellow actor Michael Massee was supposed to aim an unloaded .44 Magnum pistol *indirectly* at Lee and pull the trigger. The gun, for some reason never explained, contained a live round amongst the blanks.

Massee emptied it at Lee who was carrying an armful of groceries from which he was supposed to activate the 'squibs'. As he sank to the ground in agony, the crew thought he was still acting until he cried out, 'Cut, cut! Somebody, please say cut'. The bullet had pierced his abdomen and proved fatal the same day.

Cruel Sea, The (1953)

Pretty British actress June Thorburn features here. In 1967 at the age of thirty-six she died in an airliner crash near London. Born in Kashmir she was a former junior skiing champion before venturing into the movies.

Crusades, The (1935)

The following story may be apocryphal but it is too good to leave out. Loretta Young had the following woeful line to deliver, 'Richard, you gotta save Christianity'. DeMille took her aside and quietly told the young actress to give it more 'awe'. She returned to the set and this time gave it the full

treatment: 'Aw, Richard, you gotta save Christianity!'
DeMille groaned.

Cry Baby Killer, The (1958)

Carolyn Mitchell plays opposite Jack Nicholson in this
Roger Corman film. In 1966 she was married to Mickey
Rooney when she was shot to death by her lover, a young
man named Milos Milocevic, who was employed as a
chauffeur by French actor Alaine Delon.

Curse of the Pink Panther (1983)

David Niven (1909-1983)

Known relationships:

Barrie, Wendy
Bruce, Virginia
Dietrich, Marlene
Duke, Doris
Fonteyn, Margot
Gardner, Ava
Goddard, Paulette
Hayworth, Rita
Hutton, Barbara
Kelly, Grace
Kerr, Deborah
Keyes, Evelyn
Lamarr, Hedy
Lombard, Carole
Oberon, Merle
Princess Margaret
Rogers, Ginger
Shearer, Norma
Simon, Simone

Todd, Ann
Totter, Audrey
Young, Loretta

This was David Niven's last film. He was desperately ill and it became necessary for impersonator Rich Little to dub his voice throughout.

When David first went to Hollywood in 1934 he lived with Loretta Young's family for a year. Loretta said later: 'Because we had been a house full of women, suddenly with a man on the premises you had to start watching how you walked around undressed'. She also said their houseguest first made a play for her mother, then for her sisters and finally for her.

His first movie role was as an extra playing a Mexican cowboy. He later refused the role of Hopalong Cassidy, in a series of B films that eventually made a star of William Boyd, because he did not want to be type cast as a cowboy!

He and actor Robert Coote rented a small beach house from Marion Davies. They christened the lodgings 'Cirrhosis by the Sea', until their landlord, Marion's lover William Randolph Hearst, ordered the sign taken down. John Mills recalled that the men's change-room adjoined the women's, and had a two-way mirror installed to enable David and his buddies to observe his female guests disrobing and showering. 'We spent quite a lot of time in there, depending on the female guests of the day, of course', said Mills.

In one of his books Niven recalled his embarrassment when he sent actress Miriam Hopkins a half a dozen handkerchiefs for Christmas, and she reciprocated by sending him a brand new Studebaker!

While under suspension from MGM he gained work on the radio to make ends meet. Sam Goldwyn insisted on half of everything he earned as per their contract. After one show Niven did for Kraft, the company gave him a basket of their goods, containing cheeses, sardines, spreads and so on, plus a cheque for his services. That night he and Coote meticulously extracted half the spread from the jars, cut every cheese and sardine in half, then sent the lot accompanied by half the cheque to Goldwyn - inside half the basket.

When Columbia Pictures chief Harry Cohn's yacht developed engine trouble off the coast one day, Errol Flynn and Niven used Flynn's boat to tow him into port. As a joke they sent Harry a letter claiming half his yacht in salvage. The humorless Columbia mogul fired Niven on the spot and never allowed him to set foot inside his studio again. Errol escaped unscathed because he was contracted to Warner Bros.

When the patriotic Niven volunteered for war duty, without waiting to be called up, Goldwyn told him his contract was forthwith suspended 'until he returned or got killed, whichever came first'. Unlike Cohn, Sam did have a sense of humor, telling the actor he intended to wire Hitler and 'ask him to shoot around you'. Niven would neither write nor speak about his war exploits. Since he went into the Commandos as a lieutenant and emerged a colonel, either he was an outstanding soldier or the rate of attrition was extremely high. Or both.

In 1974, while he was presenting an Oscar at the Academy Awards night, a 'streaker' ran across the stage. 'Just think', quipped Niven. 'The only laugh that man will probably ever get is for showing his shortcomings'. The clever 'off the cuff' remark brought the house down but was it really 'off the cuff'? Conspiracy fans have since asked a few probing questions. Was his ad-lib just a tad *too* good for a spontaneous response? Was it as easy as the intruder (thirty-three year old Robert Opal) claimed it was to fool backstage security with a fake press card? Why was the man later clothed and presented to the media instead of being escorted from the building? Why were no charges ever laid? Did the Oscars ceremony need a bit of a boost that year and was Opal hired to give it one?

The man's streak on NBC that evening sparked the beginning of his brief stand-up comic career. He even managed to snag a spot on *The Mike Douglas Show* and was later hired to streak again, this time at a party for dancer Rudolph Nureyev. A further *unsolicited* streak, however, in front of the Los Angeles City Council saw him arrested and placed on probation. Five years after his moment of glory on the Oscars he was found murdered in his San Francisco sex shop.

Harry Cohn was one of the most hated people in Hollywood history, perhaps *the* most hated. It was only through the loan of mob money from Sam Giancana's Hollywood minion Johnny Roselli that he managed to gain control of the studio in the first place. He and Roselli wore identical ruby rings, provided by the mobster, declaring them to be 'blood brothers'.

On Cohn's desk sat a framed picture of the man he most admired – Benito Mussolini. On the wall behind him was a chart displaying the menstrual cycles of his major actresses. When it came to sex he left nothing to chance. He loved to fire people on Christmas Eve, especially those he didn't like. The door to his office was devoid of door handles and a button on his desk let people in or out. A bank of bright lights was set up to shine in the faces of visitors, so that he could size them up as they entered the room.

His power was absolute and he wielded it unmercifully. In the annals of Hollywood he stands out as the most loathsome of its denizens. It was simply not possible to work for Columbia and like Harry Cohn. He also spied on his workers. Microphones were planted on every sound stage and connected to an intercom in his office. That way he could hear nearly everything said on or near the sets. If he heard something he didn't like his voice would boom out over the speakers 'I heard that!' Directors George Stevens and Howard Hawks retaliated by deliberately making offensive comments about him at the tops of their voices at every opportunity. Both men were valuable company assets, so they held little fear of being sacked by their dictatorial boss.

When interviewing a starlet in his office Cohn would use his letter opener to probe the girl's mouth and check out her teeth. He would then use it to lift up her skirts to inspect her thighs. It almost goes without saying that he satisfied his sexual needs almost at will with the virtually unlimited supply of young hopefuls willing to do anything to get a contract.

His funeral service was held on two sound stages on the Columbia lot on a Sunday so nobody would miss work. About 2,000 staffers and stars attended, mostly because it was expected of them. One producer who had worked with him for years was asked if he intended going to the funeral. 'Not unless they're burying him alive', he laconically replied. When trapped into delivering a couple of kind words about the deceased, Rabbi Magnin of the Wilshire Boulevard Temple pondered for a moment, then said, 'He's dead'.

Cutthroat Island (1995)

Oliver Reed was fortunate to be removed from this disastrous picture before shooting began. At an introductory dinner the drunken actor dropped his pants in front of several key guests, including actress Geena Davis, and exhibited the eagle's talons tattooed on his penis. He was flown home at once.

Daddy's Gone A-Hunting (1969)

A year after her successful performances in *Poor Cow* and *I'll Never Forget What's 'is Name*, Carol White played opposite Paul Burke in this National General production. The married actress bedded the producer Irv Levin as soon as she won the role. The man's wife attempted suicide when she found out.

A tempestuous affair soon ensued between Carol and her co-star Burke (who was also married) that ended with White herself attempting suicide for the first time. She was depressed by a phone call from Burke on New Year's Eve, during which he gloated about being in bed with two hookers as they spoke. Once she recovered, she embarked upon a series of dalliances with several Hollywood stars, among them Warren Beatty. He regularly had sex with her as soon as his girlfriend Julie Christie went off to work each day.

By 1972 she found herself back with Burke who soon dumped her for the second time. Again she tried to kill herself and again she failed. She then chose to complicate her already sorry life even further by binging on cocaine, Valium, Quaaludes and sleeping pills. A near fatal cocktail of these substances put her in the hospital fighting for her life for the *third* time.

When she recovered she quickly married her analyst, but that relationship also collapsed. By 1976 her weight had ballooned and her looks were gone. When her ex-husband discovered her grinding broken glass into her wrists, he rushed her to the hospital in the nick of time.

Over the next decade or so her career limped along with minor bits on TV. In the mid-eighties she even tried living with a female partner in Miami, but that didn't work out either. By late 1991 the once beautiful forty-eight year-old was a mental and physical wreck.

She died in a Miami hospital from cirrhosis of the liver a month after coughing up copious quantities of blood initiated by a burst esophagus. Her two sons from her first marriage could not afford the $8,000 needed to fly her ashes back to Britain, so a final indignity saw the much-troubled lady's remains mailed home in a brown paper parcel!

Dam Busters, The (1954)

One of the code words used in the actual mission was 'Nigger', the name of the Black Labrador owned by the group leader Guy Gibson. For the movie, the socially acceptable 'Trigger' was substituted, although the Morse code signals arriving in the Ops Room actually spell out the original offending word. Richard Todd who plays Wing Commander Guy Gibson was not a tall man. At Disney Studios he was rather unkindly referred to as 'the eighth dwarf'.

Sir Michael Redgrave plays the inventor Barnes Wallis. He kept his bisexuality a secret from his wife, Rachel Kempson, for years, until he made the mistake of bringing a soldier home for a fling one evening while she was away. The man agreed to strip Redgrave and tie him to the kitchen table, but having done so he went through the actor's clothing, robbed him and left. When the cook returned from her evening off she found Redgrave naked and still tethered to the table. He was in a situation that simply could not be explained away convincingly.

Dances with Wolves (1990)

Over 2,000 buffalo from a privately owned herd were hired for this film. In addition twenty-four mock-ups were created with pneumatic breathing and kicking devices built into them. Because the herd was in South Dakota, the Indian tribe depicted in the movie had to be changed from the novel's Comanches of Texas to the Sioux of South Dakota.

Kevin Costner's parents, wife and three children all appear in his movie. They are in the family wiped out in the massacre scene at the farmhouse. His six year-old daughter Annie plays Stands-With-A-Fist as a child.

Because it was logistically impossible to film in the fall, the season was virtually etched into the landscape by utilizing 10,000 gallons of paint to give the leaves an Eastern Summer look. Even the grass of South Dakota was too brown for Costner's liking so it was dyed green!

Dangerous Liaisons (1988)

Keanu Reeves was born in Beiruit, Lebanon, of Canadian-Hawaiian parents, and raised in Australia, Canada and America. Keanu is a Hawaiian word meaning 'cool breeze over the mountains'. In 1999, his girlfriend Jennifer Syme gave birth to his stillborn child. Two years later Jennifer was tragically killed in an automobile crash.

Uma Thurman's father was one of the Dalai Lama's first American Buddhist monks. Very few Hollywood actresses have measured six feet in height. Uma is one of them, although some sources say she is only 5'11".

Swoozie Kurtz's unusual first name is derived from 'Alexander the Swoose', the name on the B-17D bomber flown by her highly decorated father in the Second World War.

John Malkovich's marriage to Glenne Headley collapsed when his affair with Michelle Pfeiffer on the set of *Dangerous Liaisons* became public. Well, I guess if you are going to cheat on your wife you might as well shoot for the stars.

Dangerous When Wet (1953)

The underwater sequence featuring Esther Williams and the animated Tom & Jerry initially met with a mixed response from preview audiences because the photography was too clear! Most people did not believe Esther was actually underwater at all. To convince them otherwise, cartoonists Hanna and Barbera were paid $50,000 to insert pink bubbles coming from her mouth whenever she spoke.

The film's finale mirrored the real life problems of distance swimmer Florence Chadwick who was attempting to swim the Catalina Channel at that time. Suffering from nausea and exhaustion, she was ready to quit until one of her support team, champion swimmer and film star Johnny Weissmuller, leapt into the water and swam alongside her offering encouragement. Esther was watching the drama unfold on television and suggested something similar be written into the script of *Dangerous When Wet*.

Argentine actor Fernando Lamas was at one time considered to be among the five fastest swimmers in the world. In 1937 he was South American Freestyle Champion, a fact he asked Esther to keep secret for him. 'So I don't end up in *all* your movies', he told her. A decade or so after they made *Dangerous When Wet* together they became man and wife. According to Esther's 'tell-all' biography, Fernando's seduction technique was anything but subtle. While driving her back to the cast's hotel after a day's shooting he initiated their romance by placing her hand on his erect penis and holding it there for the duration of the trip!

Dark Victory (1939)

George Brent was forced to flee his native Ireland as a young man because he was a member of the IRA and wanted by British authorities. During those days he worked as a dispatch rider for the top IRA man Michael Collins.

Brent began his lengthy affair with co-star Bette Davis while making this film. The romance ended the day he was asked by a beauty poll representative to name who he believed were the ten most glamorous women in Hollywood. He made the fatal (but understandable) mistake of leaving Bette's name off his list and she dropped him like a hot scone.

Dawn Patrol, The (1938)

Errol Flynn first met and propositioned Tyrone Power at a party thrown by the director of this movie, the very gay Edmund Goulding. Flynn and Goulding had already had a fling early in the production. The two screen heartthrobs disappeared into an upstairs bedroom, from which they did not emerge *for two days.*

Power's personality was a direct opposite of Flynn's. He was nervous and shy and often embarrassed by Errol's direct and coarse behavior. He hated the way Errol delighted in relating details of their trysts to his carousing pals. In particular, he was mortified by his penchant for asking him in front of all and sundry, 'Fancy a poke, sport?' Their affair was over within six months, but they remained friends until Power's early death from a heart attack at forty-five.

Douglas Fairbanks Junior's mother was not Mary Pickford, but a cotton heiress named Beth Sully. Mary was his stepmother. He was the most decorated of all the stars who went to war - any war. Of course, Audie Murphy's war record was second to none, but he was not an actor when he went off to war. Some might argue that he wasn't one after he came back either.

A lieutenant on the cruiser USS Wichita, Fairbanks did convoy duty to Malta and Murmansk. His vessel was part of the escort for the ill-fated convoy PQ17 that lost twenty-four out of thirty-five ships on its way to Russia. He was also a serving officer on Mountbatten's staff in London. By war's end he had earned the Silver Star at Ventotene, the Italian

War Cross at Capri, the Legion of Honor and the Croix de Guerre at Elba and the Distinguished Service Cross in the Mediterranean. According to Maureen O'Hara, she was quite taken by him when they co-starred in *Sinbad the Sailor* in 1947, until she discovered he wore a padded jockstrap to accentuate the bulge in his tights.

Mandy Rice-Davies, one of the call girls involved in the Profumo Affair of the '60s, met and slept with him in London. He offered to set up an interview for her at Shepparton Studios, but his producer buddy expected a *free* sample of her gratitude in advance, so she walked out. After all, business is business.

During the sensational divorce trial of Margaret the Duchess of Argyle in 1963, Doug was identified as the man in several photos receiving oral sex from the duchess.

Dead Calm (1989)

Greta Scacchi was the first choice for the female lead in this thriller, but she turned it down, so both the male and female leads were offered instead to husband and wife team Bryan Brown and Rachel Ward. They also said no. Two hundred actors were tested for the role of the heavy. Billy Zane, who was working in theatre in Los Angeles and seriously considering giving up acting, auditioned and was successful. His career took off from there.

Most of the interior cabin shots were done in sets floating in a pool in the Whitsunday Passage off the east coast of Australia. A football team from the mainland came across each morning to rock the floats from side to side to simulate ocean activity as the cast performed on board. All three stars were seasick from time to time. 'I threw up over the side for ten minutes', recalled Nicole Kidman. 'I couldn't work. I just thought, yeah, this is glamour'.

During the shoot Billy Zane fell in love with Lisa Collins (one of the actresses murdered aboard the *Orpheus*) and they married after shooting on the picture was completed. Sam Neill met and fell in love with Japanese-born makeup artist Nariko Watenabi, and they too were married.

Nicole was born in Hawaii while her Australian parents were holidaying there. She is descended from one of Australia's great cattle-owning dynasties. In 2004 the magazine *BRW* listed her as the richest Australian woman under forty, citing her estimated wealth at 107 million in US dollars ($155 million in Australian dollars).

Death Takes a Holiday (1934)

This was one of only a handful of movies the now forgotten thirties actress Evelyn Venable made. She became the model for the torchbearer depicted on the Columbia logo. It is also her soothing voice you hear emanating from 'The Blue Fairy' in Disney's 1940 classic *Pinocchio*. She retired from acting in 1943 to focus on her family.

Defiant Ones, The (1958)

We will never know how this picture would have turned out if the original casting choices of Elvis Presley and Sammy

Davis Jr had signed on. Perhaps it would have been a musical!

Robert Mitchum said he knocked back the Tony Curtis role because there was just no way a Negro and a white man would be chained together in that part of the country. He was speaking from personal experience, having spent time in his youth on a chain gang in the Deep South.

The young man with the transistor radio is Carl 'Alfalfa' Switzer, the former child star of the 'Our Gang' featurettes of the forties. Curtis adored the guy and loved listening to his stories about the old days as a child star. Evidently, the boy was swindled out of every cent he made back then. This was Carl's final appearance in a movie. A year later he was dead, shot to death in a dispute over $50.

Desperately Seeking Susan (1985)

Madonna was born on the day Elvis Presley died. For a time she was a back-up singer for European recording star Patrick Hernandez whose one and only hit was the disco monster *Born To Be Alive*. 'All those guys I stepped on to get to the top' she boasted in an interview, 'every one of them would take me back because they still love me and I still love them'.

When asked what Warren Beatty had that other men did not, she notoriously replied, 'About a billion dollars'.

Music producer Camille Barbone said of her, 'Madonna loves beautiful women, and she is into anyone sexually, male or female, who is beautiful'. The outspoken Sandra Bernhard, whose career did not survive her participation in the mind-boggling bomb *Hudson Hawk,* was strongly rumored to have been Madonna's lover. Bernhard had a book of her 'poetry' published in the nineties entitled *Love, Love, Love,* the standard of which can best be judged by one little ditty that describes her attempt to give a colleague a 'hand job' and his apparent failure to ejaculate. Keats, Shelley, eat your heart out.

In the 1970s Madonna posed nude for *Penthouse* magazine, the pictures surfacing just prior to her marriage to Sean Penn in 1985. The couple honeymooned in a Caribbean penthouse that cost them $250,000 a day to rent! The union came to an end in 1989 after Sean bound and gagged his wife over New Year's Eve following one of their fights.

Madonna once announced that she and actress Jennifer Grey, who played the female lead in *Dirty Dancing,* had enjoyed a brief lesbian relationship. It has never been confirmed, although Grey opted not to prosecute her over the comment either.

When Madonna gave birth to a baby in 1996 the pediatrician in attendance was none other than Paul Fleiss, the father of notorious Hollywood madam Heidi Fleiss. Madonna's baby to husband Guy Ritchie was christened in a $45,000 Versace jump suit. Gwyneth Paltrow was the maid of honor at their wedding. For a time Madonna lived in Bugsy Siegel's former home, the one in which he was murdered in 1947. She also owns the burial crypt alongside Marilyn Monroe's.

Rosanna Arquette was a drug addict at thirteen and cohabiting with a man by her fifteenth birthday. Her childhood was spent in communes or nudist colonies where her parents smoked pot with the kids. Her brother David wed actress Courtney Cox and is a recovering heroin junkie. Her other brother Alex works in drag shows around Los Angeles and calls himself 'Eva Destruction' or 'Amanda B. Reckonedwith'. The 1983 Toto hit song *Rosanna* was named for her. She was dating Steve Porcaro of Toto at the time.

Destination Tokyo (1943)

An FBI investigation into communism in Hollywood in 1944 came up with five names the bureau believed had 'known communist connections'. They were Lucille Ball, Walter Huston, Ira Gershwin, John Garfield and Cary Grant.

Cary made the list because of his friendship with writer Clifford Odets who directed this picture. There was also another reason. Ginger Rogers' hideous mother, Lela, had been appointed by RKO as its resident 'expert' on communism. She lodged the accusation against Grant because of a single innocuous line of dialogue he delivered in *Destination Tokyo*. When an enemy bomb stamped 'Made in America' nearly blows up his submarine, Cary's character utters the line 'appeasement has come home to roost, men', a reference to the war materials America had sold to the other side prior to its involvement in the conflict. Both Lela and the committee stupidly considered such sentiments to be Communist propaganda.

Dane Clark more or less terminated his own Hollywood career the day he flattened Jack Warner after the mogul called him a 'ham'. Warner not only tore up Clark's contract with his studio, but he also brought pressure to bear at other lots and Dane's opportunities dried up overnight. He finished his acting days in European productions.

Destry Rides Again (1939)

Marlene Dietrich told writer Erich Remarque that she seduced James Stewart while the two stars were in the wardrobe department trying on costumes for their roles in this picture. She also said she became pregnant to Jimmy, but agreed to an abortion to avoid endangering their careers.

Marlene Dietrich (1901-1992)

Known relationships with women:

Allan, Elizabeth
Arthur, Jean
Bankhead, Tallulah
Carstairs, Jo
Colbert, Claudette
Collette
Cornell, Katherine
Damita, Lili
Day, Frances
De Acosta, Mercedes
Del Rio, Dolores
Di Frasso, Dorothy
Garbo, Greta
Garland, Judy

Goddard, Paulette
Gurie, Sigrid
Keller, Greta
Lion, Margo
Louise, Anita
Munson, Ona
Nazimova, Alla
Piaf, Edith
Stanwyck, Barbara
Stein, Gertrude
Viertel, Salka
Waldoff, Claire
Warner, Ann
Winwood, Estelle
Wong, Anna May

Known relationships with men:

Aherne, Brian
Bacharach, Burt
Barthelmas, Richard
Bautzer, Greg
Beaton, Cecil
Berle, Milton
Bogart, Humphrey
Bradley, Omar Gen.
Brando, Marlon
Brynner, Yul
Cabot, Bruce
Chevalier, Maurice
Colman, Ronald
Cooper, Gary
Di Maggio, Joe
Donat, Robert
Douglas, Kirk
Fairbanks Jr, Douglas
Fisher, Eddie
Flynn, Errol
Fonda, Henry
Gabin, Jean

Gardiner, Reginald
Gavin, Mark Gen.
Gilbert, John
Hayward, Leland
Hemingway, Ernest
Howard, Leslie
Hughes, Howard
Iturbi, Jose
Kennedy, Joe Sr.
Kennedy, John F
Kennedy, Robert F
Kukrov, Georgi Marshall.
Lancaster, Burt
Lang, Fritz
Lund, John
McLaglen, Victor
Meredith, Burgess
Murrow, Edward R
Niven, David
O'Hara, John
Pasternak, Joe
Patton, George Gen.
Power, Tyrone
Preminger, Otto
Quinn, Anthony
Raft, George
Remarque, Erich Maria
Rennie, Michael
Romero, Cesar
Shaw, George Bernard
Sinatra, Frank
Spiegel, Sam
Stevenson, Adlai
Stewart, James
Tauber, Richard
Todd, Mike
Tracy, Spencer
Vallone, Raf
Von Sternberg, Josef

Wayne, John
Welles, Orson
Wilding, Michael

In the 1920s Dietrich was secretly married to Otto Katz, a
Communist agent involved in numerous espionage activities
that probably included political assassinations. The couple
had a daughter they named Maria. Katz would later fall out
of favor with his Red bosses in Prague, be arrested and
tortured (all his teeth were smashed from his head), and
then hanged as a western spy.

Marlene and Greta Garbo maintained throughout their
lives that they had never met. In fact, they did meet in
Germany, while making the silent film *The Joyless Street*,
and soon became lovers. In that movie the uncredited
Dietrich can be clearly seen in one sequence holding the
fainted Garbo in her arms as they wait in a food queue.

Marlene always considered Garbo to be her social
inferior. She also told writer-producer Sam Taylor that the
Swedish star was 'awfully big down there...she wore dirty
underclothes'. Garbo, she claimed, was extremely self-
conscious of her large genitalia.

Dietrich was a sexual predator interested in both genders.
Klaus Kinski recorded in his autobiography how she
introduced herself to actress Edith Evans. 'Marlene tore
down Edith's panties backstage in a Berlin theatre', he wrote,
'and, just using her mouth, brought Edith to orgasm'.

The sexually insatiable actress also slept with JFK at the White House when she was sixty years old. Afterwards, when asked if she had ever slept with his father, Marlene lied and said she had not. She claimed the President was 'delighted to have gotten somewhere first before the old man'.

In the early 1930s, distributors placed an advertisement in *Variety* asking Paramount not to send them any more Dietrich films. Her previous two outings were utter flops. Paramount heads gladly paid out her contract ahead of time, in effect giving her $250,000 *not* to make any more pictures for them.

In 1933, while visiting England, she tried posing as a streetwalker in Soho as an experiment. She propositioned dozens of men who were unaware of her identity, but failed to garner a single positive response.

'In Europe', she said, 'it doesn't matter if you are a man or a woman. We make love with anyone we find attractive'. She told writer Erich Remarque she must have a man every night and was unable to sleep alone. Even so, her preferences ran more to women than men.

Whenever she met a man she fancied she immediately dropped to her knees and undid his flies. She said it gave her a sense of power over him. She even boasted she did just that when first introduced to George Bernard Shaw. 'Of course, I had to do it before we could talk', she explained. Marlene, it should be said, enjoyed making outrageous statements and claims, so just how much of what she repeated actually happened is problematic.

Louise Brooks, who seemed to have something nasty to say about nearly everyone, said this of Dietrich: 'She had everyone, that one. The twist is, she preferred Chevalier to Cooper. See, Mo was supposedly impotent, at least with the ladies, whereas Coop the lady-killer supposedly had the longest handle in Hollywood.

Marlene may have been promiscuous as all get out, but she wasn't fond of being penetrated. For one thing, she liked to be in control'. When Marlene's daughter Maria became engaged, the girl refused to let her mother meet her fiancée for fear she might seduce him. She said her mother 'slept with practically everyone'.

Taking a fancy to Anne Warner (the wife of movie mogul Jack), Dietrich took her to the Sphinx Club to observe women having sex together. Mrs. Warner soon became one of her lovers and joined the 'Hollywood Sewing Circle', the euphemism for the colony's lesbian fraternity.

During the Second World War Dietrich attended the Hollywood Canteen on a regular basis, dancing with servicemen and selecting the most handsome of them for sex later in the evening.

On USO tours she seduced soldiers throughout the European theatre of war. Her well-known affair with General Mark Gavin of the 82nd Airborne Division resulted in his wife filing for divorce. When General Omar Bradley refused her request to move closer to the front lines she changed his mind by sleeping with him. 'What else could I do?' she asked Art Buchwald when relating the story to him after the war.

Next morning Bradley gave her a permit to advance nearer the front.

While touring the battlefields she would often walk into the men's bathing area and take a shower with them, then leave as if nothing had happened. Many of the GI's considered her nothing more than a tease. She preferred to have sex with officers rather than enlisted men, because the latter 'could always take a girl off into the bushes. Officers could not'.

Dietrich insisted that Adolf Hitler desired her and even sent her a Christmas tree in 1936 with instructions for her to return to Berlin. She refused him. Von Ribbentrop also tried and failed to get her to return to the German cinema. 'Hitler wanted me to be his mistress', she said after the war, 'I turned him down. Maybe I should have gone to him. I might have saved the lives of six million Jews'. In the annals of egotistical statements that one must surely take the cake.

When the Allies finally reached Berlin she was disgusted to learn that her sister Elizabeth and husband Georg Wills had been running the canteen and cinema for the staff at Bergen-Belsen Concentration Camp.

At war's end Marlene was awarded the Medal of Freedom by the US Senate (the civilian equivalent of the Congressional Medal of Honor) for her wartime work with the USO. Nazi sympathizers have several times desecrated her grave in France.

Dial 'M' for Murder (1954)

The 'M' in the title stands for Maida Vale, the London suburb in which Grace Kelly's character resides. The picture was shot in 3D but never released in that format, although copies are occasionally shown at film societies or on university campuses.

If you look closely during the scene where Grace is attacked by the hired killer, you can see a pair of scissors protruding from the man's back *before* she stabs him. Because the angle was all wrong for Grace to be filmed plunging them into her assailant's back, Hitchcock pre-placed them there and instructed the actress to raise her arm back, make a stabbing motion and then let the scissors fall to the floor. Her assailant would then turn to reveal them in his back.

Grace had a well-documented, steamy affair with her co-star Ray Milland when they made this Hitchcock thriller. What is probably less well-known is that she also seduced the actor who plays her assassin in the movie, Anthony Dawson. Fans of the first James Bond film, *Dr No* (1962), will recall him playing Professor Dent, the man who deposits the black widow in 007's bed.

Die Hard (1988)

When previews of *Die Hard* were first released, American audiences laughed and jeered Bruce Willis. They were used to seeing him playing comedy on TV's *Moonlighting* and found it difficult to accept him as an action star.

His flop vehicle *Sunset* reached the screens just after *Die Hard* finished shooting, and the combination of the reaction to the previews and the failure of *Sunset* caused nervous studio decision-makers to remove his image from the advertising posters, fearful patrons would be put off seeing the movie if they knew he was the star. They need not have worried. *Die Hard* was a monumental success that made him a super-star.

The Nakatomi Building at the center of the film is actually the Fox Plaza, a part of the Century City complex in Los Angeles.

The part of the over-confident, cocaine snorting Ellis was played by Hart Bochner, the son of accomplished Canadian actor Lloyd Bochner. Some of you might recall him playing the very British police chief in the sixties TV series *Hong Kong* that starred Australia's Rod Taylor.

If you think Alan Rickman seems genuinely shocked when he falls to his death - you are right. The stuntman holding him was supposed to count to three and then let the actor fall twenty feet onto some mattresses. To get the appropriate 'look' (and acting on the director's orders), the man sneakily released him on the count of two, hence the startled expression on Rickman's face.

Disillusioned by the disparity between pay packets for male and female actors, Bonnie Bedelia who plays Willis's wife had this to say: 'Bruce Willis was offered something like $7.5 million for *Die Hard 2*. But they offered me less than for the first one. *Less!* What do they think actors want to do sequels for anyway? It's for the money!'

Her movie career has evolved in two separate phases. In 1969 she appeared in *They Shoot Horses Don't They* and *The Gypsy Moths,* after which she spent an eternity in tele-movies before finally achieving international recognition as Holly Gennaro McLane in this blockbuster nearly twenty years down the track. Incidentally, she is the aunt of former child star Macaulay Culkin.

Willis was born in West Germany in 1955. After just receiving $16 million to make *Die Hard 3*, Willis stupidly accused *unions* of causing film making to become too costly. His hypocritical comments resulted in death threats on his new-born baby.

Alexander Godunov who plays the terrorist Karl was Jacqueline Bisset's lover for some time. In 1979 he became the first Bolshoi Ballet dancer to defect to the west. He died at forty-five from a heart attack brought on by acute alcoholism, his body lying undiscovered for two days.

Dirty Dancing (1987)

Although she plays a teenager here, Jennifer Grey was twenty-six years old when she made *Dirty Dancing*. She is the daughter of the same Joel Grey who won an Oscar for *Cabaret*. At one time or another she was engaged to Matthew Broderick and Johnny Depp.

She says that having plastic surgery on her nose was the biggest mistake of her life because she no longer looks like the girl who played Baby in *Dirty Dancing*, easily her most famous role.

Patrick Swayze was offered $5 million to do a sequel but turned it down because he felt it would not be a quality production. Grey was offered a paltry $500,000 to reprise her character. She too refused but for a different reason. She was understandably peeved at the disparity between the two amounts.

Doctor Zhivago (1965)

Doctor Zhivago was shot mostly in Spain. Tons of white marble dust was used to simulate snow on the Russian landscape.

When Jane Fonda turned down the female lead Julie Christie stepped in. The actor who plays young Yuri Zhivago is Omar Sharif's son Tarek.

Christie is one of three movie beauties who were born in India. She entered this world in Chukua in 1940. Merle Oberon was born in Bombay in 1911 and Vivien Leigh in Darjeeling in 1913. Comedian Spike Milligan and actress Googie Withers were also Indian born. British leading lady Margaret Lockwood came from nearby Karachi, Pakistan in 1911.

In the scene where Christie slaps Rod Steiger and is slapped by him in return, the stunned look on her face is genuine. The return slap was neither scripted nor even discussed. He just did it. Similarly, her desperate struggle as he kisses her was not all acting either. Method actor Rod decided the scene required some heavy French kissing, so he stuck his tongue down her throat.

Dodge City (1939)

Bruce Cabot was one of Errol Flynn's best friends and appears with him here. Marlene Dietrich considered Cabot 'the stupidest man in Hollywood, who couldn't even *read* his lines let alone remember them. When he turned up at a party he *never* put his hand in his pocket', she wailed. Then again, it is difficult to imagine Marlene shelling out for the booze and 'nibblies' too often either. Cabot was a bi-sexual and heavily into voyeurism. He replaced David Niven as Flynn's best friend after the Brit baulked at accompanying Errol on jaunts to Hollywood High School in search of young girls.

His ex-wife, actress Francesca De Scaffa, picked up between $30,000 and $40,000 supplying stories to *Confidential* Magazine during the early 1950s. She concealed a miniature tape recorder in her wristwatch and slept with at least thirty Hollywood stars in the space of two years, recording their conversations about themselves and their peers, and then selling the information to the magazine.

Double Indemnity (1944)

James M Cain the writer of *Double Indemnity* also wrote *The Postman Always Rings Twice* and *Mildred Pierce*. Cain based this story on real life killer Ruth Snyder.

Eleven name actors turned down *Double Indemnity* before Fred MacMurray was asked to do it. 'For Christ's sake', he exclaimed, 'you're making the mistake of your life. I'm a saxophone player, I can't do it'. I don't know how to act'. His entire career to that point had revolved around fluffy situation comedies and romances, with the occasional western thrown in.

George Raft was one of those offered the role before Fred. Being illiterate he had his script reader go over the screenplay for him. He agreed to play killer Walter Neff, but only if his character would be revealed at the end of the picture to be an undercover FBI agent sent to trap Stanwyck's character. Neither the writer nor the director was ever going to agree to such a drastic plot change, so George was shown the door.

Barbara Stanwyck (1907-1990)

Known relationships with men:

Boyer, Charles
Calhoun, Rory
Capra, Frank
Cooper, Gary
Douglas, Kirk
Fairbanks Jr. Douglas
Fonda, Henry
Ford, Glenn
Granger, Farley

Holden, William
Hughes, Howard
March, Fredric
Nader, George
Powell, William
Power, Tyrone
Quinn, Anthony
Raft, George
Romero, Cesar
Stewart, James
Wagner, Robert
Wayne, John

Known relationships with women:

Bankhead, Tallulah
Colbert, Claudette
Crawford, Joan
Dietrich, Marlene
Frank Fay

Married:

Robert Taylor

Orphaned at the age of four, Stanwyck went through twelve foster homes before becoming a Ziegfeld chorus girl at fifteen. Her first husband Frank Fay virtually founded the gay movement in Hollywood.

By 1939, her name was being romantically linked with both Crawford and Dietrich. At the same time it was an open secret that Robert Taylor was involved with theatre director Gilmor Brown. Studio heads brought pressure to bear on the two stars to marry and quash speculation about their sexuality before it was too late.

At the press reception after their wedding Taylor was asked if he would kiss the bride for the photographers. He politely declined, saying, 'We'll just smile and look silly, I guess'. When asked if they intended to raise horses and kids on their ranch, he answered, 'Well, we'll raise horses, definitely'. Barbara spent their wedding night at her place and Bob went to his mother's. The next morning they dashed off to their respective movie sets, Barbara to *Golden Boy* and Bob to *Lady of the Tropics*.

Compelled to live under the same roof for the sake of appearances, both stars really preferred the company of their own sex. If they were intimate it was not often. They not only had separate bedrooms, but Taylor always retired early while Stanwyck preferred to read until well past midnight.

Barbara's private moments were spent with her best friend, publicist Helen Ferguson, who would remain with her for twenty- seven years. Bob attended lots of gay parties, hung out with homosexual friends and was only mildly interested in women. To maintain the image of the macho male he went on hunting trips quite regularly, desperately trying to escape his 'pretty boy' persona. He figured an outdoor lifestyle might gain him better, tougher roles.

The legendary gay Clifton Webb referred to Barbara as 'my favorite Hollywood lesbian'. Although she did not join the 'sewing circle' as such and was always discreet about her personal life, Stanwyck's sexuality has always been veiled in secrecy. It appears she was most likely bi-sexual rather than lesbian.

When William Holden looked like being replaced in *Golden Boy* it was Stanwyck who saved his career. 'I wasn't going so well', he recalled while speaking of her at an awards night '...due to this lovely human being and her encouragement, and above all her generosity, I'm here tonight'.

Indeed, he would have been sacked after a week had she not intervened and convinced Columbia of his potential. Sometime over the next few years the two became lovers. His alcoholism, which began with a few nips to calm his nerves on the set of *Golden Boy*, ended the relationship but not the friendship.

Barbara and her first husband Frank Fay adopted a child, a boy they named Dion. By the age of six he was enrolled in a boarding school, the first of many. Stanwyck had no interest in him, whatsoever. His summer vacations were never spent at home. He was instead shunted off to camp on Catalina Island. Dion said many years later that his mother never showed him any affection and he could not recall her ever kissing him.

When he was twelve he caught a fishing spear through his leg at summer school and was hospitalized for four to five days. His mother was advised of the accident but did not even call the boy, much less visit him. Her career was her life and little else interested her, least of all her family. The only thing Dion can remember her doing for him happened when he was fifteen. She paid for a high-priced call girl to deflower the boy, figuring he needed to know the facts of life. His

Uncle Buck handled the details and afterwards told Dion to forget that Barbara Stanwyck was his mother. 'She wants nothing to do with you', he said.

Fred MacMurray once asked her the secret of acting. 'Just be truthful', she said, 'and if you can fake that, you've got it made'. The remark would not seem out of place on her tombstone.

Edward G Robinson was a paid up member of the Democratic Party and a fervent supporter of President Franklin D Roosevelt. Even so, he was forced to front the McCarthy hearings three times on accusations of being a Communist, primarily because fellow actor Adolphe Menjou reported him for showing sympathy to the union's side in a dispute!

The HUAC especially took a dim view of him loaning one of the 'Hollywood Ten' (Dalton Trumbo) $500 to tide his family over the difficult times engendered by his conviction. When they finally decided not to indict Robinson the committee had this to say. 'Well, actually, the committee has never had any evidence presented to indicate that you were anything more than a very choice sucker. I think you are number one on the sucker list in the country'. Evidently, they considered compassion and naivety to be one and the same.

Robinson was just 5'5" tall, spoke several languages and was a *bona fide* art expert who did not hit it big in the movies until he made *Little Caesar* at the age of thirty-seven. Throughout his long and generally exceptional career he was never once even *nominated* for an Oscar.

The Supporting Oscar in 1944 was taken out by Barry Fitzgerald for more or less playing himself in *Going My Way*. Bizarrely, he was nominated in both the Best Actor and Best Support categories *for the same role in the same film*. Robinson's superb scene in *Double Indemnity* where he rattles off the odds relating to various methods of suicide was worthy of a nomination at least. As usual he was out of luck.

Down Argentine Way (1940)

Betty Grable (1916-1973)

Known relationships:

Arnez, Desi
Barry, Don 'Red'
Calhoun, Rory
Cassini, Oleg
Crabbe, Buster
Dailey, Dan
Haymes, Dick
Kennedy John F
Lawford, Peter
Mature, Victor
Power, Tyrone
Raft, George
Rooney, Mickey
Shaw, Artie
Stack, Robert

Married:

Harry James
Jackie Coogan

'There are two reasons why I'm in show business', Betty often said, 'and I'm standing on them'. Her legs were insured for $1,250,000, more as a publicity stunt than anything else. She gained her first movie contract at the age of twelve, but it was soon torn up when her true age was revealed. She can be seen leading the Goldwyn girls in the 1930 musical *Whoopee!* If the birth date she has generally been attributed is correct she was thirteen years old at that time!

By her fifteenth birthday she was dating the thirty-six year-old George Raft. Her mother usually chaperoned, quite unconcerned about the indecent age difference. In fact, good old mum pushed her into show business at the age of three and was determined to make her little girl a star. After Betty finished second in a talent quest Mum slapped her face because she exhibited pride in her achievement. 'That will teach you to finish *first* next time', she said.

When Betty wed former child star Jackie Coogan, she was well aware he stood to inherit a cool $4 million on reaching his maturity in twelve months' time. Unfortunately for the newly-weds, Jackie's abominable parents had already squandered most of his earnings. The Coogan Law was created in the wake of his problems. It ruled that at least half of any child star's earnings must be kept in a trust account on the child's behalf. Jackie's folks had pumped off all but $126,000 of the $4 million he had earned.

A side effect of all this trauma was that Jackie turned to drink and the marriage failed after two years. But at least their brief union, according to Betty, was nothing if not educational. 'Coogan taught me more tricks than a whore learns in a whorehouse', she replied, when quizzed about their love life. He would go on to acquire a whole new legion of fans in his last years as Uncle Fester in *The Addams Family* TV series.

Betty grew up quick in Hollywood. By the time she was twenty nothing much fazed her about the industry or those in it. Darryl Zanuck, for example, had a nasty habit of waving his penis at women, often taking it out and resting it on his desk during interviews. 'Isn't it beautiful?' he asked her during one such meeting. 'Yes', she replied, 'and you can put it away now'. She had been around the block a few times by then and was not easily shocked or put off by sleazy studio executives.

She once aborted a baby to the rampant Artie Shaw because he dumped her to elope with Lana Turner, who he just happened to be *three-timing* with Judy Garland. In fairness to Shaw he walked in on Betty having sex with Dan Dailey on the floor of her dressing room and it griped him a little. As Dailey ran for his life Artie gave Betty a severe beating. Even so, Artie was a tad hypocritical at times.

During the Second World War a pin-up picture showing Betty clad in a bathing suit and peering provocatively over her shoulder caused a sensation. It became the most famous pin-up in history, even though the Hays Office insisted it be retouched to remove 'suggestive lines around her buttocks'.

At the Hollywood Canteen she was a special drawcard and loved to dance with servicemen, enjoying the adulation whenever she attended. Continually being 'cut in', she once danced with an estimated 300 soldiers in a single hour.

Aware that Marilyn Monroe was being groomed as the next 'Queen of the Fox Lot, she tore up her contract with the studio at the completion of *How to Marry A Millionaire*, despite it still having five more years to run.

Her marriage to trumpet player Harry James lasted for twenty-two years. Both were avid gamblers at the racetrack. Most of their friends belonged to the racing fraternity, not the movie colony.

Down Periscope (1996)

Comedian Kelsey Grammar has endured a great deal of tragedy in his life. His father was shot dead by a crazed gunman in 1969, and six years later his sister Karen was abducted, raped and murdered by three teenaged boys. Then in 1980 two of his half-brothers drowned in a scuba-diving accident off the coast of the Virgin Islands. In 1994 he was charged with having illicit sex with a fifteen year-old babysitter but the jury chose not to indict him.

Driving Miss Daisy (1989)

Although this film won the Best Picture Oscar, Bruce Beresford was not even *nominated* in the Best Director category. Nor was he invited to the awards ceremony. 'Well, they don't invite you unless you're nominated', he explained philosophically.

On Oscar night he was away in Africa shooting *Mister Johnson* when his picture picked up five statuettes. MC Billy Crystal dubbed *Driving Miss Daisy* 'the movie that directed itself'. Jessica Tandy's Best Actress acceptance speech mentioned Beresford as 'that forgotten man'. Richard Zanuck, when picking up the Best Picture Oscar, said, 'We're up here for one very simple reason, Bruce Beresford is a brilliant director'.

Dr. Kildare's Crisis (1940)

You won't find Blossom Rock's name in the credits, because at that stage in her career she was acting under the name of Marie Blake. As such, she made the Dr. Kildare series playing his receptionist Sally. Blossom was the elder sister of songbird Jeanette McDonald and in her later years became widely known for her role as Grand mama in TV's *The Addams Family*.

Dr No (1962)

Ian Fleming only wrote eleven Bond books. Many of the movies, therefore, (the total has now exceeded twenty) merely capitalize on his name and have nothing whatsoever to do with his works.

Thunderball was intended to be the first Bond film, but legal wrangles forced a change to *Dr No*. In Japan the title was read as being 'Dr? No', so the picture was initially released there as 'We Don't Want a Doctor'. The James Bond Theme, by the way, was not written by John Barry, but by a gentleman named Monty Norman who won a court case over the issue.

The role of Bond in this first picture in the series was offered to Richard Johnson, Cary Grant and James Mason, before Sean Connery was approached. Grant and Mason were interested but would not commit to any more than three films and the deal offered was for seven.

The author wanted David Niven to play 007. Roger Moore was tested but considered 'too soft' for the part and Patrick McGoohan refused it three times. When asked to play the title role, Noel Coward telegrammed his reply, 'Dr No? No! No! No!'

The film premiered in London on October 6, 1962 a day after the Beatles' debut single *Love Me Do* was released. Two of the greatest phenomenon in entertainment history, therefore, burst on the scene within 24 hours of each other.

Connery was once offered the lead in TV's *Maverick* but rejected it because he did not wish to be tied to a series. He was also considered as a replacement for Gordon Scott in the Tarzan films in 1961, but turned that offer down for the same reason.

He received a meagre six thousand pounds for his first Bond outing. He soon fell out with the producers, Harry Saltzman and Cubby Broccoli, once he realized how many millions they were making from his performance. 'I wouldn't piss on them if they were on fire', he said. Upon hearing Broccoli had suffered a massive heart attack and was paralyzed down one side of his body, Connery retorted, 'Fucking good! I hope he's paralyzed down the other side tomorrow'.

Ursula Andress arrived in tropical Jamaica without a suntan. To prepare for her role as Honeychile Ryder she was required to strip naked and allow a make-up man to paint a tan on her body from head to toe. While the poor fellow performed this thankless task, a steady stream of people on one pretext or another went in and out of the room.

Censorship restrictions prevented her from emerging out of the Caribbean exactly as Fleming had written it, naked but for a belt and a knife, with one hand covering her crotch and the other her broken nose. At the film's climax, Ursula was supposed to be attacked by dozens of large crabs while she lay chained to a ramp. When the crabs arrived in England where the scene was to be shot, however, they were found to be frozen and very dead, so the scene was shot without them. That scene does appear pretty lame when viewed today. If Dr No's intention was simply to drown her why didn't he just put her in a sack and toss her off the jetty?

Marguerite Lewars plays the photographer who slashes Quarrel's face with a broken flash bulb. She was the current Miss Jamaica in 1962 and was recruited by director Terence Young when he spotted her working at the ticket counter at Jamaica Airport. At first she was offered the role of the Eurasian girl seduced by Bond. She turned it down because her mother would never approve of her lying on a bed clad only in a towel kissing a strange man. The very first scene ever shot in a Bond film was scene number 39 of *Dr No*, the one where 007 walks past Lewars at the Jamaican airport. All her workmates gathered around to watch her perform and the poor girl became so nervous the scene had to be shot nine times. Her brother-in-law Reggie Carter plays the bogus taxi driver who picks up Bond from the airport and later suicides by biting on a cyanide-laced cigarette.

Timothy Moxon, a friend of the director, was given the small role of Stangways, the British operative in Kingston who gets shot by the 'three blind mice' in the car park. One of the killers (the one in the red cap) was Moxon's real-life dentist. Stangway's secretary (who also gets shot) is played by a woman who was rewarded with the role for offering her home for use in the scene.

The tarantula (nick-named Rosie by the crew) was pulled along on a string. Although it actually crawled on the body of stuntman Bob Simmons, a pane of glass (obviously) separated it from Connery's arm in the final close-up.

The famous Goya painting of the Duke of Wellington was actually stolen a few weeks before shooting began and was the subject of much publicity. As a contemporary joke it is shown hanging in Dr No's dining room.

Jack Lord plays Felix Leiter. Producer Cubby Broccoli was concerned he might steal the picture from Connery if he let him reprise the role in *Goldfinger,* so he was replaced by a less charismatic actor. Lord later made a couple of poor career moves in television by first knocking back the role of Napoleon Solo in *The Man From U.N.C.L.E.* series, and then passing on Captain Kirk in *Star Trek*. In the long run things worked out, however. The successful TV series *Hawaii 50* made him a worldwide star.

In 1953, Sean Connery represented Scotland in the Mr. Universe contest. In the same year he was offered a chance of a contract with Manchester United as a pro footballer, but decided to stick with acting. Five years on, many of the club's players were killed in the Munich air crash.

At the age of sixty he was voted 'the sexiest man alive'. When asked to comment, he dryly observed, 'there are very few sexy men dead'. His first wife (Australian actress Diane Cilento) gave as her reasons for leaving him, '...I finally became unable to cope with his legendary meanness with money, his suspicions and oppression of me as an actress... his entourage of hangers-on'.

Duck Soup (1933)

The satirical barbs against totalitarian regimes in this film were enough for Benito Mussolini to ban it in Italy. Oddly enough no such ban applied in Stalinist Russia. In fact, in 1934, Harpo played a concert at the Leningrad Music Hall as a guest of the Soviet Union. Of course, none of the Marx Brothers films were allowed to be shown in Hitler's Germany because the boys were Jewish.

Duck Soup flopped in 1933, but is now considered by their fans to be the best of the comedy trio's work. Its failure at the box-office saw them head over to MGM to work under the auspices of Irving Thalberg for their next offering, *A Night at the Opera*. The story goes that while they were waiting outside Thalberg's office for an interview, they lit up cigars and blew the smoke under his door. Thinking the building was on fire Thalberg rushed out and Groucho, Chico and Harpo rushed in.

Duel in the Sun (1946)

Duel in the Sun actually cost $2.9 million *more* to make than did *Gone With The Wind* seven years earlier. Jennifer Jones' heaving bosom was enough to see her publicly chastised by the Roman Catholic Church, which was disillusioned by her transformation from the title role in the saccharine *The Song Of Bernadette* a few years earlier to a brazen hussy in this. One British critic captured the essence of the film in a word when he described it as 'cornographic'.

David O Selznick took a perverse delight in coming to the set to watch his wife, Jennifer Jones, play her love scenes with other men. Director King Vidor reckoned he could hear Selznick panting during Jennifer's intimate scenes with Gregory Peck.

As a seventeen year-old Selznick received 'pocket money' of a thousand dollars a week from his father! Old man Selznick reasoned (correctly as it happened) that if the boy got used to having lots of money when he was young, it would compel him to make big money when he became an adult.

Dumbo (1941)

Dumbo was set to appear on the cover of *Time* magazine in 1941until the Japanese attack on Pearl Harbor intervened, causing the cover to be changed. This short feature made more money in its initial release than did the previous year's *Fantasia* and *Pinocchio* combined. Even though *Fantasia, Pinocchio* and *Bambi* were all critical successes, the public response was lukewarm at best. Had it not been for the US government recruiting him to make animated propaganda films during the war Disney might well have gone bankrupt.

Donald Duck's appearance was modelled on Harpo Marx. Tinkerbell, in *Peter Pan*, was based on Marilyn Monroe. Clarence Nash was the voice of Donald, Daisy, Hewy, Dewy & Lewy, and he did all the voices in six languages! 'I wanted to be a doctor', he once said of his career, 'and ended up the biggest quack in the world'.

East of Eden (1955)

Actor Ray Stricklyn recalled running into his friend James Dean at the bank shortly after Jimmy had filmed *East of Eden*. The rising new star was carrying a brown paper bag in which was stuffed $10,000. 'I don't trust Warner Brothers', he giggled, 'so I made them pay me in cash'.

Dean's brief life was greatly affected by the early death of his mother. 'My mother died on me when I was nine years old', he said. 'What does she expect me to do? Do it all by myself?' He avoided the Korean War by declaring his homosexuality to the Draft Board. For a while he attended 'The Method' school of acting but walked out after just three sessions.

Bogart said of him, 'if James Dean had lived they'd have discovered he wasn't a legend'. Elia Kazan described him as 'a pudding of hatred'.

During his brief stay in Hollywood he would spit on the portraits of Bogart, Cagney and Muni that adorned the wall of Warners' reception hall. Once, at a dinner party with Elia Kazan, Tony Perkins and Karl Malden he picked up his steak and threw it through the window. At Chasen's restaurant he would accompany his demands for service with table banging and silver clanging.

The car in which he died was nicknamed 'Little Bastard'. His last words spoken to his passenger, mechanic Dennis Stock were, 'he's got to see us'. He was wrong. The ensuing accident all but decapitated the actor. The driver of the other vehicle was unhurt. Stock, incidentally, would die in another car crash twenty-six years later.

Pieces of the wreckage of 'Little Bastard' were sold as souvenirs. Life-size plastic images of Jimmy's head went for $5 each. The James Dean Foundation set up by his family after his death sold, among other knick-knacks, James Dean spark plugs! In fact, the dead actor's trademark image has transformed his estate's worth from $96,000 into $6 million by the 1990s.

His life mask rests at Princeton University in the Laurence Hutton Collection among those of Beethoven, Keats, Thackeray and other *real* legends. Interestingly, of the three thousand 'mourners' at his funeral none were from Hollywood's acting fraternity.

East of Java (1935)

While making *East of Java,* Charles Bickford had his throat torn almost to the jugular by a 400 pound lion. The man was very unpopular with studio executives throughout his career because he often stood up for extras and other crewmembers in studio disputes. A former extra himself, he would refuse to work overtime to complete a shoot if it meant costing his former colleagues a further day's pay.

East of Sumatra (1953)

During the making of this film Suzan Ball (she was Lucille Ball's second cousin, by the way) slightly injured her leg but thought little of it. By January 1954, however, tumors had developed that necessitated the amputation of the leg if she was to survive. Three months later and wearing an artificial limb she wed actor Richard Long of '*The Big Valley'* fame. Sadly, the cancer soon spread to her lungs and she passed away in August 1955. The love of her life was Anthony Quinn. The last word she ever uttered to her husband (no doubt, to his chagrin) was 'Tony'.

East Side, West Side (1949)

The confrontation between Barbara Stanwyck (playing the cuckolded wife) and Ava Gardner (portraying the man-eater who seduces her husband) mirrored their real life situation at that time. Ava had recently enjoyed a brief affair with Barbara's husband Robert Taylor. Their affair was common knowledge and Stanwyck's ego was severely bruised by it. Consequently, their only scene together in the entire film dripped with genuine venom from both actresses.

An odd chain of events saw Nancy Sinatra Senior (the wife Frank left for Ava) become Stanwyck's best friend in her later years. Barbara died in 1990 at the age of eighty-two. A mere five days later Ava joined her in death. She was sixty-eight.

Ronald Reagan's second marriage to Hollywood also-ran Nancy Davis surprised many because her reputation in the industry was anything but snow-white. 'If I had a nickel for every Jew she's been under, I'd be rich', said the already rich George Cukor. Writer Anne Edwards recalled, 'Nancy was one of those girls whose phone number got handed around a lot'.

MGM casting director Bernard Thau was one of her lovers. Just before his death in 1983 he said Nancy was renowned for giving oral sex in the company offices, a talent he felt helped her gain a contract with the studio. Peter Lawford's last wife (in her biography about him) was equally damning when relaying a story he told her about Nancy. He recounted how he and fellow actor Robert Walker used to take road trips with Nancy to visit her parents in Arizona. In Lawford's own words she kept both men 'orally entertained' on these journeys. 'Nancy Davis was known for giving the best head in Hollywood', he said.

Easy Rider (1969)

Easy Rider cost only $501,000 to make, and is said to have recouped the entire outlay in its first week's returns - from just one theatre! Jack Nicholson admits he was stoned when he played the campfire scene. His rambling discourse on UFO's contains a muffed line that was left in the final print by Peter Fonda because Jack's marijuana-induced laugh was so believable.

No wonder. Bruce Dern saw at once that Fonda and Dennis Hopper knew Nicholson was walking away with their movie. 'Those guys killed him off because he was stealing the picture', he said. 'They'd had enough of watching Jack in the rushes'.

Nicholson, by the way, was thirty-two when he hit it big with this film. Peter's four year-old daughter Bridget can be glimpsed in a crowd scene. Former record producer (and future murderer) Phil Spector plays the cocaine dealer.

The son of Henry and brother of Jane, Peter Fonda is fortunate to have lived past his eleventh birthday. In 1950 he shot himself with a .22 caliber pistol a few months after his mother suicided. The bullet penetrated his liver and kidneys and it took three blood transfusions to save his life. Jane said it was uncertain if the act was a suicide attempt, or one engineered to gain attention from his father.

Nicholson had affairs with *three* of Dennis Hopper's ex-wives, Brooke Hayward (the author of *Haywire*), Daria Halprin (star of *Zabriskie Point*), and Mamas & Papas singer

Michelle Phillips. 'Maybe that's his trip', commented Hopper. 'I don't know. It doesn't bother me. I still like him'.

Ecstasy (1932)

Hedy Lamarr (1913-2000)

Known relationships:

Aumont, Jean-Pierre
Berle, Milton
Boyer, Charles
Brando, Marlon
Cabot, Bruce
Capa, Robert
Carson, Johnny
Chaplin, Charles
Feldman, Charles
Fisher, Eddie
Flynn, Errol
Gable, Clark
Gardiner, Reginald
Garfield, John
Granger, Farley
Henreid, Paul
Kennedy John F
Litvak, Anatole
Mayer, Louis B
Meredith, Burgess
Milland, Ray
Montgomery, George
Niven, David
Preminger, Otto
Remarque, Erich Maria
Sanders, George
Sinatra, Frank
Spiegel, Sam
Stevens, Mark

Stewart, James
Taylor, Robert
Tone, Franchot
Tracy, Spencer
Vallee, Rudy
Walker, Robert
Wilder, Billy

Married:

Gene Markey & 4 others
John Loder

Eighteen year-old Hedy Lamarr's sensational 1932 Czech film *Ecstasy* was shown in full in Nazi Germany. Then, it was suddenly banned when officials learned the star was a Viennese Jew. The picture was also banned in the USA until 1940, not on account of Hedy's origins or even the nudity, but because of the expressions on her face as she supposedly experiences orgasm. Her grimaces, by the way, were in response to the director twisting her foot off camera.

At the age of nine, Hedwig (her real name was Hedwig Keisler) was seduced by a thirty year-old woman, and at fourteen was raped by a laundryman. Howard Hughes once offered her $10,000 to pose nude for a rubber dummy he intended to mold and then sleep with! 'Why not sleep with me, the real thing?' she offered. 'Because you are too good for me', the eccentric billionaire replied.

Authorities revealed in 1997 that an anti-jamming device invented in 1940 by Hedy and composer George Antheil was the foundation for modern secure military communications. She had learned a lot about weaponry from her first husband who was a munitions maker in Germany before the war. She died in 2000 at the age of eighty-six. By the time she died in 2000, at the age of 86, neighbors said she was by then a total recluse, venturing outside only at night (with a flashlight and cane) to collect her mail.

Edge of Darkness (1943)

This film saw the emergence of newcomer Helmut Dantine, a twenty-five year-old Austrian Jew who had escaped the Nazis in his homeland and journeyed to America a year or so earlier. He was first noticed in *Mrs. Miniver*, portraying a downed Nazi flier.

Errol Flynn immediately set out to seduce the handsome Austrian, but was rebuffed by Dantine who told him he was 'saving himself' for Tyrone Power who was currently overseas on war duty. Not one to pine over lost love forever (or even for five minutes), Errol took up with a busty eighteen year-old Mexican girl named Bianca Rosa Welter instead. She would later change her name to Linda Christian and outdo both men by *marrying* Power.

Shortly after completing *Edge of Darkness*, Errol was charged with statutory rape and faced the real prospect of serving up to ten years making little rocks out of big ones if convicted. By employing the redoubtable Jerry Geisler as his attorney he managed to avoid the rap, but it was touch and go for a while. When the jury failed to reach a quick verdict and was sequestered overnight, he had his cronies employ several goons as standbys at the courthouse, ready to whisk him away to a waiting chartered aircraft destined for Venezuela should the verdict go against him.

Egyptian, The (1954)

Bella Darvi was interned at Auschwitz Concentration Camp when she was twelve years old during the Second World War, before she was discovered by Darryl Zanuck and brought to Hollywood to live with him and his wife. They created her acting name out of their Christian names, Darryl and Virginia.

Before long, Bella and Darryl were having an affair, so Virginia, quite justifiably, threw her out of their house. Writer Nunnally Johnson had a rather dry explanation for Zanuck's obvious infatuation with his houseguest. 'It's really quite simple', he said, 'Bella took him to bed. Until then, he thought sex was something you did on top of a desk'.

A regular attender at the Cannes Film Festival, Bella quickly developed a reputation for sleeping with any journalist who showed an interest in her. Several later recalled, however, that she seemed not to derive any joy from the episodes, due to her strong preference for female rather than male partners.

A most disturbed young woman, who probably never got over her time in Auschwitz if truth be known, tried to commit suicide several times. In 1971, she at last succeeded when she gassed herself in Monte Carlo at the age of forty-two.

El Dorado (1967)

El Dorado is an obvious re-do of *Rio Bravo*. Robert
Mitchum plays the drunk, as did Dean Martin in the first
film. James Caan apes Ricky Nelson's brash young
gunfighter from *Rio Bravo*. Arthur Hunnicutt does the
Walter Brennan wizened old coot thing, and a couple of
young lovelies substitute for Angie Dickinson. John Wayne,
as usual, plays John Wayne in both films. The scene where
Caan throws himself in front of a bunch of horses on Main
Street is so shabbily faked it is laughable. Not a good movie.

Enigma: Crack the Code (2001)

If you look closely at the scene where Dougray Scott and
Saffron Burrows are dancing at a club you can glimpse one of
the producers of the picture, rock star Mick Jagger, dressed
as an RAF officer sitting at a table smoking a cigarette. The
stunning Miss Burrows has been in a relationship with Fiona
Shaw (the 'baddie' in *Undercover Blues* and the private
school teacher in *Three Men and a Little Lady*) for several
years.

Erin Brockovich (2000)

The real Erin Brockovich has a small role as the waitress
who serves Julia Roberts in the diner. She is actually wearing
a nametag that reads 'Julia'. Judge LeRoy A Simmons came
out of retirement to re-enact his real life adjudication that
sent the original case further into the legal system.

Julia's brother Eric was unimpressed by her Oscar-winning performance. 'Everyone's going on about how great she was in it', he said. 'But what did she do? Wear some push-up bras. It wasn't great acting'. It is no secret the siblings have not been on speaking terms for some years. With this film Julia became the first female to receive $20 million for a role. If you ever want to aggravate an envious brother, that's the way to do it.

In Julia's hometown of Smyrna a local dentist named Dr Aspes has kept a plaque on his surgery wall for twenty-five years. It pledges the gift of a free tube of toothpaste to every child in the town, should any of his patients ever win any one of the following: An Olympic medal, a Pulitzer Prize, a Rhodes Scholarship, a Masters golfing green jacket, a Grammy Award, a Heisman Trophy for football – or an Academy Award. When Julia won her Oscar he kept his word and ordered 10,000 tubes of toothpaste from a delighted distributor.

'Kiefer and I will be together forever', said Julia Roberts in 1990. They broke up a year later, just a couple of days before they were to wed. She then took off for Ireland with his pal Jason Patric.

'I'm happier now in my life than I've ever been, despite all the chaos', was her assessment of her affair with Patric in 1991. It was over by 1993, due in part to her brief fling with Daniel Day-Lewis.

'We're in love and will spend our lives together', was her statement to the press when she wed Lyle Lovett, less than a month after first laying eyes on him. They divorced twenty-one months later. In the first eight months of their marriage they had only been able to spend ten nights under the same roof due to work commitments.

'I'm happier than I've ever been in my life'. That was in 1997, only this time she was referring to her romance with actor Benjamin Bratt. She left him in 2001 to marry Danny Moder.

'I was born to love and to be the wife of this man', she gushed as she and Moder tied the knot. Some people go through life and *never* find true and everlasting love. Julia seems able to find the 'true' bit about once a year. It's the 'everlasting' part she has trouble with.

Escape from Fort Bravo (1953)

William Campbell competently plays the over-confidant confederate soldier in this, a rare highlight in his brief and uneventful career in the movies. His ex-wife Judith Exner-Campbell, however, would achieve lasting notoriety as the mistress of John F Kennedy, mob boss Sam Giancana, Joseph Kennedy, Sammy Davis Jr and Frank Sinatra.

ET – The Extra-Terrestrial (1982)

Harrison Ford's future wife Melissa Mathison received the sole writing credit for ET based on her screenplay *ET & Me*. She is also credited with coming up with the little alien's appearance.

After spending more than a million dollars on the film, Columbia decided to drop it because the studio already owned the rights to the upcoming Jeff Bridges film *Starman*, and it was thought the stories were too much alike. Picked up by Universal, *ET* became the highest grossing movie ever made to that point. And that was despite *two* research companies decreeing it was utterly unpromising and would only appeal to children.

The confectionary Elliott uses to lure ET out of hiding is called Reese's Pieces in America. The company's business jumped by 65% after Hershey agreed to spend a million dollars on advertising.

The Mars Company passed on the opportunity to have its product, M & M's, used in the film. Unlike Columbia's researchers, Mars' so-called experts believed ET would *frighten* children.

The movie cost $10 million to make and grossed $701 million. Oops!

Over the first few weeks of its release, director Steven Spielberg's share of the profits caused his bank balance to grow by about a half a million dollars a day!

When Richard Attenborough took out the Best Director Oscar for *Gandhi* the Brit graciously went to Spielberg on his way to the podium, leaned over and whispered, 'this isn't right, this should be yours'.

In 1983, ET was runner-up for *Time* magazine's 'Man of the Year' award! Evangelist Jimmy Swaggert experienced a mental meltdown and denounced the lovable little alien as 'a beast from hell', accusing Spielberg of being 'an agent of Satan'. Jimmy evidently hails from that school of advanced thought that believes anything not found wandering about in the Garden of Eden must be the devil's work.

One of the two voices used for ET was that of Debra Winger who also appears in the Halloween scene. (She's the one wearing a mask and carrying a poodle). For the scenes where ET has to walk, a legless boy and some midgets were employed.

Harrison Ford was cast as Elliott's school principal but his part ended up on the cutting room floor. The 2002 re-issue of *ET* has the line, 'You will not go out there as a hippy' inserted in place of 'You will not go out there as a terrorist', in deference to the September 11, 2001 terrorist attack on New York.

Drew Barrymore's first appearance on film was in a tele-feature called *Suddenly Love*. She was three years old and played a boy. In 1980, at the age of five, she made *Altered States*. Drew made a sensational impression in *ET* playing Elliott's little sister.

By the age of nine, however, she was into alcohol and by ten had advanced to smoking

Marijuana. Cocaine followed before she was twelve and she slashed her wrists at fourteen but survived. Only then did she determine to dry out and start again.

In 1994, nineteen year-old Drew suddenly married a thirty-one year old bartender she barely knew. They hired a psychic priest to perform the ceremony, but that didn't help, and the union was over in less than a month. Then she married Canadian oddball comedian Tom Green in 2001, apparently after learning he had testicular cancer. They divorced in the same year.

Birthday boy David Letterman was flabbergasted on his talk show one evening when she jumped up on his desk and displayed her breasts to him. Her idea of a birthday present, she said. Openly bi-sexual, she has been quoted as saying, 'Let's just say I like women sexually. I love a woman's body, and I think a woman and a woman together are beautiful'.

Peter Coyote, who also features in the picture, once had a huge drug problem. In 1987 he said, 'I was very sick. I was dying. I was either going to stop or die. I stopped'. He later became a regular presenter on the *Time Lab* series on Foxtel.

Exorcist, The (1973)

Former Oscar-winning actress Mercedes McCambridge provided the rasping, unnerving voice of the Devil inside Linda Blair. 'Any child could have wiggled on the bed', said McCambridge. 'If there was any horror in the exorcism, it was *me*'. Her comments caused a furor as well as a dilemma for the Academy because Blair had been Oscar-nominated for her performance, largely on account of the uncanny, scary vocals that issued from her as she became the Devil. Should her nomination be rescinded because she had not given a *complete* performance? In the end the Academy chose not to rock the boat and let her nomination stand. But the damage was already done. She lost.

'I grew up fast', said Blair at the age of twenty-two. Her teenage years were spent in a haze of drugs and sex. 'I've had more relationships than some people 40 or 50 years old', she boasted. A year after her starring role in *The Exorcist*, the fifteen-year old moved in with singer/actor Rick Springfield, but left him twelve months later for a married man.

Far Country, The (1954)

Ruth Roman plays the female lead in this Jimmy Stewart western. In 1956 she and her 3 year-old son were passengers aboard the Italian liner *Andrea Doria* when it collided with another liner the *Stockholm*. The accident claimed the lives of 51 people. Ruth and the boy were unhurt. Cary Grant's wife, Betsy Drake, was also aboard and also unhurt in the tragedy.

Farewell, My Concubine (1993)

Leslie Cheung was Asia's top actor through the 80s and 90s. The Hong Kong-born actor starred in many martial arts films. He also made romantic comedies aimed at diverting attention away from his homosexuality.

In April 2003, at the age of 46, he leapt from the twenty-fourth floor of the Mandarin Oriental Hotel in Hong Kong. His prophetic last words were reported to have been, 'I'll be right down'. And he was.

Farmer's Daughter, The (1947)

James Arness, the future Matt Dillon of *Gunsmoke* fame, makes his debut here. During World War Two the 6'6" actor was wounded in the leg during the Anzio landings in January 1944. In 1950 his height gained him the title role in the science-fiction thriller *The Thing*. He suffered a great personal tragedy when his daughter, Jenny, committed suicide because rock star Greg Allman left her to marry Cher.

Fastest Guitar Alive, The (1968)

This incredibly silly vehicle is actually an espionage story set during the American Civil War starring none other than pop singer Roy Orbison in the title role! It was Roy's first and last movie. He made one too many. In the year of its release his two sons, eleven year-old Roy Jr and six year-old Tony, died in a fire in their house in Hendersonville, Tennessee.

Ferris Bueller's Day Off (1986)

Cindy Pickett and Ward Lyman who play Ferris' parents married each other in real life after the picture was shot. Alan Ruck was thirty years old when he played Cameron. Ben Stein plays the economics teacher and was a college graduate (with honors) in that field at Columbia University. Other than the roll call, all his lines spoken to the class were part of an actual economics lecture and ad-libbed.

Matthew Broderick was twenty-four years old when he played schoolboy Ferris. His real life girlfriend at the time,

Jennifer Grey, plays his sister. Mia Sara who plays his girlfriend on-screen is married to Sean Connery's son Jason in the real world.

While Broderick and Grey were holidaying in Ireland in 1987, his hired BMW collided with another vehicle killing both its female occupants. He later conceded he *may* have been driving on the wrong side of the road, but as he and Grey were the only surviving witnesses, a charge of careless driving was all that could be brought against him.

He told Irish authorities he (conveniently) had no recollection of the moments leading up to the crash. Grey said she was (also conveniently) changing a music tape at the time and saw nothing either. Already back in America by the time the case came up, he was fined one hundred pounds *in absentia* by an Irish court. Friends vow he was deeply upset over the deaths of the women.

'You don't ever feel when you're with him that you're with an *actor*', said Grey when asked what he was like. 'Actors tend to be unbearable. Matthew reads comic books instead of scripts'. Perhaps he should have taken time out from his comic books to read up on driving regulations in Ireland.

Jeffrey Jones plays Ferris's school Principal Ed Rooney. In July 2003, he pleaded 'no contest' to a charge of employing a fourteen year-old boy to pose for sexually explicit photos. Compelled to register as a sex offender in Florida, he was re-arrested in 2004 for changing domicile without notifying authorities.

Ditzy Charlie Sheen's real name is Carlos Estevez and he is the brother of *Young Guns* star Emilio Estevez. Actor Martin Sheen, of course, is their father. In 1995 Charlie was unfortunate enough to be the only 'name' identified as a client of Hollywood madam Heidi Fleiss. He admitted spending $2,000 a pop on scores of call girls working for Fleiss.

Charlie once purchased all 2,615 seats behind the left-field fence at Anaheim Stadium to improve his chances of catching a home run hit in an Angels-Tigers baseball game.

55 Days at Peking (1963)

English character actor Harry Andrews has a small part in this film. He, like Robert Helpmann, the Australian who plays the Dowager Empress's War Minister, was a homosexual. Never having married, Andrews lived with his male lover for decades.

Helpmann became chiefly responsible for the establishment of the Australian Ballet Company. In the 1940s he was the principal male dancer at Sadler's Wells and partnered the legendary Dame Margot Fonteyn.

Dame Flora Robson plays the Dowager Empress. She once had a serious affair with African-American singer Paul Robeson.

Firehouse (1987)

This is the first film in which Julia Roberts appears on screen, albeit in a very small role. Jennifer Stahl, one of the actresses who goes topless in the picture, drifted into marijuana dealing in the nineties. In 2001 she and two other persons were murdered in her New York apartment, presumably after a drug deal went wrong. The TV show *America's Most Wanted* was instrumental in bringing her killer to justice.

First Blood (1982)

The first choice to play Rambo (would you believe?) was none other than Dustin Hoffman. Dumb choice or not, at least we would have understood what he was saying most of the time.

David Morrell, who wrote the story on which *First Blood* is based, would have no part of its sequel *Rambo: First Blood Part 2*. 'On military bases they show it as a comedy', he said. 'They were rolling in the aisles, hysterical'. Even funnier was Sylvester Stallone's prediction he would one day be the second actor President of the United States. We all pray he was joking.

Five Fingers (1952)

Five Fingers was based on the World War Two thriller novel *Operation Cicero*. Darryl Zanuck decided not to use the novel's title for the film because he thought American audiences would assume it was a gangster film, related to the notorious bootlegging suburb of Cicero in Chicago.

It was circulated that the real Cicero, Elyesa Bazna, appeared on the set of *Five Fingers* and offered his services as a technical advisor (for a fee of course) to the production company. His offer was politely declined.

The character of the countess is a Hollywood fabrication. The real Cicero had help from a chambermaid and his niece, although it was mostly through his homosexual relationship with his employer, the British Ambassador, (not alluded to in the film), that he achieved the success he did. He would drug the Ambassador after their trysts and then photograph documents from the embassy safe.

During the Second World War, the wonderful Danielle Darrieux was marked for execution by the French Underground because she reputedly entertained German troops during the occupation. After hostilities ceased she was exonerated.

Her marriage to notorious lothario Porfirio Rubirosa lasted five years. He simply moved on to marry millionaire heiress Doris Duke. As of this writing (June 2015) Danielle is still living. A remarkable woman.

Flaming Star (1960)

The part of Pacer the Kiowa was written for Marlon Brando who turned it down. Elvis Presley was desperate to play a straight dramatic role instead of the lame musicals his agent kept lumbering him with, so he leapt at the chance to replace Mr. Mumbles. Unfortunately, his fans only wanted him to sing in his pictures and he was soon back on the musical treadmill.

Dolores Del Rio (1905-1983)

Known relationships with men:

Bogart, Humphrey
Chaplin, Charles
Disney, Walt
Flynn, Errol
McCrea, Joel
Onassis, Aristotle
Remarque, Erich Maria
Roland, Gilbert
Rubirosa, Porfirio
Sanders, George
Welles, Orson

Known relationships with women:

Baker, Josephine
Dietrich, Marlene
Garbo, Greta
Holliday, Billie

Mexican actress Dolores Del Rio was one of the most beautiful women ever to appear before the cameras. Ironically, this exquisite creature's sexual preferences ran to women more than men. She was also a dedicated communist. One of her last appearances on film was as Presley's mother in *Flaming Star*.

Born in Durango in 1905, she and her family were forced to flee in 1909 when Pancho Villa's forces raided the town.

Her marriage to the gay Cedric Gibbons incorporated a strange arrangement. Her sumptuous bedroom was situated on the floor above his rather sparse one. If he wished to enter her boudoir he was first required to tap on the ceiling with a broom handle, and if his wife felt so inclined she would open a trapdoor and drop down a stepladder! He later learned of her bisexuality when he came across her fondling Greta Garbo's breasts as the two women lolled by his pool.

'I thought she was the most beautiful woman I had ever seen', remembered Orson Welles after their brief affair. 'As a beauty, Delores Del Rio is in a class with Garbo', said director John Ford, 'Then she opens her mouth and becomes Minnie Mouse'.

Flesh and the Devil (1926)

Director Clarence Brown described the first pairing of Greta Garbo and John Gilbert in his 1926 silent film *Flesh and the Devil*: 'I think it was love at first sight. Then they did the love scene...it was the damndest thing you ever saw. No one else was even there. They were in a world of their own. It seemed like an intrusion to say 'cut!' So I just motioned to the crew to move over to another part of the set and let them finish what they were doing. It was embarrassing'.

Gilbert's upbringing was bizarre to say the least. His mother left him in the care of a prostitute when he was six. He would sleep on a mat in the corner of her bedroom while she serviced clients. She would tell them to pretend he wasn't there. When his mother also started turning tricks she would tell her Johns, 'Take no notice of the kid'. By the time the boy was seven he had seen it all.

His first love was silent actress Effie Stewart. That ended tragically when she was making the silent pic *Civilization* in 1916. A balcony on which she was standing collapsed and the unfortunate girl was crushed to death.

His engagement to Virginia Bruce had an odd twist to it. He agreed to leave her everything in his will, but only if he could be certain she was a virgin before they wed. Her father agreed to allow him to spend one night with his daughter prior to the wedding to verify her claim to maidenhood.

The picture generally cited as the beginning of the end for Gilbert's career is the 1929 talkie *His Glorious Night*. His 'I love you, I love you, I love you' brought titters from the audience, probably because his hammy style was more suited to silent films, or possibly because the bass had been turned down on the soundtrack at the time of recording, causing his voice to distort.

L B Mayer detested him and bore a grudge after coming to fisticuffs with the actor years earlier, so he may have arranged for the soundtrack to be adjusted to sabotage him, but Gilbert's career nose-dived for two other reasons as well.

First of all, Mayer continued to pay his salary, but refused to put him in any decent pictures or loan him out to other studios. Secondly, Gilbert's imbibing worsened dramatically with the coming of sound and the going of Garbo, as he began to drink himself to death.

On the subject of their affair, Garbo told a friend she had been 'in love with Jack Gilbert for about fifteen minutes before the fleeting sensation evaporated'. Shattered by her rejection he immediately went on a prolonged bender. At the height of his drunkenness he fired several pistol shots at a pair of lovers parked near his property and was fortunate not to be arrested.

Writer Ben Hecht said Gilbert attended a gay Hollywood party on the night before he died. While dancing with a movie queen his toupee was accidentally dislodged. Amid shouts of derision he had to retrieve it from beneath the dancer's feet, and the incident upset him visibly. He went home at once where his nurse administered a shot to induce sleep, but forgot to check on him later. He died the next morning around nine am after choking on his tongue. Some sources say Marlene Dietrich woke up to find him dead beside her; then discreetly left the house before the media and authorities arrived on the scene.

After his death the owner of the Summit Hotel in Pennsylvania purchased his bed and installed it in the newly named 'John Gilbert Honeymoon Suite' where he rented it out for twenty-four hours at a time for an exorbitant fee.

Flight of the Phoenix, The (1965)

Scottish actor Ian Bannen was the only member of the cast nominated for his performance in this excellent adventure film. Just why he was picked out of such a fine supporting ensemble is puzzling, particularly since most people would agree Hardy Kruger stole the picture.

In 1999 Bannen was killed in a car crash near Loch Ness at the age of seventy-one. He did not marry until he was forty-eight when he wed a woman he had known for seventeen years.

Flintstones, The (1994)

This was the first of the live action films based on the Hanna-Barbera TV series. The series itself was based on another TV comedy hit *The Honeymooners,* whose leading characters Ralph & Alice Kramden and Ed & Trixie Norton bear a strong resemblance to Fred & Wilma Flintstone and Barney & Betty Rubble.

The highly successful *Tom & Jerry* cartoons were also a Hanna-Barbera creation. This did not prevent MGM producer Fred Quimby, a man who was producer in name only and had nothing whatsoever to do with the project, from accepting all seven Oscars awarded to the cartoons over the years.

The names of Tom and Jerry were pulled from a hat in an office sweep at MGM. Mel Blanc provided the vocals for most of Warner Bros cartoon characters and was said to possess over a thousand of them in his repertoire. His epitaph, which he chose himself, reads 'Th...th... that's all folks'.

Another Hanna-Barbera series was the fairly successful *Top Cat*, a concept based on the Phil Silvers character

Sergeant Bilko. Arnold Stang, who played 'Sparrow' in the Sinatra film *The Man with the Golden Arm,* provided the voice for Top Cat.

Maurice Gosfield, who played the obese Private Duane Doberman in *The Phil Silvers Show,* was the voice for Benny the Ball, while veteran actor Allen Jenkins portrayed Officer Dibble. Gosfield, believe it or not, was romantically involved for some time with the former Miss Sweden, Anita Ekberg.

Flying Down to Rio (1933)

Fred Astaire's screen test in 1932 was anything but promising. 'Can't act. Can't sing, slightly bald. Can dance a little', was the studio's assessment. That wasn't much of a wrap considering he began ballet lessons at the age of four and had his own act with his sister Adele by the time he was seven!

There was not much love lost between Ginger Rogers and Fred. As Katharine Hepburn summed it up, 'He gives her class and she gives him sex'. Rogers herself said, 'I did everything Fred Astaire did, only backwards and in heels'. A pretty good point, it must be said. Then again, if Fred had danced backwards in heels he'd have done *that* better than Ginger too.

'The best singer of songs the movie world ever new', said Oscar Levant of him. 'The greatest dancer that ever lived – better than Nijinsky', said Noel Coward. Fred reputedly taught the Prince of Wales to tap dance. It is believed he was spirited into Buckingham Palace to give him lessons on the quiet.

He hardly ever rehearsed with his dancing partners. Choreographer Hermes Pan would do that, with Fred playing the woman's part. It was felt by many that Pan was his equal as a dancer. Hermes would then play Fred's part in further rehearsals with the female. When all the moves had been ironed out and synchronized, Fred and his partner would meet for the final rehearsal before filming began. Of all his partners, only Eleanor Powell (who did her own choreography) actually rehearsed with him for long periods.

The partner he had most trouble with was the statuesque Cyd Charisse. He was fifty-four when they made *The Bandwagon*, and he dreaded the lifts because she was the heaviest of his co-stars. Age and illness were also catching up with him. Even so, his agility and grace were nothing short of sensational. Cyd's husband, singer Tony Martin, said he could always tell if she had been dancing with Astaire or Gene Kelly when she returned home. With Kelly, a most physical dancer, she invariably got bruises. With Fred there were none.

It may surprise some people to know that his first screen partner was Joan Crawford in *Dancing Lady,* made in the same year *Flying Down to Rio* was released. If you have ever seen Crawford's elephantine performance in *Dancing Lady* you would appreciate why Fred never danced with her again. That woman's talent would fit in a thimble.

In his last film, the disastrous *Finian's Rainbow,* some of his routines were shot with his feet out of camera! This was not the fault of director Francis Coppola, but of the studio hierarchy who changed the format from 35mm to 70mm, and in so doing, chopped off Fred's feet!

In 1980 at the age of eighty-one he married a thirty-eight year-old lady jockey named Robyn Smith. He died in 1987. When Ginger Rogers was awarded a Kennedy Center Honor in 1992, Smith withheld rights to any film clips of Ginger and Fred dancing together for a retrospective flashback sequence, unless the center paid her. The presentation went ahead without the show.

Ginger Rogers (1911-1995)

Known relationships:

Arnaz, Desi
Ascher, Cornel
Bautzer, Greg
Evans, Robert
Gabin, Jean
Hayward, Leland
Hughes, Howard
LeRoy, Mervyn
McCarey, Leo
Meredith, Burgess
Montgomery, George
Niven, David
Powell, William
Riskin, Robert
Romero, Cesar
Stevens, George
Stewart, James
Taylor, Robert

Tracy, Spencer
Vallee, Rudy
Vanderbilt, Alfred
Walker, Jimmy

Married:

Lew Ayres & 4 others

Her mother was the dominant factor in her life and the Hollywood mother of caricature. When Ginger won an Oscar for *Kitty Foyle*, the old girl raced her to the podium to collect it – and got there first! She even arranged for Ginger to spend eternity with her, by purchasing burial plots side by side in Oakwood Memorial Park. And that is where they rest today.

Foreign Correspondent (1940)

The extremely affable Joel McCrea was married to actress Frances Dee for 57 years until his death in 1990. He left an estate worth in excess of $50 million. He made his screen debut in the CB DeMille film *Dynamite* in 1929. It appears he gained his first foothold in the industry because he was a school classmate of CB's daughter Cecilia.

Also appearing in *Foreign Correspondent* was popular English character actor Herbert Marshall. He lost a leg while serving in the Merchant Marine during World War 1. Throughout his acting career sets were specially designed to conceal his limp. Most movie fans were unaware of his handicap.

Renowned wit Robert Benchley co-wrote the dialogue, and also featured as an actor in this. His good friend Gloria Stuart, who would one day play the aged Rose in *Titanic* (more than a half century later), recalled how she and Benchley were once residents of the infamous Garden of Allah in Hollywood, during and after World War Two. Across Sunset Boulevard was Preston Sturgess's Players Restaurant, where they would often dine. Benchley declined to ever walk across the street, she said. He always took a cab from one side of Sunset Boulevard to the other.

Forever Amber (1947)

Linda Darnell's genuine fear of fire proved to be prophetic. In 1965 she fell asleep smoking a cigarette and suffered shocking burns in the ensuing fire. She died in the hospital two days later. Although she was later cremated, for some reason her remains were not interred for another ten years. No-one seems to know why this happened.

Actress Patricia Medina divorced Richard Greene because, as she drily put it, 'there weren't enough mirrors in the house for both of us'. His only real claim to fame was as Robin Hood in the British TV series *The Adventures of Robin Hood*, which ran for five years and made him a rich man. He was actually 37 years old when the series commenced, but looked much younger.

Cornel Wilde gave up his position in the US Olympic Fencing Team to become an actor in the 1930s. At the height of his popularity (so friends say) he slept with his sword under his pillow and often breakfasted dressed in doublet and hose.

Fort Apache (1948)

Newcomer John Agar made his debut in this film opposite his wife Shirley Temple. Despite being heir to a Chicago meatpacking fortune, and married to the most popular movie star on the planet, he could not make a successful career in film and faded quickly.

In fairness to him, it was no bed of roses being married to the most famous female in the world. Sick of being referred to as 'Mr. Temple', he gradually sought solace in booze. In 1953 he was arrested twice on the same day for alcohol-related offences and sentenced to four months in prison. When his daughter (by Shirley) was married he read about it in the papers. He had not been invited to the wedding.

Prior to becoming a star, Shirley unsuccessfully auditioned to become a member of the *Our Gang* cast. The guy who turned her down probably spent the rest of his life selling pencils on street corners.

Shirley was a millionaire before she was ten and the most recognized and universally loved child alive. Every birthday she was swamped with gifts from admirers around the globe. Even on her eighteenth birthday she received a staggering 135,000 gifts! Yet of the $3 million she earned in the thirties and forties only $89,000 made its way into her account. Her parents took the rest.

Perhaps out of sheer jealousy or envy (or both), many of her brethren in the industry were not as enamored of the little superstar as was the general public. Louise Brooks for one, an actress never known to mince words, called her (a trifle harshly) 'a swaggering tough little slut!'

Actor Adolphe Menjou: 'She knows all the tricks', he moaned. 'She backs me out of the camera. She blankets me and crabs my laughs. She's making a stooge out of me. Why, if she were 40 years old and on stage all her life, she wouldn't have had time to learn all she knows about acting. Don't ask me how she does it...she's Ethel Barrymore at six!'

Alice Faye described her as, 'A nice kid. We all liked her. But she was brilliant. She knew everyone's dialogue, and if you forgot a line she gave it to you. We all *hated* her for that'.

Jules Styne was sent to Shirley's home on one occasion to coach her on certain acting techniques. They were enjoying a leisurely game of badminton when Shirley's father called her to come inside. 'I'm not ready', she called back, 'and *I'll* tell you when I'm ready. I earn all the money in this household'.

Shirley said she stopped believing in Santa Claus at a very early age, when a department store Santa asked her for her autograph. President Allessandri of Chile made her the official mascot of the Chilean Navy.

When she married at seventeen and soon became pregnant, studio executives tried to sign *her unborn embryo* to a five-year contract. An emphatic 'no' was her response.

She knew only too well the kind of life a child star could expect.

From 1974-6 Shirley Temple Black (as she was by then known) served as the US Ambassador to Ghana and later to Czechoslovakia.

Comedian Will Rogers' homespun country philosophy appealed to Americans of the Depression era and he was very popular for several years. It has since been revealed he was not without his faults, however, not the least of which was an unnatural obsession with Shirley Temple. Several writers have claimed he even resorted to boring a hole through her dressing room wall so he could spy on her as she changed. In 1935, he and record-breaking aviator Wily Post died when their plane crashed in Alaska. The very likeable Rogers was genuinely mourned throughout America.

48 Hours (1982)

In 1997, Eddie Murphy was arrested after picking up a Samoan transvestite named Atisone Seuli in the heart of Boystown, West Hollywood, during the wee hours of the morning, while the actor's wife and children were out of town. Murphy's minders would claim he was merely being a 'good Samaritan' in giving the man a lift. Seuli fell to his death (apparently accidentally) from an apartment window a few months later.

When Sylvia Holland, a Diahann Carroll look-alike trans-sexual, told the *National Enquirer* that she had 'two sex encounters with Eddie, once in an alley and the second time in his car', the paper ran the story. Murphy sued them for $5 million but when the *Enquirer* made it clear it would go to court on the issue he dropped the suit.

The *Globe* also ran a story from another transvestite named Tempest. She/he told a tale of Murphy's toe-licking habits and tossed in a description of his cologne and underwear for good measure. He promptly sued the *Globe* this time. His suit contained the damning statement that Eddie 'has not paid for sex with transsexuals for ten years'. Oops! Eventually, he went on *Entertainment Tonight* and unloaded his feelings. 'This is an act of kindness that got turned into a fucking horror show. I love my wife and I'm not gay'. He also vowed he would 'never, ever play good Samaritan again'.

Described as a 'walking chemistry set', Nick Nolte was arrested for driving his motorcycle stark naked and in a 'wild manner' while under the influence of the date rape drug GHB. 'I asked someone out recently', he offered by way of explanation, 'someone closer to my age, and she said 'Oh no, you're too famous'. I got famous to get sex, and now I can't', he whined. He once awoke in a house he could not remember renting, and ordered a truckload of rocks dumped on the lawn, 'just to see what it would look like'.

For Whom the Bell Tolls (1943)

To combat the adverse effect Veronica Lake's long hairstyle was having on the efficiency of the female workforce in America during the Second World War, Ingrid

Bergman was ordered to cut her hair very short for her role in *For Whom the Bell Tolls,* in the hope it would start a new fad. It didn't.

Ingrid Bergman (1915-1982)

Known relationships:

Adler, Larry
Brando, Marlon
Brynner, Yul
Buckland, Lt Gen Simon
Capa, Robert
Cooper, Gary
Cotton, Joseph
Crosby, Bing
Fleming, Victor
Henreid, Paul
Howard, Leslie
Hughes, Howard
Kennedy John F
Meredith, Burgess
Montand, Yves
Peck, Gregory
Quinn, Anthony
Selznick, David O
Sharif, Omar
Steinbeck, John
Tracy, Spencer

Married:

Roberto Rossellini & 2 others

Bergman had no qualms about going to Nazi Germany in 1938 to make a movie. She even gave the Nazi salute while she was there without giving it a second thought. Friends say she was apolitical all her life.

Sir John Gielgud clearly thought the Swedish-born actress was an over-rated performer. 'Poor Ingrid speaks five languages and can't act in any of them', he sniffed. Alfred Hitchcock considered her to be a nymphomaniac. 'She'd do it with doorknobs', he said. She once told her husband, 'I'd like to make love to one man from each race'.

She was known to have several lovers on the go at the same time. One of them was General Simon Bolivar Buckland who was killed on Okinawa in June 1945. Another, *Life* magazine photographer Frank Capa, died when he stepped on a landmine in Vietnam in 1954.

While making *Goodbye Again* in 1961 she attempted to seduce the homosexual Anthony Perkins, by inviting him to her dressing room to rehearse a kissing scene. Aware of her reputation, Perkins refused to come in, choosing instead to stand by the door and insisting it remain open while they *discussed* the scene.

Ingrid's final years were horrendous. Cancer necessitated the removal of her left breast in 1977, followed by the right one in 1978. Radiation treatment kept her going for a few more years until she lost the use of her right hand, whereupon she doggedly taught herself to write with her left. The end mercifully came in 1982.

Four Feathers, The (1939)

John Laurie played Private Fraser in TV's *Dad's Army,* but he was a far more accomplished actor than the average TV viewer gives him credit. 'I have played every major

Shakespearean role in the theatre', he said ruefully, 'and I'm considered the finest speaker of verse in the country, and I end up becoming famous for this crap!'

He was not alone in this. The wonderfully gifted actor Alec Guinness gave scores of brilliant performances on screen and on-stage in a great many difficult and demanding roles, yet he is chiefly remembered today for playing Ben – Obi – Wan – Kenobi in the *Star Wars* films.

Four Jills in a Jeep (1944)

Carole Landis (1919-1948)

Known relationships with women:

Susann, Jacqueline

Known relationships with men:

Bautzer, Greg
Berkeley, Busby
Boyer, Charles
Chaplin, Charles
D'Arcy, Alexander
DiCicco, Pat
Dorsey, Tommy
Gardiner, Reginald
Gibbons, Cedric
Grant, Cary
Harrison, Rex
Hartford, Huntington
Litvak, Anatole
Mamoulian, Rouben
Markey, Gene
Martin, Tony
Mature, Victor
Montgomery, George

Morris, Wayne
Nagel, Conrad
Negulesco, Jean
Raft, George
Ritchie, Bob
Roach, Hal Jr.
Romero, Cesar
Rooney, Mickey
Scott, Randolph
Stack, Robert
Tone, Franchot
Tracy, Spencer
Wheeler, Irving
Zanuck, Darryl F

In 1922, her little brother Lewis was accidentally shot dead by a playmate, his death having a lasting effect on Carole's well-being. In 1934 she eloped at fifteen, but the marriage was annulled three weeks later. Undeterred, she married the same guy again six months later. After a month together he threw her out, so she hit the road for Hollywood. Tales of her getting by as a hooker in her first year there seem to be true.

Sadly, her life was cut short in 1948 when she suicided over her affair with the married Rex Harrison. She may have been pregnant to him at the time. He may have discovered her body. She had left a trunk of her love letters to Harrison with friends. He obtained them and burned them. The scandal curtailed Harrison's Hollywood career and he quickly returned to Britain.

Carole's funeral was a media circus attended by over a thousand people. At the graveside onlookers fought each other for the flowers as the services were read. 'The most revolting thing I've ever seen', said Bishop Pyman, who lay her to rest.

Three years prior to her death she embarked upon a brief affair with authoress Jacqueline Susann. The character of Jennifer North in Susann's bestseller *The Valley of the Dolls* was based on Landis.

Carole was Darryl Zanuck's regular 4pm girl in his office each day until he inevitably tired of her. Colleagues at the studio virtually considered her to be no better than a whore because of those daily sessions with the boss. In truth, she was just one of many contract players who allowed Zanuck to service them whenever he felt the urge. It was all part of the reprehensible studio system. Poor Carole had talent, beauty and brains. She was also gentle and popular with everyone, everyone that is *except* the studio executives' wives. They hated the pretty young actresses who traded sex with their husbands for work favors.

Kay Francis too was in Four Jills in a Jeep. Essentially a star of the 30s, her career was winding down by 1944. She had no pretensions about acting in meaningful roles. 'I didn't give a shit', she said. 'I just wanted the money'.

Bisexual Kay also wanted female lovers to offset the occasional male. Marlene Dietrich, Tallulah Bankhead and several studio starlets found their way into her bed. So too did Maurice Chevalier for a time.

A heavy drinker in later life, she once inadvertently sat down naked on a radiator and was severely burned. In her will, the notoriously money conscious actress bequeathed a million dollars for the training of 'Seeing Eye' dogs, much to the astonishment of her friends.

Carmen Miranda, who was known as 'The Brazilian Bombshell', was actually born in Portugal. She is one of several guest stars in the film. Between 1940 and 1944 she was at the peak of her career; earning in excess of $2 million a year.

When Fox discovered she wore no knickers beneath her swirling dress she was unceremoniously dumped, although that may have been simply used as an excuse because her peculiar vogue had become passé. It is not true she carried a supply of drugs concealed in the heels of her shoes. In fact, the lady neither smoked nor drank liquor at all.

On V-J Day in 1945 Carmen became trapped in traffic at the corner of Hollywood and Vine as crowds celebrated the Japanese surrender. She promptly climbed up on the seat of her convertible and delighted the crowd with an impromptu rhumba.

In 1955 she died suddenly from a heart attack after appearing on The Jimmy Durante Show. Her last American movie was the Martin & Lewis comedy Scared Stiff released in 1953.

4 Weddings & a Funeral (1993)

Until The Full Monty came along this was the most successful British film of all time.

Charlotte Coleman plays Hugh Grant's wacky, punkish flat-mate here. She began on British TV as one of the two children starring in Worzel Gummage. Later she starred in the popular after-school shows Educating Marmalade and Danger-Marmalade at Work. After being voted Best Actress by the Royal Television Society in 1989 for her performance in the mini-series Oranges are not the Only Fruit, her career inexplicably stalled until it was boosted again by her kooky portrayal in Four Weddings & A Funeral. She developed an eating disorder in the nineties, but it was an asthma attack that killed her in 2001 at the age of thirty-three.

Simon Callow who plays the gay Scotsman who suffers a heart attack and dies is himself gay. 'My being openly homosexual doesn't appear to have damaged my career in any way', he says.

Francis Goes to West Point (1952)

Francis the mule was made to 'talk' by placing a piece of lead in the animal's mouth and attaching a fishing line to his bridle. This was yanked each time he was required to say something, causing his mouth to move as he tried to spew out the piece of lead. He died on an Arizona ranch at the ripe old age (for a mule) of forty-seven.

Alan Royle

From Here to Eternity (1953)

In James Jones' best-selling novel, Donna Reed's character Lorene does not work at a dancehall, but as a prostitute at an establishment catering to military personnel. Neither is Karen (played by Deborah Kerr) sterile because she once had a miscarriage as she says in the film. Her many infidelities had landed her with a dose of gonorrhea. The censors, of course, insisted on the changes.

The US Navy banned showing of the film at any of its facilities because it felt it was detrimental to its sister service, the Army. Oddly enough, the Army deemed it fit to be shown at all its bases around the world, so go figure.

The Kuhio Beach east of Diamond Head in Hawaii, where Burt Lancaster and Deborah Kerr roll about in the surf, is now a tourist attraction re-named the 'From Here to Eternity Beach'. When the censors suggested the couple wear *bathrobes* during their passionate ocean embrace, Columbia boss Harry Cohn simply ignored them. And so he should have.

Joan Crawford accepted the plum role of Karen, but insisted on using her own dress designer. Cohn could not be bothered with her petty demands, so he chose Kerr instead. Harry wanted to use Aldo Ray as the middleweight fighter, Prewitt, because he was not only a boxer but one of his contract players as well. Director Fred Zinnemann would only do the film if Montgomery Clift played Prewitt, even though he and everybody else knew Monty could not punch his way out of a paper bag. It is quite evident in the fight scene on the barracks quadrangle that his double is doing all the boxing.

Clift and Frank Sinatra briefly hit it off and became friends until the singer watched with revulsion as Monty made homosexual overtones to guests at one of Frank's parties. He had his bodyguards throw his ex-buddy out.

Frank was more than happy to accept a meagre $8,000 for his role as Maggio. Eli Wallach had the front running for the part, but threw it in when he landed the lead in a Tennessee Williams play on Broadway. Sinatra's career was rejuvenated through his Oscar for this film.

When asked by his valet and friend George Jacobs if there was any truth in the story that Los Angeles crime boss Johnny Roselli had leaned on Harry Cohn at Universal to secure him the role, he replied, 'Hey, I got that part through my own fucking *talent!*' And then he winked.

Monty complained bitterly about Burt Lancaster's top billing. 'He doesn't deserve it', he moaned, 'He is a terrible actor, nothing but a big bag of wind. The most unctuous man I have ever met'. If RKO boss Howard Hughes had not refused to loan out Robert Mitchum for the top sergeant's role, Burt would not have been asked in the first place. The scene where they are sitting in the street blind drunk was played by a cold sober Lancaster and a genuinely drunken Clift.

If Donna Reed ever had any affairs she kept them very secret. Her name has never been romantically linked with anyone except her husbands. She was also considered to be the most astute businesswoman in the industry, especially in television where her gentle looks belied her tough bargaining approach.

In 1984 she was chosen as a replacement for Barbara Bel Geddes in the blockbuster TV series *Dallas,* but after a single season Bel Geddes returned and reclaimed her spot. Donna sued the show's producers and won a hefty million-dollar settlement. Within a few months she succumbed to pancreatic cancer and was dead at the age of sixty-four.

During the 1950s George Reeves achieved worldwide recognition playing Superman in the popular TV series, starring in 104 episodes over six years. Although well built (he was 6'3"), he was still required to wear foam rubber muscles as the man of steel. He could handle himself, nevertheless, and was a Golden Gloves boxing champion before he took up acting.

Portraying the comic book hero could be risky on occasion. A young boy at an autograph signing once levelled his father's Luger at Reeves with the intention of firing it into the Man of Steel's chest, and then keeping the flattened slug as a souvenir. George talked fast and convinced the boy that, whereas Superman would be perfectly safe, the ricocheting bullet might injure someone in the nearby crowd.

Late in his career he accepted a role in *Westward Ho the Wagons,* in which he played a Hamish settler, his famous face covered by a beard and hidden under a broad-brimmed hat. It was his final film. A few years later he was murdered, probably by a contract-killer reputedly hired by his former girlfriend Toni Mannix.

He and Mannix had been lovers for over nine years. Her husband, executive Eddie Mannix, knew all about it, even approved of George. But then the actor jilted her and was three days away from marrying another woman named Lenore Lemmon when he was killed.

In the 1990s the full story began to emerge. It seems Toni hired a contract killer, but then had second thoughts and tried unsuccessfully to call him off. Well, maybe. Along with receiving many anonymous death threats (up to twenty in one night), all arranged by the insanely jealous Toni, Reeves was also involved in no fewer than three car accidents in the months leading up to his murder.

He was nearly crushed between two trucks in the first one' in the second his brakes completely failed on a hilly stretch of road, and then a speeding car forced him off the highway. Was Toni Mannix responsible for these 'accidents'? Nobody really knows for sure, but suddenly life was becoming a little tricky for George.

He was shot to death in his bedroom with his own gun, a Luger he kept in his dresser drawer. Toni told the killer where to find it. No powder burns were present around his head wound, and two more bullet holes were found in the wall. Police were unable to explain how he shot himself with the gun in his right hand, when that same hand had been disabled a few days before in one of the traffic accidents.

He had clearly put up a struggle and his body sported bruises to indicate that. Nevertheless, the coroner ruled his death a suicide. This may have resulted from pressure brought to bear by Eddie Mannix whose underworld connections were enough to scare away any real enquiry. Eddie may have been protecting his wife or merely avoiding a scandal.

Lawyer to the stars Jerry Geisler was hired by Reeves' mother to investigate her son's death. Three years after he began his investigation he too was found dead, some say at the hands of the mob.

Toni Mannix never recovered from the affair. Right up to the day of her death, in 1984, she spent her time watching videos of the old Superman series over and over again. Lenore Lemmon, who apparently knew all the details but had been afraid to speak out, did so in 1996, six months before her own demise. Her life had spiraled downwards since that fateful day in 1959 and she had been working for some years as a prostitute.

From Russia with Love (1963)

In Fleming's novel, Krilencu's apartment in Istanbul had an escape trapdoor situated in a billboard depicting Marilyn Monroe's latest film *Niagara*. In the movie the billboard depicts the latest Broccoli/Saltzman production *Call Me Bwana*. Broccoli and Saltzman were the producers of *From Russia with Love*.

*B*londe Italian actress Daniela Bianchi plays the beautiful Tatiana Romanova. The former Miss Rome was also runner-up in the 1960 Miss Universe quest. She could not speak a word of English, so her entire performance was re-voiced by another actress. In 1968 Daniela made her last film and retired to wed an Italian millionaire.

The voice of the unseen Blofeld is that of British character actor Anthony Dawson. He had previously played the malevolent Professor Dent in *Dr No* in 1962.

Lotte Lenya plays the nasty Rosa Klebb, the lady with the poison-tipped daggers in her shoes. Lenya was a prostitute at thirteen who married three men in her life, all of them gay.

Pedro Armendariz plays Kerim Bey in what would prove to be his final screen role. Aware he was dying from cancer of the lymph glands, he took the role to provide future financial support for his wife. All his scenes were shot first. A mere nine days after fulfilling his commitment to the film he shot himself through the heart with an armor- piercing bullet fired from a Magnum handgun he had smuggled into his hospital room. His son Pedro Armendariz Junior would later play Hector Lopez, the puppet president of the fictional Isthmus City in License to Kill.

Full Monty, The (1997)

In China this film was titled *Six Naked Pigs*.

*T*he most likely source of the expression, 'The Full Monty', appears to have come from a British tailor's shop called Montague Burton, established in Chesterfield in 1904. An entire outfit, suit, tie, shirt and socks, could be purchased or hired (especially if you were being de-mobbed from the armed services) and was sometimes referred to as 'The Full Monty'.

Funny Girl (1968)

There was considerable Academy resentment over Barbra Streisand being granted (contrary to the rules) voting rights before she had even made a film. When she and Katharine Hepburn tied for the Best Actress Oscar, the only tie thus far in history, critics pondered what the result might have been had Barbra been unable to vote for herself.

Omar Sharif signed his contract to play opposite her in *Funny Girl* a few days before the Six Day War between the Arabs and Israelis broke out in 1967. He was an astonishing choice for the lead in the first place, being an Egyptian in a movie about a Jewish girl and a Jewish boy living in a Jewish section of Brooklyn. The film was financed by Jews, and William Wyler, the director, was also Jewish. He soon came under enormous pressure to fire Sharif from the production. 'If Omar doesn't make the film, I don't either', he warned producers. They backed off and the production went ahead as originally planned.

When Wyler was asked if he had encountered any problems directing his leading lady, he sarcastically replied, 'Not really, seeing as it's the first film she's ever directed'.

During the shoot Streisand performed at benefits supporting the Israeli war effort.

When a still from the film, depicting her and Sharif kissing, found its way into a Cairo newspaper, the Egyptian actor had to survive accusations of betraying his country. Many Arabs wanted his Egyptian citizenship revoked. Commenting on the furor, Streisand quipped, 'you think Cairo was upset? You should've seen the letter from my Aunt Rose!'

Just to complicate things further, the two stars carried on a torrid off-screen affair throughout the shoot. 'I fell madly in love with her talent and her personality', Omar said later. 'The feeling was mutual for four months, the time it took to shoot the picture. How many of my affairs seemed to last until the end of shooting? Barbra's villa served as our trysting place'. She was still married to Elliott Gould at the time.

Of his reputation with the opposite sex, Sharif had this to say: 'I make women happy, with the tenderness, love and thrills I give them...I get any woman I want because I give all of myself...they say I'm pathologically unfaithful. No. I'm never unfaithful. I simply fall in love a lot, often and fast'. He is also (in between romances that is) a world class Bridge player.

Furies, The (1950)

When Barbara Stanwyck did away with the services of a stuntwoman and opted to do her own riding in this western, some of it quite dangerous and strenuous, the aging Walter Huston chose to follow her example. 'I'm not going to let any broad show me up!' he said. Less than twenty-four hours after shooting ended he died from a heart attack, most likely brought on by the riding.

Gallipoli (1981)

The Anzac Cove sequences were staged on the beach at Port Lincoln, South Australia. David Williamson who wrote the script appears in a bit part as the tall Victorian footballer in the match played alongside the pyramids. Mel Gibson's co-star Mark Lee went back to working part-time jobs in Sydney after filming completed. His career went nowhere while Mel's went through the roof.

Bill Hunter, who plays the Aussie major who likes to listen to classical music, was a swimming champion who represented Australia at the 1956 Olympics in Melbourne. It was while working as an extra during the production of *On the Beach* that he decided to become an actor.

Mel Gibson was born in New York State but moved to Australia when he was twelve because his parents wished to keep his older, eligible brothers out of the Vietnam War draft. He has ten brothers and sisters. 'Mel Gibson is somewhere to the right of Attila the Hun', observed Susan Sarandon. 'He's beautiful, but only on the outside'.

Game of Death (1978)

In May 1973, Bruce Lee suffered what doctors described as 'a mild seizure' on the set of this film and was prescribed Dilantin, a medication often used for epilepsy. Two months later he complained of headaches and took a prescribed drug called Equagesic for relief, but died soon afterwards. Steve McQueen and James Coburn were pallbearers at his funeral. Five years further on in 1978 the cast was re-assembled and the picture completed and released.

Gangs of New York (2002)

Set in 1860 in the area of New York City known as Five Points, this picture was actually shot in Rome on sets built at great expense to replicate that section of Manhattan long since disappeared. When George Lucas visited the shoot he remarked to director Martin Scorsese that such sets could now be computer generated for a fraction of the cost. Incredibly, Scorsese was unaware of this.

Gaslight (1944)

Considered by many movie-goers to be the 'great lover' of the screen, Charles Boyer starred in many big films including *Gaslight, Algiers* and *Hold Back the Dawn*. Distressed by the death of his wife, Scottish actress Pat Paterson in 1978, he took his own life three days later.

He was probably fortunate to have even been alive in 1944. At the age of forty he joined the

French Army manning a switchboard on the Maginot Line for eleven weeks. The future French Premier Edouard Daladier convinced him he would be of more use in Hollywood making propaganda films. The Maginot Line was overrun with great loss of French life shortly after he left.

Genevieve (1953)

Kay Kendall's distinctive swooped nose was the result of plastic surgery following a car crash. She died from leukemia at the age of thirty-three, but was never told she had the dread disease and believed until her death she was suffering from iron deficiency.

Genghis Khan (1965)

Francoise Dorleac was the sister of French superstar Catherine Deneuve and plays opposite Omar Sharif in this epic about the great Mongol leader. In 1967 she was tragically burned to death after becoming trapped in her wrecked motor vehicle when it rolled into a field in France and caught fire. She was just twenty-six years old.

Gentlemen Prefer Blondes (1953)

Although they shared top billing in this, Marilyn Monroe and Jane Russell were on a vastly different pay structure. Russell was on loan from RKO and being paid $150,000, while Monroe was contracted to MGM at $750 a week and picked up a measly $9,000 for her services. 20th Century-

Fox opted to use Marilyn, rather than shell out Betty Grable's standard fee of $150,000.

Russell recalled how she would stop by Marilyn's dressing room and collect her. 'Come on, it's time to be there', was all she needed to say. 'She would get up and come with me. I think if there had been someone to do that on a lot of other films she would never have been late. She was just scared'.

In the 'Anyone Here for Love' number, Russell was accidentally knocked into the swimming pool by one of the divers on the first take. The shot was re-done, unsatisfactorily, several times until it was decided to alter the script, stick with the first take and simply add a shot of her emerging from the water. The diver who had inadvertently bumped her into the pool in the first place was fired, not because of the accident, but because he kept insisting that the inclusion of his 'bump' warranted him a credit as co-choreographer!

Doodles Weaver was the uncle of modern star Sigourney Weaver. A former member of Spike Jones' City Slickers, it is he who provides the commentary on the 'Beetle Bomb' record. Doodles used a firearm to suicide in 1983 while depressed over a heart condition.

Get Shorty (1995)

Dennis Farina plays a heavy in this. Before becoming an actor he was a detective with the Chicago Police Department for 18 years. Director Barry Sonnenfeld can be seen dressed as a Beefeater doorman in one scene. The real Chilli Palmer

(John Travolta's character) appears in the opening scene seated on the right of Farina...

Ghost (1990)

Nicole Kidman was still an unknown in Australia when she got hold of a copy of the *Ghost* script before the picture was cast. She acted out a couple of scenes and sent the video of her work to the producers, hoping to be auditioned. She did not get the part, but the tapes were seen by important people, one of whom eventually showed them to Tom Cruise who was about to cast for his upcoming *Days of Thunder*. He was impressed and took a look at her recent film *Dead Calm*. That, too, impressed him and the rest, as they say, is history.

Tony Goldwyn, who plays Swayze's supposed best friend, is the grandson of MGM mogul Samuel Goldwyn. Swayze began his show business career in 1970 as an eighteen year-old Prince Charming in the touring company of *Disney on Parade*. One of the many actors who turned down the lead was Paul Hogan. He opted instead to make the abysmal *Almost An Angel*.

Demi Moore is completely blind in her left eye. She married rock singer Freddie Moore when she was sixteen, but walked out three years later to get engaged to Emilio Estevez. Then on the eve of their wedding she walked again and four months later wed Bruce Willis.

Before she would agree to star in Disclosure in 1994, the notoriously difficult actress successfully demanded a double sized trailer, surrounded by lawn and a grove of fig trees. Her demands have earned her the nickname of 'Gimme More' in Hollywood circles. Her 'entourage costs' alone when making The Scarlet Letter, for instance, are estimated to have come to a whopping $877,000.

While heavily pregnant, she caused a furor by posing naked for the cover of Vanity Fair magazine. To promote her new film, Striptease, she removed her clothing before the cameras in David Letterman's The Late Show. No stranger to disrobing, she went topless on screen as a teenager in Blame it on Rio as well.

She and Bruce Willis were married by former rock star and ordained minister Little Richard. Shortly after their marriage collapsed, photographers snapped Leonardo DiCaprio emerging from her premises one morning. His car had been parked there all night. The forty-two year old actress met twenty-seven year old Ashton Kutcher on the set of Charlie's Angels: Full Throttle and a romance developed. They married in 2005, but divorced eight years later.

Giant (1956)

James Dean died four days after shooting concluded on this picture. When his nomination failed to win him an Oscar (Yul Brynner having thieved it for *The King And I*), Liz Taylor was outraged at the Academy's perfectly understandable reluctance to bestow on him a *posthumous* award. 'I won't go to the awards', she said, 'I won't honor any group of people who refuse to bestow the recognition due Jimmy – an Oscar for one of the brightest talents ever to come into our industry'. Uh-huh. She and the late Mr. Dean had been disappearing after each day's filming, then returning 'cow-eyed' the next morning. Not that this would have affected her assessment of his acting ability.

While *Giant* was being filmed in Texas it became customary for families from nearby areas to drop in and watch some of the day's shooting. On at least one occasion Dean unzipped his fly and urinated in front of them. He told director George Stevens it motivated him and helped him overcome his acting nerves. If he could display his penis to 2,500 onlookers without becoming embarrassed, he reasoned, then he should be OK to act confidently in front of the crew. 'I don't mean to speak ill of the dead', said co-star Rock Hudson, when asked his opinion of Dean, 'but he was a prick...selfish and petulant. On the set he would up-stage an actor and step on his lines'. He also, reputedly, refused Rock's advances, telling the older actor he 'wasn't his type'.

Taylor made plays for both men during the shoot. Hudson's wife Phyllis Gates (as well as most of the film crew) was certain an affair transpired between Rock and Liz.

G I Blues (1960)

Judith Rawlins, a young actress showcased here, dated Elvis, Bobby Rydell and Dick Haymes, whom she later married. In 1974 she committed suicide in her Bel Air home after her marriage crumbled.

In 1989 Juliet Prowse narrowly escaped death when a leopard mauled her during rehearsals for a CBS TV Special called 'Circus of the Stars'. She grew up in South Africa and became a top ballerina before venturing into movies.

After co-starring with Elvis in *G I Blues* she was engaged for a time to Frank Sinatra who had a yen for long-legged women. The engagement shocked Marilyn Monroe who was deeply involved with 'Old Blue Eyes' herself at that time, naively expecting him to propose to *her* at any moment. When Prowse refused to give up her career he ended the relationship. She died from cancer at 59.

Gilda (1946)

Rita Hayworth's legendary rendition of *Put the Blame on Mame* was not actually sung by her, but dubbed by Anita Ellis. Still, the clip is one of the great moments in cinema history, and it put Rita in a sex-symbol class of her own. 'Every man I've known', she once said, 'has fallen in love with *Gilda* and wakened up with me'.

Rita Hayworth was Ginger Rogers' first cousin, and nothing like the sex siren she played on screen. Peter Lawford described her as 'the worst lay in the world. She was always drunk and she never stopped eating'. In fairness to Hayworth, she was in her forties and sliding downhill when they were briefly involved. Considering her upbringing, it is little wonder she found lovemaking unimpressive.

Rita started out as her sleazy father's dancing partner when she was twelve years old. He regularly seduced her, but her mother, who was aware of the situation, did nothing for fear he would turn his attentions to her boys who were even younger. Dear old dad pimped his beautiful daughter to movie executives whenever he could, in exchange for promises of advancing her career.

Her life, once she shook off her father, seemed to be one long and unsuccessful quest for genuine affection, and a great many men took advantage of that. Howard Hughes, for instance, got her pregnant, but quickly had it terminated before ditching her. It must be said, nevertheless, that Rita was prepared to sleep with influential men (at least in her early days), if it would further her career.

Her first husband (another sleazebag) was a con man named Ed Judson who insisted she do just that, although she drew the line at Columbia's Harry Cohn. Rita always loathed him and successfully repelled his advances. 'Her whole life was running from him', said fellow actress Ann Miller.

When Rita finally divorced Judson in 1943, Columbia was forced to pay him off to stop him naming the industry men who had slept with his wife, even though it had mostly been at his insistence.

At various times she became engaged to Victor Mature, David Niven, Howard Hughes, Gilbert Roland and singer Tony Martin. For a while she was involved with Gary Merrill after he divorced Bette Davis, but his problems with alcohol ended that relationship, as it had his marriage.

Husband number four, singer Dick Haymes, insisted he play opposite her in an upcoming Columbia production, and threatened to pull her out of the picture if his demands were not met. Cohn countered by firing her on the spot, saying he would transform the next starlet who walked through his door into his new glamour queen. That next girl, so legend has it, was Marylin Novak, who later achieved star status as Kim Novak.

For a time, during the 1950s, Rita conducted an odd relationship with California's 'Red Light Bandit', convicted serial rapist Caryl Chessman, while he was on death row awaiting execution. Nobody knows the level of the relationship.

In 1987, she died from Alzheimer's disease, a pitiful wreck of a human being trapped in her own private hell, unable to perform the most basic of functions for herself.

Girl Interrupted (1999)

Angelina Jolie is the daughter of Oscar-winning actor Jon Voight. Her first husband, Jonathon Lee Miller, is the grandson of Bernard Lee, the actor who played 'M' in the James Bond films. When they wed in 1996 Jolie wore black leather trousers and a white shirt with her husband's name painted *in her blood* on the back. Well, you would, wouldn't you?

In 2004, she openly admitted to having a string of one-night stands in hotel rooms with various male friends. 'I decided to get closer to the men who were already very close friends of mine', she explained. 'As crazy as that sounds, meeting a man in a hotel room for a few hours and not seeing him again for a few months is about what I can handle'. She also said she was bisexual, once being in love with fashion model Jenny Shimizu. 'I probably would have married Jenny if I hadn't married my husband', she added.

She hotly denies wrecking the marriage of Brad Pitt and Jennifer Aniston, claiming she would never romance a married man, because she saw how her father's infidelities impacted on her mother. Be that as it may, her relationship with Pitt did begin while he was still married to Aniston. For all her eccentricities, Jolie works tirelessly for humanitarian causes and has stated she donates a third of her salary to charities.

Girl in the Red Velvet Swing, The (1955)

Joan Collins claims she lost her virginity to her future husband, Maxwell Reed, after he drugged her unconscious on one of their first dates and then assaulted her. She says she revived in time to find him 'trying to push a strange, soft object in my mouth'. Despite this rather dubious beginning to their relationship the couple married anyway. During their marriage Reed tried to convince her to go to bed with an old Arab sheik, who had offered *him* ten thousand pounds sterling for the privilege. Collins refused to do so and soon afterwards sought a divorce.

Another ex-husband, Anthony Newley, summed her up pretty harshly when he said, 'Joan Collins is a commodity who would sell her own bowel movement'. She once wore a dress that was so skin tight she had to be carried upstairs to make an appearance. She responded to Newley's many infidelities by telling an interviewer, 'I enjoyed being an adulteress...taking a certain vengeance for the fact that my husband was not being faithful'.

Her sister Jackie said of her, 'She always lived her life like a man. If she saw a guy she wanted to go to bed with, she went after him, and that was unacceptable behavior at the time'. Eddie Fisher recounted in his autobiography how he 'met' her up against the wall of Dean Martin's swimming pool, during an all-naked party attended by Dean, Brando and others. 'She liked men so much', he wrote', she was known as the British Open'.

Stewart Granger did not think much of her either. 'She's common and can't act', he said in 1984, 'yet she's the hottest property around these days'. Dominican playboy Ramfis Trujillo was also decidedly unimpressed. 'I picked her up on my yacht in Miami', he said. 'She was so boring, I put her ashore in Palm Beach'.

Gladiator (2000)

Russell Crowe won the lead in *Gladiator* after Mel Gibson turned it down, would you believe? Thank you, God. Connie Neilsen who plays Lucilla is Danish by birth.

When Russell walked up to receive his Best Actor Oscar for *Gladiator,* Charlton Heston theatrically whispered to him, 'As one gladiator to another, I salute you'. Why do actors do nauseating things like that?

The opening battle scenes were shot in Surrey, near London. All the ancient war machines including the catapults that fired earthen pots full of boiling oil were built from scratch. The nasty cut you see on Russell's face was inflicted when his horse collided with a tree during those opening scenes. The stitches are clearly visible as he tells Commodus he is returning home. To allow for more mobility his armor was made of foam covered with leather.

Richard Harris (who was a difficult man to befriend on-set) got along well with Crowe. 'I love the guy', he said. 'He doesn't carry that Hollywood star crap with him. There is no 'I am Russell Crowe'. He doesn't say 'did you not see *LA Confidential*? Wasn't I brilliant in it?'

During breaks in filming the cast played games of Backgammon, as well as cricket and football matches against local teams on the island of Malta where the film's Colosseum was built. The highly intelligent Joaquin Phoenix nearly always won the Backgammon games.

Oliver Reed passed away during the making of the movie. Three weeks before shooting concluded he died flat on his back in a pub from a heart attack, having just consumed eight bottles of German beer and twelve double shots of Jamaican Rum. As he ordered a whiskey he suddenly collapsed, was rushed to the hospital and declared dead fifteen minutes after arrival.

Ridley Scott considered his completed scenes to be so good he insisted on spending another $2 million computer generating the remainder of his role, rather than re-shoot with another actor. Reed's head was super-imposed on a stand-in's body for his only uncompleted scene, the one where he is slain by the Praetorian Guards. His character Proximo was originally scripted to survive, but the actor's death altered that and he was killed off by the Praetorians.

Reed came from an illustrious theatre background. His grandfather was the venerable Victorian actor Sir Henry Beerbohm Tree who founded the Royal Academy of Dramatic Arts (RADA). His uncle was the post-war filmmaker Sir Carol Reed who picked up an Oscar in 1968 for *Oliver!*

When Sean Connery walked away from the Bond series Reed was strongly considered as his replacement until his highly publicized extra-marital affair with ballet dancer Jacqui Daryl caused the producers to look elsewhere.

The contrast between a sober and a drunk Oliver Reed was quite extraordinary. His friends say he was quiet, even self-effacing when sober, and a pleasure to be with. When drunk he became an absolute monster, uncontrollable and highly dangerous. His drunken exploits were legendary.

At a posh Madrid hotel he once stripped off and climbed into the giant aquarium where he proceeded to swallow goldfish whole. At another hotel he astonished onlookers by diving into the swimming pool from his first-floor balcony. In 1964 his career was almost terminated when he was 'bottled' in a toilet by two men. The attack inflicted cuts to his face that required thirty-eight stitches.

His first wife was a nineteen year-old girl who faked her father's signature on the wedding license. His second remained devoted to him until his death. She was only sixteen when the forty-seven year old actor married her in 1985.

Godfather, The (1972)

The baby being held in the baptism scene near the end of the movie is Sofia Coppola, the daughter of the director. In 1990, the totally inexperienced Sofia would almost wreck *The Godfather Part 111* when her father placed her in the pivotal role of Al Pacino's daughter.

John Cazale plays Fredo. He and Meryl Streep had a long and close relationship until his death from cancer in 1978.

Godfather Pt III, The (1990)

Twenty-one year old actress Rebecca Schaeffer was supposed to test for a role in this picture, but never made the audition. She answered a knock on her door that morning and was confronted by a crazed fan named Robert Bardo. She chatted to him for a few moments, shook his hand and closed the door. When she opened it again after he rang her bell a second time, the man shot her to death in her doorway. Apparently, he had obtained her address from the California Department of Motor Vehicles. Schaeffer's murder resulted in legislation being introduced in California preventing the divulgence of such information in future. As so often happens, it took a tragedy to bring about a ruling that common sense should have implemented long ago.

Going My Way (1944)

Barry Fitzgerald, as previously mentioned, became the only actor to be nominated twice for the same role *in the same picture* when the Academy erroneously nominated him in both the Best Actor and Best Supporting Actor categories for this film. He won the Supporting Oscar. A few months later, he accidentally decapitated the statuette while practicing his golf swing, so Paramount forked out the princely sum of $10 and replaced it so, in effect, he wound up getting two Oscars for his performance after all.

Bing Crosby (1903-1977)

Known relationships:

Bennett, Joan
Bergman, Ingrid
Blondell, Joan
Caulfield, Joan
Craig, Yvonne
Farmer, Frances
Freeman, Mona
Hopkins, Miriam
Kelly, Grace
Murphy, Mary
Sheehan, Pat
Stevens, Inger

Married:

Dixie Lee
Kathryn Grant

Over his long career Bing Crosby sang 396 popular hit songs and sold in excess of 300 million records. Interestingly, away from the recording studio he was a life-long friend of organized crime figures. He played golf with 'Machine Gun' Jack McGurn and was a neighbor of Bugsy Siegel until the man was assassinated.

Bing was smitten with Grace Kelly when they made *The Country Girl* together. One of her previous lovers William Holden was also in the picture. Crosby was extremely disappointed when Grace refused his proposals of marriage, probably because he was already hitched. Grace was promiscuous, but she wasn't stupid. The two enjoyed intimate evenings at Alan Ladd's home (next door to Crosby's) in a section of the house that Ladd generously set aside for Bing's extra-marital flings.

An alcoholic by the time of his death, Crosby stated in his will that none of his sons was to receive a penny of his vast wealth until they were 'sixty-five years old and mature enough to spend it wisely'. No doubt the reading of the will would have been a jolly occasion for all, especially since the guy left property and cash valued somewhere between $200 and $400 million!

His sons were a sorry lot. Gary was a drunk and drug addict who claimed his father tortured him. 'That cocksucker', he told Eddie Fisher, 'I could slit his throat...slit his jugular vein and suck his blood out!' Uh-huh.

Both Fisher and Bing had an intimate relationship with Tropicana showgirl Pat Sheehan, who would ultimately wed

Dennis, another of Crosby's boys. Both Dennis and his other brother Lindsay later shot themselves. Perhaps, the thought of all that money being out of reach until they turned sixty-five unhinged them. Maybe, Dennis discovered that dear old dad had been in his wife's bed before him?

Golden Earrings (1947)

Marlene Dietrich was starring in *Golden Earrings* with Ray Milland when she heard he was complaining about having to act with 'an old hag'. She was forty-five at the time and he was forty-one. Director Mitchell Leisen recalled: 'When we were shooting the scene where he first meets her as she's stirring the stew, Marlene stuck a fish-head in her mouth, sucked the eye out, and then pulled out the rest of the head. Then, after I yelled cut, she stuck her finger down her throat to make herself throw up. The whole performance made Ray violently ill'.

Goldfinger (1964)

Pussy Galore's name worried the producers. They feared its sexual connotations might see it rejected by the censors. The publicity department at Eon Productions decided to 'test the waters' by arranging for a snapshot to be taken of actress Honor Blackman (who would play Pussy) and Prince Philip while they were attending a charity ball. The caption in the paper next day read 'Pussy and the Prince'. There were no objections so the name remained and the standby sobriquet of Kitty Galore was not required. In the novel she was a lesbian, hence her comment to Bond aboard the jet, 'I'm immune'. Blackman, by the way, was born in 1925 and nearly forty when she starred in *Goldfinger*.

A '64 Lincoln weighs about 5,000 pounds, yet when it is crushed into a lump of metal and lowered onto Oddjob's Ford Ranchero pickup (that just happens to have a maximum carrying weight of 1,000 pounds) it doesn't crush the vehicle. In fact, if we add in the gold bullion supposedly in the Lincoln's trunk, it weighed even more. This is just one of a score of dumb, poorly thought out moments in this *very* silly movie.

Desmond Llewelyn who plays 'Q' in the Bond films was killed in a car crash in 1999. None of the Bonds went to his funeral. During the Second World War he was captured by the Germans, escaped, was re-captured and escaped again! The Q is an abbreviation for 'Quartermaster'.

Gert Frobe is best remembered for his portrayal of Auric Goldfinger. Frobe's career seemed over when it was revealed he was once a member of the Nazi Party during the war. He received the benefit of the doubt after a Jewish man named Mario Blumenau (conveniently) came forward and vowed it was Frobe who once saved his family from the Gestapo. Maybe that's true. Maybe not. Maybe, a way out of the predicament was 'found'. Who knows?

Shirley Eaton, the lovely actress who got to be painted gold, was a child performer in the forties and appeared in three 'Carry On' comedies in the fifties before achieving a kind of immortality in *Goldfinger*. When she went to the picture's premiere she was astonished to discover that every line, bar one, she had spoken in the film had been dubbed. The single sentence, 'Not too early' was the only one of her lines to survive. As for her dying from skin suffocation, that is utter baloney. The human skin plays little or no part in the respiratory process.

Gone with the Wind (1939)

Irving Thalberg was responsible for L B Mayer losing the film rights to *Gone with the Wind*. 'No Civil War picture ever made a dime', he said, and that was good enough for Mayer to drop the project. Thalberg was right too, but in an industry so young it was careless of him to make so definitive a judgement so soon. The 'boy wonder' was not infallible after all.

The character of Scarlett O'Hara was based on Annie Stephens (1844 – 1934) who was the maternal grandmother of the author of *Gone with the Wind*, Margaret Mitchell, whose real name was actually Peggy Marsh. She was run down and killed by a car not long after the movie was completed.

Originally, she intended naming her heroine Pansy. The famous title was arrived at after *Bugles Sang True, Tote the Weary Load* and *Tomorrow is Another Day,* were all discarded.

The role of Scarlett eventually boiled down to four actresses, Jean Arthur, Joan Bennett, Paulette Goddard and Vivien Leigh. Vivien did not, however, secure it by chance or at the last minute. David O Selznick arranged for reporters to be present while the burning of Atlanta sequence was being shot, just so they could witness his brother arrive with Vivien in tow and proclaim he had found the Scarlett they were looking for. His words were even *scripted*.

*I*t all added to the publicity surrounding Selznick's 'nationwide search for Scarlett', and both the media and the public swallowed the story whole, not stopping to think that no producer in his right mind would start production on the biggest picture in history without knowing who was going to play the central character in it.

Paulette Goddard secretly wed Charlie Chaplin in 1936 while they were vacationing in China. Their decision to keep the marriage quiet may have been a determining factor in her missing out on the role. As far as the public was concerned, the couple had been living in sin for a few years, so the studio was wary of risking her with such a reputation.

Sixteen year-old Anne Baxter also auditioned. George Cukor the film's director at the time said hers was the best he saw. Another unsuccessful contender was Jean Arthur. Although reputedly a lesbian, she did everything in her power to secure the role, including having an alleged affair with Selznick. In all 1,400 hopefuls were interviewed, 400 read for the role and ninety tests were shot. These were done to keep the hype going *after* Vivien Leigh had already been secretly cast as far back as 1937! Goddard, Arthur and Bennett had no idea they were really being used for publicity purposes.

Forty-five year-old Leslie Howard was foolishly chosen to play the twenty-three year-old Ashley Wilkes, much to Margaret Mitchell's disappointment. And just about everyone else's for that matter. She wanted Randolph Scott to play him. She also preferred Basil Rathbone as Rhett! Howard only agreed to do the film on condition he would not have to read the interminable book.

Neither he nor Gable much liked the picture or their parts in it. They rarely met on the set either because their scenes did not coincide. Gable was actually a very insecure man and not at all sure he could carry off the role. Howard realized he was too old to play Ashley and, like many others then and now, thought the idea of Scarlett rejecting Gable in favor of him stretched audience credulity to the limit.'Gone with the Wind is going to be the biggest flop in history', predicted Gary Cooper. 'I'm just glad it'll be Clark Gable falling on his face and not me'. Even the eventual director Victor Fleming held little hope for his picture. When David O Selznick offered him a percentage of the profits instead of his fee, Fleming adamantly rejected his offer. 'This picture is going to be one of the biggest white elephants of all time', he said. He would later take his script and storm off the picture after Leigh complained he was treating her like a 'bitch'. 'Miss Leigh, you can stick this script up your Royal British ass!' were his parting words.

Ben Hecht wrote the revised screenplay without ever having read Mitchell's book! He managed to track down the original treatment written by Sidney Howard three years earlier, read through it, and then churned out the first nine reels in just seven days for a fee of $15,000. Incidentally, Sidney Howard would win the very first posthumous Oscar. He had the miserable luck to be run over and killed by a tractor on his farm soon after being nominated.

A sneak preview of the film was sprung on an unsuspecting audience attending a showing of *Beau Geste*. As that feature ended, a slide appeared on screen advising everyone to remain seated if they wished to see a preview of 'a very long film'. Anyone wishing to leave the theatre was advised to do so at once for the doors were about to be locked. When the title appeared on the screen the audience erupted into wild applause and cheering. All America had been waiting for it and this lucky group of patrons got to see the picture before anyone else. And for free.

The official premiere in Atlanta on December 14, 1939 was for whites only. None of the Negro cast was invited. Oddly enough, Atlanta's most prominent preacher, Martin Luther King Senior, *was* invited and attended with Martin Jr. At its conclusion the Mayor of Atlanta magnanimously asked the illustrious gathering for a round of applause for the Negro cast. White arrogance and condescension at its best.

When Hattie McDaniel, who plays Scarlett's nanny, beat de Havilland for the Best Supporting Oscar, Olivia ran from the auditorium to the kitchen and burst into tears. Irene Selznick went after her and told her to grow up and get on stage to congratulate McDaniel. She duly did so, smiling sweetly for the newsreel cameras.

Not only had McDaniel become the first of her race to win an Oscar, she was also the first black performer to even be invited to the presentations. The seating arrangements suggest there was considerable reluctance on the part of the organizers to ask her at all. She and her escort were placed at the back of the room near the kitchen.

After being dropped by MGM in 1953, Gable requested a personal print of *Gone with the Wind* as a memento of the two successful decades he spent at the studio. They charged him $3,000 for it!

Michael Jackson paid $1,540,000 for David O Selznick's Best Picture Oscar. Vivien Leigh's Oscar was auctioned in 1993 for $500,000. She only received $15,000 for playing the part! The picture remained the all-time box office profit maker until 1965, when it was surpassed by *The Sound of Music*.

Despite stories to the contrary, Gable may not have moved to have George Cukor replaced as director. Publicly, it was stated he did not want a known 'ladies' director in charge of the shoot, believing his performance would suffer under that style of direction. Privately, many believed he was uncomfortable knowing Cukor had first-hand knowledge of Clark's brief intimacy with William Haines in the early days when he was striving for a foothold in the industry. This, combined with Cukor's habit of continually calling him 'dearest' in front of cast and crew caused 'the King' to resent him. Much of that was true but, according to the studio, Cukor was replaced because he was unhappy with the script and Selznick tired of arguing with him about it. Opinions on which story is true still vary today.

During the 'burning of Atlanta' sequence a stuntman stood in for Gable, fighting for control of the team of skittish horses as the giant King Kong gates to Scull Island go up in flames in the background. The old Selznick backlot was set ablaze for the sequence. The horse used in this scene had fattened up since it was purchased, so dark lines were painted on its ribs to make it appear undernourished. Few patrons noticed anyway. Speaking of horses, the one ridden by Thomas Mitchell would later become the Lone Ranger's mount Silver.

Look for the bearded thug who attacks Scarlett on the bridge. He is played by the legendary stuntman Yakima Canutt. The baby you see being held by Olivia de Havilland grew up to be Raquel Welch's second husband Pat Curtis.

Vivien Leigh's breasts were (according to David O Selznick), 'smallish and tended to point outwards rather than downwards, so he ordered them 'taped upwards' with wadding stuffed around them to increase her cleavage. Did anyone *really* notice the difference?

In the scene where she kneels in the dirt and crams a fistful of radishes into her mouth, the retching noises emanating from her are actually dubbed by de Havilland. Leigh refused to make such noises herself. Actually, Olivia was by far the more genteel and ladylike of the two actresses. Vivien was notorious for her constant use of four-letter words.

Olivia's affair with billionaire Howard Hughes ended during the making of this picture, after he informed the young actress he wished to marry her - *in seventeen years' time*. She suddenly realized life with the eccentric hotshot might not be all that special. Hughes told her he envisioned a four-part plan for his life and it could not be altered. The first part was for flying, the second for constructing airplanes, the third for advancing and promoting aviation, and the fourth for marriage and retirement. That fourth segment would commence when he was fifty years old, seventeen years hence.

Two weeks after he got the heave-ho from Olivia, the eternally optimistic Hughes offered the same crazy deal to her sister Joan Fontaine *during their first dance* at the Trocadero, moments after they were introduced. She did not fancy him at all and told him so. Her very refusal intrigued the billionaire and he pestered her with many more proposals over the ensuing decade but without success.

Whereas Olivia found Gable to be distant and rather moody, Vivien got along quite well with him. The two played a board game called 'Battleship' whenever they were between takes. Olivia, who required ten minutes or so in front of a mirror to prepare for a scene, was in awe of their ability to interrupt their board game, step at once into character for a scene, and then casually return to the game as if nothing had happened.

Butterfly McQueen plays Scarlett's maid Prissy. She died from burns in 1995 after her dress caught fire while she was attempting to ignite a lantern.

Although he regularly played the English nobleman of caricature, Leslie Howard was actually the son of Hungarian-Jewish parents who immigrated to Britain not long before he was born. He suffered from shell shock in World War One and took up acting as therapy after being invalided out of action.

Bette Davis once told Michael Caine, 'did you know that Leslie screwed every woman in every movie he ever made, with the exception of me?' Joan Blondell, on the other hand, liked him a lot. 'He was a little devil and just wanted his hands on every woman around...he just loved ladies', she said.

In 1940 British Intelligence recruited him to speak to American audiences with the aim of convincing them to maintain support for Britain during the war. He died in 1943 when the DC-3 Dakota in which he was a passenger was shot down over the Bay of Biscay after being attacked by eight German Junkers. Fifty years on, the pilot who led the attack said the plane was shot down by accident. This is an odd statement because Winston Churchill was reputedly aware of the impending attack (according to several experts), but was powerless to warn the aircraft without revealing that Britain had broken the German codes.

Ona Munson, who plays Belle Watling, the kind-hearted prostitute girlfriend of Rhett Butler, was a lesbian who numbered among her lovers Greta Garbo, Marlene Dietrich and writer Mercedes de Acosta. She overdosed at the age of fifty-one.

Laura Hope Crews was the wonderful character actress who delightfully played the scatter-brained Miss Pittypat. From the money she earned making *Gone with the Wind* she built a big house on North Bedford Drive in Beverly Hills. Nearly two decades later it became the property of Lana Turner and was the scene of the Johnny Stompanato killing, involving Lana and her teenage daughter Cheryl.

Evelyn Keyes plays Scarlett's younger sister. Her autobiography detailed her active sex life in Hollywood and included tales about her three marriages (she was Artie Shaw's eighth wife and also snared John Huston and Charles Vidor along the way). She even lived with the irrepressible Mike Todd for three years.

Good News (1947)

Peter Lawford (1923-1984)

Known relationships:

Addams, Dawn
Allyson, June
Baxter, Anne
Carmen, Jeanne
Caron, Leslie
Dandridge, Dorothy
Gardner, Ava
Goddard, Paulette
Grable, Betty

Holliday, Judy
Kelly, Betty
Kennedy Jacqueline
Keyes, Evelyn
Kirkwood, Pat
Lollobrigida, Gina
Malone, Dorothy
Maxwell, Marilyn
Monroe, Marilyn
Remick, Lee
Romay, Lina
Ryan, Sheila
St John, Jill
Todd, Sally
Turner, Lana
Tyler, Beverly
Wynn, May
Young, Loretta

At the age of fifteen Lawford maimed his right arm in an accident involving a shattered windowpane and very nearly had it amputated. For the rest of his life his right hand had a claw-like appearance in its relaxed state, a deformity he usually concealed by keeping that hand in a trousers pocket, especially when being photographed. Insiders claimed his nickname 'Charlie the Seal' came from the way he clapped 'like a seal' due to his deformity. Others said it was because he 'liked to go down on women'. Sinatra told the media it pertained to his smoker's cough. In fact, there was truth in all three explanations.

His mother, May, kept Peter in girl's clothes until his teens. He was preyed upon by pedophiles of both sexes from the age of nine. From his early Hollywood days he gained a reputation as 'the screaming faggot from State Beach', due to his penchant for hanging out in public toilets and rendezvousing with men for quick sex. He was clearly bisexual. His mother actually reported his conduct to LB Mayer, hoping the movie mogul might frighten her son into giving up his nefarious lifestyle, by threatening to end his career if he did not.

Lana Turner came to his defense by giving Mayer an explicit description of her vigorous bedroom bouts with the actor, and convinced him there was no substance to the accusations. There was also talk of Lawford being caught in bed with Van Johnson, Keenan Wynn and Wynne's wife, Evie. The foursome was almost inseparable (no pun intended) but the rumors were never verified. When the Wynnes later divorced, Van married Evie within days.

Lawford did have a very serious affair with actress Lee Remick in 1961while both were married to other people. His wife at the time was Pat Kennedy, the sister of the US President John Kennedy, and a millionaire in her own right. A blind item in Hedda Hopper's gossip column warned the un-named Lawford that he was in grave danger of losing his 'million dollar baby'. When Remick ultimately refused to marry him he was quite shattered, but forced to end the relationship. Months later she was introduced to Pat at a party. 'Hello Pat, I'm Lee Remick', she said. Mrs. Lawford looked her squarely in the eye and said, 'And I'm the million dollar baby'.

Old Joe Kennedy arranged through J Edgar Hoover to have Peter's bisexuality investigated by the FBI, before he would agree to Pat marrying him. The bureau reported that the actor often frequented brothels, which seemed to put Joe's worries to rest, so the unglamorous Pat wed the financially strapped Peter without further ado.

Although he cheated on her at a rate of knots, he managed to stay on good terms with the Kennedy clan, until he blew everything by bringing along a pick-up in a black mini-skirt to Bobby's funeral! Once that happened Sinatra, too, dropped him like a hot coal for the second time in their friendship.

Once before, Frank had cut him out of the loop when he assumed Peter was having an affair with his ex-wife Ava Gardner. He renewed the 'friendship' when he needed Lawford's Kennedy connection to get him close to JFK. After the fiasco at Bobby's funeral Sinatra no longer needed the 'the brother-in-Lawford', as he called him, and Peter was once again cut adrift.

Towards the end of his life he became a drug addict and was involved in increasingly kinky, sadistic sex that involved bondage, taking razors to his nipples and using male vibrators. His fourth wife walked out of their marriage in disgust. Even a stint at the Betty Ford Clinic (he was tricked into going by friends) did nothing for his condition. He arranged for a helicopter to fly drugs into the desert behind the clinic where he simply walked out and collected them.

The end came in 1984 when his liver and kidneys collapsed, his skin turned yellow and he suffered a spasm that brought blood gushing from his mouth, nose and ears. Four years after his death his cremation and the upkeep of his cemetery crypt were still not paid for. His widow accepted payment from the *National Enquirer* in return for exclusive rights to cover the removal of his ashes and their scattering in the Pacific Ocean. During his lifetime he had borrowed tens of thousands of dollars from his friends with no interest or intention of ever paying them back.

Grease (1978)

Olivia Newton-John plays the seventeen year-old Sandy, but was actually twenty-nine when *Grease* was made. Stockard Channing, the leader of 'the Pink Ladies', was already *thirty-three* years old when she too played a high school student.

Unconfirmed tales abounded of an affair between Olivia and her co-star John Travolta on the set of *Grease*. Henry Winkler made the mistake of his life when he turned down the lead because he did not want to be typecast by the 'Fonzie-like' role. The picture was successful beyond anyone's expectations – especially Winkler's it seems.

Grapes of Wrath, The (1940)

This film was widely shown in Russia to highlight the plight of US workers during the Great Depression. It was soon withdrawn, however, when Russian audiences marveled that American sharecroppers, even the poor ones, all seemed to own cars.

Great Escape, The (1963)

James Garner was the first man to be drafted from Oklahoma for the Korean War. During a night retreat he and thirty other stragglers were mistaken for enemy troops and bombed by US jets. Accompanied by a South Korean soldier, he later ran into an enemy patrol. Holding his hands above his head, Garner pretended to be his companion's prisoner, and the two men managed to walk back to their own lines.

As a matter of interest, the Purple Heart he received (the medal all wounded US personnel are automatically awarded) came from the army's stockpile of a *million* such medals. Towards the end of World War Two, when America expected to have to invade the Japanese home islands, an order was placed for a million Purple Hearts to cover the anticipated casualties such an undertaking would incur. When the atomic bombs on Hiroshima and Nagasaki brought the conflict to a speedy end, the government was stuck with all those medals and has been issuing them in every conflict since.

Green Dolphin Street (1947)

Look for fifteen year-old Linda Christian playing a Maori named Hine-Moa. Two years later she would marry screen superstar Tyrone Power. When Power wed Linda the couple lived under the same roof as Edmund Purdom and his wife,

Tita, who was Linda's best friend. Before long Purdom was sexually involved with both Ty and Linda. Years later, after the marriages had both collapsed, Purdom married Linda.

Greystoke: The Legend of Tarzan, Lord of the Apes (1984)

Scriptwriter Robert Townes could not abide the liberties taken with his original script for this film, so he removed his name from the credits and substituted the name of his dog P H Vazak instead. To his astonishment, P H Vasak was nominated for an Oscar for best screenplay!

Andie MacDowell suffered a nervous breakdown over the movie. It was her first starring vehicle, but the producers thought her South Carolina accent was too thick, so they had Glenn Close dub over every word she had spoken in the picture.

Towards the end of his career, Sir Ralph Richardson experienced the utmost difficulty synchronizing his on stage movements with his lines. He conquered his problem by instructing himself out loud, 'one, two, clash your swords, three, four, round we go' and so on, much to the mirth of the front row of the opening night's audience at *Macbeth*, who could hear his every word.

One evening the eccentric actor was stopped by police, who found him walking very slowly along a gutter in Oxford Street in London. When asked what he was doing, Sir Ralph replied in all sincerity that he was walking his pet mouse.

Guess Who's Coming to Dinner? (1967)

Spencer Tracy was gravely ill when this film was about to be made. Consequently, nobody would insure him for the duration of the shoot. Katharine Hepburn and Stanley Kramer agreed to put their salaries in escrow in order to secure his services. If he was unable to complete it and the film had to be scrapped, their entitlements would be grabbed first to help recoup losses. As it happened, he finished the picture, but died shortly afterwards.

This picture is a cop-out. The moment Poitier was cast as the white girl's fiancée, any attempt to defend inter-racial marriage was compromised. He is simply too good-looking, too charismatic, too polished, too successful and too well off. The objective would have been much better served using a far less attractive actor portraying a far less acceptable catch.

Gunfight at the OK Corral (1957)

Burt Lancaster's first wife was an Australian trapeze artist named June Ernst. Burt was a womanizer who did not treat his conquests well, developing a heavy reputation for being violent with them. His overbearing, threatening persona frightened quite a few men too. 'Burt was really scary', remembered composer Elmer Bernstein. 'He was a dangerous guy, he had a short fuse; he was very physical. You thought you might get punched out...'

He and his best friend, Nick Cravat, came to the movies via their double act in a travelling circus. The 5'7", but enormously strong, Cravat would hold a twenty-foot long pole aloft as Burt shinnied up to its top to perform stunts. Cravat is the mute we see alongside him in *The Crimson Pirate* and *The Flame and the Arrow*. He was not really a mute, by the way. He just chose to be one in his movies because *nobody* could rid him of his thick Brooklyn accent.

In 1990 Burt suffered a stroke that left him completely paralyzed and unable to speak. Cravat visited him every day and invariably wept at his bedside. Eventually, Suzie Lancaster had to cut down his visits because they were simply too depressing. As it happened, Lancaster outlived his friend by a few months.

Guns of Navarone, The (1961)

Liverpool - born Gia Scala was a greatly disturbed lady who tried several times to end her life. Best remembered for her role as the traitor killed by Irene Papas in *The Guns of Navarone,* she was Steve McQueen's girlfriend for a few years, before her suicidal tendencies ended their relationship. As early as 1959 she attempted to jump from Waterloo Bridge in London, but was restrained by a passer-by.

In 1971, after drinking insecticide, she was administered the last rites, but survived again. Finally, in 1972, a mixture of barbiturates and alcohol did the trick and she was dead at thirty-eight. An autopsy revealed she had the beginnings of arteriosclerosis, a disease that causes lack of oxygen to the brain, a possible explanation for her erratic behavior.

Michael Trubshawe was David Niven's best friend from his British Army days on Malta. Niven always tried to insert the man's name into each of his movies, not always successfully I might add. In *The Guns of Navarone* he went one better and had the man himself inserted into the picture. Trubshawe is the chap with the large moustache who procures the Navarone squad's boat for them. He would go on to appear in a further forty films.

Guys and Dolls (1955)

Germany, for some reason, saw fit to release this film under the title *Heavy Youths and Light Girls*. Frank Sinatra and Marlon Brando did not even exchange 'hellos' throughout the entire shoot.

Writer Joseph Mankiewicz recalled Sam Goldwyn's delight in the refurbished script for *Guys and Dolls*. 'I love the re-write', said Sam. 'Now the picture has warmth and charmth'. This was just one of the legendary 'Goldwynisms' that have entered Hollywood folklore. There were many more. Just how many were actually uttered by Sam, and how many were created by the plethora of writers resident in Hollywood, is anyone's guess. Either way, they are worth a chuckle. Here is a selection of vintage 'Goldwynisms':

'It's greater than a masterpiece - it's mediocre'.
'They're always biting the hand that lays the golden egg'.
'You've got to take the bull by the teeth'.
'O', give me a smart idiot over a stupid genius any day'.
'I've gone where the hand of man has never set foot'.
'Include me out!'
'I'll give you a definite maybe'.

'We are dealing in *facts*, not realities!'

'Let's have some new clichés'.

'A verbal contract is not worth the paper it's written on'.

'Any guy who goes to a psychiatrist oughta have his head examined'.

'We've got Indians fresh from the reservoir'.

'I just flew in on a Consternation'.

'The next time I send a damn fool, I'll go myself'.

'And don't try coming back to me on bended elbow'.

'Anything that man says, you've got to take with a dose of salts'.

'He's living beyond his means, but he can afford it'.

'I'm going out for some tea and trumpets'.

'I had a great idea this morning, but I didn't like it'.

'I never put on a pair of shoes until I've worn them for five years'.

'I've just returned from 10 Drowning Street, so I know what I'm talking about'.

'It will create an excitement that will sweep the country like wild flowers'.

'Modern dancing is so old-fashioned'.

'My autobiography should only be written after I'm dead'.

'That atom bomb is dynamite!'

'There's got to be some way of stopping the word of mouth on this picture'.

'This picture will go right up the toilet'.

'I've been laid up with the intentional flu'.

'Let's bring it up to date with some snappy nineteenth century dialogue'.

'I don't care if it doesn't make a nickel. I just want every man, woman and child in America to see it'.

'Now why did you name your baby 'John'? Every Tom, Dick and Harry is named John'.

'Our comedies are not to be laughed at'.

Walter Slezak, while still dressed in his buccaneering costume, encountered Goldwyn one day on the set. 'Walter, you look very periodical', the mogul observed.

His reaction to seeing a fourteenth century sundial for the first time was, 'what will they think of next?'

Concerning criticism of himself or his movies, he insisted, 'it runs off my back like a duck'.

When told one of his pictures was too caustic, he retorted, 'Too caustic? To hell with the cost! If it's a sound story, we'll make a picture of it anyway'.

When writer James Thurber expressed concern over the amount of violence in *The Secret Life of Walter Mitty*, Goldwyn consoled him. 'I'm sorry you feel it was too bloody and thirsty', he said. 'Not only did I think so', wrote Thurber, 'I was horror and struck'.

Billy Wilder once tried to sell the MGM mogul on the idea of making a movie about the life of the legendary ballet dancer Nijinsky. Billy told him of how Nijinsky had left his male lover Diaghilev for a woman, and how the great dancer eventually became so deranged in a mental institution that he believed he was a horse. Goldwyn, who rejoiced in making 'family' pictures was aghast. 'How dare you even suggest that I make a picture like that', he ranted. Billy threw in a final plea for the idea. 'Look, if you want a happy ending, we could have him win the Kentucky Derby'. Goldwyn threw him out of his office.

For all his mangling of the English language, Sam had the courage to stand up to the McCarthyism sweeping America at a time when most of his peers toadied to the HUAC. He even went on radio and denounced the persecutions as 'Un-

American'. The HUAC chose not to call him to testify, wary of what he might say.

When asked if he was afraid television would keep movie audiences at home, he sagely replied, 'They have cooks at home, but they go out to dine'.

Harry & Tonto (1974)

Art Carney achieved enormous popularity as Ed Norton in the successful TV series *The Honeymooners*. On D-Day in 1944, the twenty-six year-old Carney went ashore on bloody Omaha beach where he was wounded by shrapnel in the leg. For the remainder of his life he walked with a limp. An alcoholic, he spent time after 1960 in a psychiatric hospital.

Harry Potter & the Chamber of Secrets (2002)

Richard Harris, who plays the wizard Albus Dumbledor, was asked which role he would like to be remembered for. He replied, 'I don't care what I'm remembered for. I don't care *if* I'm remembered. I don't care if I'm *not* remembered. I don't care *why* I'm remembered. I genuinely don't care'. He died in October 2002 - if anyone remembers. In 1968 the dyslexic actor scored a smash hit on the pop charts with the song 'MacArthur Park'.

His career was very nearly terminated following the Harrad's bomb blast in 1983. Not because he was in it, but because he publicly supported the IRA who perpetrated the attack that left six people dead. Career-wise he knew he had shot himself in the foot, so he made a hasty apology of sorts.

Heaven Knows, Mr. Allison (1957)

According to Robert Mitchum, the great platonic love of his life was his co-star in this film Deborah Kerr. 'The only leading lady I didn't go to bed with', he exaggerated. But he adored her, nevertheless, and always referred to her as his favorite actress of all time.

Like everyone else, he was pleasantly surprised to find the delightful Deborah was not the prim and proper type he had expected her to be. In the turtle-chasing sequence, for instance, director John Huston kept yelling, 'faster, go faster!', as she paddled furiously. When her wooden oar suddenly split in half, the exasperated actress turned in full nun's habit and screamed at him, 'is that *fucking* fast enough?'

The heat on location was oppressive, more so for Deborah because she had to wear the stifling nun's habit most of the time. Mitchum remembered two crewmembers being permanently employed lifting her skirts between takes and 'cooling her ass with a fan'.

When the Catholic Church sent an emissary down to the shoot in Tobago to check that the nun's character was not being cheapened in any way, Huston, Mitchum and Kerr made sure he would remember his visit. As the cameras started to roll, Bob suddenly put his hands under his co-star's breasts, while she clasped hers around his buttocks.

They then proceeded to open-mouth kiss with complete abandon. 'What is going on here?' asked the incredulous priest. 'Dammit, father', exclaimed Huston, 'now you've gone and ruined a perfectly good take'.

Heaven's Gate (1980)

After enjoying enormous success with *The Deer Hunter*, director Michael Cimino's next venture was the catastrophic *Heaven's Gate,* a project that would ultimately bring about the closure of United Artists studios. Scheduled to begin filming on April 16, 1979 and conclude by June 22 of that year, it was not finished until April of 1980!

Budgeted at $7.5 million, the picture eventually cost the staggering sum of $35 million to complete. Even then the director's cut ran for an unusable five hours! This was reduced to three and a half hours and then cut again to just two and a half. By then it had become an indecipherable mess and sank without trace at the box office. Estimates about how much money was lost vary, but $55 million seems to be pretty close when publicity costs are added in.

United Artists had virtually given Cimino a free hand when they assigned his former secretary, Joann Carelli, as line producer in charge of keeping an eye on his expenditure. She just happened to be his current girlfriend. Of the scores of extravagances indulged in by Cimino, his decision to move all the buildings constructed to *his* blueprint specifications backwards three feet (because they 'didn't look right') was one of the most preposterous. This involved an entire street of houses. His construction boss logically suggested they move the houses on *one side* of the street by six feet instead of moving both sides by three feet each, but Cimino ignored him. That moronic decision alone cost in excess of $500,000.

At a time when scarcely any movies required more than 100,000 feet of film to be shot, Cimino racked up more than *one million* feet on *Heaven's Gate*. By the end of production he would have over 500 hours of *developed* film, an unheard of extravagance.

Just when it was thought the production had finally concluded, he advised executives he would be adding a prologue and epilogue to his masterpiece. The prologue would be shot at Harvard University and run for twenty minutes. The epilogue would be shot off Newport, Rhode Island and run for about ten minutes. When both Harvard and Yale refused him permission to film on their grounds, instead of selecting any one of a hundred colleges available in America, he transported the entire crew to Oxford University in England at a cost of $4 million. The epilogue cost a further million dollars on top of that. An assistant cameraman on *Heaven's Gate* estimated later that if $20 million was spent on filming, an additional $20 million must have been spent 'to buy all that cocaine for the cast and crew'.

Hello Dolly (1969)

Walter Matthau could not abide Barbra Streisand on the set of *Hello Dolly!* 'I have more talent in my smallest fart than you have in your entire body!' he told her. 'She is the most extraordinarily uninteresting person I have ever met. I just find her a terrible bore', he added.

Here We Go Round the Mulberry Bush (1967)

For a time, during the sixties, Barry Evans was about the hottest young comedian in Britain with two TV series, *Doctor in the House* and *Doctor at Large,* both doing really well. When he suddenly pulled out of TV to concentrate on serious acting in the theatre, his career lost impetus and never really recovered. A further fairly successful series in the late seventies called *Mind Your Language* provided a brief comeback, but by the mid- eighties the likeable actor had left the industry altogether.

By 1993 he was working as a taxi driver, living in a run-down bungalow in Leicestershire and drinking heavily. In 1997, police found his body lying face down on a sofa in his bungalow. Two young men and a girl were arrested in his stolen car a few hours later and charged. One of the men was initially charged with his murder, but the case was ultimately dropped, and the local coroner recorded an open verdict on the cause of death. Evans was fifty-two when he died.

Hey, Let's Twist (1961)

A very young Joe Pesci, who was a guitarist with the Starliters at the time, has his first screen appearance here as an extra. By 1979 he was disillusioned with acting and quit the profession to open an Italian restaurant. One evening, Robert de Niro and Martin Scorsese enjoyed a meal there and asked him if he would like to play Jake la Motta's brother, Joey, in *Raging Bull*. He agreed. A decade later he won an Oscar for *Goodfellas*.

High Noon (1952)

The title song is sung by Tex Ritter, the father of actor John Ritter. This was also Lee Van Cleef's movie debut in which he plays gunman Jack Colby. He never says a word in the entire film. Sheb Wooley plays another of the outlaws pitted against Cooper. In 1958 he scored a monster worldwide hit with the novelty pop tune 'The Purple People-Eater'.

Several actors chose not to play the lead, including John Wayne, Gregory Peck, Charlton Heston and Marlon Brando. Wayne objected publicly to the final scene where (he said) Gary Cooper tossed his badge on the ground, a gesture the Duke considered almost treasonous and a point he labored long after the film's completion. 'It's the most un-American thing I've ever seen in my whole life', he bleated. Then he went off and made *Rio Bravo* 'to show how a real peace officer should act'.

To everyone's surprise he then turned up at the Academy Awards the following year and collected Cooper's Oscar for him. Gary was unable to attend the ceremony! Of course, it probably helped soothe Wayne's ruffled feathers when, in the interim, Coops apologized for making *High Noon,* saying he would not have made it had he known it was 'a Communist picture'. He was not a very bright guy.

Cooper (51) and Grace Kelly (22) had an affair during the shooting of *High Noon.* Cooper told friends, 'She looked like a cold fish with a man until you got her pants down, then she'd explode!'

Fred Zinnemann the director of *High Noon* was besotted with Kelly. In fact, he took so many close-ups of her that it threatened to ruin the picture. Editor Elmo Williams was left with the task of cutting the film to make the thing viewable. He removed 99% of Grace's close-ups and won an editing Oscar.

Gary Cooper (1901-61)

Known relationships with men:

Lawler, Anderson

Known relationships with women:

Annabella
Bankhead, Tallulah
Bergman, Ingrid
Bow, Clara
Brent, Evelyn
Chanel, Lorraine
Colbert, Claudette
Crawford, Joan

Dahl, Arlene
Dare, Dorothy
Darr, Alicia
Di Frasso, Dorothy
Dietrich, Marlene
Ekberg, Anita
Engels, Wera
Goddard, Paulette
Harvey, Lilian
Hawks, Slim
Holman, Libby
Howe, Eileen
Kelly, Grace
Lake, Veronica
Larsen, Christine
Lollobrigida, Gina
Lombard, Carole
Neal, Patricia
Oberon, Merle
Pascal, Giselle
Payton, Barbara
Stanwyck, Barbara
Velez, Lupe
Weeks, Barbara
West, Mae
Williams, Kay
Zorina, Vera

His real name was Frank J Cooper, but since his agent came from Gary, Indiana they opted for Gary as his first name. As Coops actually hailed from Helena, Montana it was considered unwise to use *his* hometown as a Christian name. Although raised in Montana by his British parents, he was educated in the UK in the years leading up to the First World War. Before becoming an actor he was a cartoonist. His stunt double was a man named Slim Talbot who always rode a horse with his elbows sticking out, something Cooper never did. Consequently, it is easy to pick the distant shots that feature Talbot and those that do not.

A car accident in his youth broke Coops' hip and left him with a permanent limp. Because of this he was classified 4F by the armed forces and exempted from war service. He was also deaf in one ear, and often did not hear people speaking to him from his bad side, a problem that over the years aggravated many people who thought he was ignoring them.

When Russian Premier Nikita Kruschev visited the USA and Hollywood in 1959, he had never heard of stars such as Marilyn Monroe or Frank Sinatra. He spoke no English, yet when he was introduced to Coops, the Premier astonished everyone by uttering the solitary word, 'yup', before walking on.

Cooper liked to pay all his bills by cheque, especially smaller ones for gas, meals and so on. He figured he could save thousands of dollars by doing so, cagily surmising that most recipients of minor cheque would prefer to *keep* one sporting his signature than cash it. Maybe he wasn't so dumb after all. Then again, director King Vidor once said of him, 'he's got a reputation as a great actor just by thinking hard about the next line'.

Well, bright guy or not, by all accounts he was a very nice one. Carl Sandberg affectionately described him as 'one of the most beloved illiterates this country has ever known'. Josef von Sternberg considered him 'one of the nicest human beings I have ever met'.

Grace Kelly (1929-1982)

Known relationships:

Aumont, Jean-Pierre
Cassini, Oleg
Cooper, Gary
Crosby, Bing
D'Arcy, Alexander
Dornhelm, Robert
Gable, Clark
Grant, Cary
Holden, William
Kennedy, John F
Khan, Prince Aly
Lyons, Gene
Milland, Ray
Miller, Mark
Niven, David
Oechsle, Jack
Pahlavi, Prince Mahmoud
Phillippe, Claudius
Sachs, Mannie
Sinatra, Frank
Tracy, Spencer

Married:

Prince Rainier of Monaco

Grace deliberately set out to lose her virginity when she was nineteen and about to leave home to try her luck in New York City. She visited a married girlfriend, whom she knew would not be at home, and seduced her husband. Grace said she needed to know all about sex *before* she left for the big city, and none of the boys she knew could be trusted to keep a secret. Once in New York she wasted no time in using sex to get her wherever she needed to be, going with a number of young men simultaneously and flitting back and forth between them at her whim. Most of them had no idea she was being unfaithful.

Actor Alexandre D'Arcy recalled how he touched her on the knee in a taxi and she instantly jumped into his arms. They went straight to his apartment and had sex, with Grace not giving it a second thought.

Drama teacher Don Richardson told how he took her to his apartment, went to make some coffee and on his return found she had taken off all her clothes and was waiting for him in his bed. 'We had no introduction to this', he said. 'There was no flirtation. I could not believe it. Here was this fantastically beautiful creature lying next to me... that night was just sheer ecstasy'.

He also recalled how she would leap out of bed on Sunday mornings, dash off to Mass, then rush back and jump naked into bed with him, 'her little gold crucifix hanging around her neck'. Their affair ended when he realized she had slept with Prince Aly Khan. Richardson knew several girls who had gone out with the Prince. 'He would give them a cigarette lighter with one emerald in it. When he fucked them he would give them a gold emerald bracelet', he said.

One evening at the climax of a private fashion show Grace put on for Richardson, she posed naked - except for one of these bracelets. She had met Aly Khan a few days before. 'I was broken-hearted', said Richardson. 'I put on my clothes and said I was leaving'. On his way out he dropped the bracelet in the fish tank. His last vision of Grace was of her, still naked, fishing about in the tank for her bracelet. 'She screwed everybody she came into contact with who was able to do anything for her...' was his final assessment of the blonde beauty. 'She screwed agents, producers and directors. And there was really no need for it. She was already on her way'.

Throughout her New York days she would do a little modelling before noon then hurry back to a boyfriend's apartment for sex in her lunch break, after which she would happily return to work. She claimed these sessions were important for her modelling career because they put lights in her eyes.

Around this time she was intimate with the Shah of Iran, Claudius Phillippe of the Waldorf-Astoria and Mannie Sachs the head of Columbia Records and a close personal friend of her father. Another of her early lovers was actor Gene Lyons. He was an alcoholic who went on to achieve a shred of fame in TV's *Ironside* before falling victim to his alcoholism in 1975. Their relationship lasted two years.

She also enjoyed a brief affair with William Holden when they made *The Bridges at Toko-Ri* together. Then she seduced Bing Crosby during the shooting of *The Country Girl*. Frank Sinatra, David Niven, Spencer Tracy and many others had her before she tied the knot with Prince Rainier of Monaco. Her prissy, white gloves image fooled few people in Hollywood.

Clara Bow, who knew something about torrid affairs and scandalous reputations herself said, 'It's been 20 years since the trial that broke my heart. If it happened today, I'd still be a whore. Grace Kelly, however, will get away with having many lovers. Know why? The damn public will never believe it!'

Zsa Zsa Gabor commented, 'She had more boyfriends in a month than I had in a lifetime...She went to bed with anyone she fancied at the time'. Hedda Hopper referred to the future princess as 'the nymphomaniac'. Author Gore Vidal said, 'Grace almost always laid the leading man. She was notorious for that in this town'.

David Niven remembered being at a dinner party in Monaco when Prince Rainier asked him who he thought of all the actresses he had slept with was the best in bed. Forgetting where he was Niven blurted out, 'Grace...er Gracie Fields'. Of all her many movie industry lovers, only Niven would attend her wedding in Monaco.

If Prince Rainier died without producing an heir, Monaco would revert back to France. That was the dilemma he faced in 1956 when he began looking around for the right woman to resolve it. Marrying a movie star (provided she was fertile) would not only produce an heir, but also give the principality's tourist trade a much-needed boost. Aristotle Onassis prepared a list of candidates, at the top of which was Marilyn Monroe, the number one star in the world at that time. When *Life* magazine asked her if she thought the prince would marry her she replied, 'Give me two days alone with him and of course he'll want to marry me'. But she was too late. He had already met Grace.

Rainier had hoped for some time to marry his lover Gisele Pascal, but his spiritual adviser Father Francis Tucker considered it a poor match, so he told the prince Gisele was barren and the union was called off. Later she married someone else and had a child. Rainier was inconsolable.

Grace's father was unimpressed by royalty and said so. He particularly resented having to pay Rainier a dowry of $2,000,000. 'He's getting my daughter. Isn't that enough?' he complained. When asked by an interviewer what he thought of his future son-in-law, Mr. Kelly could only say rather crudely, 'The Prince comes up to Grace's titties'. His comment did not make it into the article.

All of Grace's movies were banned in Monaco for many years. The population did not wish to see its princess kissing other men on the screen. Off screen, however, both she and her husband took lovers. By the 1970s they no longer shared the same bedroom, and soon ceased sharing the same country as Grace lived more and more in Paris. In 1976, she bedded producer Robert Dornheim who was sixteen years her junior.

Her affair with Cary Grant did not begin when they made *To Catch a Thief* in the years before her marriage. Both were involved with someone else at the time. They renewed acquaintances in the 1970s and were lovers for seven years. Towards the end of her life she had numerous flings with a series of young men she called her 'toy boys'. Per Mattson a thirty-three year old Swedish actor was one. Another was New York restaurateur Jim McMullen who spent a passionate week with her in Monaco. She also picked up executive Jeffrey Fitzgerald on the Concorde and they, too, became lovers. When her daughters began to hit the scandal sheets, Grace confided to her biographer Gwen Robyns, 'How can I bring up my daughters not to have affairs, when I am having affairs with married men all the time?'

The Sunday Times ran a story prior to her death in 1982 suggesting she had joined the Solar Temple, a cult whose initiation rites into the sect involved nude massage and ritual sex. In October 1994 twenty-three members of the cult were found dead in a farmhouse in Cheiry, Switzerland, victims of what appeared to be either a suicide pact or possible mass murder.

The car accident that ended Grace's life was probably caused by her suffering a mild stroke while she was at the wheel. The vehicle lost control and plunged 120 feet over a cliff and landed on its hood. She was placed on a life support system but it proved pointless and the machine was switched off.

High Society (1956)

High Society is a musical remake of the 1940 film *The Philadelphia Story*. To fulfil her studio contract, Grace Kelly still had one more film to make before she could quit the movies and marry Monaco's Prince Rainier. That film was *High Society*. Rainier accompanied her to the set each day and appeared puzzled by the private jokes passing between his fiancée and her co-stars Frank Sinatra and Bing Crosby.

Being far removed from the Hollywood grapevine, the prince genuinely believed Grace's chaste screen image and thought she was a virgin. She had simply informed his doctors when they examined her hymen that it had been broken playing hockey in high school. Rainier was certainly unaware her co-stars on *High Society* had both slept with her.

The engagement ring she wears in the movie is the same one given to her by Rainier a couple of months prior to the shoot. The home where *High Society* was mostly filmed was Clarendon Court in Newport, Rhode Island. Its owner Claus von Bulow was the millionaire once charged with murdering his wife Sunny, the story of which was retold in the Jeremy Irons film *Reversal of Fortune*.

The biggest blunder in Academy Awards history saw writers Elwood Ullman and Edward Berends nominated for the screenplay of this film when, in fact, they had actually written the screenplay for a Bowery Boys movie of the same name. Too embarrassed to admit their error, the Board of Governors announced they had indeed nominated the Bowery Boys picture, a ludicrous statement ultimately corrected by Ullman and Berends who graciously withdrew from the final ballot.

Hook (1992)

Glenn Close can just be identified playing a bearded pirate in this. Other cameos include musicians David Crosby,

Quincy Adams and Phil Collins. A very young Gwyneth Paltrow plays Wendy Darling as a girl.

Hop-along-Cassidy (1935)

Robert Mitchum got his start in Hopalong Cassidy oaters playing bad guys in half a dozen or so of these B-Graders. When William Boyd made *The Volga Boatman* for DeMille in 1926, a thirteen year-old schoolgirl named Grace Bradley fell madly in love with his image on the screen. She set her heart on one day marrying him, and a decade later met the cowboy star in Hollywood when she was a struggling starlet. They married in 1937.

By the early thirties his career was rapidly sliding downhill, due in part to the antics of another William Boyd whose behavior was being attributed to the wrong man. The opportunity to make the Hopalong Cassidy pictures, in which he wore all dark blue clothing (not black as you might have thought), turned his career around. The dark blue was a deliberate ploy to offset his natural silver hair and twin pearl-handled pistols.

Surprisingly, he was not really the cowboy type. In fact, he could barely ride a horse at all until much later in his career. His early scenes on horseback, (those conducted above a canter), were performed by his double and stuntman Ted Wells.

Horse Feathers (1932)

Thelma Todd who plays the female lead in this Marx Brothers romp was a very likeable comedienne of the 20s and 30s known as 'The Ice-Cream Blonde'. 'She was a favorite with everybody on the lot', said Hal Roach, 'from the lowest employee to the highest'.

In 1935 the pretty thirty-year old actress died, possibly murdered on the orders of gangster Lucky Luciano with whom she was having an affair, and probably because she refused to let him use her Sidewalk Café Restaurant as a gambling den. Her live-in lover Roland West confessed on his deathbed decades later to being *responsible* for her death, but whether he meant directly or indirectly is not known.

Thelma's body was found in her garaged car one morning. Her blood-spattered face and coat along with several cracked ribs were explained by the coroner as being the result of her having fallen against the steering wheel as she succumbed to carbon monoxide poisoning. Nobody bought that story for a moment. Besides, there were other factors that did not seem quite right.

Although the key was turned in the car's ignition, the motor was off and there were still two gallons of gas in the tank. Furthermore, her maid was certain Thelma's body had been moved between the time she first found it and the arrival of the police. None of these anomalies was considered by the coroner to have any significance.

Although he placed the time of death at around six am on the Sunday morning, a Mrs. Wallace Ford testified to a Grand Jury that Todd rang her at four pm on *Sunday* afternoon. Another unexplained anomaly was the state of the dead woman's slippers. A policewoman who re-enacted the 270 steps climb to Thelma's garage, found her shoes were considerably scuffed and caked with dirt. Thelma's slippers found on the floor of her car were spotless.

Just prior to her death Thelma confided to a friend, 'I've fallen in love with a tough bunch of characters. I'm not sure what I'm going to do about it. I'm really frightened for the first time in my life'.

Witnesses overheard her arguing with Luciano at the Brown Derby Restaurant in Beverly Hills earlier in the week. 'You'll open a gambling casino in my restaurant over my dead body', she told the mobster. 'That can be arranged', was his sinister reply. She then foolishly threatened to go to the DA, unaware he was a mob pawn who regularly reported to Luciano.

As often happened in Hollywood in the thirties, money more than likely changed hands to ensure her death was investigated in a rudimentary manner. On the very day her corpse was discovered, Busby Berkeley was due to appear in court on three counts of vehicular manslaughter. It has since been theorized that corrupt civic and police officials were 'persuaded' to tidy up the Todd death quickly. Two scandals at once was something the studios did not need.

There were originally six Marx brothers, but one of them (Manfred) died in childhood. Julius became Groucho because he was moody. Leonard was nicknamed Chico because he liked to chase the chicks. Adolph played the harp so of course he was dubbed Harpo. Milton was referred to as Gummo because he always wore gumshoes, and Herbert was named after a chimpanzee called Zeppo.

Harpo played piano in a whorehouse in the early days. Although the mute in the act, he was the most articulate of all the brothers. A favorite of the New York literary crowd, he was a member of the famed Algonquin Club, a collection of noted writers, humorists and intellectuals. He was also friend to many of the powerful men in Hollywood, including Sam Goldwyn

Chico also had connections. He was a regular player at the Thursday night Bridge parties conducted at the home of Irving Thalberg and his wife Norma Shearer. Goldwyn and Joe Schenck were also regulars. 'Chico, I would say', said Jack Benny, 'loved women and gambling – period'.

Groucho, too, was a gambler, and like many Hollywood identities did not much care with whom he gambled. He and Phil Silvers (of *Sgt. Bilko* fame) lost a great deal of money in a crooked game with mobster Johnny Roselli, the same Roselli who ended his days in several pieces bobbing about in an oil drum in the Atlantic in 1976.

On a bond-selling tour during World War Two, Groucho soon realized he had to wear his greasepaint eyebrows and moustache because nobody recognized him without them.

On the same tour, while he was at the White House, a be-ribboned general asked him if he knew where the first lady, Mrs. Roosevelt, might be. 'She's upstairs filing her teeth', he replied, an obvious reference to Eleanor's decidedly equine features.

Zeppo developed a company that made, among other devices, the clamp mechanism used for the atom bombs dropped on Japan. By war's end he was a millionaire. He divorced his wife and moved to Palm Springs with a showgirl twenty years his junior.

Summoned to Hollywood to discuss a movie contract with MGM, the brothers tired of waiting for executive Irving Thalberg to arrive, so they stripped naked in his office and toasted marshmallows in his fireplace until he did.

On another occasion they were invited to speak at a noon executive luncheon in New York City. While in the elevator on its way to the fourteenth floor they again decided to strip off and surprise the gathering. When the lift doors opened the naked trio leapt out, only to discover they had alighted at a luncheon for female telephone employees!

Playwright George Bernard Shaw said his fifth favorite actor was Sir Cedric Hardwicke - after the four Marx Bros.

Horse Soldiers, The (1959)

African-American tennis star Althea Gibson plays Constance Towers' maid Luki in this John Ford western.

The superb character actor Strother Martin was a former Junior Springboard Diving Champion who initially went to Hollywood as a swimming instructor.

Houdini (1953)

Houdini is a prime example of Hollywood refusing to let the facts get in the way of a good story. In this movie Harry Houdini is dumped into the icy Detroit River, bound and chained inside a trunk. Once out of the trunk he struggles to find the hole in the ice that is his only escape route, *until* he hears the voice of his mother calling him and directing him to the hole and safety. According to the movie script, she is in another city altogether, and has died at the precise moment he heard her voice guiding him to safety.

In reality, however, things were a little different. He did escape from the Detroit River during a stunt in 1906, but it did not include a trunk, nor was the river iced over, and his dear old mother died *seven years* after that day. In fact, Harry simply dived off the Bell Isle Bridge and emerged from the water soon afterwards.

The movie would have us believe that the Water Torture Cell worried Houdini, both physically and spiritually, and this led to it ultimately being responsible for his death. Rubbish. Harry had performed the trick hundreds of times over fourteen years. It held no terrors at all for him. He died from peritonitis, hastened by a punch to the midriff from a fan during a moment of bravado on Houdini's part. Nothing more mysterious than that.

House of Cards (1968)

Born in Stockholm, Inger Stevens learned to speak English without an accent, but then had to fake one for her starring role in the TV series *The Farmer's Daughter*. She was emotionally flattened when Bing Crosby unexpectedly dumped her to marry Kathryn Grant. Inger thought their relationship was solid, until she turned on her television one evening to hear he had eloped with Grant. In the sixties she found it increasingly difficult to get good roles because of her marriage to black athlete Isaac Jones. At the age of thirty- six she committed suicide with sleeping pills.

How the West Was Won (1962)

Yvonne de Carlo's stuntman husband Robert Morgan was thrown from the train during the fight on the log truck sequence and seriously injured. Wheels passed over his body three times and he was extremely fortunate to survive, although his leg was later amputated. He sued the studio for $1.4 million, but witnesses were allegedly threatened with their jobs if they supported his accusations of negligence. Deprived of any substantiating witnesses he lost the case.

It was on the set of this picture that Debbie Reynolds met Agnes Moorehead. Her son, Todd Fisher, has openly stated that the two actresses were lovers from then until Moorehead's death in 1974. Debbie denies being bisexual or lesbian.

How to Marry a Millionaire (1953)

This was the first film to be shot in Cinemascope, but the second to be released. Darryl Zanuck chose the more spectacular *The Robe* to launch the new process in the cinemas. When Anita Loos wrote *How to Marry a Millionaire*, she modelled the character of Lorelei Lee on Paulette Goddard who was reputed to be one of her lovers.

Three in-jokes occur in the film. Betty Grable wrongly identifies a trumpet player heard on the radio as Harry James, who was actually her real life husband at the time. Lauren Bacall speaks of 'that old fellow what's-his-name in *African Queen*', referring to *her* real-life husband Humphrey Bogart. And Marilyn can be seen reading *Murder by Strangulation*, a dig at her fate in the movie *Niagara* released later that same year.

Hurricane, The (1937)

Jon Hall was the star of this film. Once married to the lovely Frances Langford, his career was over by the late forties, so he took to pioneering underwater camera equipment, later used to great effect in the Esther Williams films. In 1979, after being bedridden for many months with bladder cancer, he ended his life with a firearm.

I am a Fugitive from a Chain Gang (1932)

The story was based on the real life trials of a man named Robert Burns, who was convicted in Georgia of stealing $5.29 worth of food in 1920 and sentenced to ten years hard labor. Georgian state authorities tried unsuccessfully to have the picture banned.

I Claudius (1937)

Only twenty minutes of film was completed on this 1937 movie featuring Charles Laughton as the stammering Emperor Claudius. Director Josef Von Sternberg clashed repeatedly with the perfectionist Laughton and budget problems quickly arose. When co-star Merle Oberon was seriously injured in a car crash the project was abandoned. It now appears her accident was used as an excuse by the studio to cut and run with the troubled production's insurance money.

Laughton's health was impaired for the remainder of his life after he was gassed at Vimy Ridge during the Great War. His wife, actress Elsa Lanchester, always claimed she was unaware of his homosexuality until well into their marriage. Even so, he desperately wanted to father a child, but Elsa could not conceive, more than likely on account of a botched abortion she underwent while in burlesque in her younger days.

Shelley Winters recalled Marilyn Monroe saying to her, when they roomed together in their pre-stardom days, that she thought Laughton was 'the sexiest man alive'! The more I find out about Marilyn, the more she worries me.

Merle Oberon (1911-1979)

Known relationships:

Aherne, Brian
Bautzer, Greg
Beatty, Admiral David
Bey, Turhan
Brando, Marlon
Brent, George
Cagney, James
Chevalier, Maurice
Cini, Giorgio
Cochran, Steve
Colman, Ronald
Cooper, Gary
Donat, Robert
Fairbanks Jr, Douglas
Fisher, Eddie
Gable, Clark
Granger, Stewart
Harris, Richard
Harrison, Rex
Henreid, Paul
Hillary, Richard
Howard, Leslie
Hughes, Howard
Hutchinson, Leslie
Khan, Prince Aly
Mander, Miles
Niven, David
Prince Philip Mountbatten
Ross, Rex
Rush, Richard
Ryan, Robert
Schenck, Joseph M
Sinatra, Frank
Taylor, Rod
Zanuck, Darryl F

Married:

Alexander Korda & 3 others

Hollywood Warts 'N' All

Merle was born with a heart defect in Bombay to a Ceylonese mother and a British engineer father who was killed on the Somme in 1915. Throughout her life she kept her mother's identity a closely guarded secret, passing her off for decades as her hired servant and maid. When the old lady died, Merle had her buried in an unmarked grave in Micheldever, Hampshire, then commissioned a portrait of a brown haired, blue eyed, white woman and hung it in her living room, telling everyone it was a picture of her mother.

Oberon always maintained she was born aboard a ship passing by the island of Tasmania. One year before her death in 1979, the people of Tasmania (still believing the charade) hosted a reception in her honor commemorating the origins of their most famous female star.

Working as a 'hostess' under the name of Queenie O'Brien at the Café de Paris in London in her teens, she is believed to have sold her body to make ends meet when times were tough. Cecil Beaton said of her, 'Merle is almost a nymphomaniac. She makes love because she likes it, because of the money. She is as promiscuous as a man, enjoying a quick one behind the door'.

Dietrich hated her with a passion, referring to her as 'that Singapore streetwalker' and 'a real common piece'. Columnist Sheilah Graham said of her, 'She was always in awe of her fellow movie stars. When she was having an affair with Jimmy Cagney during a bond-selling tour in World War 2, she interrupted their sex by saying, 'Just imagine, I'm in bed with Jimmy Cagney'. I hear it somewhat diminished his ardor'.

Her over-use of makeup to whiten her complexion caused a severe skin disorder, curable only by the removal of all the top skin from her face, an extremely painful process. It was while she was being treated for this disorder that she met and fell in love with a severely burned British fighter pilot named Richard Hillary. His face and hands were destroyed when he was shot down in flames over England. She restored his virility in her Ritz Towers apartment and had very strong feelings for him. Some months later he pulled some strings and resumed flying, but was shot down a second time and killed. Oberon was hysterical for several days and quit the film she was working on.

Her affair with Leslie Howard ended when his wife Ruth walked in on the couple having sex on the floor of his dressing room. Engaged to Joseph Schenck at the time, Merle returned his ring once the story got around. Schenck sold it that evening to Douglas Fairbanks who used it to become engaged to Lady Sylvia Ashley.

While in her late fifties, Merle seduced newcomer Richard Harris after a party at her home. Harris wrote in his memoirs how he had fantasized about her since childhood and was thrilled just to get an invitation to the party! The married Senator Edward Kennedy once invited her out, but she turned him down, stating she was concerned everyone would recognize them. He told her the American people would like him no matter what he did. Kennedy arrogance in all its glory. Chappaquiddick would prove him wrong.

Imitation of Life (1959)

Sandra Dee's mother married for the second time when her daughter was five years old. Her stepfather insisted Sandra sleep between the newlyweds on their honeymoon. 'I'm not marrying your mother', he told her. 'I'm marrying both of you'. He was soon having sex with both of them as well, and did so until his death seven years later.

At the age of sixteen (although the studio pretended she was eighteen) Dee married singer Bobby Darin. She had already been suffering from anorexia for four years and the problem would continue to plague her well into her twenties.

Indiana Jones & the Last Crusade (1989)

Harrison Ford cut his chin in a car accident in Northern California when he was twenty. The cut is 'explained' in this film when River Phoenix, playing the young Indiana Jones, has his chin cut by a whip. Actually, Sean Connery is only twelve years older than Ford in real life, but plays his father here.

There are two mistakes evident when Hitler gives Indiana his autograph. First, he signs it 'Adolf' instead of the German form of 'Adolph'. Secondly, he signs with his right hand. Hitler was left-handed.

In Old Chicago (1938)

Alice Brady won the Best Supporting Oscar for *In Old Chicago*, but was laid up at home with a broken leg on presentation night. A 'representative' accepted the statuette on her behalf and was never seen again. The Academy later gave her a replacement.

Alice Faye was also in this film. Although not a great singer, she knew how to sell a song better than most other artists. 'I'd rather have Alice Faye introduce my songs than anyone else' said none other than Irving Berlin. She won her role in this picture by replacing the recently deceased Jean Harlow.

In the Name of the Father (1993)

In preparation for his role in *In the Name of the Father,* Daniel Day-Lewis went without sleep for several nights, lived in a specially constructed cell on the set, ate cold porridge and prison slops, and underwent hours of interrogation by real life detectives.

Being a method actor, Daniel Day-Lewis insisted on being carried everywhere and spoon-fed by crewmembers on the set of *My Left Foot* to enhance his performance. He is also said to have learned to write with his foot and remained in a wheelchair for the entire six weeks of the shoot. For his role in *The Crucible* he arrived at the New England location weeks early, just so he could personally help construct his character's seventeenth century cottage.

His wife Rebecca Miller is the daughter of playwright Arthur Miller. Had Marilyn Monroe lived and stayed married to Arthur she would now be Daniel Day-Lewis's mother in law!

Intolerance (1916)

Robert Harron's future appeared bright when he starred as 'boy' in this D W Griffith epic, but when DW chose Richard Barthelmess over him to star in *Way Down East* in 1919, the bitterly disappointed young actor shot himself.

Florence Lawrence was known as 'The Biograph Girl' during the first decade of the twentieth century, and was earning the then tidy sum of $25 a week as the most popular actress in silent movies, even though the public did not even know her name. In 1910 she fell out with Biograph and was snapped up by Carl Laemmle the head of the Independent Motion Picture Company. He raised her salary to a staggering $1,000 a week!

Once he had her signed, Laemmle placed a bogus story in the press stating she had been killed in a streetcar accident in St Louis. Then he followed up with a second story captioned, 'We Nail a Lie', in which he accused competitors of falsely claiming his star was dead! He then arranged for Florence to make a personal appearance in St Louis, to prove she was alive and well. Hundreds turned out to see the subject of this 'real life mystery', and in the crush tore the buttons from her coat as souvenirs. Laemmle had cleverly created the world's first movie star.

By 1938, however, her career was well and truly over and she grew deeply depressed. She chose to take her life in agonizing fashion by eating ant paste, her death scarcely causing a ripple in an industry that had long since passed her by.

In Which We Serve (1942)

Noel Coward once made a pass at David Niven, but was rebuffed by the dapper Brit who politely reminded him he was old enough to be his father. From then onwards Coward always referred to him as 'son'. It was their standing private joke.

Incidentally, Coward wrote the tune *Mad About the Boy* as a tribute to his 'friend' Cary Grant. Noel once told writer Gore Vidal that he had never had sex with a woman in his life. 'Not even with Gertie Lawrence?' asked Vidal incredulously. 'Particularly not with Miss Lawrence', was the indignant response.

Irma La Douce (1963)

Shirley MacLaine, as nearly everyone knows, believes wholeheartedly in reincarnation. 'I believe that in previous lives I have been an elephant princess, a kidnapped maiden, a peg-legged pirate and a court jester beheaded by Louis X1', she told *Sunday Today* in 1986. Her old friend Dean Martin refused to buy it. 'Shirley, I love her. But her oars ain't touching the water these days', he said. Yves Montand, in the same vein said, 'Shirley MacLaine – who does she think she isn't?'

Isadora (1969)

The last words spoken by the subject of this movie, the exotic roaring twenties dancer Isadora Duncan, were about as prophetic as they come. 'Farewell, my friends', she called in French as she climbed into her Bugatti open-top sports car in 1927. 'I am off to glory!' Whereupon she put her foot on the accelerator, her long scarf became entwined in the rear wheel spokes, and as the vehicle began to roar away her neck was snapped, killing her instantly.

Island in the Sun (1957)

Joan Fontaine received a stack of hate mail (mostly from Ku Klux Klan members) following her love scenes in this picture with black actor Harry Belafonte. When rumors spread that she and Belafonte were off-screen lovers as well the letters increased, causing the intervention of the FBI.

It Happened at the World's Fair (1963)

Yvonne Craig plays one of Elvis Presley's love interests here, the one he croons 'Relax' to, as he attempts to seduce her. Off the set they enjoyed a brief fling. These days she is best remembered as Batgirl in the campy *Batman* TV series of the sixties.

After Elvis she lowered her sights somewhat and wed fifties singer Jimmie Boyd, the young, buck-toothed kid who made a fortune from his million-selling hit singles 'I Saw Mommie Kissing Santa Claus' and 'Tell Me A Story'.

Eleven year-old Kurt Russell makes his screen debut here playing the young boy Elvis pays to boot him in the shins a couple of times. In the 1970s he almost quit acting to pursue a career as a minor league baseball player of considerable promise, but an injury put paid to that ambition. His father Bing Russell played the deputy sheriff in the long-running *Bonanza* series on TV.

It Happened One Night (1934)

Clark Gable and Claudette Colbert were forced by their respective studios to make this picture. Neither star thought it would amount to anything of consequence. Constance Bennett, Myrna Loy, Miriam Hopkins and Margaret Sullavan all turned their noses up when approached to play the female lead. 'I said it was just a silly comedy', Hopkins later lamented.

Gable was especially angry at being farmed out to the lowly Columbia outfit, so he rolled up for the first day's shooting quite drunk. Ten years after winning an Oscar for the picture he gave the statuette to a small boy. 'Having it doesn't mean anything', he explained, 'Earning it does'. Years later it was purchased at auction by Stephen Spielberg for $607,500 and donated to the Academy.

When Gable removed his shirt and revealed he was not wearing anything underneath it, the sales of singlets plummeted throughout America. Such was the impact of movies in pre-war America. Underwear companies even tried to sue Columbia over the issue.

Bob Clampett, the inventor of Bugs Bunny, says he got the idea for the 'wascally wabbit' from watching Clark chewing on a carrot in *It Happened One Night*.

The 'walls of Jericho' scene was inserted because Colbert would not agree to undress before the cameras. At first she refused to lift her skirt for the hitchhiking sequence as well. After viewing her stand-in's efforts, however, she changed her mind. 'My legs are better than hers,' she remarked, and shot the scene.

Convinced she had no chance of winning an Oscar, Colbert was at the railway station ready to depart on a holiday when she received news of her victory. She clambered into the sidecar of a police motor-cycle and rushed to the Biltmore Hotel to pick up her statuette.

At the previous year's Oscars, director Frank Capra suffered the embarrassment of rushing to the podium thinking he had won the Best Director award, only to discover that the 'Frank' called out by presenter Will Rogers was the other one who had been nominated, Frank Lloyd. Instead of announcing the winner's full name, Rogers had simply held the Oscar aloft and said, 'Come and get it Frank'. Capra leapt from his seat as the spotlight played on the auditorium looking for the winner. 'Over here, I'm over here!' he called. Only then did he see Lloyd heading for the stage. The sheepish Capra slunk back to his seat. The mix-up was supposed to end announcements on a first name basis forever, but the following year presenter Irvin Cobb teased Capra again when he called out, 'Come up and get it, Frank'. But this time it was for real. He had indeed won for *It Happened One Night*.

Claudette Colbert (1903-1996)

Known relationships with men:

Bautzer, Greg
Boyer, Charles
Chevalier, Maurice
Cooper, Gary
Gable, Clark
Henreid, Paul
Howard, Leslie
Johnson, Kerry
MacMurray, Fred
McCrea, Joel
Power, Tyrone
Stewart, James
Sturges, Preston
Taylor, Robert
Tracy, Spencer

Known relationships with women:

Crawford, Joan
Dietrich, Marlene
Garbo, Greta
Hepburn, Katharine
Hull, Verna
McDaniel, Hattie
Parlo, Dita
Stanwyck, Barbara
Tashman, Lilyan
Trevor, Claire

To ensure she was never photographed from the right side, Colbert, so the story goes, would paint that side of her face green before takes, if a director refused to take her seriously on the subject.

Noel Coward had no time for her. 'I'd wring your neck if you had one', he once told her. She did indeed have a perceptibly short neck. It was disguised on film by clever use of clothing, angles and lighting.

Her views on the 'casting couch' system of advancement in the movie industry were quite candid. 'The casting couch – the only one of us who ever made it to stardom without it was Bette Davis', she said.

Marlene Dietrich (who once had a fling with her) often referred to her as 'an ugly shop girl'. For some reason Dietrich considered all her female lovers to be her social inferiors. She really was a terrible snob. On retirement Colbert moved to Barbados with her alleged girlfriend actress Claire Trevor.

Clark Gable (1901-1960)

Known relationships:

Adams, Edie
Allan, Elizabeth
Angeli, Pier
Astor, Mary
Blondell, Joan
Bruce, Virginia
Carmen, Jeanne
Colbert, Claudette
Colby, Anita

Crawford, Joan
Davies, Marion
Davis, Nancy
De Carlo, Yvonne
De Havilland, Olivia
De Mille, Katherine
De Scaffa, Francesca
Dorfler, Franz
Evans, Madge
Frederick, Pauline
Gardner, Ava
Goddard, Paulette
Granger, Dorothy
Grey, Virginia
Griffith, Corinne
Harlow, Jean
Harrison, Joan
Hawks, Slim
Hayward, Susan
Hyer, Martha
Kelly, Grace
Lake, Veronica
Lamarr, Hedy
Lilly, Doris
Loy, Myrna
Maxwell, Marilyn
MovitaYoung, Loretta
O'Brien, Dolly
Oberon, Merle
Oliver, Edna May
Page, Anita
Parker, Denise
Parsons, Louella
Powell, Eleanor
Rogers St Johns, Adela
Shearer, Norma
Sothern, Ann
Totter, Audrey
Turner, Lana

Van Doren, Mamie
Velez, Lupe
Weeks, Barbara
White, Elaine
Winters, Shelley

Married:

Carole Lombard & 4 others

One of Gable's wives, Ria Langham, was seventeen years older than him. Another Josephine Dillon was fifteen years his senior and it is said their marriage was never consummated. He married Dillon because she was a drama coach and he needed a personal tutor. He married Langham because she was rich and he needed the money.

Despite this interest in older women (albeit for less than romantic reasons), he still found time to bed scores of younger ones. While he and MGM press agent George Nicholls were admiring a group picture of MGM actresses one day, Clark smugly commented, 'Aren't they beautiful? And I've had every one of 'em'.

Gay actor, turned interior decorator, William Haines confided to his good friend Joan Crawford the details of his intimacy with Gable when the future 'King of Hollywood' was just another struggling young actor in the early days. 'I fucked him in the men's room of the Beverly Wilshire Hotel', he bluntly informed her. 'He was that desperate. He was a nice guy, but not a fruitcake'.

Joan confided in friends also. 'He wasn't a satisfying lover. I often tried to distract him from my bedroom. But he had more magnetism than any man on earth', she said. Clark and Joan were intimate for decades, and it was to her he went for solace the night his wife Carole Lombard died.

Because he was enjoying a last minute tryst with a young un-named actress, he sent a flunkie to the airport to meet Lombard, unaware her plane was overdue. Carole was apparently concerned her husband was being unfaithful with either Crawford or his current co-star Lana Turner, so she decided to fly back from Indiana, because it was quicker than taking the train. He suffered a guilt complex over her death for the rest of his life.

After her death he signed on with the US Air Force as a navigator, flying missions over Nazi

Germany. Shattered by his loss, he volunteered for combat missions and continually requested to be trained as a gunner. 'No officer mans a gun', said his CO, 'the guy's crazy. He's trying to get himself killed'. When Herman Goering placed a $5,000 bounty on his head, dead or alive, Gable's CO was instructed to protect his aircraft with extra bomber escorts. The CO was a relieved man when the actor was sent home after just five missions.

Off-screen he was penny-pinching, shy and rather dull. Ava Gardner considered him dumb as well. 'Clark is the sort of guy, if you said 'Hi ya Clark, how are you? - he'd be stuck for an answer', she said.

It's a Mad, Mad, Mad, Mad World (1963)

Starlet Lisa Gaye has a small role as a policewoman in Spencer Tracy's office. Her career never rose to any great heights, even though she was quite attractive and the real life sister of established star Debra Paget.

Dick Shawn, who plays Ethel Merman's son, but who is probably best remembered as 'LSD' in Mel Brooks' *The Producers*, died on stage during a performance in Los Angeles in 1987.

Three years after the release of this film, Mickey Rooney's wife Barbara was shot to death by her lover, a former stuntman named Milos Milocevic, who then turned the gun on himself. Milocevic was formerly married to a high priced Hollywood call girl named Cynthia Bouron. She would hit the headlines briefly when she brought an unsuccessful paternity suit against sixty-six year old Cary Grant in 1970. In 1973, her body was found in the trunk of a stolen car parked in a Hollywood supermarket car park. She had been bludgeoned to death. Her killer was never found.

Ethel Merman plays the insufferable mother-in-law of Milton Berle. Off the screen she was an abusive drunk and a loud-mouthed, vulgar bigot who referred to African-Americans as 'niggers' and to anyone else she disliked as 'commie Jews'. For each of her Broadway shows she demanded 10% of the tickets for herself so she could sell them at inflated prices to touts.

During her long affair with Sherman Billingsley who owned the Stork Club in New York, she would often tease the doorman by throwing up her skirt as she entered the club, revealing her disdain for the use of underwear. Their affair ended when Billingsley refused her offer of a half a million dollars to divorce his wife and marry her instead.

Merman and actor Ernest Borgnine parted after just thirty-eight days of marriage. The chapter in her autobiography on Borgnine has on it his name, followed by a single blank page. The bisexual Judy Garland was reputed to be one of her lovers.

Milton Berle (1908-2002)

Known relationships:

Ball, Lucille
Bara, Theda
Darnell, Linda
Davis, Nancy
Dell, Myrna
Dietrich, Marlene
Hughes, Mary Beth
Hutton, Betty
Jergens, Adele
Kilgallen, Dorothy
Lake, Veronica
Lamarr, Hedy
McPherson, Aimee Semple
Miller, Ann
Monroe, Marilyn
Negri, Pola
Sheridan, Ann
Turner, Lana

Berle was once familiar to American TV viewers as 'Uncle Milty', courtesy of his long running prime time show. In

Hollywood he was a real ladies' man possibly because he was considered to be the proud owner of the largest genitalia in the business, or at least equaling that of Forrest Tucker.

When asked to win a bet for his golfing cronies against a visitor who claimed *he* was entitled to that claim, Berle said, 'All right', but I'm telling you now, I'm only going to show enough of it to win'. He won. 'They say that the two best hung men in Hollywood are Forrest Tucker and Milton Berle', said Betty Grable, adding with a grimace, 'what a shame. It's never the handsome ones. The bigger they are, the homelier'.

In old age he was, to put it bluntly, a dirty old man. When he was eighty-three he invited a twenty-four year old woman over to his restaurant table, where he asked if he could put his head between her breasts. Before she could answer he said, 'I have something big and beautiful too. Here, have a feel'. He then forced her hand onto his crotch.

For reasons she never fully explained the young woman agreed to a date with him! 'I barely got through the front door before he attacked me', she recalled. 'He took his pants off and I got the shock of my life. Here was a man in his eighties standing stark naked before me and he was huge! To my horror, he forced me to give him oral sex. But Milton didn't get excited. Then he joined me down on the floor and we tried to make love, but it was just a total bust'. Well, she sounds like an innocent young thing.

At the age of eighty-eight he had an altercation with a thirty-three year old bellman at the Taj Mahal Hotel. The man accused Berle of squeezing his crotch and ruining his sex life after taking offence at something the man said. The incident was settled out of court. When he died of colon cancer in 2002, the funeral directors set up 150 chairs in the auditorium, expecting a big turnout for the one-time 'King of Television'. Just four of them were occupied by the time the service commenced.

It's a Pleasure (1945)

During the 1940s Marie McDonald's studio billed her as 'The Body', a name she thoroughly despised. For the 1945 film, *It's a Pleasure*, she was compelled to die her blonde hair red because the film's star, Sonja Henie, had a clause in her contract guaranteeing 'no other blondes' in her movies.

In 1957 McDonald was supposedly kidnapped and then found unharmed forty hours later. It turned out to be a publicity stunt to boost her flagging career. It didn't work. In 1965 she took a lethal overdose, which the coroner generously ruled as 'accidental'.

Ivanhoe (1952)

At the commencement of this movie we see Robert Taylor embark upon what can only be described as the most optimistic quest in history. Convinced King Richard is alive *somewhere in Europe*, he hops on his trusty steed and rides the poor thing all over the continent while he sings a little ditty he hopes the King will hear and respond to (assuming he is still alive, of course). The plan is simplicity in itself.

Well, simple-minded actually. He merely rides around *every* castle in Europe warbling and hoping.

Joy of joys the plan works! He arrives in Austria, and King Dick hears his little tune from his castle cell, (just as well he wasn't underground in a dungeon), and tosses down a note he happens to have prepared for just such a contingency. There is, however, an unexpected chink in this brilliantly thought out plan because the note is written in *Austrian*. Since Richard only spoke and wrote in French (he never did get a handle on English either, by the way), we have to wonder how and why he chose to contact his savior (who was clearly an Englishman) in a language neither could understand. Ivanhoe takes the note to the first Austrian he comes across and forces him to translate it, yet when the parchment appears on the screen – you guessed it - *it is written in English*.

After such a start we just know our hero will overcome whatever obstacles he encounters over the next 100 minutes or so of the movie. And he does.

Elizabeth Taylor (1932-2011)

Known relationships:

Beatty, Warren
Bernstein, Carl
Bowie, David
Damone, Vic
Dean, James
DiCicco, Pat
Donen, Stanley
Farrell, Colin
Finch, Peter

Goldblum, Jeff
Hamilton, George
Hudson, Rock
Kashoggi, AdnanReagan, Ronald
Lawford, Christopher
Lawford, Peter
Lerner, Max
Loew Jr, Arthur
Long, Richard
Luna, Victor
Mankiewicz, Joseph
Mature, Victor
Pawley, William
Prince Rainier of Monaco
Reynolds, Burt
Sinatra, Frank
Steiger, Rod
Taylor, Robert
Thompson, Marshall
Wagner, Robert
Winters, Jason
Wynberg, Henry
Zahedi, Ardeshir

Married:

Eddie Fisher
Michael Wilding & 4 others
Richard Burton (twice)

Liz's mother, Sara, had a lengthy affair with director Michael Curtiz. Her father, who was gay, was intimate with renowned homosexual designer Adrian, the husband of actress Janet Gaynor.

By the age of fourteen Liz was as developed as most grown women would love to be. At 35-22-35 she presented a censorship problem by insisting she show off her newly acquired cleavage. The censors could not have that, so they in turn insisted she wear an *orange* in her cleavage during camerawork, and instructed cameramen to move back if they could see the orange through their lenses. An original idea if ever there was one.

At sixteen she played the wife of thirty-seven year old Robert Taylor in *Conspirator*. On completion of filming each day she had to dash off to a tutor to do her schoolwork. 'How can I concentrate on my education', she complained, 'when Robert Taylor keeps sticking his tongue down my throat?'

Bob had problems of his own, and asked cameraman Freddie Young to only shoot him from the waist up because he was embarrassed about the erections he was getting while kissing the voluptuous teenager. When Liz's bathrobe accidentally fell open and displayed her breasts during one scene the offending shot was destroyed on studio orders. Of course, just how many of these 'offensive out-takes' are ever *really* destroyed is another question altogether.

Liz's marriage to Nicky Hilton had been over for two years by the time she made *Ivanhoe* in 1951. He was a heroin addict, an alcoholic and addicted to gambling when he married the seventeen year-old beauty. He was also a wife beater as she quickly found out. Their marriage was not even consummated until the third night because the groom was hopelessly drunk for a couple of days.

He also had no interest in her movie career and even less in movie stars in general. At their engagement party when she asked him if he would like to meet Spencer Tracy and

Joan Bennett, he gave them a cursory glance and told her to 'skip it'.

Like most of her husbands and lovers, Nicky was possessed of an enormous penis. Actress Terry Moore described it as 'wider than a beer can and much longer. 'To make love to him was akin to fornicating with a horse', she said. Liz confessed to her hairdresser she liked well-endowed men. Eddie Fisher, John Warner, Henry Wynberg and Hilton were all in that category.

In 1999, Liz admitted she miscarried after Hilton kicked her in the stomach while in one of his rages. 'I saw the baby in the toilet', she said. 'I left him after nine months of marriage after having a baby kicked out of my stomach'. Even so, she continued to meet him afterwards from time to time for sex if the urge grabbed her.

Immediately after divorcing Hilton the eighteen year-old Taylor was proposed to by forty-four year-old Howard Hughes. Actually it was more like a business proposal. He offered her father a million dollars for her hand, and the man was sorely tempted, but Liz detested Hughes and declined the offer for him. Next morning, the incurably optimistic billionaire dumped an attaché case full of diamonds, rubies and emeralds on her bare tummy as she lay by the hotel pool. 'Get dressed', he ordered, 'we're getting married'. She again refused and he reluctantly gathered up his baubles and gave up the chase. Later, still miffed, he would say in an interview, 'Every man should have the opportunity to sleep with

Elizabeth Taylor – and the rate she's going, every man will'. Well, every man but one it would seem.

Her second husband, actor Michael Wilding, was bisexual and an epileptic. She knew this before marrying him, but neither condition appeared to overly bother her. A reporter summed up the media's disbelief that a woman as vivacious as Liz could deign to wed a man as dull as Wilding, when he wrote, 'the bride wore a dove gray suit, the groom wore an air of surprise'.

A few years after they divorced, Wilding became both Liz's and Richard Burton's agent. When Michael's paramour Marlene Dietrich heard of the marriage she fumed. 'It must be those huge breasts of hers', she snapped. 'He likes them to dangle in his face'. What a little ray of sunshine Marlene was.

Husband number three was entrepreneur and wheeler-dealer Mike Todd. Liz seemed extremely happy with him (as indeed she did, initially, with them all) but he flew his airplane into a mountain before we could find out if they would have gone the distance.

The next starter in the Elizabeth Taylor Marriage Stakes was singer Eddie Fisher. Angela Sweeney, who was his voice coach and former girlfriend, described him as a sexual dynamo. 'He had an organ the size of Sinatra or Cooper', she said, 'and his ability to have sex as often as a dozen times a night was unreal. He would reach climax and immediately have another erection'. She thought his sexual prowess was due to the amount of 'speed' he ingested.

Liz was still wed to Fisher, but heavily involved with Burton, when the latter arrived uninvited at her apartment one evening in Rome, as she and Fisher were entertaining guests. A very drunk Burton walked in and began to sprout Shakespeare at the top of his voice. Then, turning to Liz he roared, 'You are my girl, aren't you?' 'Yes', she quietly answered. 'If you're my girl', he said, 'come over here and stick your tongue down my throat'. She walked to him and kissed him passionately in front of her guests as Fisher slowly stood up and left the room. Weeks later Eddie rang her at home and Burton answered the phone. 'What are you doing in my home?' the exasperated singer asked. 'What do you think I'm doing?' sneered Burton, 'I'm fucking your wife'.

When her longtime friend Peter Lawford visited Liz in 1983 at the Betty Ford Clinic where she was attempting to cure her alcoholism, he brought with him a man he introduced as his cousin. In fact, the financially strapped actor had sold the story of her BFC stint to the *National Enquirer* for $15,000. The 'cousin' was a reporter.

Marriages five, six and seven, to Burton (twice) and senator John Warner just the once, are covered elsewhere in this book so we'll move on to number eight, the one to bulldozer driver Larry Fortensky in 1990. He was a patient she met at the clinic and another alcoholic. The wedding took place at Michael Jackson's Neverland estate and the controversial megastar himself gave the bride away. As the couple took their vows an enterprising reporter actually parachuted into the wedding party from a helicopter!

Of all her trips to the altar her union with Fortensky was the most bizarre. He was a blue-collar worker without money, a monosyllabic man who had never even been on an airplane until she took him to Tangier for some jet-set celebrity bash. When he took her to MacDonald's for lunch it was the first time in her life she had ever been in one of *their* establishments. All they had in common were their alcoholism and their sexual attraction. The alcoholism accelerated as the attraction waned over the eight years they were together. They were from opposite ends of the social spectrum and might just as well have been from two different planets. The greatest surprise is that it lasted as long as it did.

The inimitable Oscar Levant once quipped about her numerous marriages, 'always a bride, never a bridesmaid'. 'Her five husbands', he added, 'have absolutely nothing in common, except Liz'. (Oscar had died by the time she married numbers six through eight).

One of her lovers in the eighties was Saudi arms dealer Adnan Kashoggi, the uncle of Dodi Fayed who later died with Princess Diana in the car crash in Paris in August 1997.

Liz had sex with Frank Sinatra three times by her count. Keen on wedding him, she brought the subject up almost immediately, and Frank took to his heels, especially when he discovered she was pregnant with his child. According to his pal Jilly Rizzo she went to Mexico for an abortion, although she steadfastly denied this.

Alan Royle

One evening at the Ingemar Johanssen-Floyd Patterson title fight at Madison Square Gardens, a complete stranger went up to her as she sat ringside, reached down and pulled out one of her breasts! Turning to the nearby members of the crowd, he yelled, 'Ladies and gentlemen, I ask you – isn't this a beautiful sight?' For once in her life Liz was speechless. She majestically put her breast back where it belonged and watched the bout.

Her eight husbands were not exactly knights in shining armor, far from it. Hilton was an alcoholic and drug addict who beat her and died young from his excesses. Wilding was an alcoholic, epileptic who died broke. MikeTodd was a shady character known to beat his women. Fisher was another alcoholic and addicted to drugs. Burton was a hopeless alcoholic through both their marriages and drank himself to death. John Warner allegedly used her to further his political ambitions and then discarded her. Fortensky was yet another alcoholic wife-beater. When it came to choosing husbands Liz was an eight-time loser.

I Wanted Wings (1941)

Ray Milland was an avid parachutist in his leisure hours. When the opportunity arose, therefore, to don a 'chute while testing an airplane for this movie, he leapt at it. Before he had a chance to exit the aircraft, however, the pilot aborted the jump because he was short on fuel. Upon returning to base Milland was mortified to learn that the 'chute he had so eagerly donned was not a real one. It was only a movie prop!

Jailhouse Rock (1957)

Judy Tyler was the twenty-three year-old who played Peggy Van Alden, Elvis Presley's girlfriend, in *Jailhouse Rock*. Three days after shooting concluded she and her husband were killed in a car crash. Apparently, Presley was infatuated by the recently wed girl and refused to watch the film because of her death.

Jaws (1975)

Peter Benchley has a cameo in the picture as a reporter on the beach. He is the grandson of humorist Robert Benchley and wrote the novel on which the movie is based. It in turn was founded on the 1916 Jersey shark attacks that shocked America. When he strongly objected to the intended ending he was thrown off the set.

The shark weighed twelve tons and took fifteen men using a system of hydraulics to operate it. In the first rushes its eyes crossed and its mouth wouldn't close. Over the course of filming its skin sometimes peeled off, the fins occasionally went in different directions and the salt water tended to turn its teeth pearly white, which required divers to blacken them from time to time. It even sunk once. Other than that it worked perfectly.

The part of Chief Brody's wife went to Lorraine Gary who just happened to be the wife of Sid Scheinberg, the President of Universal. The tension between Robert Shaw and Richard Dreyfuss was genuine. They could not stand each other. The sounds of Susan Backlinie drowning (she was the first

355

victim) were achieved by laying her on her back under a microphone and pouring water down her throat.

The character played by Dreyfuss was supposed to be eaten by the shark while he was in the water inside his 'shark-proof' cage. The twenty-four feet long shark, however, could not be made to appear convincing when it was required to attack the cage. It was decided, therefore, to film a genuine sixteen footer off the coast of Australia, place a midget inside the cage and have the real shark attack him.

Unfortunately, the excellent footage of the real shark attacking the cage was taken *before* the midget could be put inside it. There was a further difficulty. The little guy required *midget* air tanks that only contained twelve minutes of air. That issue quickly became moot, however. After witnessing the attack on the empty cage, the man, understandably, refused to get in it again. In the end, it was agreed to use the footage of the shark attacking the empty cage, but have Dreyfuss evacuate it just in time. Preview audiences stood and applauded his survival. The 'severed head' sequence, one of the scariest moments in the film, was shot as an afterthought in the swimming pool of the film's editor.

In the five months it took to film on Martha's Vineyard, Dreyfuss got to know nearly every waitress on the island. Most were pretty college girls working on their summer vacations. Insiders said he 'cut a swathe through them'.

When John Williams first played the musical score for Spielberg, the director laughed and said, 'that's funny, John, really. But what did you really have in mind for the theme of *Jaws*?' Since then, of course, the *Jaws* theme has become one of the most recognized pieces of music in movie history.

Months before the picture opened Spielberg put to Universal executives his idea of selling to patrons little chocolate sharks that, when bitten, would squirt cherry juice. 'We'll clean up', he said. Wiser heads prevailed and the studio vetoed the idea.

Robert Shaw was half drunk when he delivered the monologue on the sinking of the USS Indianapolis and got the date wrong. It went down on July 30, 1945, not on June 29.

A tank of compressed air will not explode if struck by a bullet as depicted in the film's finale. It will merely decompress and shoot backwards, much like a pricked balloon only more forcefully. While on the subject of the finale, where did the three barrels attached to the shark disappear to when it attacked Brody?

Jaws – the Revenge (1987)

Judith Barsi was a promising child star appearing in a few films, among them Jaws – The Revenge. When she was eleven years old her father shot her dead as she slept and then killed her mother as she came to the girl's aid. He then turned the gun on himself.

Jazz Singer, The (1927)

The first talking picture was a huge gamble for Warner Brothers and cost $500,000 to make. Only two theatres in all of America were capable of utilizing the sound techniques incorporated in the film. If 'sound' did not take on, Warners were out of business.

Technically speaking, *The Jazz Singer* was mostly a silent movie that merely incorporated a couple of musical and dialogue sequences, and it was by no means the result of a new invention. The ability to put sound on film existed from the early days of movies. Edison and others had accomplished it, but deemed the concept impractical and too costly to pursue.

MGM's wonder boy Irving Thalberg was dead wrong when he told his boss, LB Mayer, 'Novelty is always welcome, but talking pictures is just a fad'. Consequently, MGM initially tried to ignore the new innovation.

When the studio came to its senses, the job of 'sound production manager' was allotted to Norma Shearer's brother Douglas. He came up with the idea of having the actors *mime* the words to already recorded music, to save on production costs. The first song to receive this treatment was *The Wedding of the Painted Dolls* in *Broadway Melody*. The film went on to win the Best Picture Oscar.

John Gilbert's voice brought giggles from theatre patrons in his first talkie, but this was more a technical hitch than anything else and was remedied in his next film. His main problem was his inability to discard his mannerisms and gestures that were those of a silent actor. He could not, or *would* not, tone them down. Just how much was done behind the scenes by Mayer to finish his career off altogether is still being debated. Mayer, who hated him and bore a grudge, continued to renew his contract, but would neither use him in decent films, nor loan him out. Lack of exposure saw his public move on to other idols.

Eddie Cantor was the first choice for Jolson's role in *The Jazz Singer,* but he wanted too much money, so the Warner brothers started looking elsewhere. George Jessel was approached next, but he too refused when he heard he would be accepting a Cantor reject. Jolson only agreed to do it after being guaranteed he would get twice his normal fee, one for his acting and one for his talking! He also wisely accepted some Warner Bros. stock as part of the deal.

Jessel owned one of the most renowned and extensive collections of pornography in Hollywood. His last wife was a sixteen year-old starlet whom he married when he was in his forties. He once described Jolson as 'a no good son-of-a-bitch, but the greatest entertainer I've ever seen'.

Jolson was born in Sprednik, Lithuania in 1886, and was a man obsessed with his own celebrity status. By all accounts, his brother Harry was equally talented, so Al paid him $150 a week to stay out of show business!

More than any other performer, Jolson craved public adoration and he didn't care whose toes he stepped on to get it. In 1921, while appearing in a Broadway show entitled *Bongo,* he suddenly walked to the front of the stage and asked the audience if it would rather hear him sing a few of his songs. Much to their disgust the rest of the cast were dismissed, and he sang until the early hours of the morning.

On another occasion he was actually in the audience (watching *Show Girl* on Broadway), when he suddenly leapt to his feet and began to sing along with the show, to wild and thunderous applause. The cast's reaction to this intrusion has been lost to history. Similarly, while wed to Ruby Keeler, he jumped up from the stalls again and sang her a love song, disrupting yet another show.

Jeremiah Johnson (1972)

Will Geer, who plays the mountain man who hunts 'griz', was a former member of the Communist Party and the long-time lover of gay activist Harry Hay. TV enthusiasts will recall him playing grandpa in *The Waltons*.

It would appear this film was inspired by the story of the legendary mountain man John 'Liver-Eatin' Johnson. Like Jeremiah, he went off into the mountains and married a Flathead woman who was killed by the Crow while he was off hunting. And like Jeremiah he killed a Crow in retaliation and that brought a host of disgruntled Crow warriors bent on his assassination. John, however, was not quite as 'civilized' as Jeremiah in his outlook. Over the next fifteen years he is said to have slaughtered 247 members of the tribe – and eaten their livers! Then, just as in the movie, he came across a monument erected by the tribe that was dedicated to his exploits, so he had a change of heart and stopped killing them before he single-handedly wiped out an entire race of people. Well, that's the story, anyway. In later years he worked as a sheriff in Cheyenne, Wyoming.

Jesse James (1939)

Tyrone Power (1914-1958)

Known relationships with men:

Arnaz, Desi
Brando, Marlon
Dantine, Helmut
Flynn, Errol
Gilmore, Jonathan
Goulding, Edmund
Herron, Mark
Hudson, Rock
Hughes, Howard
Moran, Jackie
Purdom, Edmund
Romero, Cesar
Selzer, Richard
Zanuck, Darryl F

Known relationships with women:

Brooks, Phyllis
Callahan, Margaret
Carroll, Madeleine
Charisse, Cyd
Colbert, Claudette
Crawford, Joan
Dandridge, Dorothy
Darr, Alicia
Day, Doris
Dietrich, Marlene
Ekberg, Anita
Faye, Alice

Fleming, Rhonda
Gabor, Eva
Gabor, Zsa Zsa
Gam, Rita
Garland, Judy
Gaynor, Janet
Goddard, Paulette
Grable, Betty
Hayworth, Rita
Henie, Sonja
Johnson, Evie
Loy, Myrna
Matthews, Jessie
O'Hara, Maureen
Pampanini, Silvana
Peron, Eva
Roblee, Mary
Simon, Simone
Stanwyck, Barbara
Tierney, Gene
Turner, Lana
Wheelan, Arleen
Wyman, Jane
Young, Loretta
Zetterling, Mai

Married:

Annabella
Linda Christian & 1 other

When Daryl Zanuck first laid eyes on Power he said the young man looked like a monkey. Ty was so hairy that electrolysis had to be used to separate his hairline from his eyebrows. Rita Hayworth and Barbara Stanwyck had similar treatment for the same problem. Ginger Rogers, on the other hand, refused electrolysis to remove the 'peach fuzz' that covered her entire face. Photographs of her were airbrushed instead.

Actress Alice Faye once considered Power's proposal of marriage, but decided against it. 'I decided he was too fond of the boys for it to work out', she explained. 'He was the best looking thing I've ever seen in my life'. Anne Baxter too said he was 'the handsomest man I ever saw'.

His first marriage to bisexual actress Annabella was arranged by the studio to curb stories about both stars' sexual preferences. Annabella lost her virginity to Errol Flynn. Ty was also one of his lovers.

In his final years, his looks deteriorated by too much alcohol, Power reputedly indulged in group sex parties that greatly saddened his many friends, especially Van and Evie Johnson who were very close to him. During a fencing scene with George Sanders in 1959, on the set of Solomon and Sheba, the forty-four year old Power suffered a heart attack and died before reaching the hospital.

Two months later his son Ty Junior was born. Rock Hudson was named as his godfather. Power's funeral was a circus. Crowds arrived with boxed lunches and cheered as each star drove up to the chapel. Loretta Young turned up direct from the set of a TV show dressed in full Geisha costume.

Jezebel (1938)

Director William Wyler and star Bette Davis had a passionate affair during the making of Jezebel. When Bette had reservations about marrying him, primarily because she did not want her children to grow up with a Jewish father, Wyler sent her an ultimatum. If she did not say yes by the following Wednesday he would marry someone else.

Unaware of the contents of his letter, she did not get around to opening it until it was too late. He married starlet Margaret Tallichet on the Wednesday and Davis was shattered. Not opening his letter was the biggest mistake of her life, she later said. For all that, the marriage was no rebound affair. Wyler and Tallichet stayed together for forty years. Ironically, the next project that saw Davis directed by him was the melodrama The Letter. She later admitted to aborting his baby during their romance.

John & Yoko: A Love Story (1985)

British actor Mark Lindsay was all set to play John Lennon in this 1985 telemovie, until it was discovered his real name was Mark Chapman, the same as that of Lennon's real life assassin. Lindsay was forced to relinquish the role when executives became concerned the public might not believe it was simply a coincidence.

Johnny Belinda (1948)

Jane Wyman was still married to Ronald Reagan when she fell in love with Lew Ayres on the set of *Johnny Belinda*.

Ronnie knew about it and publicly gave her permission to cuckold him. 'Right now, Jane needs very much to have a fling', he said. 'And I intend to let her have it'. After their divorce she told a reporter her husband was 'about as good in bed as he was on the screen'. Ronnie probably took that as a compliment.

Johnny Eager (1941)

The statuesque Beryl Wallace plays Mabel in this. In 1948 she, her impresario lover Earl Carroll, and forty-two others died when their plane crashed into Mount Carmel, Pennsylvania.

Johnny Guitar (1954)

Mercedes McCambridge's feud with Joan Crawford on the set of *Johnny Guitar* became the stuff of legend. They despised each other. Years later McCambridge, restraining herself following Joan's death, said of her, 'She was a mean, tipsy, powerful, rotten egg lady'.

Sterling Hayden also stars in this film and could not stand Crawford either. 'There is not enough money in Hollywood to lure me into making another film with Joan Crawford', he said.

Joy in the Morning (1965)

Richard Chamberlain and his co-star Yvette Mimieux fell out during filming, mostly over her continual taunts about his masculinity. Years later, the French magazine *Nous Deux* reported that he 'came out' during an interview with one of its journalists. Chamberlain's manager was quick to refute the claim on his behalf. Nevertheless, it was quite true, as his biography has since confirmed, albeit decades on.

Jurassic Park (1993)

More children saw *Jurassic Park* in Pakistan than saw all the films released in that nation over the previous forty-five years!

Richard Attenborough asked director Stephen Spielberg for a marvelous death scene. 'Would you prefer a marvelous death scene or a marvelous sequel?' the director laconically asked. Attenborough opted for the extra money and turned up in the sequel.

The concept upon which this film is based is complete balderdash. Using dinosaur DNA to reproduce dinosaurs is virtually impossible. Only a single dinosaur gene (found on a 20 million years old magnolia leaf) has thus far been recovered. The building of a complete organism requires thousands of different genes and *every one of them* is needed for revivification.

The most favorable conditions are necessary just to enable a single gene to survive intact. The chances of these thousands of genes being found intact are negligible, but the problems do not end there. Even a complete set would require a similar complete set of *maternal* gene products already in place within an egg for an embryo to form. A case of impossibility heaped upon impossibility.

The adding of frog DNA to complete the recipe (as suggested in the movie) would simply produce an undeveloped blob. Frogs are not even remotely near dinosaurs genealogically.

Incidentally, Tyrannosaurus Rex and most of the other dinosaurs depicted in *Jurassic Park* stem from the Cretaceous Period and not from the Jurassic Period. Another anomaly occurs when Sam Neill's character says a T-Rex reacts only to movement. Paleontologist or not, there is simply no way he could know that.

Karate Kid, The (1984)

Ralph Macchio was twenty-two years old when he played the 'kid' in this film, and twenty-seven when he portrayed him for the final time in The Karate Kid 111 in 1989.

Kind Hearts & Coronets (1949)

Apart from being a fine actress, Valerie Hobson was also the wife of British War Minister John Profumo, the politician whose career was wrecked when he became involved with call girl Christine Keeler in the 1960s. Unfortunately for him, Keeler was also carrying on an affair with a Soviet attaché named Evgeny Ivanov. Profumo lied to the House of Commons and his very real expectations of becoming Britain's next Prime Minister went up in smoke.

To her great credit Hobson stood by her husband until her death in 1998 at the age of eighty-one. For much of her later life she was involved with Lepra, a leprosy relief charity organization. Her husband, too, devoted himself to charity work in London's East End.

Dennis Price was a bisexual and an alcoholic. Although most of his acquaintances were aware of his sexual preferences, he tried hard to keep it quiet. Hermione Baddeley recalled noticing bruises on his body one evening after they had made love. 'Some of my boy friends knock me about, too', he said. 'I quite enjoy it'. He died in 1973 from cirrhosis of the liver.

Best-remembered as Captain Mainwaring in the TV series *Dad's Army*, Arthur Lowe was unfortunate to fall in love with a self-serving, drunken nymphomaniac who made his life hell. Joan Cooper Lowe played Private Godfrey's sister in the series. Although an amateur actress, she insisted on appearing in whatever shows her husband featured in, a demand that saw him miss his one chance at Hollywood. He spent his best years in minor theatre work in the sticks in England, just so she could 'act' with him. When he died in 1982 she could not even find time to attend the funeral. The widow Lowe was too busy touring.

King Kong (1933)

Adolph Zukor rejected this project outright. He thought the concept of a giant gorilla falling in love with a young woman was just plain stupid. 'You know what a fifty-foot gorilla would see in a five-foot girl?' he scoffed. 'His breakfast!' He's right too. From a scale perspective this dumb story is the equivalent of a guy falling in love with a lady cockroach.

We know it's a fantasy and all, but if Kong could climb up the Empire State Building, why couldn't he climb over the wall on Skull Island?

In this early version, stop-start animation was used for the sequences involving the giant ape. One such sequence showing him walking through the jungle was accomplished using a small rubber model surrounded by jungle consisting of hundreds of tiny budding plants. Because the process required scores of miniscule moves by the model, each one photographed separately, the thirty seconds of actual film took days to complete. When it was finished and the film was run, all the tiny plants that had gradually opened over the days of shooting suddenly bloomed, as if by magic, and ruined the scene. The entire process had to be repeated, this time changing the plants every few hours.

Another problem with stop-start animation involved the lighting. Light globes gradually dim throughout a day's shooting and this gradual fading, while indiscernible to the naked eye in real time, is quite evident when a piece of animated film is run. Consequently, the globes, too, had to be changed several times daily.

A scene (since lost), showing four sailors hurled into a ravine from a log bridge and devoured by giant spiders, stopped the preview audience in their tracks when it was screened in San Bernardino. It was just too grisly for audiences of that time, so the director removed it from the released print.

The director, Merian C Cooper, led a highly adventurous life. He fought against Pancho Villa in Mexico and was shot down behind enemy lines in World War One. In the Second World War he was interned by the Russians in various camps while fighting as a volunteer in the Polish Army.

When Fay Wray, who plays the girl offered up to Kong, asked about the identity of her male co-star she was told, 'You will have the tallest, darkest leading man in Hollywood'. Shots of Kong peeling away her clothing were cut from the original release but were restored in the late sixties. In 1999 an original poster for the picture sold for an incredible $244,500.

King of Kings, The (1927)

HB Warner was a British actor (unrelated to the famous Warner Brothers) who was cast as Jesus in this classic silent film. He was a fifty year-old has-been, chosen by DeMille because he needed a face for Jesus that was not readily recognizable to audiences, but someone who knew how to act. Nobody was greatly surprised when an inebriated Warner (he was a hopeless alcoholic) was discovered stark naked atop an equally naked female extra in his dressing room prior to the picture's release. The young lady threatened to tell the press she had 'slept with Jesus' unless she was sufficiently remunerated. Such a disclosure would have sunk the film so DeMille paid up.

King's Row (1942)

Writer Gore Vidal said of the future President of the United States, 'When Ronald Reagan's career in show business came to an end he was hired to impersonate, first a California governor and then an American president'. When Jack Warner was told Ronnie was running for Governor of California he exclaimed, 'No! No! Jimmy Stewart for governor. Reagan for his best friend'.

Just as he was starting to gain recognition for his performance in *King's Row*, Reagan's rise to stardom was interrupted by America's entry into the Second World War. He joined the services and his career never fully recovered from the hiatus. He stayed in the States (in fact he never even left California), but in all fairness to him, without his contact lenses he was practically blind and totally unfit for active service in a combat unit. William Holden served in the same Army Air Force unit at Culver City. They did *not* get along. Adjutant Reagan kept him at attention for twenty-five minutes while he recited the regulations to him word for word.

First wife, Jane Wyman, left the future President because, 'I just couldn't stand to watch that damn *King's Row* one more time'. Although he only had the second lead in the picture, Ronnie was forever running it on his home screen for the entertainment of his dinner guests, much to her disgust.

He was also an incessant talker. She recalled him describing a baseball game to Ann Sheridan *ball by ball*.

When Wyman interrupted and told him that Ann had no interest in baseball whatsoever, he ignored her and continued with the story until its end. He was formerly a baseball commentator on the radio. 'Don't ask him the time', Wyman warned a friend. 'He'll tell you how to make a clock'.

He was Governor of California before he reached the White House. In a revealing radio interview in 1979 he torpedoed his credibility by telling listeners, 'most air pollution is caused, not by chimneys and vehicle exhausts, but by *plants and trees'*. So, of course, America made him President.

Ann Sheridan also features in *King's Row*. The studio dubbed her 'the Oomph Girl', a nickname she rightly thought was both ridiculous and meaningless. One of her former lovers, Jack Benny, said of her, 'Annie was just a plain, simple girl. She liked her sex simple and her liquor plain. And she liked both of them a lot'.

She had a body like a skinny young man. In fact, she was so devoid of a figure that the studio deemed it necessary to construct for her a chest harness to wear, complete with size 36" rubber breasts. Whenever the contraption annoyed her she would fling it at someone nearby, saying, 'Here, hold my tits will ya?" When required for a scene it was not uncommon to hear her voice booming across the set, 'OK. Who's got my tits?'

Krakatoa: East of Java (1968)

Any casual glance at a map will show Krakatoa as being *west* of Java, not east. Evidently, they don't teach cartography in Hollywood.

In 1997, just six weeks after his daughter Daisy took her own life, Brian Keith shot himself. He was suffering from emphysema and lung cancer and her loss proved to be the final straw.

Kramer vs Kramer (1979)

Justin Henry was just shy of his ninth birthday when he became the youngest ever Oscar nominee for his performance in this movie. He was earlier nominated for a Golden Globe and burst into tears when his name was not read out as the winner. At the Oscars he lost again to seventy-eight year old veteran Melvyn Douglas who refused to attend the event. 'The whole thing is absurd', sniffed the winner. 'Me competing with an eight year-old!'

Meryl Streep recalled when she and Dustin Hoffman first auditioned for this film. 'He came up to me and said I'm Dustin (burp) Hoffman, and he put his hand on my breast. What an obnoxious pig, I thought'.

Krays, The (1990)

Two members of the pop group Spandau Ballet were chosen to depict the brothers Kray. Real life brothers Gary and Martin Kemp were surprise choices but gave convincing performances.

Kremlin Letter, The (1970)

If, like a lot of other people, you are wondering why a letter of any sort (Kremlin or otherwise) does not feature in this movie, you are not alone. Producer Richard Zanuck had no idea either. Director John Huston replied, 'damned if I know', when he was asked the same question. When Noel Behn, who thought up the title *and wrote the book*, was asked about it, he responded, 'Yeah. That confused me to'.

Ladies' Man, The (1961)

Twenty year-old Karyn Kapcinet made her debut in this Jerry Lewis comedy. Two years after its release she was found strangled in her West Hollywood apartment, the murder never being solved. In an interview in 1976, her father said, 'we have a good idea who did it, but nothing we could ever prove'.

Lady and the Tramp (1955)

The Catholic Church found itself universally lampooned after it condemned Disney's classic *Lady and the Tramp* because it portrayed an unwed couple!

Singer Peggy Lee wrote the lyrics for her song *He's a Tramp* and several other tunes featured in the film. Paid a paltry $3,500 for her efforts, she sued Disney for a percentage of the film's profits (up to $90 million at the time), and succeeded in gaining a several million dollars payout.

Lady Sings the Blues (1972)

Many Academy members were offended by methods adopted by Diana Ross's boyfriend Berry Gordy Junior to win her votes in the race for the Best Actress Oscar. Ironically, she might have won on her merits had she not been shot in the foot by Gordy. He took out daily, full-page spreads in the trade papers, featuring Diana in her role as junkie Billie Holliday, one of which showed her sitting on the toilet dressed only in a bra! He also spent a pile on expensive gifts and lavish dinners for members, expecting them to vote for her out of gratitude. Many did not. As a final unintentional nail in her coffin he *publicly* christened her new poodle 'Oscar'. Enough was enough. Diana became an also-ran.

Land of the Pharaohs, The (1955)

Joan Collins only won the lead in this costumer because the girl who tested before her made a complete mess of it. Ivy Nicholson was told by director Howard Hawks to 'just react naturally' when actor Jack Hawkins slaps her. So she sunk her teeth into his arm! Exit Ivy, enter Joan.

Lassie Come Home (1943)

A male dog named Pal acted as Lassie, as did another three Pals over the next few years through to 1951. There was even a radio show starring the famous pooch, in which Pal would do the barking while a human imitator provided the panting, wheezing and growling. Is nothing sacred?

Last of the Mohicans, The (1992)

Wes Studi, who plays the Huron Indian Magua, is a full blood Cherokee and was a schoolteacher before taking up acting. As well as his portrayal of a Huron here, the former Vietnam War veteran has so far played a Mohawk in *The Broken Chain*, a Crow in *Dances with Wolves* and the Apache shaman Geronimo in *Geronimo: An American Legend*.

The part of the Mohican Chingachgook is played by one of the founders of the American Indian Movement (AIM), Russel Means.

Laura (1944)

Dana Andrews plays the detective who falls in love with Laura, and was the real life brother of actor Steve Forrest. Andrews' career was ruined by alcoholism. In 1972 he did a series of TV advertisements for Alcoholics Anonymous. 'I'm Dana Andrews, and I'm an alcoholic. I don't drink anymore, but I used to - all the time'.

Gene Tierney (1920-1991)

Known relationships:

Albert, Eddie
Arnez, Desi
Aumont, Jean-Pierre
Douglas, Kirk
Fonda, Henry
Hartford, Huntington
Kennedy John F
Khan, Prince Aly
Manciewicz, Joseph

Mature, Victor
Morley, Robert
Power, Tyrone
Rosenberg, Leland
Rubirosa, Porfirio
Stauffer, Teddy
Sterling, Robert
Tracy, Spencer
Vallee, Rudy
Zanuck, Darryl F

Gene Tierney plays the title role. Her first child, Daria, was born deaf and hopelessly retarded due to Tierney's exposure to German measles during her pregnancy. A star struck young woman who was suffering from measles, had risen from her sickbed to attend the Hollywood Canteen during the war, where she came in contact with the actress. 'Everyone told me I shouldn't go', the woman herself told Tierney when she again approached her at a tennis match years later, 'but I just had to. You were my favorite'.

It may or may not be connected to her tragic tale, but Agatha Christie's 1962 book The Mirror Crack'd centers on a famous actress who poisons a woman because she gave her German measles during her first month of pregnancy. It was not widely known, but Tierney suffered from mental instability throughout the forties when at the height of her popularity.

Clifton Webb was a ballroom dancer in the 1920s, before he opted to change to acting as a profession. Although he first appeared in a movie in 1920, it would be a further twenty-four years before he scored his first speaking role, which happened to be in Laura.

Throughout his career he always took his mother, Maybelle, to public appearances as his escort. When she died in 1960 he was inconsolable, so much so that Noel Coward rather unkindly referred to him as 'the world's oldest surviving orphan'. Openly gay, he was close to Rudolph Valentino in their youth and is said by several historians to have been James Dean's mentor in the early fifties.

Lavender Hill Mob, The (1952)

Arthur Mullard gained popularity in Britain through his appearances in shows such as *Bootsie & Snudge, Vacant Lot* and *Hancock's Half Hour*. After his death, his daughter Barbara told how he used her as a sex slave from the time she was thirteen, a fact known to her mother who chose to hold the girl responsible! Mullard often beat his wife, even knocking out some of her teeth on one occasion. She would later commit suicide. In his will he left Barbara just five thousand pounds, the remaining 245 thousand pounds going to (believe it or not) the National Children's Home.

Lawrence of Arabia (1962)

At times during filming in Jordan the temperature in the shade reached 51.7 degrees Celsius (125 degrees Fahrenheit) and actually caused thermometers to explode. Marlon Brando and Albert Finney both rejected the role of Lawrence. French actor Alain Delon refused the role of Sheriff Ali and the General Allenby part was turned down by Cary Grant. Noel Coward did not appreciate Peter O'Toole's portrayal of Lawrence. 'If you'd been any prettier', he told him, 'the film would have been called *Florence of Arabia*'.

The Arab League banned the picture because they said it showed their people in a bad light. President Nasser, however, took the time to watch it and gave it the green light to be screened uncut in Egypt where the picture broke all existing records. Nevertheless, it is still banned in most Arab countries and has never been shown in Turkey for reasons apparent in the film.

Although it was never suggested in the movie, the real Lawrence had homosexual relationships with both Sherif Ali and the young Arab boy Dahoum. In fact, the whole picture is more fiction than fact. Lowell Thomas, the writer portrayed as Jackson Bentley by Arthur Kennedy, was particularly unimpressed. 'They only got two things right – the camels and the sand', he said. There is, for example, no evidence whatsoever of Lawrence even being present when the Turkish column was massacred, much less participating in the slaughter. That aside, Thomas' broad criticism seems overly harsh.

Sam Spiegel, who made both *Lawrence Of Arabia* and *The Bridge On The River Kwai*, was the producer of caricature, a loud, fat cat, movie mogul, complete with cigar, gold chains, pinky rings and a bevy of voluptuous women always at his chubby fingertips. Before hitting it big with

'Lawrence' he was deported from Britain for writing bad cheque and perpetrating other frauds.

When he was found dead in his bathtub on the French West Indies island of St. Martin, the hotel manager asked another guest, actor Peter Ustinov, to give him the kiss of life. 'Alive or dead, I would not kiss Sam Spiegel', he shuddered.

Libeled Lady (1936)

The dress worn by Jean Harlow in this film is the same one in which she was buried in June 1937.

Lifeboat (1944)

Hitchcock's penchant for making brief personal appearances in his films struck a snag in this one because almost all the action takes place in a lifeboat on the high seas. He overcame this seemingly insurmountable problem by having a newspaper float by in which there appears a picture of him advertising weight reduction.

Lifeboat was mostly filmed in a large studio tank, equipped with an entry and exit ladder attached to the side. Tallulah Bankhead never wore underwear and delighted in ascending the ladder *ahead* of the all-male cast, and descending *after* them.

A cameraman actually complained to Hitchcock about her habit of exposing herself. When the director told him the problem was not really his department, the man asked, 'Well, whose department is it then?' 'I would say wardrobe', replied Hitchcock, 'or possibly hair dressing'.

The bi-sexual actress loved to exhibit herself whenever the opportunity arose, especially at parties where she would often perform cartwheels and handstands atop pianos, as always minus her underwear. She was also promiscuous as all get out with either sex. One of her myriad lovers, actress Patsy Kelly claimed, 'Tallulah had more girlfriends than Errol Flynn'. And she had more boyfriends than girlfriends.

During the course of the production she made it her business to seduce co-star John Hodiak the moment she learned he was generously endowed. The following morning, much to his embarrassment, she loudly proclaimed to the cast and crew that he was, indeed, 'a two-hander'!

Walter Slezak was good as the ruthless and cunning German U-Boat commander rescued by the occupants of the lifeboat. An Austrian by birth he loathed the Third Reich, yet had to contend with Bankhead referring to him throughout the shoot as 'that Goddam Nazi'. In 1983 he committed suicide by shooting himself.

Tallulah Bankhead (1902-1968)

Known relationships with women:

Astaire, Adele
Barrymore, Ethel
Carpenter, Louisa
Collier, Constance
Cornell, Katherine
Crawford, Joan
Day, Frances

De Acosta, Mercedes
Dietrich, Marlene
Francis, Kay
Garbo, Greta
Holiday, Billie
Holman, Libby
Johnson, Kaye
Kelly, Patsy
Le Gallienne, Eva
Levien, Sonya
Lillie, Beatrice
Logan, Ella
McDaniel, Hattie
Munson, Ona
Nazimova, Alla
Scott, Lizabeth
Stanwyck, Barbara
Tashman, Lilyan
Taylor, Laurette
Thorndike, Sybil
Vaughan, Sarah
Williams, Hope
Winwood, Estelle
Yurka, Blanche

Known relationships with men:

Armstrong, Louis
Barrymore, John
Benchley, Robert
Bernstein, Leonard
Boyer, Charles
Brando, Marlon
Brynner, Yul
Bushman, Francis X
Chaplin, Charles
Churchill, Winston
Cook, Donald
Cooper, Gary
Dantine, Helmut

De Bosdari, Anthony
Dorsey, Tommy
Du Maurier, Gerald
Durante, Jimmy
Fairbanks Jr, Douglas
Flynn, Errol
Fonda, Henry
Grant, Cary
Hodiak, John
Howard, Leslie
Hughes, Howard
Hutchinson, Leslie
Johnson, Kerry
Lord Arlington
March, Fredric
Marx, ChicoWilliams, Hugh
Marx, Groucho
Meredith, Burgess
Montgomery, Robert
Murrow, Ed
Raft, George
Ray, Johnnie
Remarque, Erich
Ryan, Robert
Sanders, George
Strut, Napier
Tilden, Bill
Wanger, Walter
Weissmuller, Johnny
Whitney, John
Williams, Tennessee

The list of her non-celebrity lovers is much longer. She boasted of having more than 5,000 of them!

At one Hollywood soiree, she rushed over to Errol Flynn, roaring, 'Errol dahling', and buried her face in his crotch. That same evening she encountered Lillian Gish who commented on how well the years had treated them both. 'Dear Lillian', retorted Tallulah, 'here we are still surviving after all these years. You with your face lifted and your vagina dropped, and me with my vagina lifted and my face dropped'.

She came to Hollywood in 1932 to make *The Devil and the Deep,* 'for the money, and to fuck that divine Gary Cooper', she openly told all and sundry. She soon got her wish and contracted a dose of gonorrhea from Coops into the bargain.

In a ladies powder room one day she discovered there was no toilet paper in her cubicle. Peering under the door into the next stall, she asked the lady there if she could spare some. When informed there was no paper in that cubicle either, she proposed, 'Well then darling, do you have two fives for a ten?'

When asked by a lady friend if she 'remembered the minuet' she responded with, 'dahling, I can't even remember the men I *slept* with'. She delighted *most* of George Cukor's Christmas guests one year when she slipped out of her dress, grabbed a bunch of violets and lay naked on a marble bench in his foyer posing as Goya's *Nude Maja*. A matronly grand dame of the theatre was flabbergasted.

At another shindig, actor Ivor Novello was not amused when he and the other guests were treated to the sight of their hostess wearing a see-through dress with, of course, nothing underneath it. She promptly put her legs up on the dining table and then slid off revealing herself to the throng.

After witnessing this and listening to her interminable chatter about herself, Novello and his lover, Richard Rose, decided enough was enough and got up to leave. 'Dahling, I haven't shocked you, have I?' mocked Tallulah. 'You haven't shocked me at all', he replied, 'but you have bored me intensely'.

She managed to offend just about everybody in Hollywood, in particular the hierarchy. At a studio bash one evening she serenaded LB Mayer to the tune of *Bye Bye Blackbird*, incorporating her own lines, 'pack up all my cares and woes, here I go, singing low, bye, bye, Jewbird'. LB smoldered. When he chastised her about her outrageous private life, she checkmated him by threatening to publicize her romps with several of his top stars, both male and female.

Her first words on meeting Joan Crawford were, 'dahling, I've had an affair with your husband. You'll be next'. She often said she called everybody darling because she simply could not remember names. 'I once introduced a friend of mine as Martini. Her name was actually Olive', she said.

She defined herself as 'ambi-sextrous'. One of her more outrageous stunts was to sprinkle some of Marlene Dietrich's gold dust hair spray on her own pubic area, and then expose herself to passers-by on the set, exclaiming, 'Guess what I've been doing?'

While touring with Dietrich's nineteen year-old daughter, Maria, the middle-aged Tallulah caused an uproar in Columbus, Ohio, when she was observed blind drunk and buck naked chasing the unfortunate girl through the corridors of a hotel. She often hosted nude orgies in her apartment and delighted in answering the door completely naked to deliverymen, telegram boys, or whomever, delivering her standard greeting, 'Darling, come in. What'll you have?'

By 1940 she was using marijuana, cocaine and other chemicals in rectal suppositories. Tennessee Williams said she would insert one and 'turn into a Zombie and pass out on the floor'. Williams actually wrote the character Blanche Dubois in *A Streetcar Named Desire* specifically for Tallulah, but by the time it was ready to be produced she was too old for the role.

In a surge of patriotic fervor during the Second World War, she swore off all alcohol 'until the British re-take Dunkirk'. She resorted instead to drinking Spirits of Ammonia in Coca Cola, unaware its alcohol content was around 65%. When the love of her life, a British fighter pilot named Lord Arlington, was shot down and killed in the Battle of Britain, she was heartbroken and mourned him until her death.

The Stork Club's owner Sherman Billingsley dropped by her New York flat one evening with two friends in tow and found her in bed, as usual stark naked. When she informed him he had been 'chosen' to service her for the night, he took fright and bolted. His companions stayed behind and with Tallulah formed a *ménage a trois* for the evening.

A *Time* magazine researcher once asked her press agent, Irving Hoffman, about her reputation as a nymphomaniac. 'For instance', he enquired, 'have you ever made it with her?' Hoffman lowered his voice and said, 'She'll kill me if she ever hears I've said it, but the answer is 'no'.

Her marriage to John Emery (who was said to be the illegitimate son of John Barrymore) was merely one of convenience. 'It was his no-comings rather than his shortcomings that destroyed the union', she said. She joined him for a brief fling years later, 'just to prove that there were *still* no hard feelings'.

In 1965, while appearing in *Die, Die My Darling* with Donald Sutherland, the sixty-three year old Tallulah startled him by walking into his dressing room completely nude. 'What's the matter darling?' she asked. 'Haven't you ever seen a blonde before?' Throughout her life she surrounded herself with young men who were mostly gay and ready to satisfy her every whim. She referred to them as her 'caddies'.

When a stranger in the street asked her late in life if she really was Tallulah Bankhead, she replied, 'what's left of her'. 'They used to photograph Shirley Temple through gauze', she once commented. 'They should photograph me through linoleum'.

She made no apologies for her behavior. 'If I had my life to live over again, I would make the same mistakes, only sooner'. She was a substance abuser all her life. 'My father warned me about men and booze', she said, 'but he never mentioned a word about women and cocaine. Cocaine isn't habit forming', she added, 'I should know. I've been using it for years'.

At dinner parties or in restaurants, she would loudly exclaim to a recently arrived actor, 'I've slept with every man at this table and you're gonna be next'. Often she would embrace the frumpiest woman at a gathering and bellow, 'you must know by now that I'm mad about you!'

She all but wrecked a society wedding by loudly proclaiming about the bride and groom, 'I've had both of them, darling – and neither of them is any good'. When asked if she kept a diary, she responded, 'only good girls keep diaries. Bad girls don't have time'. The incomparable Tallulah Bankhead died during the 1968 Asian flu epidemic. Her last words were 'codeine...bourbon'. Beryl Reid, perhaps, best summed up her life: 'At least she didn't die wondering'.

Life of Brian (1979)

This movie was made by Hand Made Films, a company owned by ex-Beatle George Harrison. In fact, George has a cameo as Mr. Papadopolous of 'the Mount' who utters a single word, 'ullo', in a distinct Liverpudlian accent. *Life of Brian* was banned in its entirety as blasphemous in Runnymede England, even though not a single cinema existed within the council's boundaries.

Graham Chapman, who plays Brian, was a homosexual who died from AIDS in 1989. When the National Viewers and Listeners Association wrote to the Monty Python crew warning them that one of their stars was gay, the cast wrote back assuring the group, 'We have found out who it is and we have taken him out and killed him'.

'Graham Chapman was a looney', said fellow Python Eric Idle, '...who could reduce any drinking party to a shambles by consuming half a distillery and then crawl round the floor kissing all the men and groping all the women'.

John Cleese's wife Connie Booth played the maid in his hit TV series *Fawlty Towers*.

Lili (1953)

Best remembered for playing Kitty in the western TV series *Gunsmoke*, Amanda Blake made just four films for MGM and this was one of them. Married five times, the last of these to a bisexual estate agent, she was virtually sentenced to death by him when he gave her AIDS. Being a forty-cigarettes a day smoker, she also contracted cancer of the tongue in 1974, but it was AIDS that killed her fifteen years later.

Limelight (1952)

In this movie Buster Keaton and Charlie Chaplin perform a vaudeville duet. Chaplin, whose film it was, drastically cut down Keaton's performance when he became concerned it might upstage his own. Made in 1951, *Limelight* won an Oscar for Best Score in 1972! By Academy rules a picture does not become eligible for Oscars until it has been shown in a Los Angeles theatre, and that did not happen in this case until twenty years after it first saw the light of day.

Lion King, The (1994)

This was the highest grossing animated film of the 20th century, raking in a massive $772 million. It was originally supposed to be titled King of the Jungle, until someone astutely pointed out that lions do not live in the jungle.

Lipstick (1976)

Margaux Hemingway appears in this as the rape victim, Chris McCormick. Her younger sibling Mariel also gets a bit playing her little sister. Margaux overdosed on phenobarbital in 1996 at the age of forty-one, her decomposing body only being identified later through dental records. She was the fifth member of her ill-fated family to suicide.

Little Big Man (1970)

Wild Bill Hickock was shot dead in the Number Ten Saloon in Deadwood in 1876 by a demented little cross-eyed man named Jack McCall. Demented or not, Jack was not quite as dumb as he looked. When asked why he shot the famous gunfighter in the back of the head instead of facing him down, he replied, 'I didn't want to commit suicide'.

Curiously, the bullet that ploughed through Bill's skull lodged in the hand of one of his poker-playing pals, a man named Captain Frank Massey. He purposefully carried the slug, still embedded in his hand, for the remainder of his life, and delighted in announcing to anyone who would listen, 'Gents, the bullet which killed Wild Bill has come to town'. It was a great way to get free drinks.

Little Miss Marker (1934)

Dorothy Dell plays the nightclub singer Bangles Carson in this Shirley Temple vehicle, and was a childhood friend of Dorothy Lamour. In June of the year this picture was released, she was killed instantly, with her lover, when their car plunged down an embankment and struck a telephone pole. She was not yet twenty years old.

Little Women (1933)

When Joan Bennett's husband, Walter Wanger, found out about her affair with Hollywood agent Jennings Lang, he confronted the man and shot him in the testicles! The outcome from all this was Lang lost a testicle and Joan lost her career. The public chose to blame her entirely for the altercation, and she was quickly abandoned by her studio as well. Wanger served a couple of months' prison-time.

Lives of a Bengal Lancer (1934)

Richard Cromwell features here as Lieutenant David Stone, the son of the Lancers' CO. He was married to the young and naïve Angela Lansbury at the time, but walked out on her within the year, unable to cope with his homosexuality. His sexual preferences were known to nearly everyone except his nineteen year-old bride. Howard Hughes was one of his lovers, in fact. Cromwell later played Henry Fonda's brother in *Jezebel*, but then his career lost momentum.

Lodger, The (1925)

Ivor Novello was the star of this silent version of *The Lodger*. He also wrote the classic World War 1 song *Keep the Home Fires Burning*. Sometime after that, he was paid to help write the script for the first Tarzan movie, and it was he who came up with the immortal line, 'Me Tarzan , you Jane'.

Because he was a matinee idol in Britain, it was decided to alter the ending of *The Lodger*, and show him *not* to be the killer. The same thing happened with Cary Grant in *Suspicion* over a decade later, and for the same reason. By 1932, Novello's star was on the wane, so the sound remake had him turn out to be the killer after all.

Some sources claim he was the only man known to have had a sexual relationship with Winston Churchill.

Lolita (1962)

In a 1979 *Screen International* interview Shelley Winters said, 'When I did *Lolita* with James Mason, I had to be given drugs to calm me when I was doing a scene in bed with him. In *Alfie,* when I was supposed to be on top of Michael Caine, I had little pillows placed all over his body so we wouldn't touch'.

Shelley Winters (1920-2006)

Known relationships:

Blake, Robert
Brady, Scott
Brando, Marlon
Colman, Ronald

Connery, Sean
Cord, Alex
Dailey, Dan
Douglas, Kirk
Finney, Albert
Flynn, Errol
Gable, Clark
Garfield, John
Granger, Farley
Hayden, Sterling
Holden, William
Hughes, Howard
Ireland, John
Kennedy, Joe
Kennedy, John F
Lancaster, Burt
Mailer, Norman
Mitchum, Robert
Olivier, Laurence
Quinn, Anthony
Ray, Nicholas
Stevenson, Adlai
Thomas, Dylan
Tierney, Lawrence
Tone, Franchot
Walker, Robert

Married:

Anthony Franciosa & 3 others

Of her tempestuous marriage to Tony Franciosa, Shelley said, 'I'll never forget the night I brought my Oscar home, and Tony took one look at it and I knew my marriage was over'.

As a young starlet she was invited by Yvonne de Carlo to a party at Errol Flynn's home. While there she observed both

Flynn and Clark Gable being treated by a doctor in an adjoining room. 'He cut a little flap of skin on the back of the right shoulder blade, inserted some kind of capsule into it, then put a stitch in the skin, closing it... no regular doctor has been able to explain it to me', she recalled. 'But that's what I saw'.

De Carlo went off with Gable and Shelley spent the weekend romping with Flynn. She light-heartedly wrote in her memoirs of the 'terrible' dilemma that confronted her; whether to sleep with Clark Gable or Errol Flynn. She nailed Gable later. Dilemma solved.

In the twilight of her career she looked for work on television. When asked by a young executive (who clearly did not know her) to read for a role, she stormed out and went home. Returning the following morning, she produced not one, but *two* Oscars, which she plonked down on the table in front of her. 'Now', she said to the same young man, 'do you still want me to read?'

Sue Lyon gained international fame playing the title role in Lolita. Married at seventeen, she caught her husband in bed with another woman and divorced him. Her second union was to a black American football player a couple of years later. Prejudice against mixed marriages caused them to flee to Spain to live, but that marriage also ended on the rocks.

In 1973, the by then twenty-seven year old actress decided to wed a convicted murderer who was serving a life sentence in a penitentiary. They divorced a year later.

Eddie Fisher claims he and Richard Burton were briefly intimate with her. According to him, she wanted to find out for herself which man was the better lover, so she tried out each in turn.

Longest Day, The (1962)

For the shooting of the Omaha Beach landing, a separate camera was trained on each of the major stars. They were instructed to stay within their prescribed beach location and not to wander out of the camera's scope, regardless of what occurred around them. Eddie Albert lost track of his allotted area and wandered about in confusion while the cameras continued to roll. The shots of him ended up in the final cut because his bewilderment looked perfectly natural.

Among the myriad of stars gathered together for this film was the lovely Irina Demick who scored the role of a French Resistance fighter. The ageing Darryl Zanuck, whose project it was, had finally left his much-maligned wife and was squiring Miss Demick at the time.

Zanuck was refused the use of US Army tanks and landing craft for his epic, until he hit upon giving Peter Lawford a part in the film. Lawford, being the brother-in-law of John F Kennedy, approached the President about the problem and Zanuck got everything he required.

Richard Todd plays John Howard, the leader of the Parachute Regiment that attacks Pegasus Bridge on D-Day. Back in 1944, Todd himself was involved in the raid as a young paratrooper. In one scene in the movie he is required to have a brief conversation with a young officer who was meant to be *him* back in 1944! 'I was in effect standing beside myself talking to myself', he said.

Jeffrey Hunter has a brief but memorable role as the young Marine who succeeds in blowing a hole through the German fortifications on Omaha beach, but is killed in the process. In 1969, at the age of forty-three, he fell down some stairs and underwent brain surgery to save his life, but died after the operation.

Curt Jurgens spent World War Two in a Hungarian concentration camp because of derogatory remarks he made about Nazi Propaganda Minister Joseph Goebbels. French actress Arletty had her head shaved and was jailed for two months following the Liberation of France because she slept with a German Luftwaffe officer during the war. 'My heart is French', she said in her defense. 'But my arse is international'.

Long Gray Line, The (1955)

Maureen O'Hara recounted walking in on director John Ford in his office one day, only to find him passionately kissing 'one of the most famous leading men in the picture business.' She would not disclose who it was. On another occasion, he deliberately tried to embarrass her at a meeting by drawing penises of all shapes and sizes as they spoke.

On the set he continually berated and insulted her in front of the entire crew. 'Well, did Herself have a good shit this morning?' he would roar at the top of his voice. 'Come on, move that big ass of yours!' was another of his much-used insults. He had been writing her letters for months professing his love, but she continued to ignore them.

Long, Long Trailer, The (1954)

This comedy features the husband and wife team of Lucille Ball and Desi Arnaz, the greatly loved stars of television's *I Love Lucy* series. Arnaz was a bisexual Cuban who fled the island during the 1933 revolution. At high school in the USA his best friend was Al Capone Jr. His endless succession of lovers was only matched by his utter lack of discretion. The combination placed a fatal strain on his marriage.

In 1944, Lucy tired of Desi's womanizing and filed for divorce. He called her the night before the hearing, took her to dinner and then spent the night with her in a hotel room. The next morning she got up and attended the hearing as planned, then returned to him at the hotel for an afternoon and evening of lovemaking. By California law a couple having sex together at any time during the one year 'cooling off' period following the filing, automatically invalidate the petition. Next day the divorce was called off and they remained together for a further seventeen years!

When *I Love Lucy* was being planned, CBS did not want Desi Arnaz in the series at all. Lucy told them, 'No Desi – no Lucy', so he was reluctantly taken on board. To the studio's dismay he then insisted on top billing! *That* problem was resolved by calling the program 'I Love Lucy'. Desi, being the 'I', gave him first billing, so to speak.

A spin-off from the series was planned to star Vivian Vance and William Frawley, the character actors who played Ethel and Fred Mertz in the show. Vance rejected it out of hand, despite being offered $50,000 just to do the pilot episode. 'I loathed Bill Frawley', she said, 'and the feeling was mutual. Whenever I received a new script, I raced through it, praying that there wouldn't be a scene where we had to be in bed together'.

Frawley was an alcoholic and a mean-spirited man who did not get along with anyone on the set. He was furious when he learned of Vivian's refusal (he needed the money), and refused to speak to her again, except when work necessitated it. He dropped dead from a heart attack while strolling on Sunset Boulevard in 1966.

When Lucy and Desi bought RKO Studios following their enormous success with the series, Lucy's first action was to fire the man who fired *her* back in 1935 when she was a struggling young actress. She sold the studio (Desilu) in 1968 to Gulf & Western for $17 million.

When it was decided her TV character should have a child to coincide with Lucy's real life pregnancy, the network forbade the use of the word 'pregnant' in the script. It was finally agreed her condition would always be referred to as 'expecting'. Throughout this period the company had clerics from the four major American religions on the set during all filming, to monitor any script references that might be seen as offensive to either the Catholic, Protestant, Jewish or Baptist faiths. 'Desi is a loser, a gambler, an alcoholic, a skirt-chaser...a financially smart man but self-destructive. He's just a loser'. So said Lucy when the couple divorced, and she was right. He would often go to the Hollywood Burlesque Theatre and collect five or six strippers or chorines, then take them back to his hotel suite for sex. They would wait in the parlor, drinking his liquor, while he took them one at a time into the bedroom until he had serviced them all.

Phyllis Diller found working with Lucy difficult. 'Lucille Ball was a control freak', she said. 'Had to be in charge of everything. Never saw a woman who took her comedy so seriously'.

Lost Weekend, The (1945)

Fearing a loss of sales, the liquor companies of America unsuccessfully offered the studio $5 million to shelve this picture about a hopeless alcoholic. It was made in the days when test marketing of new films was conducted by having cards filled out by preview audiences. Billy wilder was the director and he recalled perusing one such card. It read: '*The Lost Weekend* told me that it was a great movie, but I should take out all the stuff about drinking and alcoholism'.

Lost World, The (1960)

Towards the end of filming some genius at Fox decided to cut overheads by removing the coffee urn from the set. Cast and crew instantly went on strike and refused to return to work until it was restored. At a nearby sound stage Marilyn Monroe was making *Let's Make Love* when she heard of the dispute. 'I'll get your coffee back!' she told her friend Michael Rennie. 'I'll go on strike too, until they return your coffee'. And she did. The urn was back on the set that day.

Love Affair (1994)

This is Katharine Hepburn's final movie appearance, in which she plays the spirited aunt of Warren Beatty. For reasons known only to her she agreed to utter the 'f' word, the only time she did so on screen in her entire career. Now *why* would she do that and become another one of the herd after all those years?

Love at First Bite (1979)

During the Vietnam War George Hamilton conveniently dated Lynda Bird Johnson, the daughter of US President Lyndon Johnson. On being drafted for combat duty, George allegedly used the connection to have his call-up deferred on the grounds of being 'his mother's and his brother's sole support'. A hue and cry ensued. By the time he was re-classified as A1, in March 1967, he was twenty-seven years old and too old for the draft.

Love Happy (1950)

This was the final Marx Brothers film and it is not very good. The picture was slapped together to help pay off some of Chico's massive gambling debts. Whereas Harpo never gambled at all, Chico could never stop. When asked how much he had lost over the years, he replied, 'Find out how much money Harpo has. That's how much I've lost'.

The climactic rooftop chase among neon signs was added at the last moment because financing of the picture had run out. Companies were paid to have their names put on the signs.

Marilyn Monroe has a 38 seconds scene here, for which she received just $500 plus a screen credit, 'Introducing Marilyn Monroe'. It was actually her *fourth* film. She recounted how the 58 year-old Groucho whispered to her off camera, 'you have the prettiest ass in the business.' Then he propositioned her. 'I'm sure he meant it in the nicest way', she said. As far as we know, she turned him down.

Chico Marx died in 1961 at the age of seventy-four. Harpo was the next to go, three years later, aged seventy-five. 'He inherited all my mother's good qualities', said Groucho of him, 'kindness, understanding, and friendliness. I got what was left'. Both Groucho and Gummo shuffled off in 1977 and Zeppo was the last to go in 1979.

Love is a Many Splendored Thing (1955)

Because this film starred his wife Jennifer Jones, David O Selznick sent scores of memos regarding all aspects of its direction to director Henry King, even though Selznick was not actually producing the picture. Finally, an exasperated King sent him an ultimatum. King could either stop production to read the memos, or continue production and not read them. Selznick got the message.

Lovely to Look at (1952)

Zsa Zsa Gabor (1917 -)

Known relationships:

Attaturk, Kemal
Bautzer, Greg
Burton, Richard
Carson, Johnny
Connery, Sean
Guinle, Jorge
Hays, Hal
Henreid, Paul
Hervia, Anton
Hilton, Nicky
Hughes, Howard
Johnson, Edward
Karl, Harry
Kennedy, John F
Khan, Prince Aly
Kissinger, Henry
Klotz, Herbert
Lanza, Mario
Paley, William
Pignitari, Baby
Power, Tyrone
Prince Philip Mountbatten
Ritchie, Bob
Rubirosa, Porfirio
Russo, Gianni
Sinatra, Frank
Stompanato, Johnny
Todd, Mike
Tone, Franchot

Trujillo, Ramfis

Married:

George Sanders & 8 others

This is one of several movies in which Zsa Zsa Gabor provided decoration. In fact, she was more like a professional guest star or cameo than a genuine movie actress. When she danced the Twist at the Peppermint Lounge one evening, writer Earl Wilson was on hand to record the moment. His article started the dance craze that swept the world.

Just how much of her autobiography, *One Life Is Not Enough*, is fact, and how much is fabrication, will probably never be known. Among her claims are the following:

She was named Miss Hungary at the age of fourteen, but was disqualified because of her age. This appears to be true.

Her claim that she was Junior Fencing Champion of Hungary is questionable.

She says she married a thirty-five year-old Turkish diplomat when she was fifteen. Apparently true. The union was never consummated, which seems highly unlikely in light of her later form.

Instead, she says she lost her virginity in the same year to none other than the redoubtable fifty-one year old legend Kemal Attaturk and was his mistress for several months. That *might* explain her husband's failure (or reluctance) to consummate their marriage, but her stories are open to much speculation.

While wed to billionaire Conrad Hilton she managed to find time to simultaneously sleep with her stepson Nicky.

Her marriage to George Sanders foundered because, as she often said, both were in love with the same person – George. She did concede that he was *one* of the true loves of her life. Bizarrely, he once dared her to seduce a Catholic priest. So she did.

Her sixth husband, Jack Ryan, was the designer of the original Barbie Doll.

In the seventies she was asked to be the spokesperson for the worldwide launching of the Hungarian toy, the Rubik's Cube, presumably because she herself was Hungarian. She received a fee of $25,000 for doing absolutely nothing and surprised nobody with her opening words on the podium: 'What am I here for dahlink?'

Her arrest and eventual conviction in 1989 over an altercation with a traffic cop (she slapped his face), unaccountably made headlines around the world. Her husband Prince Frederick von Anhalt Duke of Saxony scarcely helped her cause when he sniffed to the media, 'the rich and famous should be judged differently. This city couldn't live with the little people's tax money'. The judge thought otherwise and slapped Zsa Zsa with three days jail, 120 hours community service and a $12,350 fine. Hopefully, the fine enabled the city to live just a little bit longer.

'I have never hated a man enough to give his diamonds back', she once admitted. 'I am a marvelous housekeeper.

Every time I leave a man I keep his house'. That last remark has been attributed to at least a dozen other celebrities, so she probably did not originate it.

In the middle of Dominican playboy Porfirio Rubirosa's lengthy affair with Zsa Zsa he heard of the failure of heiress Barbara Hutton's latest marriage. Since he was almost broke, he switched his affections to her instead, and within a week or so she accepted his proposal of marriage. The union lasted fifty-three days. The divorce settlement left 'Rubi' with gifts valued at over a million dollars, plus $2.5 million in cash. In all the exercise netted him the equivalent of $66,000 a day while it lasted.

Not content with ripping off Hutton he next turned his attention to Doris Duke, also one of the wealthiest women in the world. 'Rubi was sweet', said Duke, 'but we weren't married more than a few hours and he was already diddling the maid'. His method of seduction was about as basic and crass as it gets. He would ask a woman to dance with him and immediately place her hand on his penis (which seemed to be forever in a semi-erect state). If she reacted unfavorably, he would move on to another and try again. French waiters still refer to their peppermills as 'Rubirosas' in deference to his reputed sixteen-inch (?) organ. He died in a car crash in France in 1965 at the age of fifty-six.

Loving You (1957)

Elvis Presley's parents, Gladys and Vernon, appear as extras in a concert audience during this film. His mum's maiden name, incidentally, was the same as film star Mary Pickford's real name, Gladys Smith. After his beloved mother died in 1958 Elvis refused to watch *Loving You* ever again.

While making *Loving You* he enjoyed affairs with two of its players. Barbara Hearns had a bit part and Dolores Hart was his co-star, not only in this but also in *King Creole* the following year. Miss Hart would later retire from movies and become a nun, calling herself Sister Dolores. We don't know how many nuns slept with Elvis, (assuming they were intimate, of course), but it would be a good bet Sister Dolores may very well be the sole member of a unique club.

Love Me Tender (1956)

The original title for this picture was to have been The Reno Brothers, but once Elvis Presley's yet to be recorded single Love Me Tender received advance orders for 400,000 copies, the name was quickly changed to cash in on the tune's anticipated success.

Elvis's hair is considerably darker when he sings the title tune than at any other time in the movie. That is because the song was added later, after he had dyed his hair black. When he arrived in Hollywood for his movie debut in this picture he was actually a blond.

It was only after his stint in Germany on National Service that he emerged with bluish-black hair. His biographers say he dyed his locks black to emulate his hero Roy Orbison. It is difficult not to laugh at him in this film as he belts out Rock & Roll and swivels his hips to the squeals of the young ladies of the town. After all, unless we've been grossly misinformed, the birth of Rock & Roll did not take place during the American Civil War! I doubt very much if there were a lot of silly, squealing teenagers about either.

Debra Paget was just fourteen and still at school when 20th Century Fox signed her to a contract in 1948. The gorgeous youngster successfully fended off the advances of Elvis away from the cameras.

In 1958 she married for the first time, but it lasted just four months. Her second effort in 1960 fared even worse, and was over inside twenty-two days. In 1964 she wed a Chinese-American oilman who was a nephew of Madame Chiang Kai Shek, but that too ended in divorce in 1971.

Ma & Pa Kettle (1949)

Marjorie Main was born Mary Tomlinson to a clergyman and his wife. As a teenager she ran away from home to avoid disgracing her family with her lesbianism. In New York City she befriended another teenager, Ruby Stevens and the two spent their days chasing work in burlesque and their evenings in the gay bars of Harlem. The ubiquitous Oscar Levant was their driver on these jaunts. Stevens would later change her name to Barbara Stanwyck. Marjorie plays Ma Kettle in all nine of the very popular Kettles comedies that were inspired by the 1947 hit comedy *The Egg And I*. Seven of them featured Percy Kilbride as Pa Kettle. He was killed in a car crash in 1964.

Madness of King George, The (1994)

The original title was to be *The Madness of King George 111,* but that idea was canned when it was deemed a real possibility that most Americans would not go to see it, believing they had already missed *The Madness of King George 1 & 2.*

Just before the Academy Awards ceremony in 1995, for which Nigel Hawthorne was nominated for his starring performance in this film, he and his partner were 'outed' by *Advocate* magazine in America. Back home in England the press reaction was vicious and extremely hurtful to both men.

Magnificent Obsession (1954)

In 1953, Joan Crawford saw the early cuts of this picture starring the still to be famous Rock Hudson and thought him most desirable. 'He's a combination of Gary Cooper and Robert Taylor', she remarked, and invited him to her home for a meal and a swim in her pool. While Rock was showering, so the story goes, she stripped, turned out the lights and slid into the cubicle with him. 'Close your eyes and pretend I'm Clark Gable', she supposedly said before seducing him.

Hudson's screen test for 20th Century Fox was so bad the studio used it for years to show aspiring young actors what *not* to do in front of the cameras. After trying to succeed as an actor for a number of years, his big chance came when he starred in *Magnificent Obsession*. He sneaked into the preview theatre with his friend Jack Navaar, watched for a few minutes and then quietly left. Navaar found him hunched over the steering wheel of his car sobbing. The actor knew from the audience reaction he had finally made it. It had taken him twenty-five films to get there.

As Hudson himself said when commenting on 'Rock' as a choice of Christian name, 'it's better than Crash or Brick which were the other two suggestions'. Gay agent, Henry Willson, (one of his lovers) came up with the name. Doris Day who was aware of Hudson's homosexuality, commented, 'I call him Ernie because he is certainly no Rock'. The quip went un-noticed at the time. What was noticed (and also not commented on in public) was his habit of whiling away his time on the set between shots doing needlework. In fact, he became quite an aficionado.

When *Confidential* persisted with its threat to run a story exposing him as gay, Universal quickly ordered him to wed his secretary Phyllis Gates in an effort to pre-empt it. She was not told of his sexual preferences. After two years of marriage (and several beatings) she eventually learned the truth. Rock and his cronies then spread false rumors that *she* was bi-sexual and had been caught in lesbian situations. The stories paved the way for his divorce and put the public in his corner.

Confidential only lasted from December 1952 until 1957 but it stirred up a mountain of trouble in the interim. Its editor, Howard Rushmore, employed private eyes such as former cop, leg breaker, and all-round tough nut Fred Otash, to dig up the dirt on celebrities big and small. Rushmore used disgruntled partners, dismissed employees, hookers, bartenders and anyone else he could find to gain information, often providing them with miniature recorders or hidden cameras. When it all came tumbling down in 1957 he climbed into a cab on Manhattan's East Side, *shot his wife through the head*, and then put the gun in his mouth and pulled the trigger. Few grieved him.

A wag sent out invitations to a bogus wedding between Rock and gay comedian Jim Nabors. Even though it was untrue, the ensuing publicity caused Nabors' variety series to be cancelled and effectively wrecked his career. For some reason the public pilloried Nabors but forgave Hudson. As far as we know, the two men were platonic friends until then, but not lovers. Sadly, that friendship ended at once, neither man willing to talk to the other again for fear of tabloid gossip and consequences.

Early in his career Rock went to great lengths to conceal his homosexuality, but by the time he was making the TV series *MacMillan and Wife* all that had changed. Reasonably secure in the knowledge that most of Hollywood knew about him yet protected his image, he began to indulge in orgies at his home where up to fifty gay young men would actively participate.

Shortly after learning he had AIDS he was required to kiss actress Linda Evans during a scene in the TV series *Dynasty*. In those days it was widely believed the transfer of saliva could spread the disease. He went ahead with the scene anyway, rather than risk the publicity and awkward questions a refusal might engender. Evans had her concerns over the scene also and gargled antiseptics afterwards. When asked why she took such a risk she ingenuously replied, 'I didn't want to hurt his feelings'.

Magnificent Seven, The (1960)

Yul Brynner (1920-1985)

Known relationships:

Bankhead, Tallulah
Baxter, Anne
Berg, Nancy
Bergman, Ingrid
Bloom, Claire
Crawford, Joan
Dietrich, Marlene
Ekberg, Anita
Garland, Judy
Hodge, Vicki
Jurado, Katy
Lollobrigida, Gina
Monroe, Marilyn
Reagan, Nancy
St Cyr, Lili

Married:

Virginia Gilmore & 3 others

Actor Patrick Newell, who worked with Brynner on *The Long Duel,* said the bald star's ego knew no bounds. Whatever subject was brought up in conversation, Brynner claimed to have excelled at it at some time or another. Co-star Trevor Howard openly showed his disgust on several occasions by simply walking off as he described his imagined prowess in all manner of sporting achievements.

He was also thought of as the stingiest, cheapest man in Hollywood. Even the miserable Peter Lawford could be shamed into picking up the tab at a restaurant once in a while. Brynner simply did not pay. Not ever. For the last forty-five years of his life he wore only black clothing. He believed it made him look 'less bulky, less like an overweight wrestler', he said. He died on the same day as Orson Welles.

Magnum Force (1973)

Robert Urich plays the vigilante cop Mike Grimes here. His second wife Heather Menzies was Louisa von Trapp in the monumentally successful *The Sound of Music*. Urich died from cancer at fifty-five.

Male and Female (1919)

While making *Male and Female*, Gloria Swanson had to contend with a real lion standing over her in one scene. She rushed off to director Cecil B DeMille's office and hysterically told him she was too distraught to appear on the set the following day. His response was to open a box of jewels on his desk and suggest she select a trinket to calm her nerves. 'I picked out a gold mesh evening bag with an emerald clip', she recalled, 'and immediately felt much better'. She was back at work in the morning.

Maltese Falcon, The (1941)

Mary Astor (1906-1987)

Known relationships:

Asher, Irving
Barrymore, John
Bogart, Humphrey
Colman, Ronald
Fairbanks, Douglas
Fowler, Gene
Gable, Clark
Hughes, Howard
Huston, John
Kaufman, George
Lyon, Ben
Saunders, John
Taylor, Joseph

Her career seemed over in the 30s, after explicit details of sex romps with writer George Kaufman were found in her diary and leaked to the press. The public, however, chose to forgive her and her career actually flourished, culminating in her most famous role as the femme fatale in *The Maltese Falcon* The leaked excerpts were reproduced in the press, with the offending words edited out. Readers had a ball filling in the blanks.

'He ...... the living daylights out of me', was one that reached the tabloids. Another read, 'It was wonderful to ....the sweet afternoon away... I don't know where George got his staying power! He must have ... three times in an hour!'

After attending a show together she wrote, 'my hand wasn't in my own lap during the third (act)... it's been years

since I felt up a man in public, but I just got carried away…'
She raved over Kaufman's sexual endurance. 'His powers of
recuperation are amazing, and we made love all night long…
it all worked perfectly and we shared our fourth …… at
dawn…It seems that George is just hard all the time…I don't
see how he does it. He is perfect'. Another excerpt: 'He
greeted me in his pajamas and we flew into each other's
arms. He was rampant in an instant…he tore out of them and
I was never undressed by anyone so fast in my life'.

During the custody trial for their daughter, her husband's
maid gave details of *his* behavior while the couple were
separated. She described how starlet Norma Taylor and three
other Busby Berkeley blondes spent succeeding nights with
him in his bed. She also told of a stand up fight in full view of
his daughter, which the starlet conducted clad only in red toe
polish. The judge eventually awarded Mary the family
mansion and full custody of her little girl. The diary was
impounded by the court and kept locked away, until 1952,
when it was allegedly burned without its entire contents
being made public.

Astor struggled with alcoholism later in life and
attempted suicide at least once in 1951. Of her lifestyle in the
1930s she later wrote, 'I was sick, spoiled and selfish,
prowling like some animal seeking monetary satisfaction.
Sexually, I was out of control'. It was rumored for decades
she and Bette Davis had an affair, but both women
vigorously denied it.

Mame (1974)

Lucille Ball was sixty-three years old when she made this diabolical picture. What possessed the studio to put the over the hill Lucy in a vehicle that was a gilt-edged success on Broadway for Angela Lansbury is anyone's guess. Even with soft focus, her sixty-three years blazed like a beacon across every scene. When asked her age in the film, her character replies, 'Somewhere between forty and death'. Surely she cringed uttering such a laughable line.

As for her singing, well, it was nothing more than a tuneless croak. In fact, to cover for the star's inadequacies as a singer and dancer, the tunes were *slowed down* so she could cope. She reputedly told reporters that Lansbury did not want the role because she was sick of it. Besides, she was in Ireland visiting her son, Lucy said. Neither statement was true. Angela both wanted the movie role and clearly deserved it. The problem, she said later - she was never asked.

Man Bait (1926)

Former Mack Sennett bathing beauty Marie Prevost stars in this silent picture, the highlight of a minor career that failed to make the transition to sound. By 1937, the thirty-eight year old was down and out when she died alone in her apartment. Alone, that is, except for her pet dachshund. Several days after her death Marie's body was found, surrounded by empty whiskey bottles, her whining dachshund alongside her. The ravenous animal had chewed both her arms and legs into bloody stumps!

Manhattan Melodrama (1934)

This movie became famous through its relationship to Public Enemy Number One, John Dillinger. It was after watching *Manhattan Melodrama* on July 22, 1934, that he emerged from the Bioscope cinema in Chicago and was gunned down by FBI agents. His current girlfriend Ann Sage sold him out for the $10,000 reward.

Man Who Loved Cat Dancing, The (1973)

A scandal erupted when a cameraman, obsessed with Sarah Miles, shot himself in a fit of jealousy because she was allegedly intimate with her co-star Burt Reynolds.

Man Who Shot Liberty Valence, The (1962)

Despite many stories to the contrary, John Wayne was only an average football player. Woody Strode, by comparison, was a star player at UCLA before entering the movie business. Strode also served in the armed services during World War Two, whereas Wayne did not. The two men got into a brawl during the making of *The Man Who Shot Liberty Valence*, after director John Ford needled Wayne on both issues.

Man Who Would be King, The (1975)

Michael Caine's wife, Shakira Baksh, makes her only screen appearance as the princess in this version of Kipling's novel. She was a former Miss Guyana, in 1967 when she was eighteen, and ran third in that year's Miss World pageant.

Caine quotes his mother as giving him the following advice: 'Be like a duck...remain calm on the surface and paddle like hell underneath'.

He chose the name Caine when he looked out of his window and saw a film marquis advertising *The Caine Mutiny*. If a different film had been showing, he quips, he might now be known as Michael 101 Dalmations. Actress Valerie Perrine described him as, 'without doubt, the nicest human being I've ever worked with'.

Man with the Golden Arm, The (1955)

Kim Novak (1933 -)

Known relationships:

Adams, Nick
Bandini, Mario
Brando, Marlon
Chamberlain, Wilt
Davis Jr, Sammy
Fisher, Eddie
Grant, Cary
Guinle, Jorge
Hemmings, David
Ireland, John
Kennedy, Robert F
Khan, Prince Aly
Krim, Mac
Mathews, Kerwin
Quine, Richard
Rubirosa, Porfirio
Sinatra, Frank

Trujillo, Rafael

Married:

Richard Johnson & 1 other

Novak came from a Polish background. Her boss at Columbia, Harry Cohn, referred to her as 'that fat Polack' behind her back. At her first screen test the director advised everyone, 'don't listen to her, just look'. The head of publicity told her, 'you're just a piece of meat, that's all'. Promoted by the studio as 'the Lavender Blonde', she was compelled to live in a lavender apartment decked out by the studio. She hated it.

Frank Sinatra (1915-1998)

Known relationships:

Bacall, Lauren
Bartok, Eva
Baxter, Anne
Beatty, Adelle
Berg, Nancy
Bisset, Jacqueline
Campbell, Judy
Carmen, Jeanne
Caron, Leslie
Churchill, Pamela
Crawford, Joan
Davis, Nancy
Dickinson, Angie
Dietrich, Marlene
Duke, Patty
Ekberg, Anita
Exner, Judith
Gabor, Eva
Gabor, Zsa Zsa

Garland, Judy
Hamilton, Kip
Holiday, Billie
Horne, Lena
Kelly, Grace
LaMarr, Hedy
Lane, Abbe
Lange, Hope
Lee, Peggy
Lollobrigida, Gina
Loren, Sophia
Lynley, Carol
MacLaine, Shirley
MacRae, Sheila
Maxwell, Marilyn
Meredith, Judi
Monroe, Marilyn
Moss, Kate
Novak, Kim
Oberon, Merle
Onassis, Jackie
Princess Alexandra
Princess Soraya
Principal, Victoria
Provine, Dorothy
Prowse, Juliet
Reed, Donna
Remick, Lee
Shore, Dinah
Smith, Keely
St John, Jill
Stevenson, Venetia
Taylor, Elizabeth
Tsu, Irene
Turner, Lana
Vanderbilt, Gloria
Weld, Tuesday
White, Carol
Wood, Natalie

Alan Royle

Married:

> Ava Gardner
> Mia Farrow
> Barbara Marx & 1 other

The rather weedy Frank actually weighed 13 pounds 8 ounces at birth, yet never grew taller than 5'7". The left side of his face was scarred and deformed by the forceps used to remove him from his mother's uterus. They also punctured his eardrum, which later caused him to be classified 4F during World War Two and unfit for service.

He never learned to read a single note of music in his life, but nobody pulled a crowd like Sinatra. In 1980, when the Golden Nugget Casino was built in Atlantic City, it was to Sinatra the owners turned to ensure a quick return on their investment. He was paid $10 million over three years, plus generous stock options, and given access to private jets, helicopters and limousines. Free accommodation in any one of the six deeply luxurious suites usually reserved for high rollers, with rooms for his entire entourage, were thrown in. And he was worth every penny of it. His first appearance over a four- day engagement brought in $20 million in revenue to the casino. One gambler alone lost $3.7 million.

When Frank left his first wife, Nancy, he kept a list of all the major Hollywood beauties on the back of his dressing room door, and crossed them off as he seduced them. He would receive regular up-dates on which starlet or Broadway actress was 'hot', what their sexual tastes ran to, and their availability status. Nancy still entertained hopes of a reunion, but eventually called it quits on hearing of his affair with Ava Gardner.

Songwriter and friend Jimmy Van Heusen spoke of Sinatra's attitude toward his women. 'Before bed, he would be so charming...a perfect gentleman...it was the next day that we'd find the other Frank' he said. 'He wouldn't even go near her...humped and dumped. The minute the conquest was achieved, kaput. The girl could pack her bags. I saw so many of them leave his home in tears'.

For most of his life he used women for sex and then discarded them. All except Ava, that is. He was crazy about her, but simply unable to remain faithful to her, or to any woman for that matter.

He was vindictive as hell. If friends crossed him, or even if he *thought* they had, he wrote them off – forever. Quite often they were unaware of why they found themselves suddenly *persona non grata*. He never accepted, or even listened to, explanations or excuses. The 'traitor' was simply cut off completely from his circle. On the odd occasion when he was mistaken on such issues he *never* apologized or offered second chances.

When Robert Mitchum was once asked whom he would least like to fight, he replied 'Frank Sinatra. Because no matter how many times you knocked him down, he would keep getting up until one of us was killed'.

HRH Prince Charles was asked how he found Old Blue Eyes. 'Terribly nice one minute and...well, not so nice the next', he replied. Robert Aldrich called him 'an unpleasant man. No one has yet worked out what really makes him tick'.

Lewis Milestone perhaps summed him up best. 'If you line up twelve people who know him you'll get twelve different versions of his character and behavior'.

For all that, he could be extremely generous when the mood took him, especially to his friends. He bought Sammy Davis Jr's home in Beverly Hills for him. When Sammy died in 1990 he gave his widow a million dollars to clear her debts and retain the home. Rosalind Russell knew of his generosity. 'I guess there is just reams that could be written about the things he has done for people, which no one knows other than the recipients. He likes it that way'.

As a partner in the Sands Hotel he was known to pay the college tuition fees or medical bills of coffee shop girls who were struggling to make ends meet. If any customer at the casino abused a waitress he would issue orders to 'get the bastard off my property'.

He was also one of the first show business personalities to visibly take a stance on civil rights issues. He spoke out against racial prejudice at high schools and, in 1945, participated in a ten-minute film entitled *The House I Live In*. The film won a Special Academy Award for its efforts to convince teenagers of the stupidity of such prejudices. He also insisted on any black musicians travelling with him being afforded the same hotel and restaurant privileges he and the other white members of his troupe enjoyed.

His Negro valet, George Jacobs, recalled their first meeting. He was waiting outside a Hollywood party for his boss to emerge and in desperate need of a cigarette, so he asked the first person to come along. It happened to be Frank Sinatra. The singer, who was at the nadir of his career at the time, said he did not have any on him and went in to the party. A few minutes later he came out with a bowl of smokes. Within a year Jacobs was working for him.

Wherever he went Frank carried a stack of $100 bills folded into tight little squares, which he used for tipping busboys, waitresses, bellhops, parking attendants, and anyone else who looked after him. He would either quietly press the bill into their hand or order one of his entourage to, 'Duke him a hundred'.

He also had a sense of humor and was quite a prankster. When good friend Joe E Lewis was locked in his high rise Beverly Wilshire apartment for non-payment of rent, he wired Sinatra for help. Frank sent him a parachute.

On another occasion he arranged for a contractor to accompany him to agent Swifty Lazar's apartment, where they bricked in the man's clothes closet, painted the area the same color as the wall and then sneaked out.

As big a star as he was, Sinatra was himself star-struck by Fred Astaire. He once followed the legendary dancer around the studio lot, keeping out of sight and whispering to his companion, 'Look at how he moves. Just look at him!'

In a 1965 *Life* interview, in response to a question concerning his extravagant sex-life, Frank responded, 'If I had as many affairs as you fellows claim, I'd be speaking to you today from a jar in the Harvard Medical School'. Few believed him. He used hookers when starlets, bar girls and female fans were unavailable at a moment's notice. He had an aversion about going to bed alone, convinced that sex improved his voice, especially before a recording session.

Remarkably, his very first gold record did not come until 1965 when he recorded a love song (with his daughter Nancy) entitled *Something Stupid*, a tune the wags in the industry referred to as 'The Incest Song'. Gold records aside, it would take four full days to play every song he recorded in his lifetime.

So many people wanted to attend his funeral that the family decided to have tickets printed! Anyone without one was refused admittance, and it had to be collected personally from Ticketmaster. Even Nancy Reagan had to stand in line to collect hers.

Man with the Golden Gun, The (1974)

Zsa Zsa Gabor wrote in her autobiography of a party at Britt Ekland's home, during which the guests were invited into the hostess's bathroom to observe her sitting stark naked in a bathtub full of cocaine.

She was once married to Peter Sellers. Their daughter, Victoria, roomed with Hollywood madam Heidi Fleiss for a couple of years. 'Mum goes for boy lovers', she rather disloyally revealed when asked about Britt.

Herve Villechaize plays the diminutive Nick Nack in this, but his real claim to fame was as Ricardo Montalban's assistant, ('De plane! De plane!') in the hit TV series *Fantasy Island*. When he demanded the same huge salary as Montalban, studio executives fired him on the spot and his career never recovered.

Despite his short stature, Villechaize's organs were normal size, and the squeezing of them into his tiny ribcage caused the actor great pain as he got older. He was unable to sleep on his back and was often compelled to crouch against his bed in order to get any sleep at all. One evening in October 1993 he decided to end his misery. He turned on a tape recorder, put a gun to his chest and fired a bullet into his heart. 'It hurts...it hurts. I'm dying, I'm dying', were his pathetic final words.

Marathon Man (1976)

Dustin Hoffman is a method actor. For a scene in *Marathon Man*, in which his character has gone days without sleep, he stayed awake all night to prepare himself for the shoot. Upon observing his condition and mental struggle to bury himself in the character, co-star Lawrence Olivier laconically offered a suggestion. 'Why don't you just *act*?'

Marnie (1964)

Alfred Hitchcock's conduct towards his star, Tipi Hedron, while shooting this picture was less than exemplary. She had previously starred for him in *The Birds* and he had become somewhat obsessed with her by the time they made *Marnie*. After propositioning her in her trailer and being refused (yet again), he chose only to speak with her through his associates from that time onwards. He also vowed to ruin her career. It appears he may have succeeded, because she rarely featured in a film after *Marnie*.

Her daughter, Melanie Griffith, recalled a present Hitchcock gave her when she was a child. 'He was macabre. When I was a little girl he sent me a gift of a replica of my mother, Tippi Hedren, in a coffin. This was his idea of a joke. He had a sick sense of humor. After that, my mother never worked for him again'.

Mary Poppins (1964)

When Julie Andrews won the Best Actress Oscar for *Mary Poppins,* which was shot in the same year as *My Fair Lady*, she did not fail to take a swipe at the studio that chose Audrey Hepburn over her to play Eliza Doolittle. 'I'd like to thank all those who made this possible', she said, 'especially Jack Warner'. Actually, she was not even Disney's first choice to play Mary Poppins. Walt wanted Bette Davis, but in the end chose Julie, so he said, because he preferred the way she whistled!

Maytime (1937)

Jeanette MacDonald and John Barrymore did not get along when they made *Maytime*. Her predilection for stealing scenes from her co-stars incurred his considerable wrath. 'If you wave that loathsome chiffon rag you call a kerchief once more while I'm speaking', he roared, 'I shall ram it down your gurgling throat!'

McLintock! (1963)

Stefanie Powers can speak seven languages: English, Polish, Russian, French, Spanish, Italian, Swahili and Mandarin Chinese. An extraordinary woman in many ways, she even learned to bullfight in her teens in Mexico where she was dubbed *La Pecosa* meaning 'the freckled one'.

I've tried it all', she admits. 'Even smoking heroin, though thank God I had a guardian angel to get me out of it'. Her first husband, actor Gary Lockwood, was a violent drunk who often beat her. Sixties fans may recall the series he starred in on television called *The Lieutenant*. William Holden, on the other hand, adored her. 'How many women would accompany a man upriver in Northern New Guinea, wind up with dengue fever, and not complain?' he said. 'Not many'.

Mexican Spitfire (1939)

Lupe Velez (1908-1944)

Known relationships:

Borzage, Frank
Cabot, Bruce

Chaplin, Charles
Colman, Ronald
Columbo, Russ
Cooper, Gary
Cortez, Ricardo
Dempsey, Jack
Durante, Jimmy
Fairbanks Sr, Douglas
Fairbanks, Jr, Douglas
Fleming, Victor
Flynn, Errol
Gable, Clark
Gilbert, John
Jessel, George
Johnson, Jack
Lahr, Bert
Maresch, Harald
Mix, Tom
Moore, Clayton
Quinn, Anthony
Remarque, Erich
Robinson, Edward G
Roland, Gilbert
Scott, Randolph
Skelton, Red
Tibbett, Lawrence
Vallee, Rudy
Williams, Guinn

Married:

Johnny Weissmuller

Her mother started Lupe working in burlesque houses at a young age in Mexico. By the time the girl was fifteen she was being sold to the highest bidder. In Hollywood she had scores of lovers ranging from actors to stuntmen, cameramen and stagehands. If she fancied a man she bedded him. Actor Leon Ames described her as 'the twistiest, most sensuous looking thing I have ever seen'. An avid fights fan, she would often climb into the ring and attack referees when she felt they had judged Mexican boxers harshly.

Completely uninhibited, she would jump up on a restaurant table, strip all her clothes off, and perform a wild Mexican dance for stunned patrons. On the set she would lounge around minus any underwear with her legs spread wide apart, thoroughly enjoying the parade of males who stopped by to admire the view.

At parties, naked as usual, she would liven up proceedings by rotating her left breast, first in one direction and then the other. She would enrage her husband, Johnny Weissmuller, by suddenly pulling her skirt over her head while talking to a group of people, simply to prove she scorned the use of lingerie.

Lupe had a long-running madcap affair with Gary Cooper. When he ended it, she fired a shot at him in a railway station as his train pulled out for New York City. She would often call him on the set and engage him in phone sex while the crew and director were forced to wait to complete a scene.

Another lover was cowboy star Tom Mix, but she jettisoned him when his star started to wane. Clark Gable was yet another, but it was he who sent her packing. He was wary of her fondness for spilling details about her love life. 'She'll be all over town telling everyone what a lousy lay I am', he said.

Russ Columbo and fighters Jack Dempsey and Jack Johnson seduced her too. Even Randolph Scott took a shot before he met Cary Grant.

Lupe not only loved passionately, she was also vindictive. Her greatest hatred was reserved for millionaire oddball Libby Holman. Holman was near-sighted yet far too vain to wear spectacles, so Velez would urinate outside her dressing room door each night hoping she would slip in the mess and injure herself!

Upon learning she was pregnant to Harold Ramond, a man who had no intention of marrying her, she determined, as a devout Catholic, to go out in a blaze of glory and self-pity, rather than abort the child. After eating a spicy Mexican meal she dressed in her finest clothes and downed copious quantities of booze along with 75 Seconal pills. She then lay down on a bed of flower petals, hands clasped across her chest and waited to die with dignity. Unfortunately, the food reacted with the booze and pills and she vomited. She was discovered next morning with her head jammed in the toilet bowl. She was thirty-five. Her suicide note to Ramond read in part, '...you did not want us. Now we will never be disgraced'.

Mildred Pierce (1945)

Realizing her career was hanging by a thread, Joan Crawford desperately wanted the lead in *Mildred Pierce* to stage a comeback. Director Michael Curtiz's response was, 'why should I waste my time directing a has-been?' It was unprecedented for an established star (even one on the skids) to screen test for a role alongside minor members of the cast, but she was willing to do whatever was necessary to secure the part. By purposefully doing the test looking drab and dowdy she won out over Barbara Stanwyck who had been more or less promised the role.

Bette Davis, who had first refusal on every good script at Warners, had already said 'no'. She did not want to play the mother of a sixteen year-old. Once the role was hers Joan quickly abandoned the dowdy look for her trademark glossy star image, which brought her into direct conflict with Curtiz. He called for her to be replaced by Stanwyck a week into the production, but Joan countered by insisting producer Jerry Wald fire Curtiz! A compromise was reached and filming recommenced. It was an uneasy truce, with Curtiz calling her 'phony Joanie' to her face, and 'that rotten bitch' behind her back. She went on to win the Oscar she so badly needed, enabling her career to struggle along for another twenty years or so.

On Oscar night she feigned an illness, so she would not have to attend. She was simply too terrified of losing. On hearing the result on the radio, she dashed out of bed and took a shower, emerging 'coiffed, perfumed, resplendent, radiant', recalled daughter Christina. Photographers arrived and snapped her (back in her sickbed) clutching 'Oscar' to her bosom. The picture knocked every other winner off the next morning's front pages. Just as she had intended it would.

She originated the practice of hiring a publicity man to secretly run an Oscars campaign. Henry Rogers and Warner Brothers producer Jerry Wald manipulated the media (in particular columnist Hedda Hopper) into believing Joan's performance in *Mildred Pierce* was certain to win an award.

Rogers was so successful, he repeated the procedure for Olivia De Havilland the following year and she also won. But his third effort (for Rosalind Russell) backfired and she lost out to Loretta Young in what was considered to be one of Oscar's great upsets. It wasn't really. Russell was only odds-on favorite because Rogers had *created* a betting market and installed her at the top at ridiculously short odds. All smoke and mirrors stuff.

Joan Crawford (1906-1977)

Known relationships with women:

Arzner, Dorothy
Bankhead, Tallulah
Chatterton, Ruth
Colbert, Claudette
Garland, Judy
Parker, Denise
Raye, Martha
Stanwyck, Barbara
Tashman, Lilyan

Known relationships with men:

Anderson, Eddie 'Rochester'
Andrews, Dana
Aumont, Jean-Pierre
Barry, Don 'Red'
Bautzer, Greg
Bern, Paul

Bogart, Humphrey
Borzage, Frank
Brian, David
Brown, Johnny Mack
Brynner, Yul
Carson, Jack
Chandler, Jeff
Cochran, Steve
Cooper, Gary
Cooper, Jackie
Cortez, Ricardo
Craig, James
Cudahy, Michael
Curtis, Tony
Donlevy, Brian
Douglas, Kirk
Egan, Richard
Fisher, Eddie
Fleming, Victor
Fonda, Henry
Ford, Glenn
Gable, Clark
Garfield, John
Gilbert, John
Gleason, Jackie
Granger, Farley
Grant, Cary
Hawks, Howard
Heflin, Van
Hudson, Rock
Hughes, Howard
Ireland, John
Johnson, Kerry
Kennedy, John F
Kimberly, James
Lang, Jennings
Lederer, Francis
Lyles, A C
Mankiewicz, Joseph

Martin, Charles
Martin, Tony
Mayer, Louis B
McCoy, Tim
Miller, David
Mitchum, Robert
Montgomery, Robert
Nader, George
Newman, Paul
Norris, Edward
Novello, Ivor
Nype, Russell
Oakie, Jack
Power, Tyrone
Preston, Robert
Rapf, Harry
Ray, Nicholas
Romero, Cesar
Rubirosa, Porfirio
Sachs, Manny
Scott, Zachary
Selznick, David O
Shaw, Artie
Shaw, Peter
Sherman, Vincent
Sinatra, Frank
Sterling, Robert
Stewart, James
Taylor, Robert
Tracy, Spencer
Vallee, Rudy
Vanderbilt, Alfred
Wagner, Robert
Walters, Charles
Wayne, John
Weissmuller, Johnny
Whitney, John
Winchell, Walter

Married:

Douglas Fairbanks Jr
Franchot Tone & 2 others

Crawford's entire body was smothered from head to toe in freckles, which were airbrushed out of publicity stills and covered with make-up for the cameras.

She was born in 1904 and not 1908 as most sources indicate. All her life she pretended to be four years younger than she actually was. Thought by everyone to be a teenager when she wed Douglas Fairbanks Jr, she was actually twenty-four and some years older than him. The groom's famous parents Doug Senior and Mary Pickford did not go to the wedding. Joan's promiscuity was common knowledge around town, so as far as they were concerned their son had married a cheap tramp and gold digger. They weren't far wrong.

After being named as co-respondent in two divorce cases in 1928, she was warned by L B Mayer at MGM to clean up her act or her career would be over. It was then she set her cap for young Fairbanks who fell for her hook, line and sinker.

Known as Billie in her childhood days, the inordinately over-sexed Joan was discovered by her mother having sex with her stepfather when she was eleven years old! Two years later she began sleeping with her brother, and in her late teens was arrested in Chicago on prostitution charges while working in mob speak-easies. Once in show business she used her body to scramble up the ladder, bedding executives, writers, directors, musicians and other actors as the need arose.

In her early twenties she appeared in at least two pornographic movies during her starving chorus girl days in New York, although MGM would deny such accusations once she became a star. In the meantime, the studio quietly tried to buy up all the prints and stills of *Velvet Lips* and *The Casting Couch,* her two starring vehicles. The second of these involved her stripping and giving oral sex followed by full intercourse to a 'producer'. Copies still exist in private collections today.

It was during those early days she contracted VD for the first time and underwent the first of several abortions. 'I happen to know', said Veronica Lake, 'that Joan Crawford and Tallulah Bankhead couldn't have babies because of the illegal abortions performed on them.' Although Joan always denied having female lovers, even she would have been hard pressed to explain away a photograph published in 2002 showing a young, busty Joan in the arms of an equally busty lady. Both women were naked.

She began her affair with Clark Gable while still married to Fairbanks. Writer Adela Rogers St. John recalled coming across the duo going at it behind the bandstand at the Cocoanut Grove, while their respective spouses were seated out front. 'Adela! Darling!' exclaimed Crawford. Gable just grinned. The next morning St. John received a note from Joan. 'I bet you were *thrilled* watching', she wrote. Obviously, the romance was not a very well-kept secret.

Visitors to the set of a couple of pictures starring the lovers were embarrassed to hear them in the throes of passion in Crawford's trailer during breaks in filming.

According to former child star Jackie Cooper, he was seduced by her in the pool-house at her home when he was seventeen. 'She was an extraordinary performer', he recalled. 'I was learning things that most men don't learn until they are much older - if at all'. They repeated the performance eight or nine times over the next few months. 'When I left, she would put me on the calendar for the next visit. I could hardly wait', he warmly recalled. Then just as suddenly it was over. One night after one of their bouts she coldly told him, 'put it all out of your mind. It never happened'.

Crawford was candid when asked if she had ever been on the casting couch. 'Well, it sure as hell beat the cold, hard floor', she snapped. Bette Davis remarked, 'she slept with every male star at MGM except Lassie!' She seduced hundreds of men, even succeeding briefly with John Wayne, although he denied it until his dying day. 'Hell, she's been trying for years', said Wayne. 'I don't take her calls, that's all'. It was known he preferred subservient lovers (and Joan was anything but that) so the liaison was short-lived. She also swore like a sailor and that turned Wayne and a lot of other conservative men off. 'I have great admiration for her as an actress, but she's a slut', said L B Mayer. 'Her whole life is an act. She is what she is, a cheap flapper who likes to get laid'. When asked what age she preferred her men she replied, 'oh, anyone over fifteen is OK!' She wasn't joking.

MGM conducted a nationwide competition to select a suitable name for her. Somehow Lucille LeSeur just didn't sound right. An advertisement promised a cash prize of $500 for whoever came up with the winning name. In the event of a tie each successful entrant would get $500 apiece. The name 'Joan Arden' was about to be declared the winner when miserly studio executives had second thoughts about shelling out $1,000 to the two successful applicants. Instead, it was announced there already existed a Joan Arden in the industry, so Joan Crawford was to be Lucille's new moniker. Her autobiography disputes this, but Maurice Rapf, whose father was a studio head at the time (and one of her lovers), insists his recollection is accurate.

Her brief affair with Spencer Tracy ended during a rehearsal for a radio show. As she continually stuttered and stumbled over her lines he lost his temper. 'For Christ's sake', he exclaimed. 'I thought you were supposed to be a pro!' That was the end of that!

As she did with most female stars in Hollywood, Marlene Dietrich loathed her. 'That terrible, vulgar woman with the pop-eyes beats her children', said Dietrich, who was scarcely a model mother herself. 'But what do you expect from that class? A cheap tap dancer!'

'I never liked Joan Crawford at all', said Louise Brooks. 'Never. I hate fakes. She was an awful fake. A washerwoman's daughter! I'm a terrible snob, you know'. The comments say more about Dietrich and Brooks than they do about Crawford.

Joan enjoyed revealing her body to casual acquaintances. She would often greet her dates in her bedroom, offering them cocktails while she dressed in front of them. Comedian Jackie Gleason met her at a party and went home with her. 'She was neat', he recalled. 'Minutes after I (bleeped) her she got up and started making the bed with me still in it".

She met Yul Brynner backstage after seeing him in the Broadway production of *The King And I*, and even asked him for a photograph. The next morning he sent Joan a large *nude* portrait of himself and by that afternoon they were at it like a pair of minks in his dressing room. It's probably time for the term 'dressing room' to be re-named the 'undressing room', given the amount of seduction that seems to take place there.

When attending a function alone, Joan would select a man from those present to later drive her home. Once there, the man would be invited in for a drink and would invariably stay the night. 'There was a steady flow of men', said a former servant. 'They came and went at all hours. If she had a date, I used to see her take him by the hand at the end of the evening and lead him upstairs...As I recall, a few gentlemen were reluctant'.

While some of her casual lovers, like Kirk Douglas for instance, thought sex with Crawford was cold and clinical, most of the men she seduced rated her as an extraordinary performer in bed. Attorney Greg Bautzer who bedded half the sex queens of Hollywood said, 'a night with Joan was better than a year with ten others'.

439

Although she certainly enjoyed rolling about with men, she also experimented with her own gender. Her budding friendship with Marilyn Monroe ended when she made a pass at the up and coming new sex symbol. She grabbed MM's breasts while they were trying on dresses. 'She was one of those girls who went back and forth', was the description Louise Brooks gave her. 'Mother had lesbian proclivities', wrote daughter Christina. It was not unusual for Joan to completely undress in front of studio staff members of either gender in her dressing room while casually discussing studio business.

She would not smoke from a cigarette packet that had been opened by anybody other than herself. There were no fewer than twenty-six telephones in her home and she spent an average of four hours a day speaking on them. She wore slippers adorned with bells as she walked about the house, so her servants would always know where she was at all times.

On the set she employed a man to pay her compliments. Before each scene it was his job to whisper, 'Miss Crawford, you are a great actress. Miss Crawford, you are beautiful and ageless'.

Fellow actor Ray Stricklyn recalled her being a surprise guest of honor at a Costumers Ball at the Ambassador Hotel in 1958. He later learned she only agreed to make an appearance if the designers presented her with an award naming her 'Best Dressed Actress in Films', which they duly did.

Six months before she died Joan wrote her will and left nothing at all to her adopted children Christina and Christopher, 'for reasons well known to them both', it read. 'She was a neurotic bitch, she used us only for publicity', moaned Christopher after her death.

Joan adopted them in 1939, even though she was single at the time. Mob boss Meyer Lansky, an acquaintance from her speak-easy days, arranged it through his black market connections. When Bette Davis gave birth in 1947 and attracted all the media's attention, the jealous Crawford went interstate and returned with *two* new babies she named Cathy and Cindy. 'I intend to adopt four more', she told *United Press*, 'Two boys and two girls. I already have the names picked out. Carol and Cal and Connie and...I forget'. All the names began with the first letter of her surname. Even her dog was named Cliquot and her parakeet was called Crazy Crawford.

Christina penned a best-selling novel entitled *Mommie Dearest*, in which she described her mother as a child abuser. Just how much of it is true is debatable, but by most accounts it seems she treated her two oldest children badly. Not everyone, however, appreciated Christina or believed her book. At Joan's funeral, her long-time friend Myrna Loy stood up and walked out of the chapel when Christina arrived - and the book had not yet been published! Betty Barker who was Joan's secretary for thirty-five years insisted she never witnessed any of the events depicted in the book. 'Christina wrote it for the money', she said.

Then again, actress Jane Greer recalled visiting Joan in the late forties and accidentally observing young Christopher strapped into his bed one evening. Others remembered looking on aghast as Joan would pull down the boy's pants in front of an entire gathering and spank his bare buttocks. In a media interview at that time she expounded her theories on child control. 'I spank them daily', she boasted, 'Spare the rod and you have brats'. Her determination to raise her children as 'little ladies and gentlemen' was the height of hypocrisy given her own track record.

Even best friend Helen Hayes was disturbed about her parenting techniques. 'Joan tried to be all things to all people', she said. 'I just wish she hadn't tried to be a mother'. Christopher said he visited his mother in 1962, fifteen years before her death, to show her his daughter for the first time. 'It doesn't look like you', said Joan after giving the baby a brief glance. 'It's probably a bastard'. 'I walked out', he said. 'It was the last time I saw her'.

Good friend Debbie Reynolds has always maintained Crawford committed suicide because she was unable to live with the ravages of stomach cancer.

Million Dollar Mermaid (1952)

This picture stars Esther Williams as the Australian aquatic star Annette Kellerman, the woman who gained instant notoriety in America in 1907 by being arrested on a beach in Boston for wearing a one-piece bathing costume. Out of that single incident she created a movie and swimming extravaganza career that saw her remain in America for over sixty years, until she made a belated return visit to Australia in 1970.

Esther dived fifty feet off a platform in the film's finale and broke three vertebrae in her neck. An aluminum crown she was wearing in the sequence dangerously affected her entry into the water, and the impact came within a hair's breadth of making her a paraplegic. Even so, she spent the next six months encased in plaster.

Esther and Victor Mature, both of whom were married to others at the time, had a steamy affair that started one evening in her dressing room. (Don't they all?) 'That first night', she wrote, 'we made love over and over and into exhaustion'. By the time shooting ended so too had the romance. (Don't they all?)

Esther recounted in her autobiography how she and two friends were stopped at a roadside bar for a drink one day, when a young fan excitedly approached her. 'Esther! Esther Williams! Nobody will believe me', he cried. After giving the lad her autograph, she astonished her friends by quickly lowering the top of her dress and exposing her breasts to him. The boy gaped and staggered off. 'The guy said nobody would believe him', she explained to her dumbstruck friends. 'I just wanted to help him out. I made sure that nobody would'.

Mogambo (1953)

This is a remake of the 1932 picture *Red Dust*, and was shot on location in Kenya. Both versions feature the same leading man, Clark Gable, a most unusual occurrence considering they were made twenty years apart. 'Mogambo', by the way, is the Swahili word for 'passion'. All the actors and crew were issued with weapons for the five months of the shoot, due to the Mau Mau uprising in Kenya at that time.

British actor Donald Sinden was staggered by the vast disparity between the money paid to American actors and that paid to their British counterparts in the 1950s. He received fifty pounds sterling a week for his services, while the aging Gable was paid 750 pounds sterling per week *for living expenses* - on top of his enormous salary. Admittedly, Gable was the star, but British actors worked for peanuts in those days.

Upon hearing of complaints by the locals about her nude shower sequence, Ava Gardner responded by stripping naked and running through the village in front of the entire crew and the African extras. She then took another shower in full view of everyone. She went to Gable's tent one evening demanding to know why he had not yet had sex with her. At the time he was intimately involved with the other female star, Grace Kelly. Besides, Ava was an old flame and he had tired of her. On another evening Kelly and Gable were caught *en flagrante* by Sinden when he drunkenly staggered into their love nest by mistake. He apologized profusely and was quickly ordered out by 'the King'.

Interestingly, Ava told writer Gregory Speck a different story about her relationship with him. 'I had been in love with Clark ever since I was a little girl in North Carolina', she said, '...we became very good friends, but there was never any flirtation...I'm sorry I never had an affair with Clark, but I worshipped him as a fan, and I adored him as a person'. There is considerable evidence to the contrary, however.

At a dinner for the British Ambassador to Uganda, Ava and John Ford (the director of *Mogambo*) were discussing her husband Frank Sinatra. 'What do you see in that 120 pound runt you married?' asked Ford. 'Well', she replied, 'there's ten pound of Frank and 110 pound of cock'. The Ambassador laughed heartily.

Ava flew to London for an abortion during filming. After the shoot was over she was again pregnant to Sinatra who visited her on location. That pregnancy too was aborted. Meanwhile, 23 year old Grace and 52 year old Clark were splitting their spare time between fishing, skinny-dipping in Lake Victoria, and rolling about in his bed.

Ava Gardner (1922-1990)

Known relationships:

Bautzer, Greg
Bey, Turhan
Brando, Marlon
Brooks, Paul
Bryan, Paul
Burton, Richard
Cabre, Mario
Carroll, John
Chiari, Walter

Cohen, Mickey
D'Arcy, Alexander
Damone, Vic
Daniels, Billy
Davis Jr, Sammy
Davis, Freddy
Dominguin, Luis
Duff, Howard
Evans, Robert
Farrow, John
Feldman, Charles
Franciosa, Anthony
Gable, Clark
Granger, Farley
Guinle, Jorge
Hanna, David
Hartford, Huntington
Heflin, Van
Hemingway, Ernest
Hughes, Howard
Huston, John
Kennedy, John F
Kind, Jimmy
Kiner, Ralph
Lamas, Fernando
Lancaster, Burt
Lawford, Peter
LeRoy, Mervyn
Mankiewicz, Joseph
McQueen, Steve
Mitchum, Robert
Niven, David
Peterson, Chris
Prinz Langenberg
Reis, Irving
Remar, David
Rubirosa, Porfirio
Ryan, Frank
Schenck, Joseph

Scott, George C
Sharif, Omar
Siegel, Benny
Stack, Robert
Stompanato, Johnny
Taylor, Robert
Terrail, Claude
Torme, Mel
Trabert, Tony
Viertel, Peter
Walker, Robert

Married:

Artie Shaw
Frank Sinatra
Mickey Rooney

She was actually born Ava Gardner, but L B Mayer liked everyone to think he created his stars out of 'non-entities', so he invented a phony real name for her and then changed it back to Ava Gardner! Only in Hollywood. Mayer said of her screen test, 'She can't talk. She can't act. She's terrific!' How right he was.

At nineteen, and in Hollywood only six months, she wed twenty-one year-old Mickey Rooney who was at the zenith of his career. She met him a week after her arrival in Culver City. Still a virgin on her wedding night, she was terrified, but soon found she quite enjoyed herself and looked forward to a repeat performance in the morning. Rooney had more important things to do. He went off early to play golf! They divorced sixteen months later. In his autobiography Mickey ungallantly chose to describe Ava's vagina and nipples in glowing detail, which we won't go into here.

While Ava worked hard each day on her lessons at the studio, and looked forward to quiet evenings at home, Rooney dreaded such evenings. 'I went nuts sitting around', he said. 'I had to have people around. Action. I dreaded those long evenings at home'. Ava became bored with parties night after night, but that would change in years to come. Mickey was also insanely jealous of anyone who even looked at his wife. He flew into a rage at a party when he saw her dancing with actor Tom Drake, even though *everyone* (including Rooney) knew Drake was gay and totally disinterested sexually in her or any other woman.

Her parting words to her husband prior to their divorce were, 'You know Mick I'm damn tired of living with a midget'. They met again briefly on the eve of his being sent overseas in the army. The next morning he asked her if she would marry him again. Ava promised to wait for him until the war was over, but she soon broke her promise.

Although she only married three times herself, Ava's husbands collected *nineteen* wives between them. She once said, 'All I got out of Hollywood was three lousy husbands'. One of them was bandleader Artie Shaw who demanded total subservience from all his wives in every aspect of their lives.

He was also an intellectual who insisted they improve their minds at every opportunity. Kathleen Windsor, the author of *Forever Amber,* was married to him after Ava. She said he chose the books she could read and the clothes she could wear. He even dictated how she should think on every conceivable subject, and tolerated no difference of opinion.

Lana Turner, another of his wives, commented, 'Artie was my entire college education'. Ava's response to all his posturing was more down to earth. 'I left before he had a chance to flunk me', she said. He once berated her for reading *Forever Amber*, because he considered it trash. Ava laughed out loud when she heard later he had married its author! At the height of his popularity, in 1938, Shaw was earning a massive $60,000 a week!

Howard Hughes once slapped Ava so hard he dislocated her jaw. She responded by knocking him unconscious with a heavy bronze bell. It was Hughes who Rooney found at her apartment when he returned home on leave from the army. After a brief fight, the threesome settled down to drink two bottles of Dom Perignon. As Rooney left, Hughes' parting advice was, 'Mickey don't get your ass shot off'. Ava's affair with Hughes ended when she learned he was bugging her car and employing spies to monitor her every movement.

Her affair with George C Scott began on the set of *The Bible* in 1965 and ended after he, too, beat her badly and even threatened her life. A friend told her ex-husband Frank Sinatra about it and he used his mob connections to 'convince' Scott to give her up – or else.

While Ava was making *The Flying Dutchman* in Madrid, stories flew about that she was cheating on Frank with a bullfighter named Mario Cabre. This silly young man became so enamored of her he actually hired a hall and recited poetry he had written, extolling his undying love for the actress. After a few minutes of this drivel he left the stage, amid raucous laughter and catcalls. Undeterred, he pursued her endlessly until, one evening, she got very drunk and let him have his way. Sinatra never forgave her.

Esther Williams recalled seeing her dancing the flamenco on a tabletop in Spain in her declining years. 'Ava was wearing a skirt that revealed everything as she twirled, 'Esther remembered. 'She was not wearing panties. My heart went out to Ava and what she had become. Here she was, desperately self-destructive, and keeping company with a drunken band of gypsies. Sometimes, she would just disappear with them for days'.

Around that time (the 1970s) the Ritz Hotel in Madrid banned all movie people from its premises, after Ava became drunk and urinated in the ornamental fountain in the lobby. Many of those latter years were spent in Spain, where she went through a succession of bullfighter lovers. In the end, however, she moved to London to live out her days in relative seclusion. In 1990, she died from chronic lung disease and the lingering effects of a stroke. She was sixty-seven. In her will she left a maid and a limousine to her pet dog, Morgan.

Money for Nothing (1993)

The real life subject of this tale was a longshoreman named Joey Coyle, who found a million dollars that had fallen out of an armored car. He committed suicide shortly before the picture was released.

Monster's Ball (2001)

The torrid sex scene between Halle Berry and Billy Bob Thornton was left to the two stars to - 'just go for it', to let it happen, so to speak. Halle agreed to do it *only* if Billy Bob was just as naked as she had to be. So they shot the scene with both actors clad only in 'pasties'. These are self-adhesive strips usually attached with Velcro to the private parts in order to avoid the fatal NC-17 rating, the 'no admittance to under eighteens' kiss of death that, inevitably, leads to box-office failure.

Berry was second in the Miss USA contest and third in the Miss Universe quest of 1987. The winners must have been something special! In 2000 she was severely beaten by an ex-lover (Wesley Snipes was the man named, but he denies everything) and was left with partial hearing loss.

Moon-Spinners, The (1964)

Silent star Pola Negri's last Hollywood role was in this 1963 Disney flop, in which she parodied herself. It was her first appearance on screen since 1943.

Upon arriving in America in the twenties, Negri made it clear she expected to be treated as a major star. She demanded, and was given, all the trappings, and soon became the embodiment of the movie star of caricature. Her motor vehicle was a long white Rolls Royce limousine, trimmed in ivory with white velvet upholstery. Door handles and fittings were of solid gold and the horn adorned with a golden snake's head sporting ruby eyes. Her chauffeurs wore white uniforms on sunny days and total black if it rained.

She ordered a tiger cub and often paraded it on a leash as she walked along Sunset Boulevard. A white lapdog and two Russian wolfhounds rounded out her image. On the set she was a law unto herself, turning up at whatever time suited her. On one occasion she insisted on orchid petals covering the studio floor before she would condescend to begin work, then ordered them removed when she found they gave her hay fever. Her private life was anything but private because she preferred it that way. She was a voracious headline seeker who lived to be the center of attention.

Her on-again, off-again affair with Charlie Chaplin, and a phony feud with Gloria Swanson (dreamed up by their agents), were planned campaigns to keep her in the public eye. Then she topped everything off with a cross-country dash to Valentino's deathbed, spending two full hours with his body and posing for news cameramen 'as if she was shooting a picture'. She even claimed he proposed marriage to her with his dying breath.

Tallulah Bankhead described her as, 'that lying lesbo, a publicity hound'. This was after Pola had 'fainted' several times at *both* of Valentino's funerals, and each time in front of the cameras. At the second service, after doing her fainting thing, a photographer called to her, 'hey Pola, the light's not good on your face. Will you do it again? She happily complied.

As her star began to fade, she sued a French magazine that wrote she was once Adolf Hitler's mistress. Years later when asked if it was true, she replied, 'Why not? There have been many important men in my life'. Others say she never even met Hitler. She responded to a question regarding her love affairs by saying: 'There were so many of them, I scarcely remember'. At least, that was true.

Moonstruck (1987)

Nicolas Cage's character's name was scripted as Ronnie Paolo, but when location scouts discovered the Cammareri Brothers Bakery in Brooklyn (one that still used a coal fueled oven) his surname was changed to Cammareri.

Julie Bovasso was the dialogue coach who helped Armenian/Native American Cher and Greek Olympia Dukakis with their Italian accents. She also plays Cher's Aunt Rita in the film.

Cher was extremely nervous and excited when she won the Best Actress Oscar for this film and forgot to thank the director Norman Jewison or the writer John Shanley in her acceptance speech. Several days later she took out a full-page ad and thanked them properly.

Mortal Storm, The (1940)

Dan Dailey, who plays a Nazi Brown Shirt hoodlum in *The Mortal Storm,* was a cross-dresser who was once picked up by Hollywood police while he was walking about in drag. He had a particular penchant for Linda Darnell's gowns, and was known to make midnight raids on the studio wardrobe department to try them on.

Margaret Sullavan, who plays James Stewart's love interest, had earlier been married to his best friend, Henry Fonda. They divorced when Fonda caught her cheating with producer Jed Harris. Another former spouse, Leland Howard, recalled a disturbing habit she acquired in later years. 'Hell, Maggie knew all about highway pick-ups before they became fashionable, or rather, infamous', he said. 'The wonder of men', she once told him, 'is that no two of them is alike, especially when making love'.

She overdosed in 1960 at the age of forty-eight, either unable to contend with her increasing deafness, or from ingesting incorrect medication by accident. She had always been tone deaf and unable to hear herself speak.

Mrs. Miniver (1942)

There were 488 feature films made in 1942, the most ever for a single year. This one picked up the Best Picture Oscar. Nazi Propaganda Minister Joseph Goebbels raved about it. 'What a wonderful propaganda for the Allied cause', he exclaimed after viewing the finished production. 'What a wave of sympathy for the British and hatred for the Germans comes out of this film! Surely this isn't merely a work of art; it is also excellent propaganda'.

Winston Churchill thought its morale value was 'worth more than a flotilla of destroyers'. In fact, both he and Roosevelt were so impressed with the closing speech delivered by the village vicar (played by Henry Wilcoxen) that they had it printed on leaflets and dropped behind German lines in Occupied Europe.

Neither Walter Pidgeon nor Greer Garson wanted to make the picture. Pidgeon was wary of director William Wyler's reputation for perfection. He was known as 'Ninety Take Wyler' and Pidgeon could not really be bothered. But he was forty-four years old and in need of a hit, so he took the job. Garson, like Norma Shearer before her, rejected the title role at first because she would be playing a mother with a son old enough to go to war.

Wyler and his camera crew took thousands of feet of combat film on bombing raids over Germany. Ever the perfectionist, he once asked their pilot to fly closer to the flak, so he could get better pictures! Unfortunately, the pilot's response is lost to history.

LB Mayer was most reluctant for Helmut Dantine to play the downed German pilot as a bona-fide, hate-filled Nazi. Still concerned about the German film market, (although Berlin had not accepted his films for over two years), LB warned Wyler to refrain from depicting Dantine's character as despicable. If he did so, another director would be ordered to shoot over it. 'We don't hate anybody. We are not at war', explained Mayer. However, when Japan and America entered the conflict before the film's completion, he had a sudden change of heart. 'Make the pilot a Nazi son of a bitch', he ordered.

Unknown newcomer Peter Lawford has a single line of dialogue in the film and is barely noticeable. He rushes up to Garson crying, 'The Jerries are over London in the hundreds. Looks like a big show!' You must look fast to spot him.

It has always intrigued me how this picture came to be identified with the average British family's determination to withstand the blitz and defy the Nazi hordes. After all, the average family did not live in a two-story home; and the average British husband was not an architect.

In 1943, Greer Garson surprised everyone by marrying Richard Ney, the young actor nine years her junior who plays her sappy son in the film. The MGM publicity machine was initially unaware of the romance, blissfully issuing a press item that read: 'Miss Garson bought a vacation cottage at Pebble Beach. Richard Ney hurries to the beach for a dip every lunch hour...even on the coldest days'. Oh yes, he was 'having a dip' alright.

MGM kept their subsequent marriage a secret for fear it would jeopardize the picture's believability if fans knew. Ney was actually on leave from war service when the movie was made. The couple divorced in 1947. It would not be unfair to say that his performance has to be one of the most irksome in movie history. He was actually more hateful than the German flier played by Dantine.

Contrary to popular belief, Greer's acceptance speech for her Oscar for *Mrs. Miniver* did not last for an hour at all. It went for five and a half minutes, although it probably felt like an hour to those who had to endure it. It did, however, bring about time limits being placed on acceptance speeches from then onwards.

Her monologue actually lasted longer than the entire *inaugural* Oscars presentations. They had taken only five minutes in total. In fairness to Garson it was after one o'clock in the morning by the time the ceremony got around to her, and everybody had pretty much had enough of the speechifying by then. Her opening words were, believe it or not, 'I am practically unprepared...'

The delightful character actor Henry Travers was on the British stage *for thirty-nine years* before he made his first screen appearance at the age of fifty-nine. Of his more than fifty films he is probably best remembered for his portrayal of the ill-fated stationmaster in this, and for his whimsical angel in *It's A Wonderful Life*.

Mr. Smith Goes to Washington (1939)

James Stewart chose to endure the very painful process of having two drops of bi-chloral mercury administered to his vocal chords at regular intervals, in order to achieve the effect of a hoarse throat for his filibustering scene.

Mummy, The (1999)

If you look closely at the library sequence, you can see a male double replacing Rachel Weisz atop the ladder in the long shots. In the mob sequence where everyone is chanting 'Imotep', watch for a man who appears to be blind coming towards the camera. In fact, his eyes have been 'computer-removed', because he kept ruining take after take by looking directly into the lens. The exasperated director simply erased the offending eyes from the final print.

The sequence showing the steamer docked on the Nile was actually shot at the Tilbury docks on a wintery day. The palm trees, sand dunes and pyramids were computered in to replace the real background. The sinking of the riverboat was shot on a man-made lake in England.

Murder by Death (1976)

Estelle Winwood plays Elsa Lanchester's nurse. 'I did have one homosexual husband - at least', she once said, 'Guthrie McClint, who loved his fellow man – often. In what can only be described as an astonishing career, this lesbian character actress made her stage debut at sixteen in 1898 and her last movie *Murder By Death* in 1976 at the age of 94. She lived to be 102 years of age.

One-eyed actor Peter Falk plays Sam Spade. When he went in search of a contract from Harry Cohn at Columbia he experienced first-hand the cold-blooded nature of the most detested man in Hollywood. 'Thank you Mr. Falk', said Cohn, 'but for the same money I can get an actor with *two* eyes'.

Murders in the Rue Morgue (1932)

Sidney Fox was just 4'11" tall, a dark-haired beauty who stars opposite Bela Lugosi in this early version of Poe's classic story. Although she began her career playing Bette Davis's sister in the 1931 picture *Bad Sister,* her star did not rise, despite her coquettish acting style. In 1942 at the age of thirty-one she was found dead from an overdose of sleeping pills.

Mutiny on the Bounty (1935)

This film was particularly unfair on Captain Bligh. He was not the martinet they depicted although he was difficult to get along with. As far as flogging goes, by British Navy standards of the time he was quite lenient. His achievement of sailing an overloaded, open boat 3,000 miles is quite simply the greatest feat of seamanship in the annals of the British Navy or, for that matter, any navy.

There is some doubt that Fletcher Christian died on Pitcairn Island. A shipmate vowed he saw him in England years after the mutiny, while the poet William Wordsworth who had once attended school with the future mutineer, left a letter saying he was convinced he had returned to England.

My Best Friend's Wedding (1997)

Bi-sexual Rupert Everett joined the heroin set in London for a while; then worked as a 'rent boy' before succeeding in movies. 'Let's face it', he said, 'I'm just a sex machine to both genders. It's all very exhausting'. He was also a model for cosmetics giant Yves St. Laurent before turning to acting.

My Cousin Vinny (1992)

Austin Pendleton objected to his character (the defense lawyer) having to speak with a stutter, claiming it was a 'sick joke' because Pendleton himself stuttered. The hilarious 'two utes' scene originated in a conversation between Joe Pesci and director Jonathan Lynn, when Pesci spoke just like that. Lynn thought it funny enough to incorporate an extra scene into the picture.

Unconfirmed rumors have abounded for some time in Hollywood that Jack Palance read out the wrong name when he announced Marisa Tomei as Best Supporting Actress for *My Cousin* Vinny. Not that it matters much if he did. Her performance was so enjoyable it is doubtful if many people care if there was a blunder or not.

My Fair Lady (1964)

Although it won the Best Picture Oscar, *My Fair Lady* lost money at the box-office. At its peak on Broadway, however, tickets were in huge demand. Well-to-do couples were sent freebies in the mail by burglars who then ransacked their homes while the recipients attended the show.

When Warners asked Cary Grant to play Professor Higgins he turned them down flat. 'Not only will I not play Higgins', he said, 'but if you don't put Rex Harrison in it, I won't go to see it!' Grant has been quoted in some books as having made the same statement regarding Robert Preston when Cary was offered the lead in *The Music Man*.

Coming from the middle class area of Walton -on- Thames, Julie Andrews experienced great difficulty in mastering a cockney accent for her role as Eliza Doolittle in the Broadway production of *My Fair Lady*. In fact, she was compelled to hire a phonetics expert to coach her. Oddly enough, the expert was *an American*. Even so, she should have got the movie role, but Jack Warner simply would not risk a costly production with a female lead that was not a household name in America. Had Audrey Hepburn refused it, the next cab off the rank was Elizabeth Taylor, who desperately wanted the role.

Audrey Hepburn was thirty-four when she played Eliza Doolittle in this. Hollywood could no more bring itself to nominate her for *My Fair Lady* than it could Natalie Wood for *West Side Story* in 1962. Because Marnie Nixon did the singing in both films, the Academy considered both actresses had only given *half*-performances.

Audrey was born in Belgium. As a young girl in World War Two she carried messages concealed in her shoes for the Resistance during the German occupation. It is not often remembered, but like Marilyn Monroe she too serenaded JFK with 'Happy Birthday Mr. President', on his *last* birthday in 1963. She was also said to have been one his myriad lovers.

Audrey always carted along twenty or more pieces of luggage containing all her favorite possessions, vases, pictures etc. whenever she travelled. Upon arriving at a hotel she would laboriously unpack them all and 'set up home'. When it became necessary to move on she would carefully repack the lot for her next destination. By all accounts this universally loved lady was as delightful a human being off the screen as she was on it.

Gladys Cooper, who plays Rex Harrison's mother, was a pin-up girl for British troops in World War One. Even Bette Davis admired her. 'One of the few actresses I felt privileged to play a scene with', she magnanimously admitted. Gladys succumbed to a virus in 1971. Her dying words were reminiscent of her screen persona. 'If this is what virus pneumonia does to one, I really don't think I will bother to have it again'.

George Cukor directed *My Fair Lady*. When word reached Sam Goldwyn that his top director was gay, he called George into his office to discuss the matter. Clearly uncomfortable with the situation, Sam asked, 'you must answer me truthfully, because I must know. Tell me, are you a...homosexual?' Without hesitation Cukor gave him a one-word answer, 'dedicated'. That was the end of their chat and the meeting. Goldwyn never broached the subject with him again.

Rex Harrison had only one eye and wore a toupee in his films. While wed to Lili Palmer he fell in love with the dying British actress Kay Kendall. In a most bizarre arrangement, he and Palmer agreed to a divorce to enable him to briefly marry Kendall, the understanding being they would re-marry after Kay died. Kendall passed away within two years but the couple never remarried. Although Rex treated her abominably at times, Kay adored him. 'I love you with all my heart', were the last words she whispered to him before slipping away.

Harrison's much talked about nickname was born out of his decidedly 'un-sexy' persona. On the set of *The Foxes of Harrow* the crew began calling him 'Sexy Rexy' because he was anything but that. The studio picked up on it and the sobriquet stuck.

Maureen O'Hara wrote that many people believed Rex and his lover, Carole Landis, signed a suicide pact shortly before she went through with her part of the bargain. Rex, they say, chickened out. A studio employee supposedly found the note and destroyed it. A trunk full of love letters between the two lovers went missing on the day Carole died. Harrison was said to have destroyed its contents.

Not many of his peers cared very much for him, because he was usually abrasive, sour and self-centered most of the time. And he lived up to that description right to the end. His final words to his youngest son Carey were, 'Drop dead!' To his other son Noel he said, 'There was something I always wanted to tell you. I could never stand the sound of your fucking guitar'. Noel was an Olympic skier and pop singer who enjoyed brief success with a single in the sixties entitled *A Young Girl of Sixteen*.

My Forbidden Past (1951)

Ava Gardner and Robert Mitchum began a serious affair on the set of this RKO film. She went so far as to phone his wife Dorothy and ask her to release him. Dorothy, who was always aware of her husband's many indiscretions, calmly told her to ask Bob if he wanted to go through with it. When push came to shove he did what he always did - he stayed with his wife. Although he found Ava to be the most desirable woman he had ever encountered, when asked about her he crassly spoke of her fondness for 'golden showers' and left it at that.

My Geisha (1962)

To attain the desired 'Japanese look' for her role in *My Geisha,* Shirley MacLaine wore pieces of condom cut into almond shapes that were stuck to her eyelids and then concealed under make-up.

Hot on the heels of his affair with Marilyn Monroe during the making of *Let's Make Love,* French actor Yves Montand moved to seduce MacLaine when they were on location in Japan making this picture. He successfully bet her husband he could make her fall in love with him before shooting completed. Her husband, incidentally, lived in Japan and Shirley lived in America throughout their seemingly pointless marriage. He gallantly advised her of the details of the wager *after* the affair had been consummated. Montand, as always, soon moved on to other women.

My Man Godfrey (1936)

Carole Lombard (1908-1942)

Known relationships:

Barrymore, John
Columbo, Russ
Cooper, Gary
Cooper, Harry
Gilbert, John
Hughes, Howard
Kennedy Jr, Joe
Kennedy, Joe
March, Fredric
Niven, David
Quinn, Anthony
Raft, George
Randall, Addison
Raymond, Gene
Riskin, Robert
Romero, Cesar
Selznick, David O
Sennett, Mack
Stack, Robert
Stewart, James
Sturges, Preston

Married:

Powell, William
Gable, Clark

Lombard was discovered playing ball on the street when she was twelve years old, and was in her first movie by the end of the same year. Starting out as a Mack Sennett Bathing Beauty (via his notorious casting couch), she was one of very few of these young girls to go on to a successful acting career.

A born practical joker, she first met her future husband, Clark Gable, at a Hollywood party when she arranged to arrive in an ambulance and be carried into the gathering on a stretcher. She responded to questions about her love life with 'the King' by saying, 'He's a lousy lay. A few inches less and they'd be calling him the 'Queen of Hollywood'.

Everybody loved her, bosses, fellow actors and the public. She swore like a longshoreman almost every time she opened her mouth, yet nobody seemed to think any less of her for it. It was part of her appeal in an environment where such language is not exactly infrequent. With Lombard what you saw was what you got. In an industry built on pretense, she was utterly unpretentious, and that made her special.

When asked what made her a star, after several years of trying under the name of Carol Lombard, she responded in typical fashion, 'I think it was adding that fucking 'E' that did it'.

 George Raft recalled being in her dressing room one day when she suddenly stripped in front of him and proceeded to peroxide her pubic hairs! 'Relax George', she said, 'I'm just matching my collar and cuffs'. She also had undeniable talent, particularly in light comedy. 'The greatest star in the world', said director William Wellman of her, 'the greatest actress'.

Tragically, she was killed in an air crash in 1942 while returning from a Bond-selling tour. Her mother, who was also killed in the crash, was terrified of air travel and begged her to return by train. In the end they tossed a coin to decide and, as fate would have it, Carole won.

At a stopover she used her considerable charm to avoid being 'bumped' from the flight in favor of some military personnel. An hour or so later the aircraft slammed into the side of a mountain. The forward section, where Carole was seated, was compressed into a chunk about ten feet long by the impact. Her remains were identified through the earrings she wore. MGM fixer, Eddie Mannix, volunteered to trudge through the snow to the crash site, rather than see Gable make the harrowing journey.

Before leaving on her ill-fated trip, Carole sent Gable a blow-up sex doll as a joke, 'to keep him company'. He in turn bought her its male counterpart, complete with huge erection. He had planned to present it to her when she got home.

On January 15, 1944, Irene Dunne christened the liberty ship S.

S. *Carole Lombard* at its launching. Captain Clark Gable stood nearby openly weeping.

The openly gay Franklin Pangborn always played prissy hotel managers, bankers or floorwalkers in his later films such as this one. Early in his career he was inexplicably cast as a villain before his comedic gifts became apparent.

My Own Private Idaho (1991)

Rodney Harvey stars in *My Own Private* Idaho. He also appeared with his girlfriend, Drew Barrymore, in *Gun Crazy*. In 1998, the thirty year-old actor's body was found in a hotel room, sitting up in bed with an empty syringe protruding from the left arm.

Myra Breckinridge (1970)

The director of this awful movie was a former British pop star named Mike Sarne, who just happened to snare Brigitte Bardot for a while in his private life. His biggest hit was a tune called *Come Outside.* He sang it with the help of a young woman named Wendy Richard. She would find her own niche in British television comedy as Miss Brahms in the popular series *Are You Being Served?*

Mae West and Raquel Welch feuded throughout the production of *Myra Breckinridge.* The animosity began after Raquel arrived on set wearing a black dress with white ruffles. Mae's contract stipulated only she could wear black and white in the picture.

Raquel stormed off and disappeared for three days. She eventually returned wearing a black dress with a blue ruffle, the blue being so pale it might just as well have been white. Mae was furious but she had been checkmated.

Nanook of the North (1921)

Nanook the Eskimo, the subject of this acclaimed documentary, died from hunger soon after the movie was released.

National Velvet (1944)

Anne Revere won an Oscar for her portrayal of Mrs. Brown in *National Velvet.* After two more nominations she vanished from the screen for twenty years, a victim of the McCarthy witch-hunts of the early 50s. 'I'm a free thinking

Yankee rebel', she defiantly told the HUAC, 'and nobody's going to tell *me* what to do!' Nevertheless, they did, and her Hollywood days were placed on hold for a couple of decades. It is believed she was named by fellow actor Larry Parks.

Donald Crisp, who plays her husband and Velvet's father, served as a trooper with the British Army in the Boer War. During World War One he was an officer on General Pershing's staff. He was still doing his bit in the Second World War as a Colonel in the OSS.

The studio thought eleven year-old Liz Taylor's breasts were not developed enough to play the adolescent Velvet. Within three months, however, she grew from a training bra into a B-cup and the part was hers. Until then Katharine Hepburn had been earmarked for it.

Taylor's brother Howard and Roddy McDowall's sister Virginia each had bits in the production. Stories that Liz's back problems originated when she fell from her horse while shooting the Grand National sequence are not true. She was even a poor rider on the flat, so putting her mount over jumps was out of the question. A stuntman was used.

Jackie 'Butch' Jenkins plays Velvet's freckle-faced baby brother and was very popular with the public for a few years. His career abruptly ceased in 1950 when he developed an uncontrollable stutter. He later successfully ran a string of car wash establishments.

Neptune's Daughter (1949)

Mel Blanc was the voice of Bugs Bunny, Porky Pig and a score of other Warners cartoon characters. He has a small role as one of Ricardo Montalban's sidekicks in this film. His son Noel took over providing the voices for his father's characters following Mel's death in 1989. In 1991, Noel was seriously injured in the same helicopter crash that almost cost the aged Kirk Douglas his life.

Network (1976)

'I'm not even sure that winning is all that important', Oscar-nominee (and eventual winner) Peter Finch told a reporter in the lead-up to the awards. The comment was made during one of *three hundred* interviews the actor gave promoting both himself and the movie, and all in the space of just five months. In fact, it was while he was waiting to do yet another one that he collapsed and died from a heart attack in a hotel lobby. The Academy has a ruling against posthumous nominations, but because he died shortly *after* the ballot forms went out it was powerless to do anything about it.

Finch was born in London and lived in France and India before moving to Australia and getting work in the fledgling radio industry in the 1930s. He was a life-long Buddhist. His son Charles had little time for him. 'I just can't bring myself to say anything nice about my father', he said. 'He brought nothing but anguish and hardship to our lives'.

Never-ending Story II: The Next Chapter (1990)

Jonathan Brandis, the juvenile star of this film, committed suicide in 2003 at the age of twenty-seven.

Niagara (1953)

Henry Hathaway, the director of *Niagara*, accentuated Marilyn Monroe's swaying gait by shortening the heel on one of her shoes. He was showcasing the sexiest woman on the planet and he knew it. Her dresses are deliberately skintight and it is obvious she is not wearing any underclothes. She also inserted little round buttons in her bras to give the appearance of firm nipples. 'Mine won't get hard', she explained, 'they're the wrong sort'.

The red dress she wore, while writhing about singing 'Kiss', kept riding up to her waist throughout the ten to fifteen shots it took to complete the number. Because she habitually wore no underwear the crew respectfully covered her from the waist down in a horse blanket after the first few takes.

The shower sequence nearly drove Hathaway mad because she kept pressing up against the wet curtain and revealing her attributes. In the end he gave up and later had the special effects department darken down the film to get the segment past the censors.

One evening, during the shoot, a nude Marilyn chose to walk over and stand in front of her bedroom window, giggling at a group of youths peering at her from below. 'I remember her standing stark naked in front of her room window which looked out over the street', recalled actor Max Showalter, 'Come in and look! Why are all those men looking up here?' she called to him. He told her it was obvious why they were there. 'You haven't got a stitch of clothing on, so they're all down on the street looking up at you'. 'Oh, they are?' she innocently answered. He believed his explanation genuinely surprised her.

Max was assigned by Darryl Zanuck to occupy the room adjoining Marilyn's, and instructed to keep an eye on her. She insisted the door between the two rooms be kept unlocked, except when her fiancée Joe DiMaggio was visiting the set. 'I remember it was just before she shot her first scene', recalled Showalter. 'In the middle of the night, stark naked, she came in and jumped on my bed'. 'Please don't do anything to me, just hold me', she said. 'Nudity', he said, 'meant nothing to her'.

Marilyn Monroe (1926-1962)

Known relationships with women:

Carmen, Jeanne
Lytess, Natasha
St Cyr, Lili

Known relationships with men:

Bacon, Jim
Berle, Milton
Bolanos, Jose
Brando, Marlon
Brazzi, Rossano
Brynner, Yul
Carroll, John

Cassini, Oleg
Chaplin Jr, Charles
Chaplin, Sydney
Curtis, Tony
Davis Jr, Sammy
Feldman, Charles
Fisher, Eddie
Greene, Milton
Guinle, Jorge
Hughes, Howard
Huston, John
Hyde, Johnny
Jessel, George
Kazan, Elia
Kennedy, John F
Kennedy, Robert F
La Vey, Anton
Lawford, Peter
Lyon, Ben
Martin, Dean
Marx, Chico
Mitchum, Robert
Montand, Yves
Odets, Clifford
President Sukarno
Ray, Nicholas
Reagan, Ronald
Robinson Jr, Edward G
Rooney, Mickey
Roselli, Johnny
Rubirosa, Porfirio
Runyon, Damon
Sanders, George
Schenck, Joseph
Seigel, Benny
Sinatra, Frank
Slatzer, Robert
Spiegel, Sam
Terrail, Claude

Todd, Mike
Tone, Franchot
Torme, Mel
Wagner, Robert
Welles, Orson
Winchell, Walter
Zanuck, Darryl F
...plus scores more men (and a few more women) from all walks of life.

Married:

Jo DiMaggio
Arthur Miller & 1 other

Marilyn's maternal great grandfather hanged himself. Both her maternal grand-parents died in asylums and her mother was still incarcerated in one when Marilyn died. Marilyn was born Norma Jean Mortenson and illegitimate. She lived in ten foster homes, then was two years in an orphanage, followed by yet another foster home. She told of being seduced by an elderly boarder at one of these when she was eight or nine. She also claimed she was sexually abused by a foster mother from about the age of six.

Her first husband was Jim Dougherty, whom she wed when she was sixteen in 1942. He worked in a factory alongside a young Robert Mitchum. 'Marilyn was not a very sexy girl. No sex appeal whatsoever', recalled Mitchum. She was also extremely shy. Dougherty, incidentally, would one day train the SWAT team that participated in the fiery finale of the Patty Hearst kidnapping decades later.

By 1948 Marilyn's shyness had totally disappeared and she was working as a stripper in burlesque. Her marriage long since over, she operated as a streetwalker off Sunset Boulevard, picking up men in bars at $15 a trick. In those early days she underwent possibly a dozen abortions, many of them little more than backyard butcheries that more than likely destroyed any real hopes she had later of bearing children.

In 1949, to make ends meet, she agreed to do a nude calendar for a paltry $50 fee. It went on to earn in excess of $750,000 for the calendar company that released it a few years later. 'Sure I posed', she said, 'I was hungry', Asked if she had anything at all on at the time, she famously replied, 'Oh yes, I had the radio on'.

Writer Will Fowler recalled her being stoned at a party in her apartment that year. 'She just took off her clothes', he said. 'She liked to show her body off to men. She used to do anything that men would ask her, really just as a favor. She just walked around stoned and naked. It was as much her idea as ours.' On another occasion agent Milt Ebbins was astonished when she walked in on a meeting he was having with director Elia Kazan, wearing just the top half of Kazan's pajamas.

By about 1950 she was ensconced in seventy year-old movie mogul Joseph Schenck's guest bungalow and servicing him when required. Schenck required an injection to give him an erection for a short period. Upon receiving it he would call Marilyn to rush to the main house and satisfy him before its effect wore off. Fox Studio boss Spyrous Skouras was another aged executive who traded career advancement promises for sex with her. There were many, many others.

By the time she was thirty she had undergone, by her own count, thirteen abortions. According to some sources the last of these was performed on July 20, 1962, just two weeks before her death. The child was reputedly conceived to John F Kennedy. It might even have been his brother Bobby's. It is doubtful Marilyn even knew whose it was.

For a while she lived with Columbia voice coach Fred Karger and his mother. He repeatedly refused to marry her, claiming he did not want a celebrity for a wife. Oddly enough he later wed Ronald Reagan's ex-wife Jane Wyman.

Future producer Nico Minardos had a seven-month affair with her in 1952 when he was just a youth. 'She could never have a climax', he said, 'though she would try so hard. She had such sexual psychological problems'. He also thought she was 'one of the most beautiful girls I've ever seen, waking up in the morning without make-up. Absolutely gorgeous...and yet she was a lousy lay'.

Even at the height of her career she was required to service studio executives. She once told a journalist friend she had 'gotten hooked on sex' going from one-night stand to one-night stand. 'Copulation was, I'm sure, Marilyn's uncomplicated way of saying thank you', said writer Nunnally Johnson. Marilyn said she had sex with just about anyone who asked her, male or female, and had done so for as long as she could remember. She resented men who *expected* sex, however, and usually rejected them.

Although not bi-sexual in the usual sense, she sometimes found solace in the arms of women, particularly after she had been passed around by directors, producers and actors and was feeling low. Barbara Stanwyck was reputedly one such source of comfort. 'People tried to make me into a lesbian', Marilyn said later. 'I laughed. No sex is wrong if there's love in it'.

It was TV's Ben Casey, actor Vincent Edwards, who arranged her blind date with his pal baseball legend Joe DiMaggio at the Villa Nova Restaurant. She confided to writer Ben Hecht that she and Joe had sex in the back of her car a few hours after they met. What DiMaggio did not know was that she was intimate with at least four others during the two years he courted her prior to their wedding. Her wedding gift to him was a set of nude photographs of herself from her calendar series, the ones too explicit for publication.

Their marriage was doomed from the start. He was neat and conservative while she was sloppy and craved attention. Both enjoyed immense fame, but Joe's star was on the wane, while Marilyn was at her professional peak. Above all, DiMaggio was extremely jealous, yet his wife flaunted her sexuality as part and parcel of her trade as a screen sex siren. These problems coupled with their complete lack of any common interests were insurmountable. As she told studio friend Jet Fore, 'Joe's biggest bat is not the one he uses on the field. If that's all it takes, we'd still be married. But at some point you had to get out of bed and start talking'. In the end they could scarcely speak to each other without fighting.

Nunnally Johnson recalled an incident on the set of one of Marilyn's movies that disenchanted him with the actress once and for all. The entire crew resented Marilyn because she continually fluffed her lines and kept everyone on the set hours after they should have been finished for the day. Finally she got it right and Johnson, feeling she was in need of a friendly face, walked over to her and said comfortingly, 'Don't worry darling, that last one looked very good'. Marilyn gave him a puzzled look and said, 'Worry about what?' Johnson swore never to attribute human feelings towards her again.

When the world's greatest sex symbol married the Pulitzer Prize-winning author Arthur Miller, *Variety* ran the following headline: EGGHEAD WEDS HOURGLASS.

Night and Day (1946)

This biography of songwriter Cole Porter's life bears little resemblance to the truth. Porter would not sell the rights to it unless certain aspects of his lifestyle were omitted. The producers were not permitted to mention his excessive drinking, his flamboyant homosexual lifestyle, nor his lavender marriage to an older, extremely wealthy woman.

Friends thought it particularly funny that the gnomish, physically incapacitated, owl-eyed songwriter was to be portrayed by the world's number one sex symbol, Cary Grant. Actually, Porter wanted his close friend Fred Astaire to play him, but Fred would not touch the project. So, the story is a complete fabrication, the picture is as dull as dishwater – but who cares? The music is simply the best.

Actors Monty Woolley and Jack Cassidy were two of Porter's many male lovers.

Night of the Hunter, The (1955)

For some reason Robert Mitchum had a thing for urinating in public whenever he got drunk and embittered – which was often. At one location, he did it all over a hotel lobby settee in front of a horde of his fans that had travelled some distance just to meet their idol. He also urinated over a young woman who propositioned him in a bar one evening. While in France he even tried to personally extinguish the Eternal Flame in Paris!

When the assistant director on *The Night of the Hunter* told him he was too drunk to perform, he went over to the man's car, opened the door and relieved himself for some considerable time on the front seat. He did it again in front of the cameras and crew in *Ryan's Daughter*. During his one and only stint at the Betty Ford Clinic he repeated the performance, this time in the swimming pool after refusing to join the other 'guests' in some aquatic regime ordered by the staff. The man had a problem.

Lillian Gish plays the feisty old lady who protects the children from Mitchum's character. She and her sister Dorothy once had the opportunity to buy the Sunset Strip, back in the early days of Hollywood, for the princely sum of

$300. After discussing the pros and cons, they opted to buy a dress each instead!

When Bette Davis asked director Lindsay Anderson if the rumors about Lillian being a lesbian were true, he replied: 'Don't ask me, Bette. Ask her long-time girlfriend'. For what it is worth, Lillian never married and never had children. She left her entire fortune to her good friend Helen Hayes, but there is not a word anywhere that indicates either lady was gay, much less in a relationship other than platonic.

Night Shift (1982)

Kevin Costner can be glimpsed as an extra in the morgue party scene. Future leading lady Shannen Doherty is the Brownie who attacks Henry Winkler in the elevator. The annoying saxophone player on the subway is director Ronny Howard.

Noah's Ark (1929)

A major scene in this film required the flooding of the gigantic Temple of Moloch, an operation involving the dumping of 15,000 tons of water on hundreds of extras. Chief cameraman Hal Mohr walked off the picture when he expressed concern for the safety of the extras and was ignored by studio executives. The sequence went ahead on the orders of director Michael Curtiz and studio head Darryl F Zanuck. Three extras died and another lost a leg. Several more were crippled. Zanuck did his best to keep the story out of the newspapers.

It was Zanuck who wrote most of the Rin Tin Tin scripts that put both the canine star and himself on the road to success at 20th Century-Fox. As soon as Zanuck arrived from Nebraska he began a passionate affair with the delectable Dolores Costello, but it didn't last. Later, as a studio mogul, he maintained a ritual of having sex with a female employee in the back room adjoining his office every day at 4 pm. Actresses and starlets were selected to appear at these sessions, among them Carole Landis who was reputedly one of his regulars.

Henry Fonda described him as 'a narrow bastard with only two interests in life, making movies and satisfying his cock'. Zanuck insisted on all male stars at Fox shaving their chests. The bald-chested Tyrone Power didn't care, but William Holden and John Payne were particularly irked by this regulation.

None but the Brave (1964)

In 1964, while making *None but the Brave* in Hawaii, Frank Sinatra and Howard Koch's wife, Ruth, were swept out to sea while swimming. Actor Brad Dexter, whose greatest claim to movie fame was as one of the original Magnificent Seven, swam out and kept them afloat until surf riders reached them. Out of gratitude Frank made Dexter the producer on some of his films for a while.

North by Northwest (1959)

The title *North by Northwest* has nothing whatsoever to do with the plot. Somebody must have just liked the sound of it for a title.

Sophia Loren was designated for the female lead until contractual problems saw her replaced by Eva Marie Saint. Because director Alfred Hitchcock could not get permission to film at neither Mount Rushmore nor the United Nations building, he was compelled to have both built into sets for the film.

Although Hitch directed hundreds of women over the decades he knew very little about them or their physiology. When Saint informed him she was indisposed because of her period he had to be told what it was.

Jessie Royce Landis who plays Cary Grant's mother was actually a year *younger* than him in real life. Saint was thirty and Cary fifty-four when they played the romantic leads. For some reason Hollywood producers have never thought twice about making pictures in which a fifty to sixty year-old man provides the love interest for a much younger woman. Studios recoil in horror, however, at the prospect of a young man getting it on with a much older woman. On the odd occasion when such a scenario is required, the older woman is usually a tramp and the young man a naïve and immature victim.

In *Charade,* shot in 1962, Cary was by then fifty-eight while his co-star Audrey Hepburn was only thirty-three and looked a good decade younger than that. Audiences conditioned to such things accepted their romance as completely normal and natural. Perhaps, decades of young starlets submitting to lecherous elderly Hollywood executives has the latter believing this is par for the course in the real world as well.

North to Alaska (1960)

Ernie Kovacs was hilarious as the cigar-chomping conman in this western comedy. Two years after its completion he was killed in a car accident. Police attending the scene surmised he had been reaching for a lighter to ignite his cigar, and took his eyes off the road momentarily.

French actress Capucine played Michelle "Angel", her favorite flower was the capucine (French for nasturtium). Rumors have abounded for decades that the French beauty was a transsexual, but they have never been confirmed. When asked if she and William Holden had consummated their affair, the predominately lesbian actress said: 'He desired me more than I desired him. I have had romantic or sexual liaisons with women. It happened because I was so strongly attracted'.

Despite his own sexual ambivalence, actor Dirk Bogarde came very close to marrying her. But it was not to be. In 1990, the beautiful but troubled actress, while suffering from profound depression, threw herself from the balcony of her eighth-floor apartment in Switzerland.

When he was sixteen, Fabian was literally plucked off the street because of his looks and transformed into a pop singer. He toured Australia that year and did five shows at the Sydney Stadium. Not only could he not sing to save himself, his manager had to shout the lyrics to him from off-stage throughout his performances He couldn't remember the words either.

Not as a Stranger (1955)

Not as a Stranger was released in Hong Kong under the exhausting title: The Heart of a Lady as Pure as the Full Moon over the Place of Medical Salvation. Whew!

Four of Hollywood's most renowned boozers, Robert Mitchum, Frank Sinatra, Broderick Crawford and Lee Marvin, are featured in this picture. The notorious 'Wrong Door Raid' involving all four gentlemen took place around this time.

It all started when Joe DiMaggio could not locate his fiancée, Marilyn Monroe. His good buddy Sinatra (who was servicing Marilyn behind Joe's back, by the way) said he knew where she was, and was prepared to take his pals there and drag her out by the hair, if need be. The group drove to where Frank was sure she was staying, burst into room 3A as per his instructions, and were confronted by an octogenarian lady who did not resemble the blonde sex goddess in the remotest way. She immediately called the police, complaining of being broken into by a handful of famous movie stars. No charges were laid because everybody denied everything.

Nothing but Trouble (1991)

The title of this movie pretty much sums up the life of its rapper star, Tupac Shakur. He was born in 1971 to Alice Williams one of the founders of the Black Panthers. She was also one of the twenty-one Panthers arrested (she was acquitted) in 1969, on charges of conspiring to bomb public places in New York City. His father, too, was a Panther and his stepfather went to prison for sixty years in 1971 for his involvement in a Brinks truck robbery.

Exposed to drugs at an early age (his mother was a crack addict), Shakur was dealing in narcotics by the time he turned seventeen. In November 1993, he was charged with the rape and sodomy of a nineteen year-old woman in a Manhattan hotel room. While out on bail he was gunned down in the lobby of a Times Square building and robbed of $40,000 worth of jewelry. Miraculously he survived. A witness to the crime was murdered in Queens a year later, so no one was ever charged.

Sentenced to four and a half years in prison for sexual abuse, Shakur married a young college student while he was inside, just so he could enjoy conjugal visits. The union was soon annulled. Released in 1996, he scored great successes with three rap albums, not that it did him any good in the long run. In September of that year he was shot to death as he sat at traffic lights in his limousine in Las Vegas. He was twenty-five.

Ocean's Eleven (1960)

During the shoot at the Sands in Vegas, Presidential candidate John F Kennedy spent a week with Sinatra & Co as their guest. Sammy Davis recalled Peter Lawford telling him that the casino owners had gifted JFK with a satchel containing a million dollars for his campaign. He said he saw it in Jack's private room along with four showgirls 'donated' for his amusement.

The friendship between Davis and Sinatra appears to have been genuine, although many people say Sammy ingratiated himself with 'the Boss' by allowing himself to be the butt of Frank's racial quips, both on-stage and off. Be that as it may, Sinatra went to bat for Davis numerous times, *especially* over racial issues. When Sammy was denied the purchase of a home in a white neighborhood because of his color, Sinatra solved the problem by buying every house in the street to enable his pal to live in the home of his choosing. For all his bad press, Sinatra could be extremely generous and made contributions to many charities over the years, always anonymously.

From the age of three Sammy was on the road with the family vaudeville act. Consequently, he never spent a single day in kindergarten or school in his life. When child welfare came sniffing about, he was either hidden or disguised in whiskers as a midget.

No matter how famous he became he was still the victim of racial discrimination wherever he went. Even when he was head-lining at the Sands Hotel in Vegas, a couple of high-rolling southerners spotted him in the hotel pool one morning and insisted it be drained before whites could use it again. It was. Bob Hope once asked him during a golf game what his handicap was. 'I'm one-eyed, I'm Jewish and I'm black', Sammy replied. 'What's yours?'

His betrothal to white actress Mai Britt threatened to destroy Sinatra's ties with the Kennedys, so Sammy released Frank from his duties as best man at the wedding. With the Presidential elections coming up, Kennedy could not afford to alienate the southern vote, and was set to cut Sinatra adrift if the wedding plans went ahead with 'Old Blue Eyes' as best man. Once the election was over, Sinatra and the rest of the Rat Pack were free to attend the wedding as previously planned, without recrimination on Davis's part. Sinatra was genuinely moved by the gesture.

Sammy's engagement to Kim Novak in 1958 created even bigger problems. Two gangster associates, twice removed from Columbia head Harry Cohn, reputedly took him into the desert outside Vegas, held a sharpened stick to his one remaining eye and threatened to blind him altogether unless he left Novak alone and married a black woman at once. Within a week he had tied the knot with an African/American showgirl named Loray White. He paid her $25,000 for the privilege and the marriage was never consummated. In fact, until he announced his intention to marry the startled Miss White in the middle of his Vegas performance one evening, she had never even dated him before. Harry Belafonte was best man. A few months later the couple secretly divorced.

By 1967 he was hanging out with the Rolling Stones, Jimi Hendrix and Mama Cass Elliott, dropping acid, snorting coke, smoking pot and drinking heavily. One night he sang a single song in his cabaret act and then trouped off stage believing he had completed a full concert.

In 1941, Cesar Romero was sacked from the Cisco Kid films because he persisted in playing the hero in 'a gay way'. Nicknamed 'Butch' by his friends, he numbered among his many lovers Tyrone Power and Desi Arnaz. In the 1960s he played 'the Joker' in the camp TV series *Batman*.

Oh, God! (1977)

One of the great love stories of Hollywood is that of George Burns and Gracie Allen. Together for nearly forty years they do not, however, reside together in death. Gracie was a Catholic and George was Jewish so the closest he could get to her in the cemetery was in the nearby Episcopalian section.

One-Eyed Jacks (1961)

Pina Pellicer is the young actress who portrays Karl Malden's daughter in this film directed by Marlon Brando. She and Brando had a brief affair during shooting, although she was involved with several women at the time. The extremely timid and sensitive girl had already attempted suicide by slashing her wrists as a seventeen year-old. Brando bedded her and then ditched her. Three years later she took her own life over a lesbian relationship that went amiss. She was twenty-nine.

One Flew Over the Cuckoo's Nest (1975)

Jack Nicholson was away on a skiing holiday until day six of the shoot, so he was initially unaware that some of the supporting cast were, in fact, inmates of the hospital. When Michael Douglas observed him at the break for lunch suddenly put down his plate and walk off, he hurried to the actor and enquired if there was a problem. 'Man', replied Nicholson, 'these guys don't quit. I'm eating lunch and nobody breaks character, nothing. What's going on here?'

During filming, Louise Fletcher worried that some of her fellow actors had come to view her as the real Nurse Ratched. To prove she was a normal woman, she called the cast together and assured them, 'I'm not the monster'. She then stripped off her clothes and stood, topless, before the group to emphasize her point.

Ellen Burstyn, who won an Oscar in the previous year for *Alice Doesn't Live Here Anymore*, went on television and urged Academy voters to boycott the awards in protest at the shortage of good female roles. Fletcher who was nominated for her performance in 'Cuckoo' was extremely miffed. Why, she asked, did Miss Burstyn not insist on a boycott when *she* was nominated instead of waiting until when she was not? Point taken. Fletcher went on to win anyway.

One Hundred Men and a Girl (1937)

In between making movies Adolphe Menjou would travel to the unemployment office in his chauffeur-driven Rolls Royce and collect his $90 a week unemployment cheque! An extreme right-winger, he happily named names during the McCarthy witch-hunts of the fifties.

Not everyone in Hollywood, of course, was in favor of the witch-hunts. The Committee for the First Amendment chartered a plane for several movie celebrities to fly from Los Angeles to Washington on October 26, 1947, to protest the proceedings. Included in the group were Humphrey Bogart, Lauren Bacall, Danny Kaye, John Huston, Sterling Hayden, Gene Kelly and Ira Gershwin. On December 2, however, one of them got cold feet. Bogart issued a statement calling his participation 'ill-advised and even foolish'.

On Golden Pond (1981)

Until Katharine Hepburn and Henry Fonda made *On Golden Pond* together at the end of their careers, they had never once officially met throughout their fifty years in Hollywood. On the set she gave him a small gift, a felt hat that was once her lover Spencer Tracy's favorite. Fonda wore it in the first scene they shot.

Fonda was extremely fortunate to survive World War Two. As a lieutenant aboard the destroyer USS *Curtis,* he was on shore leave when a Kamikaze destroyed the area on board where he usually worked. He later won a Bronze Star for his part in detecting and plotting the sinking of a Japanese submarine.

On Her Majesty's Secret Service (1969)

While shooting the sequence where Bond is attacked by four helicopters, British cameraman Johnny Jordan was seriously injured when two of the choppers collided. His leg was very badly gashed and later amputated. His rotten luck continued when, in 1969, he was thrown from the fuselage of a B-25 and killed while filming *Catch-22*.

Only the Valiant (1951)

Barbara Payton plays the female lead here, alongside Gregory Peck with whom she had a brief affair. In fact, she tended to bed all her leading men. After her marriage to Franchot Tone collapsed, she alternated between him and Tom Neal for a while, until the latter caught her *en flagrante* with Franchot and beat him senseless. It almost goes without saying that the sexually industrious Howard Hughes, and the equally energetic lawyer Greg Bautzer, also found their way into Barbara's boudoir. Dennis Hopper had her in a back booth of a bar when she was hawking her body around Sunset Boulevard in the late fifties and early sixties.

After her career dried up she became involved with gangsters, and at one time testified on behalf of her mob boyfriend, providing him with a much-needed alibi. She was also a central figure in a statewide multi-million dollar drugs ring, uncovered by authorities, and was fortunate not to do time in prison. By 1958 she was an alcoholic and drug abuser, and in 1964 was arrested for prostitution. Liver failure resulted in her skin turning yellow and her front teeth falling out. In 1967 her system gave up and she was dead at thirty-nine.

On the Beach (1959)

In Australia, in 1959, to make *On the Beach,* Ava Gardner alienated the press and most of the population when she supposedly told the press: 'I'm here to make a film about the end of the world and this sure is the place for it'. It now appears the comment may have been an invention by a journalist named Neil Jillett.

On the Waterfront (1954)

Shortly before this picture was made, screenwriter Budd Schulberg, director Elia Kazan and actor Lee J Cobb, all informed on their colleagues to the HUAC during the McCarthy hearings. Kazan named names in 1952 to save his career. Among those he sold out was writer Clifford Odets. Initially, Marlon Brando refused the lead because he considered Kazan to be a stoolpigeon. When he later changed his mind, he said it was because the director guaranteed him time off to visit his shrink.

When Kazan came on stage in 1998 to receive an honorary award from the movie industry, he did so to tepid applause. Nick Nolte, Ed Harris and others sat determinedly, with arms folded, as the cameras played on them. Comedian

Chris Rock set off a chorus of boos when he referred to Kazan as 'a rat'. As for the stoolpigeon himself, he made no apologies for his actions nearly a half a century before, actions that saw eight of his colleagues' careers terminated.

There is no doubt a blacklist once existed, although the studios steadfastly denied it. When one director complained to Jack Warner that he had been refused a job because of it, Warner retorted, 'there is no blacklist and you're not on it!' Ironically, J Parnell –Thomas, the chairman of the HUAC committee in October 1947, ended up in Danbury Federal Penitentiary, convicted of payroll padding. He served time alongside two of the Hollywood Ten that *his* committee had convicted for contempt of court.

Even though Eva Marie Saint clearly plays the leading lady in this film, she was successfully nominated in the Best Supporting Actress category, the idea being to keep her clear of the Judy Garland – Grace Kelly contest for Best Actress. The Supporting Oscars were supposed to give non-leading performers an opportunity to be recognized, but over the years that has certainly not always been the case.

'I don't like Mr. Brando', remarked Rod Steiger who plays his brother in the film. 'I'll never forget or forgive what he did to me in *On the Waterfront*. I did the take with him when the camera was on him, but when it came time for the camera to be on me - he went home! I had to speak my lines to an assistant director. It must have just burned him up that we came out even in that scene, despite what he did'.

Although he never contradicted nor confirmed stories that he and his roommate in the early days (Wally Cox of TV's *Hiram Holiday*) were lovers, Brando did say in an interview, 'Like many men I have had homosexual experiences, and I'm not ashamed of them'.

Writer Truman Capote claimed to have had sex with him too, but there is no proof of this either. The tiny, drug-addicted, alcoholic Capote was not much liked. He tended to get acquaintances to confide in him, and then he would blab their confessions to the media. Brando was one such victim. 'The little bastard spent half the night telling me his problems', he moaned. 'I figured the least I could do was tell him a few of mine'. Capote had just informed the media of Brando's homosexual past.

'Marlon Brando got, for an aggregate of twenty minutes on screen in *Superman* and *Apocalypse Now,* more money than Clark Gable got for twenty years at MGM', said Billy Wilder. After seeing Brando in *A Streetcar Named Desire*, Joan Crawford asked him to be in her new picture *Sudden Fear,* in the role of her young husband. He sent word back to her that he wasn't interested in 'doing any mother-and-son pictures at the present time'. He went straight to the top of her hate list.

Lee J Cobb was a brilliant actor, especially on the New York Stage, but his reputation was forever sullied by the McCarthy witch-hunts. When his good friend, writer Alvah Bessie, asked him for a $500 loan to tide his family over while Bessie was in prison for a year as one of 'the Hollywood Ten', Cobb lied and told him he did not have the money.

Then, in 1953, the stoolpigeons came home to roost when actor Larry Parks named Cobb as a communist to the HUAC. To get out from under, Cobb promptly named twenty people to the Committee, including character actor Sam Jaffe. He not only betrayed his friends, but he also publicly praised the Committee for the job it was doing. To testify was, he said, 'a privilege...I can only say that I am sorry for those who haven't, and that more haven't done so'.

'OUR GANG' Series of shorts (1930s and 40s)

Three of the child actors who feature in this immensely popular series died tragically. A fourth was charged with murder in 2002.

Freckle-faced Jay R Smith appears in twenty-five of these short comedies playing 'Speck'. In 2002 his corpse was found in the Nevada desert. A vagrant he had befriended was later charged with his murder. The equally freckle-faced Carl 'Alfalfa' Switzer was shot to death over a $50 bet in 1959, a year after he played his last role, a miniscule bit in Charlton Heston's version of *Ben-Hur*.

The delightful Scotty Beckett made his acting debut in an *Our Gang* short at the age of three. Later, he played the young *Anthony Adverse*, the young dauphin in *Marie Antoinette*, and the young Paris Mitchell in *King's Row*. From then on his life began its downward spiral. By nineteen he was drinking heavily.

In 1954 he was arrested for carrying a concealed weapon and, three years later, was again arrested for carrying hard drugs. In 1960 he was jailed for six months for assaulting his step- daughter with a crutch. Two years went by before he slashed his wrists and survived. In 1968, he succeeded in fatally overdosing with sleeping pills at the age of thirty-nine.

Robert Blake was also a former member of the *Our Gang* children in the thirties, listed under his real name of Mickey Gubitosi. In the forties he was seen playing Little Beaver in the Red Ryder series of B westerns, alongside 'Wild Bill' Elliott. When he was a child his father sexually abused him, and often tied the boy under the house for days on end, forcing him to eat his meals like dog from a bowl on the floor.

In 2002, Blake was charged with shooting to death his wife, Bonny Lee Bakly. She was murdered while sitting in his parked car outside a restaurant in Los Angeles. Police arrived on the scene to find Blake pacing up and down and vomiting. He told them he had left his revolver *on the table* at the restaurant, and had gone back to retrieve it. His wife, he claimed, was shot in his absence. He was not believed, and he and his chauffeur were charged in April 2002 with conspiracy to murder. In March 2005, to the amazement of most of America, they were acquitted. Los Angeles District Attorney Steve Cooley, when asked to comment on the verdict, described Blake as 'a miserable human being'. The jurors he described as 'incredibly stupid'.

The dead woman was a scam artist and bigamist who sold nude photos of herself to wealthy, gullible men whom she later married, fleeced, and then discarded, usually without bothering to get a divorce. One was an eighty-one year-old Montana man whom she left one hour after the wedding. Blake was her *ninth* husband.

Paint Your Wagon (1969)

Jean Seberg plays the female lead in *Paint Your Wagon*, alongside Clint Eastwood and Lee Marvin. Whereas Lee received a million dollars as male lead, by comparison Jean was paid a paltry $120,000. Her marriage to Romain Gary received its *coup de grace* from her affair with the equally married Eastwood on the set of this film.

Seberg was plagued by mental illness throughout the seventies and committed to asylums in 1970, '74 and '79. The FBI also hounded her because of her political affiliations and intimate involvement with the militant Black Panther Hakim Jamal, a radical who advocated the killing of all whites (presumably with the exception of the one he was bedding). She introduced him to Vanessa Redgrave, and even managed to squeeze $10,000 out of Marlon Brando for the Black Panther cause. Jamal stayed at Redgrave's London home for a while, prior to his murder at the hands of his fellow Panthers who tired of his duality.

Jean then took up with another Panther (Raymond 'Masai' Hewitt), which brought her under even closer FBI surveillance. J Edgar Hoover leaked it to the press that her soon to be born baby was fathered by the black militant. The child was stillborn, however, and the greatly disturbed Seberg opted to display its corpse in a glass casket to prove to the world it was white!

By 1973 she was grossly overweight, her self-esteem was at an all-time low. To prove to herself she was still attractive to men, she began having sex with complete strangers in elevators and hotel rooms. Just before her death she went into a weight loss farm for six weeks, emerging as svelte as ever, but the sudden loss of poundage had tipped her mentally over the edge. For some time she became convinced her refrigerator was spying on her! One evening she threw herself in front of a train but was rescued. On another occasion she hacked at her wrists with a steak knife during a meal in a restaurant.

The end came when she wrapped her naked body in a blanket, drove to the Paris airport, climbed into the back seat of her Renault, and downed a stack of barbiturates. Her body lay undiscovered for nine days. One year later her former husband, Romain Gary, also killed himself. He left a note that read: 'No connection with Jean Seberg. Lovers of broken hearts are kindly asked to look elsewhere'.

Paleface, The (1948)

Iris Adrian plays Pepper in this Bob Hope vehicle. 'I never went with actors', she said. 'Basically, they're bums who got lucky in the looks department'. Given that assessment of her peers, it came as no surprise when she bypassed all the

Hollywood hunks and married a pro-football player. Of course, it could be argued that sportsmen are bums who got lucky in the muscles department, but we won't go into that.

Iris was never a major star but she does have one claim to fame. As far as I know, she is the only Hollywood actor to meet her end in an earthquake! She was eighty-two years old when the San Andreas Fault caught up with her in 1994.

Pandora's Box (1928)

The enigmatic, outrageous and exquisite Louise Brooks plays the flower girl Lulu in this classic silent film made in Germany. She (typically) won a contract with Famous Players-Lasky by stripping and lying down on producer Walter Wanger's office couch at their first meeting.

Her promiscuity began at fourteen when she became sexually involved with a much older man in Wichita, Kansas. Taking lovers of either gender wherever she went, Lulu, as she was known, was deemed the ultimate hedonist. 'The best lovers I ever had were homosexuals', she said. She always insisted she was not a lesbian, despite her lusty affair with Greta Garbo. By her own count she bedded 430 lovers of both sexes. She even wrote an explicit book on her life, but at the last moment decided to burn it instead of having it published. George Cukor described her as 'a beautiful nothing'.

Lulu started out in show business as a fifteen year-old dancer in New York and was soon in George White's Scandals. Tiring of that, she drifted into movies for the extra money. When she refused to sleep with Columbia mogul Harry Cohn, he vowed to get even with her. Years later, when she was down and almost out he offered her a place in the chorus of the 1937 musical *When You're In Love*. He then released stills of her in the line captioned, 'Louise Brooks, former screen star, who deserted Hollywood seven years ago… Louise courageously begins again at the bottom'.

Her bridges well and truly burned behind her, she worked in New York City as a sales clerk through the late forties and early fifties. Her final years were spent as a recluse, more often than not being 'kept' by wealthy men. She died at the age of seventy-nine in 1985.

Papillon (1973)

Steve McQueen was unruly, unpopular, almost deaf in one ear, and notorious as the stingiest of tippers. He rarely got along with his fellow actors. One of those he really detested was his co-star in *Papillon*, Dustin Hoffman, whom he described as 'an over-acting ham'. Norman Jewison, who directed McQueen in *The Cincinnati Kid* in 1965, said, 'I can honestly say he's the most difficult actor I've ever worked with'.

Robert Mitchum had this to say: 'Steve McQueen was notorious for orgies. Honest to God Roman-type sex orgies. The guy always needed an audience. Even sex…he had to make it into a party'.

When his wife, Neile Adams, confessed to a brief affair with actor Maximillian Schell, he flew into a rage and put a gun to her head. She was pregnant at the time, so he forced her to abort the baby in case it was Schell's.

Paradise Garden (1917)

This is one of the few films featuring minor actress Virginia Rappe, the girl who would find unwanted fame as the so-called 'victim' of Roscoe 'Fatty' Arbuckle's sex-crazed assault in a 1921 scandal that rocked Hollywood.

When her picture first appeared on the sheet music cover for *Let Me Call You Sweetheart,* it brought about a call from Hollywood to come out and screen test for an acting job. All she initially got from this was a bit part in *Fantasy.* She did, however, manage to infect half the Mack Sennett Company with the 'crabs' during her years there. She also had five abortions between the ages of fourteen and sixteen and was pregnant again at the time of her death, to a forty year-old sculptor she barely knew. She suffered from chronic cystitis and the resultant abdominal pains often caused the twenty-five year-old to tear off her clothes, especially when she got drunk.

It took three trials to finally exonerate Arbuckle of the charge of raping her and causing Rappe's death. By then his career was in tatters. The Hearst press was especially relentless in its persecution of the comedian, intent on throwing him to the wolves, before details of other orgies involving a number of movie moguls could emerge.

Headlines such as: 'Arbuckle Dances While Girl Is Dying' and 'Arbuckle Cries: I Have Waited For Five Years, And Now

I've Got You', pitilessly attacked him, before and during his trials. Years later, Hearst told a crony that the Arbuckle case sold more newspapers than the sinking of the *Lusitania*.

It was argued by Arbuckle's attorney that the comedian had gone to Rappe's aid at a party when he accidentally discovered her vomiting in one of the bedrooms of the St. Francis Hotel. He called for an ambulance at once and the girl was rushed to the hospital. The official autopsy report found she was pregnant, had VD, and had died from peritonitis.

A scheming crony of hers, one Bambina Delmont, attempted to extort money from Arbuckle and it was her accusations that ultimately led to him being charged and tried for rape. Delmont's past record of blackmail, extortion and prostitution was kept secret by the prosecution throughout the trial. The papers clambered all over the story, trampling Arbuckle's name in the mud as they did so. Stories that the dead girl had been assaulted with a bottle or a jagged piece of ice were printed willy-nilly by the Hearst papers, then picked up by other publications. All of them implied he had violated the girl and caused her death. None had any foundation in fact.

District Attorney Matthew Brady went public proclaiming he would have the funnyman convicted. Privately, he was aware that Delmont's accusations were untrue, but he had political aspirations that would be well served if he gained a conviction. Paramount head Adolph Zukor, it was later revealed, paid Brady a substantial amount towards his handling of the trial. Zukor and Arbuckle had been at loggerheads for some time over the comedian's refusal to help promote Paramount productions. It was even thought Zukor might have arranged the St. Francis party to get Fatty into trouble with the authorities.

The first trial resulted in a hung jury because a single juror with known ties to Brady defied the other eleven who voted for acquittal. The second trial was bungled by Arbuckle's attorney who mistakenly thought the evidence presented in the hung trial would be enough to clear his client, so he chose not to put Fatty on the stand. This trial too resulted in a hung jury. Again, there was a prosecution 'stooge' among the jurors, the solitary 'hold-out'.

By the time the whole truth emerged at the third trial, the jury took just five minutes to acquit the beleaguered comedian. Brady's refusal to place his key witness (Delmont) on the stand in *any* of the trials was finally seen for what it was. The members of the jury submitted a written testimonial, apologizing to the actor for the ordeal he had suffered, and exonerating him of any blame, whatsoever. But the damage had been done. The man who once drove about in a $25,000 Rolls Royce and earned in excess of a million dollars a year had been wiped out by the court costs. Worse still, he was vilified throughout America.

Six days *after his acquittal* he was banned from the movie industry by the newly appointed Will Hays of the Hays Office, the instrument put in place by the studios to self-monitor their conduct before government censure took that option out of their hands. The ban was later lifted but, of course, it was much too late to salvage Roscoe's career. He found some directorial work under the pseudonym of William B Goodrich, and was just getting on his feet when he died from a heart attack in 1933 at the age of forty-six. His third wife actress Addie McPhail lived until 2003, dying at the age of ninety-seven.

Parent Trap, The (1961)

Walt Disney was used to getting his own way. When he billed Hayley Mills over Maureen O'Hara in this film, in direct contravention of his contract with the Irish actress, O'Hara insisted he abide by their agreement. He sent her a message: 'Sue me and I'll destroy you'. Aware of his power to do just that, she opted not to file papers against him.

Party, The (1968)

Pretty Claudine Longet, who was the ex-wife of singer Andy Williams, plays the female lead in this Peter Sellers comedy. In 1977, she shot and killed her lover, Croatian Olympic ski racer Vladimir'Spider' Sabich, as he went to rendezvous with another woman in Aspen, Colorado. Her attorney, Ron Austin, somehow managed to get her conviction reduced to one of 'criminal negligence' and she served just *twenty-one days* in jail before walking free. Austin and Longet later became husband and wife.

The busty Carol Wayne (39-24-35) plays the minor role of June Warren. Less than twelve months after posing nude for

Playboy in 1984 she was dead. She and a used car dealer named Edward Durston travelled to Manzanillo on the Mexican Gold Coast for a holiday. On arrival at their hotel an argument developed and she stormed off alone towards the beach. Three days later her body was found in Santiago Bay. She had been dead about two days.

When no sign of alcohol or drugs were detected in the autopsy, local police suspected foul play, a suspicion that increased when Durstan suddenly left the area. In the end, however, there was no evidence to support a murder theory, so an 'accidental death' verdict was recorded. It may just have been coincidental, but the same Edward Durstan was the last person known to be with the daughter of TV celebrity Art Linkletter, when she supposedly jumped out of her apartment window in 1969 after taking LSD.

Patton (1970)

Patton's son, George Patton III, made it to Major General and served in both Korea and Vietnam. 'I do like to see the arms and legs fly', the chip-off-the-old-block commented. He once attended a party wearing a peace medallion and carrying the bullet-scarred skull of a Viet Cong soldier!

George C Scott refused to attend the Oscars when he won for *Patton* in 1970, describing the Academy Awards as a 'meat parade'. A month before the ceremony he accepted the New York Film Critics' Best Actor Award for the same role! The question often asked since then is why did he wait until *after* Oscar nominations had closed before writing to the

Academy and advising it of his intention to refuse a statuette if he won?

His affair with Ava Gardner ended after he bashed her once too often. He broke her collarbone in Rome and then assaulted her again in their Savoy suite in London. This time she called the police and had him locked up. He returned to his wife for a time, but became deeply depressed getting over Ava and wound up in a Connecticut sanitarium. His ex-wife Colleen Dewhurst said of him, 'George C Scott. Fine actor. Big drinker. Wife beater. What else do you want to know?' Nevertheless, she did fall for him twice.

Peg 'O' My Heart (1932)

William Randolph Hearst was in his fifties when he first saw seventeen year-old Marion Davies in the Ziegfeld Follies in 1915. They soon became lovers. His wife Millicent understandably detested Marion, referring to her as 'that harlot', yet steadfastly refused to divorce her enormously rich husband. It seems she was angry, but not stupid.

Hearst provided Marion with a mansion in Santa Monica that contained 118 rooms and 55 bathrooms! Her dressing room consisted of fourteen rooms in itself. The salon was solid gold, the crystal chandeliers were from Tiffany's and there was also a porcelain room, formerly the property of a Chinese princess. The tycoon's extravagance when it came to his lover was boundless. He once had the stage and walls of a theatre adorned with 100,000 pink roses for one of her premieres in New York City.

He always thought Marion disliked alcohol, so he banned it from all his parties at their fabulous San Simeon estate, although cocktails and wine were permitted. Guests such as David Niven used to smuggle in booze for after dinner drinks in the guest bedrooms. Marion would sneak off and join them.

She remained Hearst's companion for thirty-five years, but they never married. She had occasional lovers over that time, but did not marry until four months after he died at the age of eighty-eight in 1951. By then Marion was fifty-four years old. Her last years were spent in a haze of alcohol and the morphine she needed to relieve the ravages of mouth cancer. The Patty Hearst who made the headlines after being kidnapped by militants and participating (apparently willingly) in a bank robbery in 1974 was William Randolph's granddaughter.

Perfect (1985)

Down the list of credits appears the name of Paul Baressi, the man who went to the press in 1990 vowing he and John Travolta had once enjoyed a two-year affair in and around the time they made *Perfect*. Travolta, not surprisingly, has vehemently denied the story. Even though Baressi has since retracted his claims, he still insists Travolta took him to Hawaii for a few weeks of 'togetherness', whatever that means.

Pete Smith Presents (1935 – 1950s)

Pete Smith churned out shorts on American suburbia for nearly two decades, winning a Special Oscar for them in 1953. In 1979 he committed suicide by leaping from the roof of a nursing home.

Peyton Place (1957)

It took studio executives five hours to talk Lana Turner into playing the role of Constance MacKenzie in this. She was thirty-seven years of age, she argued, and too young to play a mother. Only after it was pointed out to her that Joan Crawford's career was resurrected through portraying a mother in *Mildred Pierce* did she come around.

Her daughter Cheryl broke down when she attended the Hollywood premiere of Peyton Place and saw her mother's performance. 'They were all too familiar, those icy, dangerous looks mother gave', wrote Cheryl later. 'The imperial manner and tight-assed way of crossing a room, the way she would turn and punch home a line...the techniques mother used to intimidate and control me came not from a well of feeling but from her bag of actress tricks'.

Lana's friends held their collective breaths when Cheryl published her memoirs, expecting a *Mommie Dearest* styled hatchet job. But Cheryl dismissed their concerns. 'Mom wasn't around much in my life for a *Mommie Dearest*', she said. 'She qualifies perhaps for a long cameo role'.

Lana Turner (1921-1995)

Known relationships:

Arnaz, Desi
Barry, Don 'Red'
Bautzer, Greg
Berle, Milton
Berman, Pandro S
Bernstein, Leonard
Bey, Turhan
Bowman, Lee
Broccoli, Cubby
Burton, Richard
Calhoun, Rory
Cassini, Oleg
Connery, Sean
Cooper, Jackie
Daniels, Billy
Dominguin, Luis
Dorsey, Tommy
Douglas, Kirk
Downs, Johnny
Evans, Charles
Evans, Robert
Fisher, Eddie
Flynn, Errol
Gable, Clark
Garfield, John
Goodman, Benny
Guinle, Jorge
Harrison, Rex
Hartford, Huntington
Haymes, Dick
Hodiak, John
Hughes, Howard
Hutton, Robert
Johnson, Kerry
Kennedy, John F
Kind, Jimmy
Krupa, Gene
Lamas, Fernando

Lawford, Peter
LeRoy, Mervyn
Louis, Joe
Mabry, Moss
Martin, Dean
Martin, Tony
Mature, Victor
Meyer, Johnny
Michael, Marc
Montalban, Ricardo
Montgomery, George
Morris, Wayne
Newman, Paul
Pero, Tylor
Peterson, Chris
Power, Tyrone
Raft, George
Reagan, Ronald
Rich, Buddy
Romero, Cesar
Rooney, Art
Rooney, Mickey
Shaw, Peter
Siegel, Benny
Sinatra, Frank
Stack, Robert
Stewart, James
Stompanato, Johnny
Taylor, Robert
Torme, Mel
Tracy, Spencer
Wagner, Robert
Wapner, Joseph
Westmore, Bud
Ziegler, Ronald

Married:

Lex Barker
Artie Shaw & 5 others

Lana Turner's father was a mine foreman who was murdered following a crap game when she was nine. His beaten and stabbed body was found minus a sock, the one in which he kept his winnings.

She was discovered at fifteen playing truant from school and drinking Coca Cola in the Top Hat Café (*not* in Schwab's Soda Fountain, as has often been quoted). In October 1939, she was reported to be the first Hollywood star to wear nylons (they had just been invented). As a matter of interest, nylons were named for New York and London, the hometowns of their two inventors.

She lost her virginity to Hollywood lawyer and perennial escort of beautiful actresses, Greg Bautzer, although Mickey Rooney always claimed he was the first. She married bandleader Artie Shaw to spite Bautzer who had stood her up that evening. 'I thought of someone who would make Greg mad and jealous', she explained. 'So I called Artie. After midnight, Artie said it would be nice if we got married'. The predatory Shaw was heavily involved with Judy Garland at the time and Betty Grable was pregnant to him.

When an MGM executive chastised Lana for picking up a gas station attendant for casual sex, she fobbed him off, saying, 'don't worry honey, who's gonna believe it?' Another executive said of her, 'she was amoral. If she saw a stagehand with tight pants and a muscular build, she'd invite him into her dressing room'.

Her makeup man, Del Armstrong, recalled her often saying, 'I want that one', and she would get him. 'She was always the aggressor', said Armstrong. 'But once she slept with a guy, she'd lose interest, except with Tyrone Power'. 'Ty was the love of her life', said her friend Esther Williams. 'She never got over him'.

'She's not even an actress...only a trollop', said Gloria Swanson. 'Probably the worst actress that ever made the top', said John Cromwell. Tennessee Williams was even more scathing. 'Couldn't act her way out of her form-fitting cashmeres', he said.

She was a sexual athlete most of her life. Of one of her seven husbands, Robert Eaton, she said, 'he's the first man to keep up with me in the sack'. She told a friend they would lock themselves in the bedroom for days making love. Unfortunately for the marriage, Eaton liked to 'keep up with' other women at the same time. While she toured Vietnam in 1967, he did some 'keeping up' in their marital bed. Her over-protective mother saved the stained linen as proof of his infidelity, and presented it to her daughter when she returned home. Exit Mr. Eaton.

Frank Sinatra, rightly or wrongly, blamed her for destroying his marriage to Ava Gardner. Someone told him Ava, Lana and Barbara Payton were holed up in a hotel room enjoying a three-way sex session. He found them together in various stages of undress and refused to believe Ava when she told him they were 'just kidding around'. Some biographers argue that Lana swung both ways, an opinion based entirely on that tale, but it seems highly unlikely. It is the only time *any* of those ladies' names have been mentioned in a same gender situation.

Lana married seven times and had one child. 'I expected to have one husband and seven babies', she said. She is believed to have aborted pregnancies to Rooney, Shaw and Power. Her romance with Fernando Lamas was a fiery one. It ended after he gave her one beating too many.

Then came a small time hoodlum named Johnny Stompanato. He was nicknamed 'Oscar' because his penis when erect was said to be about the same size as an Oscar statuette. Their affair ended suddenly when he was stabbed to death at her home. The official explanation was that Lana's fourteen year-old daughter Cheryl, knife in hand, accidentally ran into him as she went to her mother's assistance during a heated argument.

Many people believe Lana may have killed him and Cheryl, being a minor, took the blame to save her mother's career. After Cheryl's acquittal an unknown man yelled from the back of the courtroom that the killing was the result of 'mother - daughter rivalry'. Stompanato may have been abusing Cheryl and Lana found out about it.

Her seventh and last husband Eric Root penned *The Private Diary of My Life with Lana Turner,* in which he claims she told him, 'I killed the son of a bitch, and I'd do it again'. Root also discovered evidence that gangster Mickey Cohen arranged for tape recordings to be made of Lana and Stompanato having sex. According to Root, photos of her sleeping naked were secretly taken as well, and peddled for hundreds of dollars.

His version of the killing suggests that LA detective Fred Otash helped Turner concoct her story. The reason there was scarcely any blood found on the floor near Stompanato's body, according to Root, was because Lana stabbed him in her bed as he slept. She and Otash then moved the body and cleaned up the bed before calling the police. 'The bed looked as if a hog had been slaughtered in it', Root wrote. In 1961, the Stompanato family received $20,000 in a private settlement from Lana after they sued her for $750,000 over the killing. She said she paid the money to avoid the trauma of another trial.

Daughter Cheryl went into business with her father Stephen Crane a few years later. They made millions from the string of Kon Tiki restaurants he sold in 1978. She then went into real estate, and has since found contentment in a solid relationship with her lover Joyce LeRoy. In 1962 Harold Robbins wrote *Where Love Has Gone*, a novel loosely based on the incident.

Picnic at Hanging Rock (1975)

Sometime during her marriage to Rex Harrison, Rachel Roberts began to slide into mental illness, filling her diaries with bizarre fantasies of personal degradation at the hands of slave drivers and others. Soon her illness manifested itself in her public behavior.

John Valva, a bit part player in *Cleopatra*, recalled how she went around at a party for the cast and unzipped the flies of all the men in the room. Earlier that same evening, at a studio premiere party for Harrison, she threw a tantrum over the attention photographers were bestowing on Liz Taylor and Richard Burton. Climbing onto a tabletop, she pulled up her dress and shouted, 'Here's my pussy. Take some pictures of it!' At another London party she crawled across the room to where Robert Mitchum and his wife were chatting to a group of guests, and proceeded to undo his flies with her teeth!

Invited aboard Burton's yacht Kalizma, she sunbaked in the nude, and then ran about minus her panties, hitching up her skirts and inviting the actor to seduce her. So he did. Richard Gere said of her: 'She had good legs. How do I know? Because she was forever throwing her dress up over her head!'

Harrison described their marriage: 'Put pure and simple, Rachel was an absolute bitch, and pure hell to live with'. On one occasion at a restaurant, she tried to nail her husband's hand to the tablecloth with a steak knife. In 1980, deeply troubled, the poor woman ended it all by downing a quantity of Nembutals and Mogadons, followed by a lethal dose of some kind of insecticide.

Places in the Heart (1984)

When asked about the Oscars in a 1986 *Playboy* interview, Sally Field said, 'When I won my first one, I was so contained. Numb. All I could think of was, 'don't fall down'. I didn't have any underwear on'. Her second Oscar acceptance speech was for her performance in *Places in the Heart*. It has become the source of great embarrassment to her over the years. 'The first time, I hardly felt it because it was all so new', she began, '...But now I feel it...you like me! You *like* me! I can't deny the fact that you like me. Right now, you *really* like me!' Well, at least no one can accuse her of employing a writer.

Plank, The (1967)

Jimmy Edwards was a bluff, hearty comedian who sported a huge handlebar moustache and achieved immense popularity on British radio in the long-running *Take It From Here* series. The winner of a Distinguished Flying Cross in World War Two, he wore his eleven-inch moustache to cover facial scars suffered during the conflict. His wife of eleven years divorced him after discovering he was still having sex with men, despite promising her on their wedding night to give up the practice.

Pocketful of Miracles (1961)

Director Frank Capra said he lost his taste for movie making while shooting this film 'because Glenn Ford made me lick his boots'. Ford was married to dancer Eleanor Powell from 1943-59. She later became a church minister.

In 1946 a fan wrote a letter to him that read, 'I am 22, pretty, but I never saved my money. You did. That is the real reason I would like to marry you. Please let me know soon as I have also written to Dick Powell and Larry Parks'. That is quite possibly the most honest marriage proposal in history.

Poltergeist (1982)

Heather O'Rourke is the little girl who plays Carol Anne Freeling and utters the catch phrase, 'they're back'. Sadly, she died from septic shock, resulting from a bowel obstruction at the age of twelve in 1988.

Even more tragic was the fate of Dominique Dunne who plays her older sister in *Poltergeist*. In the same year the picture was released the twenty-two year old was strangled to death in the driveway of her home by her boyfriend, a chef named John Sweeney.

Her killer served just two and a half years of his 62 years sentence before being released. When he returned to his chef's job at a Los Angeles restaurant, Dunne's parents picketed the establishment displaying signs reading: 'The hands that will prepare your meal tonight also murdered Dominique Dunne'. He was fired soon afterwards.

Postman Always Rings Twice, The (1981)

Jack Nicholson wanted to do the sex scene with, as he called it, 'a full stinger'. He tried for forty-five minutes to 'fluff himself', but was unable to get an erection, 'because I knew everyone was waiting down there to see this thing', he said. It would seem that even the greats are prone to the odd case of stage fright. Censors are certainly more lenient now than ever before, but an erect male member is still very much a no- no, so what was he thinking?

Pretty Woman (1990)

The original script was titled *3000*, with Julia Roberts' character a hopelessly drug addicted hooker dumped back on the streets after her week with the wealthy client who pays her $3,000 for her services. Too grim by far for the Disney people, so they and director Garry Marshall turned to *Cinderella* for a happy ending and a smash hit. Ironically, this tale about a prostitute became the most successful Disney film *ever* up to the time of its release in 1990.

The opening full-length body shot of Roberts stopped short of her head. That was because the body shown belonged to stand-in Shelley Michelle. In fact, even the body on the publicity poster was not Julia's, but that of another double named Donna Scoggins. Gere's body, too, on the poster is not his.

Julia has had a 'no nudity' clause inserted in all her contracts since *Pretty Woman*. Despite appearances to the contrary, she is quite shy when it comes to displaying her body. 'I just don't feel that my algebra teacher should ever know what my butt looks like', she explains. In deference to her shyness, Marshall cleared the set completely for her bathtub scene (including the cameraman). Julia climbed into the bath wearing a swimsuit, removed it underwater and did her scene. She then exited, still naked, but completely alone as the camera continued to roll.

Marshall secretly instructed Gere to snap shut the jewelry box as Julia attempts to touch the necklace it contained, hoping to get a spontaneous reaction. Her reaction was one of genuine surprise and brought forth a guffaw from her that was kept in the film.

Unsubstantiated rumors of an off-screen romance with Gere resulted in Julia's boyfriend, Dylan McDermott, rushing to the set from Morocco to check for himself. She broke up with him soon afterwards. Apparently, her future husband, Lyle Lovett, carried about a tape of *Pretty Woman* with him on tour before he had even met her. 'He must have watched it a hundred times', a friend remembered.

Pride and Prejudice (1940)

Clark Gable had a *slight* preference for older women, quite a lot older in fact, although in all honesty the man would settle for just about any woman he could lay his hands on. Insiders claimed he even had a brief fling with Dame Edna May Oliver who plays Lady Catherine de Burgh in *Pride and Prejudice*.

He often seduced unknown 'plain Janes' as well. They were always grateful for some quick sex with a movie star, he said, and did not pester him or go running to the newspapers afterwards. Dame Edna, by the way, made only one more film after this one before dying from an intestinal disorder in 1942.

Pride of the Yankees, The (1942)

The reason why there is very little baseball action in this picture about Lou Gherig's life is because the director found it impossible to disguise Gary Cooper's complete lack of sporting ability. He had no idea how to throw, catch or hit a ball. His dud hip even made running the bases a major problem.

Professionals, The (1966)

The exquisite Claudia Cardinale is a native of Tunisia, and once represented her country at basketball. Photographer Conrad Hall described her as, 'a cameraman's dream, a perfect piece of nature. There is not much you can do wrong in photographing her'.

In 1958, nineteen year-old Claudia was raped by an un-named man and gave birth to a son nine months later. For years she pretended the boy was her younger brother. In the 1960s, she caused a stir by wearing a mini-skirt to an audience with the Pope. In this writer's opinion, she resides comfortably in his top ten sexiest actresses of all time.

Psycho (1960)

The opening scene showing Janet Leigh's character and her boyfriend in bed together was the first of its kind to appear in a mainstream Hollywood film. The Production Code Office, as usual, told Hitchcock to remove it, but he simply ignored their instructions. Incredibly, the censors were more concerned about a toilet being flushed in one scene than they were about the slicing and dicing in the shower sequence.

Leigh was required to work for seven days on the shower sequence, much of the time wearing only moleskin 'pasties' over her private parts. Her 'killer', Tony Perkins, was away in New York rehearsing a play the whole time, so the scene that changed his career actually took place without him!

Perkins was a bi-sexual, reputed to have had a seven-year relationship with actor Kevin McCarthy, the star of the B thriller *Invasion of the Body Snatchers*. When questioned about their affair many years later, McCarthy stretched his credibility to the limit by claiming he was not even aware Tony was gay!

Tab Hunter was also reputed to be one of Perkins' lovers. Author Truman Capote claimed he rejected Tony's advances because, 'I don't like blood', he explained, 'and Tony's a sadist. He likes to see blood'.

Perkins claimed he knocked back offers of sex from Ingrid Bergman, Brigitte Bardot, Ava Gardner and Jane Fonda, but managed to bed Victoria Principal. All of these ladies have denied his claims, Principal curiously adding, 'It was, for both of us, a special time in our lives'. What was?

Later in life he married and became a father. He adored his wife Berinthia Berenson who was with him until his death in 1992. He left behind a touching message for his sons given to them after his death. It read: 'Boys, don't try to find a woman as wonderful as your mother to marry because if you do, you'll stay single your whole lives'. His son Osgood played the young Norman Bates in *Psycho 2* in 1983.

Pt 109 (1963)

This biopic about the wartime experiences of John F Kennedy was given the go-ahead by the President himself on three conditions. First of all, he demanded it remain historically accurate. Second, any monies coming to him from the project were to be given to PT109 survivors or their next of kin. Third, he must personally choose the actor to portray him. After viewing several audition tapes he settled for the relatively unknown Cliff Robertson.

On the eve of World War Two, Kennedy embarked upon an affair with Danish beauty queen Ingrid Arvad, a woman described by Adolf Hitler, no less, as 'the perfect example of Nordic beauty'. If her FBI dossier can be believed, she was an intimate of the Fuhrer as well.

Kennedy's obsession with sex continued throughout his life. His crewmates in the US Navy nicknamed him 'Shafty', because of his seemingly endless quest for women. He even had a nickname for his penis, referring to it as 'Lay More'.

In 1951, he very nearly married Alicia Purdom, the wife of actor Edmund Purdom. Old Joe Kennedy despised the British and vetoed the idea. Nine years later, when Purdom was about to divorce his wife, he threatened to name JFK as co-respondent. A 'quickie' Mexican divorce was arranged and the whole affair was hushed up.

One FBI informer reported witnessing JFK and Senator Estes Kefauver having sex with two women in Kennedy's apartment in front of other guests. The two men then reputedly switched partners and did it again. Nude pool parties at the White House (while Jackie was away) were commonplace and involved Jack, brother Bobby, a couple of their intimate cronies and several young women. 'I'm not through with a girl till I have had her three ways', Jack once told a colleague.

Marilyn Monroe told friends she only slept with the President once, and that was at Bing Crosby's Palm Springs home on March 24, 1962. This is undoubtedly untrue as there were numerous witnesses who saw them together dozens of times. Peter Lawford, for instance, recalled taking photographs of them naked in a bathtub as she performed oral sex on the President. J Edgar Hoover had tape recordings of them having sex in Lawford's home and elsewhere. When Bobbie Kennedy threatened to replace him as head of the FBI, Hoover warned the brothers that any such action would result in the release of the tapes to the public.

Jack spent two or three days prior to his inauguration in a Palm Springs holiday cottage with actress Angie Dickinson. When asked years later about having sex with the President, she replied, 'it was the best twenty seconds of my life'. Both Jack and his father were renowned for being quick and inconsiderate lovers. Conquest was more important to them than consummation.

Jayne Mansfield let Jack seduce her when she was eight months pregnant. 'He was very considerate of my condition', she said. He had stripper Blaze Starr in a closet while her regular boyfriend, Governor Earl Long, was next door at a party. Judith Exner-Campbell claimed she visited the White House twenty or so times to indulge him. At the time she was also servicing mob boss Sam Giancana.

Two young, blonde college graduates working at the White House, Priscilla Wear and Jill Cowan, code-named 'Fiddle and Faddle' by the President, were employed ostensibly as secretaries to Pierre Salinger and Evelyn Lincoln, but in reality were backup playthings for Kennedy. They were on stand-by to satisfy him either singularly or in tandem, usually in the White House pool. They did very little typing.

Public Enemy, The (1931)

The breakfast scene in which Jimmy Cagney grinds half a grapefruit in Mae Clarke's face was based on a similar incident involving notorious Chicago gangster Hymie Weiss. He shoved an omelet in his girlfriend's face one morning at the breakfast table because she would not stop talking.

Mae had just divorced Fanny Brice's brother, Monte, amid considerable acrimony from both parties, when the picture was released. Monte was thereafter seen attending the Strand Theatre every day for months while *The Public Enemy* played there. He would arrive just before the grapefruit scene, watch with glee as Cagney ground it into his ex-wife's face, then get up and walk out.

Pulp Fiction (1994)

The actress who leaps onto the restaurant table in the opening scene and screams expletives at a rate of knots is Amanda Plummer, the daughter of Christopher Plummer, the actor who played the Baron von Trapp in *The Sound of Music.*

Quentin Tarantino convinced John Travolta to take the role of a hit man in *Pulp Fiction* because it might be his last chance to turn his ailing career around. He reluctantly accepted the part for a paltry $150,000. Within two years his signing price soared to $18 million a movie.

The actor (apparently having forgotten Tarantino's input) put his new- found fame down to his belief in Scientology. When Germany refused to recognize Scientology as a religion he made an impassioned plea to Congress, asking it to sanction Germany for religious oppression. He was unsuccessful.

Quiet Man, The (1952)

John Ford paid a measly ten dollars in 1936 for the option on Maurice Walsh's *Saturday Evening Post* story on which this film is based. It took the writer a further sixteen years to realize any further return on his story. In the final analysis, he ended up with only $6,260 from a film that earned millions.

These days the village of Cong in Ireland, which was the location for the shooting of the picture in 1952, sports 'The Quiet Man Hostel', where the film is still screened every night of the week.

All four of John Wayne's children can be seen in Maureen O'Hara's cart in the Innisfree race scene. Her real life brother Charles plays Hugh Forbes and another brother, Jimmy, portrays Father Paul. Barry Fitzgerald's real life brother Arthur Shields plays Reverend Playfair.

The Quiet Man should have won the Best Picture Oscar that year. It was not the greatest picture ever made, but there was not a lot to beat in 1952. Instead, the Academy voters suffered from collective brain drain and gave it to Cecil B deMille's woeful *The Greatest Show on Earth*. There have been some abysmal choices for Best Picture down the years, and CB's lousy circus flick is right at the top of the list.

Fans of the wonderful Victor McLaglen will be mortified to learn he was not Irish at all, but English. He was no friend of Wayne's either. He loathed the Duke's extreme right wing ideals.

As a young man he served in the Boer War, prospected for gold in Canada, wrestled and boxed his way across America, and dived for pearls in the South Seas. In a travelling carnival for a time, he let his chest be used as an anvil for men to break rocks on. Once, he even went six rounds with the World Heavyweight Boxing Champion Jack Johnson. What a guy!

The story goes that Maureen O'Hara, while shooting a swashbuckling sequence in one of her pirate movies, leapt from the battlements to the floor, fifteen feet below, and carried on sword-fighting without a pause. The entire stunt crew fell to their knees in admiration.

Elsa Lanchester once said of her: 'She looks as if butter wouldn't melt in her mouth, *or anywhere else.*' Be that as it may, she was an extraordinarily beautiful woman who rightly earned her title, 'the Queen of Technicolor'. With her green eyes, flaming red hair, hourglass figure and feisty persona, she was the Irish colleen of folklore, who also managed to give a whole new meaning to the pirate picture genre.

It is interesting to note that she makes no mention of any affair with Anthony Quinn in her autobiography *'Tis Herself*, yet Quinn devotes several passages to it in his. They actually made six films together between 1942 and 1991, one more than she made with John Wayne, yet she mentions Tony's name just four times, and offers not a single word about him, other than that he was in the cast. When she came out of twenty years' retirement to make *Only the Lonely* in 1991, guess who played her love interest? It was Anthony Quinn. Coincidence? Maybe.

It was O'Hara who put the first nail in the coffin of the muckraking *Confidential* Magazine, when she successfully sued the editor over a story accusing her of having sex in the back row of a cinema with a Latin-American lover. She proved in court that she was not even in the country on the date specified, and won a large settlement. Before long, the magazine went broke and not before time either.

By the sixties, it was anything goes in the fan magazine trade. Outrageous headlines and bogus tales were the order of the day. For example, 'Robert Redford's Wife Kidnapped!' was one such heading. The story, in fact, referred to Redford taking a day off from his busy schedule to sneak his wife away for some time alone with her!

Another one read, 'Martin Marriage Collapses...Dean Admits The One-Year Old Baby In His House Is Another Woman's!' The baby in question was indeed another woman's. It was his *grandchild*. The 'collapse' referred to his wife protesting about babysitting the infant.

'Liz Caught With Nude Young Man...How She Explained To Her Children'. This one referred to Liz Taylor's attendance at the Oscars night when a 'streaker' appeared onstage.

'Liza Minnelli Fears Judy's Ghost Wants Her Newborn Baby', screamed yet another headline. Liza had merely mentioned that her mother Judy Garland would have enjoyed having a grandchild, had she lived to see it.

Quo Vadis? (1925)

In this silent version of the Douglas novel, the lions were starved for three days to enhance their ferocity. As luck would have it, one of them escaped and fatally mauled an extra. Executives demurred at killing an animal worth quite a bit of money, so they mulled about trying to determine how best to get the beast away from the body. Only when it began devouring the corpse did someone make the decision to have the hapless animal shot.

Raiders of the Lost Ark (1981)

Indiana Jones was named after a pet Alaskan malamute dog owned by the wife of George Lucas. Harrison Ford only got the part of Indiana because Steven Speilberg's first choice, Tom Selleck, was unable to obtain a release from his *Magnum PI* television series in time to accept it.

Spielberg's fiancée, Amy Irving, was all set to play Miriam Ravenwood, but was replaced by Karen Allen when he heard rumors of her affair with Willie Nelson on the set of *Honeysuckle Rose*.

The most remembered scene in the movie is the one in which Indiana confronts a huge master swordsman in the marketplace. Ford was ill with diarrhea on the day of shooting and in no condition to fight a prolonged battle, so Spielberg had him simply shoot the swordsman dead. The scene is now considered a classic.

There is simply no way a German military force would have been permitted in Egypt in 1936. The country was part of the British Empire. For that matter, the German soldiers are clearly Afrika Korps and that did not even come into being until 1941.

If you look closely when Indy is surrounded by hundreds of snakes in the Well of Souls, you will see that many of them are merely chopped lengths of garden hose. It is also evident a pane of glass separates him from the real ones in one shot.

During the Second World War, Denholm Elliott was a prisoner of the Germans and held for a time in the infamous Colditz Castle. He plays the Dean at Indy's university here. Off-screen he was a bisexual alcoholic who died from AIDS at the age of seventy in 1992.

His first wife was lovely Virginia McKenna, the star of *Born Free*. His second wife Sandra and he had an open marriage. He could bring male friends home to his part of the house, while she had a live-in boyfriend for much of the time in her part.

Raintree County (1957)

While making this film Montgomery Clift was involved in a terrible car crash shortly after leaving a party at Liz Taylor's home. Trapped against the steering wheel, his face a pulverized mess, he was choking on his own blood (and two of his teeth that had lodged in his throat), when Liz arrived on the scene. She stuck her fingers in his mouth and pulled out the broken teeth, probably saving his life. He later had one of the teeth mounted on a strand of silver and presented to her as a necklace.

His injuries were horrific, and included a crushed jaw and sinus cavity, severe concussion, broken teeth, a lacerated lip, four broken ribs, a perforated eardrum and extensive other facial lacerations. His face mended in time, but he was psychologically scarred by the carnage. When he resumed making *Raintree County* several weeks later he was twice found wandering about stark naked in the middle of the night at the cast's hotel. He also over-dosed on sleeping pills and was fortunate to survive.

Random Harvest (1942)

Susan Peters was Oscar- nominated for her role in *Random Harvest*, and showed genuine promise as an up and coming actress of note. Tragically, her career was cut short on a hunting trip when a bullet accidentally discharged from her gun and lodged in her spine. Paralyzed from the waist down, and confined to a wheelchair for the remainder of her brief life, she became a recluse and died from a chronic kidney infection at the age of just thirty-one.

Rasputin & the Empress (1932)

The real Prince Felix and Princess Irina Yusupov sued MGM, not for depicting him murdering Rasputin (which he readily admitted), but because the film claimed the Mad Monk had raped the Princess. MGM made the mistake of assuming the Yusupovs were dead when they were very much alive and living in London. In fact, Felix lived on until 1967.

The subsequent court case cost the studio hundreds of thousands of dollars. In 1935, in the wake of the Yusupov libel, MGM introduced a final caption into its films, following the credits list. It read: 'The events and characters depicted in this photoplay are fictitious. Any similarity to persons living or dead is purely coincidental'. A similar caption accompanies every movie today.

Raw Wind in Eden (1958)

Jeff Chandler and Esther Williams fell in love while making this film. Still undecided if she should accept his marriage proposal, Esther was shocked one evening when he appeared before her dressed in a red wig, women's clothes, stockings, high heels and make-up. Chandler had been cross-dressing for decades and revealed his secret to her in the hope she would accept him anyway.

She asked how he considered himself when they made love, and he replied, 'I'm a beautiful woman making love to a beautiful woman'. She ended the relationship on the spot. In 1961 he died after a minor back surgery operation went wrong. A major artery was accidentally cut and despite 54 blood transfusions he was dead at the age of forty-three.

Reach For the Sky (1956)

The real Douglas Bader was signed to double for distance shots of Kenneth More in *Reach For the Sky*. He would only do so, however, if *all* his friends depicted in the novel were also portrayed on the screen. When told this was simply not possible he, rather petulantly, withdrew his services.

One of Kenneth More's earliest jobs in the theatre was to keep an eye on the audience at the Windmill Theatre, the only British venue permitted to feature naked women on stage (provided they did not move, that is). More's duties were to report any instances of men masturbating! 'A4, wanker, *Times*', was the code, for instance, indicating a gentleman was pleasuring himself in that particular seat while using a copy of *The Times* to conceal his actions. Theatre bouncers would then apprehend the culprit and evict him. It would be interesting to learn what More wrote on his tax returns under the 'job description' heading.

Rear Window (1954)

Raymond Burr had everyone believing that he had been shot in the stomach fighting the Japanese on Okinawa during WW2. Like most of his 'studio' history this was a fabrication. In the 1960s he would become a superstar on television as Perry Mason and Ironside. He plays the killer in Hitchcock's *Rear Window*.

Burr's private life remained a closely guarded secret throughout his tenure at the top of the TV pile. In 1963, at the height of his Perry Mason fame, he secretly married his lover Robert Benevides in a gay ceremony on their ranch in California. Studio biographies maintained he wed three women, was widowed twice and divorced once, yet none of his family ever met any of those wives. In truth they never existed. Although a homosexual, he did enjoy an affair with the much younger Natalie Wood. Whether or not it was consummated is unknown. On his death he bequeathed his entire thirty-two million dollar fortune to Mr. Benevides.

William Hopper, the one-eyed son of gossip columnist Hedda Hopper, played Paul Drake in the *Perry Mason* series and was, according to at least two biographers, in love with Burr for years. Tony Curtis recalled how difficult it was for the young man to make friends in Hollywood. 'We all felt that Hedda's son, Bill, was a spy', he said.

Rebecca (1940)

For a short while Sunset Boulevard was renamed Rebecca Lane. David O Selznick had managed to con the Governor of California and the Mayor of Los Angeles into doing so as a publicity stunt to promote his movie.

Second string actor Brian Aherne dated Olivia De Havilland before he married her sister Joan Fontaine. The latter complained of him spending most of their wedding night describing his torrid affair with Marlene Dietrich. 'I grew increasingly numb', Joan wrote.

Dame Judith Anderson, the Australian actress who won an Oscar for her portrayal of the malevolent Mrs. Danvers, was a confirmed lesbian who steadfastly refused to come out of the closet. She described her two marriages as, 'very short, but far too long'. In 1984 she played Minx Lockeridge in the short-lived TV series *Santa Barbara*.

Sir C. Aubrey Smith, the extremely tall English character actor featured here, was once the captain of the Surrey cricket team as well as captain of England on tours of South Africa and Australia.

Rebel Without a Cause (1955)

According to a number of biographers and historians, director Nicholas Ray created some kind of perverted record (even for Hollywood), by having sexual relations with all three of his stars in this film - Natalie Wood, James Dean and Sal Mineo. What made that record even more reprehensible was that Wood and Mineo were under-age at the time. Dennis Hopper who was also in the picture claims he too was seducing Natalie, claiming she was, sexually, very active for a fifteen year-old. Not only was she sleeping with Ray and Hopper, she also found time to have it off with Dean in the back seat of his car one evening while they were parked on the Hollywood Heights.

Columnist Rona Barrett recalled seeing Nick Adams exhibiting his genitalia at a party. 'He publicly opened his fly...to prove he was a manly man', she said. Adams died from an overdose at thirty-six. A friend found him in his living room, leaning against a wall with his eyes wide open. The coroner's official verdict was 'accident; suicide; undetermined', which is obviously coroner-talk for 'beats me!' The police found no sign of drug paraphernalia at the scene, yet the cause of death was deemed to be probably due to the drug paraldehyde (a substance prescribed for alcoholics) and Promazine intoxication.

Sal Mineo was in street gangs from the time he was eight years old and headed for reform school, until the movies changed his life. His overnight success in this film went straight to his head, however, and he lived the high life to the full as his gigantic ego took over. Unfortunately for him he

535

was too short and too ethnic for the beach boy films of the sixties, and his popularity abruptly fizzled.

He was all set for a comeback playing one of the Arab boys in Lawrence of Arabia, until his previous performance as an Arab-killing Jew in Exodus resulted in Jordanian authorities refusing him entry into the country for the shoot. He was dropped from the production and that, as they say, was that.

By 1961, he was reduced to playing an ape in Escape from the Planet of the Apes in order to pay the rent. The bi-sexual actor had flings with Tuesday Weld and, allegedly, Yul Brynner, but his career had definitely stalled. In 1979, his troubles ended when a man named Lionel Williams stabbed him through the heart in Sal's own driveway - 'just for the hell of it' the killer said.

Red Dust (1932)

Less than twelve months after making *Red Dust*, Clark Gable reputedly knocked down and killed a woman while he was driving his car when drunk. LB Mayer offered a junior executive a job for life with the studio if he would swear he was driving the vehicle. The young man served twelve months gaol for involuntary manslaughter and secured a job for life at MGM. Gable was never officially implicated in the death. Several writers since then have suggested that the young man was, in fact, none other than an assistant director named John Huston, but there is no proof of this.

At the age of sixteen Jean Harlow eloped with a millionaire's son who gave her $250,000 as a wedding present. They soon divorced. When she became pregnant by her second husband in 1929, her mother and stepfather arranged for an abortion to avoid damaging her burgeoning career. Husband number two tired of his meddling in-laws and left her.

Before hitting it big she often frequented Barney's Beanery on Santa Monica Boulevard where she picked up men for casual sex. This practice intensified after her next husband, writer Paul Bern, was shot dead around the time she was making *Red Dust*. Wearing a black wig as a disguise, she seemingly embarked upon scores of one-night stands in an attempt to learn sexual techniques she hoped might give her some measure of satisfaction.

'When it came to kissing', said Jimmy Stewart, 'Harlow was the best'. She was also completely at ease with her own nakedness and known to answer jibes about her low-cut gowns by exposing her breasts on the spot. While shooting the bathing scene in *Red Dust*, she delighted in standing up in the nude whenever the camera stopped rolling. Ava Gardner would emulate her behavior years later in the re-make, *Mogambo!* Jean's hair was regularly dyed to maintain its platinum blonde sheen until it became so damaged she was forced to wear a wig. She also dyed her pubic hair the same color.

Her stepfather was a shady character named Marino Belle. He arranged dates for her with his gangster friends including the infamous 'Bugsy' Seigel. In the meantime, he swindled her out of her fortune by pretending to invest the money in bogus schemes. He introduced her to New Jersey mob boss Abner 'Longy' Zwillman and she soon became intimate with him. The homely- looking gangster sent her monthly cheque until she married Bern in 1932. 'Longy' also delighted in showing his gangster pals a locket he possessed containing a tuft of Harlow's pubic hair! She married Bern, a gentle man whom she genuinely liked, but she quickly became involved with Gable soon after his death.

A lot of information has emerged in recent years about how the MGM fixers worked overtime to besmirch Bern's reputation, and to convince the public that he took his own life, basically because he felt ashamed of his inadequacy in bed. It was all totally untrue. It appears now that his common law wife turned up at his home that day, having read of his marriage to Harlow, an argument ensued, and she shot him in the head. Her body was found in a river a few weeks later, an apparent suicide.

MGM could not have its star Jean Harlow being found to be a bigamist, so the 'fixers' moved in and created the whole suicide scenario, complete with fake suicide note, and sold it, lock, stock & barrel to the gullible public. The local police simply agreed to whatever line the 'fixers' came up with, and poor Paul Bern went down in history as a rather pathetic excuse for a human being.

MGM's second in command, Irving Thalberg had been Bern's very good friend and detested L B Mayer's media release of details about the dead man's sexual deficiencies and problems. The strategy was to make Harlow appear the victim of an impotent husband who killed himself from shame because he could not satisfy his beautiful young wife. The story bandied about portrayed him as a grossly under-endowed wife beater. He was none of those things.

A bizarre incident occurred at his memorial service. The funeral director stood beside the casket and offered those assembled an opportunity to bid a final farewell to the deceased. The casket was then mechanically moved into an upright position, and the top of the lid slowly slid down to reveal Bern's face staring out at the congregation. John Gilbert vomited, Thalberg burst into tears, as did Harlow, and Gable ran from the room, appalled at this final indignity.

Fifty years further down the track, another old friend Samuel Marx extensively investigated Bern's death. He claimed Dorothy Millette did meet with her husband on the night of his death, stripped off near the pool and offered her body to him. He too disrobed and embraced her whereupon she picked up a pistol and shot him in the temple.

The studio 'fixers' arrived next morning and cleaned up the mess. They oiled the gun to remove her fingerprints and placed it in Bern's dead hand after laying his body on the bedroom floor. It all sounds a little *film-noirish,* but Marx was convinced he had solved the mystery. There are a few details that are not quite right in Marx's analysis, however. Bern was certainly shot in his bedroom as he emerged from taking a shower, there being blood and brain matter on the ceiling there, but most of the rest stands up.

Harlow's death at twenty-six from uremic poisoning has also been the subject of much speculation. Studio hype blamed kidney damage she supposedly sustained from a beating she received from Bern. Not true at all.

Others say her religiously fanatical mother refused her medical aid until it was too late. There is evidence that Mrs. Bello was a religious nut, who sat in Jean's room night after night praying out loud for hours trying to provide her with 'a direct link to God'. When Gable and a couple of studio executives insisted Jean go to the hospital, Jean's mother assured them she had 'told the sickness to leave Jean's body', so it would. When the stricken actress complained of feeling hot, her mother advised her to *think about* feeling cold! Even when it was evident Harlow was beyond help and actually dying, all Mrs. Bello could say was 'there is no death'. Gable and the others eventually pushed the woman aside and rushed Jean to the nearest hospital, but it was already far too late to save her.

Her death brought out the worst in MGM. The studio took out full page advertisements showing the company lion dressed in white tie and tails, tears pouring down his face, and placing a wreath on a tombstone that read: JEAN HARLOW IN MEMORIUM. Below it was a scroll listing her screen credits.

Her funeral got the full treatment. Jeanette MacDonald warbled *Indian Love Call* and Nelson Eddy belted out *Ah,*

Sweet Mystery of Life. The silver and bronze casket rested under a portrait of Sir Alfred Lord Tennyson, with a volume of his poetry opened at 'Crossing the Bar'. MGM saw fit to give the dead star's mother a pension of $500 a month for life, evidently as some kind of compensation for the loss of her daughter.

Gene Raymond also starred in *Red Dust*, playing Mary Astor's husband. In real life he was married to Jeanette MacDonald for twenty-eight years, but in name only. Jeanette continued her on again – off again affair with Nelson Eddy throughout the marriage, and Raymond persisted with his homosexual trysts. He spent their wedding night with the equally gay Buddy Rogers who had just married Mary Pickford. Both couples were on their honeymoons!

After making *Flying Down to Rio* and *Red Dust* for RKO, Raymond was found to be in an intimate relationship with a teenage boy whose parents threatened to press charges. RKO paid them off and then quietly let the actor go.

Sometime after that Jeanette forked out $1,000 hush money to bail him out of jail on a morals charge when he was arrested at a club for homosexuals. Refusing a divorce and aware a scandal would destroy his wife's career, he continued in similar vein for decades. In 1948 he was again arrested for seducing young boys.

Red River (1948)

John Wayne was bitterly disappointed when he was overlooked in the Oscars for his role in this film – and rightly so. 'Montgomery Clift was in this picture too, you know', he said later, 'and they wanted to give that poor kid an Academy Award so bad that they simply forgot about me. Clift was acting they said. Duke's only playing himself. But hell, I played an old man in that, and I was only 40'.

Richard Farnsworth doubled for Clift in some of the action sequences. He had to. As every director in Hollywood knew, Monty threw a punch like a girl. Farnsworth had been a stuntman since he was sixteen, doubling for Roy Rogers and other cowboy stars. He is probably best known now for his Oscar nomination for *Comes a Horseman* and as Anne Shirley's benefactor in *Anne of Green Gables*. In 2000, while suffering from an incurable cancer, he shot himself.

Red River was touted as being John Ireland's big chance to become a star via his showy role as a gunfighter. He blew it when he made an enemy of director Howard Hawks by seducing Joanne Dru during filming. Hawks himself had aspirations in that direction and became extremely jealous and bloody-minded over the issue. The upshot was he chopped Ireland's role down to almost nothing, and the actor missed his only real chance at stardom.

Ireland made the front pages of the tabloids in 1959 when he was forty-five years old and involved in an affair with sixteen year-old Tuesday Weld. 'If there wasn't such a difference in our ages I'd ask her to marry me', he said. 'That and her mother are the only things stopping me'. No wonder.

Reluctant Debutante, The (1958)

When this film was shot Kay Kendall and Rex Harrison had just married. Everyone, it seems, knew Kay was dying from leukemia – everyone except her. 'It was difficult trying to be funny', recalled Angela Lansbury, 'when you knew a brilliant light was about to be extinguished'. Kay passed away a year later at the age of thirty-three, one of the most delightful British comediennes of all time.

Remember My Name (1978)

Berry Berenson was long married to actor Anthony Perkins and acted in three movies herself, *Cat People, Remember My Name* and *Winter Kills*. On September 11, 2001 she had the misfortune to be aboard American Airlines Flight 11 when it slammed into the north tower of the World Trade Centre in New York. She was returning from a holiday in Cape Cod when she met her fate.

Riders of the Purple Sage (1925)

Between 1926 and 1967 one quarter of all the movies made in America were westerns. There were 227 produced in 1925 alone. Since the sound era began in 1927, over 4,000 have been made. Television, too, has turned out a huge number of western series, an amazing 48 shows running simultaneously in 1959 alone, when the genre was at its peak!

'Broncho' Billy Anderson made over 400 westerns between 1903 and 1920, one and two-reel shorts mostly, that he churned out for about $800 a time, but taking in around $50,000 for each one, an enormous amount for the time.

Many western stars of silent movies used to stage their first appearance in a film for maximum effect. Ken Maynard, for example, would swing open a door, then pose, to enable the audience to applaud his entry into the story. In the silent era Universal Studios erected spectator galleries for the public to watch its movies being made. A small entrance fee was charged, a forerunner to today's highly lucrative studio tours.

Although Tom Mix was purported to have been a Rough Rider fighting in the Mexican and Boer Wars, (as well as an illustrious few years as a US Marshall), the truth was very different. He was actually a deserter from the army and his cowboy days were marked only by an arrest on a horse stealing charge. The truth did not, however, stop him from selling maps of his body marked with the 'twenty-one wounds' he received in combat, complete with descriptions of how each one was inflicted!

He always spoke slowly because he had trouble all his life with his ill-fitting false teeth. At the zenith of his career it was Tom Mix movies that kept the Fox Studios afloat. Earning $20,000 a week, he owned a palatial home situated at the end of a mile-long drive. It sported a huge neon sign that winked his initials into the night. He admitted in his later years that his stunts were all 'doubled' for him or faked. In 1924, his wife shot and wounded him because he beat her. Then, midway through the thirties, he suddenly went broke after a million dollar investment in a circus went sour.

He was just beginning to make a comeback when he was killed in a freakish car accident in 1940. When his corpse was pulled from the wreck, it was found to be virtually unmarked. A steel suitcase in the back of the vehicle, full of $20 coins, had struck him in the neck, however, killing him instantly. A statue of a rider less horse was erected at the site of his death near Florence, Arizona.

Buck Jones was a spectacularly popular cowboy actor of the 1930s who perished in the disastrous Coconut Grove nightclub fire in Boston on November 28, 1942. For decades it had been assumed that he lost his life because he repeatedly returned into the burning building to rescue others, but that was simply not the case. His body was found at the table with his friends, all of them having been overcome by the smoke. As happened far too often in the Hollywood of studio days, somebody changed the truth, probably to put more bums on seats at theatres featuring the dead star's films.

Riders of the Whistling Pines (1949)

In 1978, Gene Autry, Hugh Hefner and rock star Alice Cooper established a fund to rejuvenate the Hollywood sign. Since then this famous landmark has become the butt of several inspired pranks. Using black plastic sheeting to cover up one of the letters, anonymous wags converted it to read 'Holywood' to celebrate the Pope's 1987 visit to Los Angeles.

It became 'Hollyweed' for a while following the relaxing of laws on marijuana, and then 'Ollywood' in tribute to Oliver North's over-rated performance at the Senate 'Iran-gate' hearings. The sign originally read 'Hollywoodland', but a mudslide during the Second World War took away the last four letters and they were never replaced.

By 1973 the famous sign had had become so dilapidated it was decided to build a new one. Hank Berger, a man with a nose for a profit, purchased the scrap iron from the original, chopped it into one-inch squares, and then sold them to film buffs for $29.95 apiece.

Riders of the Whistling Pines was just one of scores of second features churned out by Gene Autry over twenty years, from the 1930s to the 1950s. Even he was bemused by their popularity. 'I'm no great actor and I'm no great rider and I'm no great singer', he said. 'But whatever it is I'm doing, they like it'. Considering himself a role model for children, he refused to smoke or drink on screen, or to hit anyone smaller than himself.

His 1950 recording of *Rudolph the Red-Nosed Reindeer* became the second biggest selling single in history up to that time. Only Bing Crosby's *White Christmas* sold more. A follow-up single with an Easter theme entitled *Peter Cottontail* was also a million-seller.

Crosby, Dinah Shore and several other big-time artists knocked back the chance to record 'Rudolph', and Gene was only offered it because nobody else was interested. It eventually sold 100 million records in scores of languages, and has since been covered by over 400 artists.

In 1980 Autry was named the eighth richest man in California. One year later at the age of seventy-four he married a woman of thirty-nine. A long-time friend of Richard Nixon, he purchased the Los Angeles Angels baseball team, and was still heavily involved in the game when he passed away in 1998 at the ripe old age of 91.

Right Stuff, The (1983)

Dennis Quaid plays astronaut Gordon Cooper in this greatly underestimated film. 'I wanted to play NASA astronaut Gordon Cooper in *The Right Stuff* a year before they even thought about the movie. I mean, *he fell asleep on the launch pad!*' a justifiably impressed Quaid exclaimed during an interview. All things considered, it doesn't get much cooler than nodding off atop a rocket that's about to blast off for the moon.

Rio Bravo (1959)

In 1985, Ricky Nelson's chartered aircraft caught fire when an on board heater mal-functioned. Although the pilot managed to land, the fire had already engulfed the passenger section killing everyone including Nelson. Untrue stories abounded afterwards that he and his fellow musicians had been free-basing cocaine on board and caused the conflagration themselves. The victims' families received $4.5 million in damages from the airline. He is probably best remembered in his brief movie career for his role as the young gunslinger in *Rio Bravo*.

In his youth Dean Martin delivered bootleg liquor, ran numbers and craps games for hoodlums, and fought as a prizefighter under the sobriquet of 'Kid Crochet'. He worked at the Club Alabama in New York City, an establishment owned by Louis Buchalter (a.

K.

A. Louis Lepke), the killer who ran Murder Incorporated. When Lepke went to the electric chair, Martin sat with his family throughout the execution. .

He was ten years older than his comedy duo partner Jerry Lewis. When Sinatra first saw their act at mobster Frank Costello's Copacabana Night Club in 1948, he was unimpressed by Dean. 'The Dago's lousy', he observed, 'but the little Jew is great'. At the Copa the duo earned $5,000 a week at a time when the average national income was just $1,500 per annum!

When they took their show from the east coast to California, they did so with financial backing from gangster Mickey Cohen. In fact, most of their early bookings were in Mob establishments. Lewis initially had no idea who his employers were, but Dino knew most of them from way back.

They were his friends and associates. They did favors for him and he did favors for them.

Both men consistently cheated on their wives. For a while, they were seen openly cavorting around town, Dean with June Allyson who was then married to Dick Powell, and Jerry with John Payne's wife Gloria de Haven.

Jerry's over-weening ambition was in direct contrast to Dino's lackadaisical approach to everything, including his career. Whereas Dino just wanted to enjoy himself, his partner was on an ego trip that spiraled out of control. Jerry took charge of everything, even selecting the musical arrangements for Dean's songs. In fairness to Lewis, however, if he had not done so their extraordinarily successful rise to the top might never have happened. Martin was just too laid back to initiate anything. If the duo was approached in a bar or restaurant and offered work at some club or casino, Dean would simply jerk his thumb at Lewis and say, 'talk to the Jew". He had no interest in details. Only in having a good time.

Their break-up was inevitable and it was not an amicable one. By then, Lewis was virtually treating Martin as his employee, ordering him about and criticizing his lack of zeal. The final straw came when he told Dean to don a policeman's uniform for a comedy sequence in *The Delicate Delinquent*. Dean had grown up in tough neighborhoods, hating policemen, and had no intention of wearing the uniform. Heated words were exchanged and Martin walked out. Once the duo had fulfilled certain contractual obligations they went their separate ways. They did not speak again for twenty years.

As a solo performer, one that was not in demand, Dean devised his 'drunk' persona for his stage act. It was a roaring success. He did not actually have a drinking problem until his later years, but to stay in character he always carried a glass with him even on the golf course. It usually contained apple cider.

Oddly enough, virtually everybody he worked with agreed that, off camera, he was by far the funnier of the duo, a fact Lewis's fragile ego could never come to terms with. In 1957, within a year of the breakup, Dean debuted solo at the Sands in Vegas. An instant success, he found himself doing six-week stints there, twice yearly, for the next thirty years. He was paid $300,000 a year for just twelve weeks work, a workload that suited him to perfection.

He was one of only a few people who could talk back to Sinatra and still retain his friendship. Very much his own man, he would often wander off to his hotel room to read comics or watch westerns on TV, rather than join Frank and his cronies in all night binges and partying. When his hit song 'Everybody Loves Somebody' knocked the Beatles off the number one spot on Billboard, he good-naturedly cabled Elvis Presley who had long been an admirer of his. 'If you can't handle the Beatles, I'll do it for you, pally', the cable read.

The Dean Martin Show began on TV in 1965 and remained the most successful program on the tube throughout the next decade. Initially, he didn't want to do it, but the salary of $40,000 a week for one day's work changed his mind. In fact, he rarely needed more than about three hours in the studio each week to fulfil his commitment. By 1967 the pay per episode had jumped to an unprecedented $285,000! Not bad for just 3-4 hours work.

His daughter Deana recalled the day his XKE Jaguar broke down on Sunset Boulevard 'for the umpteenth time'. He stepped out of the vehicle, produced a derringer from his boot and shot it as he would a horse with a broken leg. It was typical of his zany brand of humor.

In 1987, his son, Dino Jr, flew his Air National Guard Phantom Jet into the side of Mt San Gorgonio near Palm Springs and was killed. He was thirty-five. By a strange coincidence, ten years earlier Dolly Sinatra, Frank's mother, died when the airplane in which she was a passenger collided with the same mountain.

Martin never got over his son's death. In his final months he would sit in his private booth at his favorite bar, preferably alone, listening to his albums being played in the background and drinking quietly. When asked what he was doing he would reply, 'waiting to die'. After declining major liver and kidney surgery to prolong his life, he passed away on Christmas Day, 1995.

On December 28, 1995 the city of Las Vegas turned off the lights on the Strip for one minute as a sign of respect for the popular entertainer. The only previous time this had happened was when Sammy Davis Junior died. Dean was buried in a crypt at Westwood Village Memorial Park a few yards from Marilyn Monroe. The plaque on his tomb reads: 'Everybody Loves Somebody Sometime'.

As from the year 2002, the date June 7 has been declared a public holiday in the state of Ohio. Martin was born in Steubenville, Ohio on that day in 1917. It was the first time anywhere in the United States that an entertainer had been so honored.

Barbrara Sinatra was once asked how she could possibly count Angie Dickinson as a close friend, considering the lengthy affair Angie once had with her husband Frank. 'If I went by that rule I wouldn't have any friends at all', she answered with a laugh. Apparently, Angie keeps an autographed photo of the late JFK, inscribed, 'Angie: To the only woman I ever loved'. In a 1985 Photoplay interview she remarked, 'no question – the more powerful men are, the more sexy they are'.

River of no Return (1954)

The sequences shot aboard the raft on the Bow River required the use of stunt doubles for Robert Mitchum, Marilyn Monroe and the boy Tommy Rettig. The studio would simply not let them venture into the river unless they were in some way attached to the bank. The double for Rettig was a midget named Harry Monty who once played a Munchkin in Garland's *Wizard of Oz* fifteen years earlier. Close-ups of the trio were shot in an indoor tank back in Hollywood in front of a giant process screen, with men tossing buckets of water over the actors and firing steel-headed arrows into the logs at their feet.

Director Otto Preminger detested Marilyn's unprofessionalism. 'A vacuum with nipples', was his personal opinion of her. It was Marilyn's drama coach, Natasha Lytess, who insisted she enunciate every syllable of every word clearly and distinctly, a practice that sounded utterly phony and drove everybody to distraction. Nunnally Johnson, while exasperated by her antics, nonetheless appreciated her for what she was: 'She is a phenomenon of nature, like Niagara Falls or the Grand Canyon. You can't talk to it. It can't talk to you. All you can do is stand back and be awed by it'. Amen.

Rettig was warned by his priest not to socialize with Marilyn because she was 'a woman of ill repute'. She was visibly upset when the boy told her. He would go on to star in the TV series *Lassie*. After acting roles dried up he went to California with his *fifteen year-old* wife and began growing marijuana. Arrested twice for doing so, he was placed on probation, but graduated instead into smuggling cocaine. Arrested again he was sentenced to five years in prison, but the charges were later dropped on appeal. In 1980 he was yet again arrested on drug charges. He died in 1996.

Rory Calhoun plays the bad guy. When *Confidential* Magazine was set to print an expose on the homosexuality of Rock Hudson and Anthony Perkins, Universal convinced the editors to hold off by offering them a stack of cash and a lesser story regarding Calhoun's prison record. The story stalled his career. At one of his divorce hearings his wife, Lita Baron, cited no fewer than seventy women as proof of his adultery! He could have named a couple of hundred more.

Road to Singapore (1940)

Bob Hope was one of the richest men in America, with his worth estimated in the 1970s to be in the vicinity of $500 million. He arrived in Hollywood in 1938 with $100,000 he had earned in vaudeville and on Broadway, and immediately began buying up land in the San Fernando Valley at $30 an acre.

A team of thirteen writers would take scripts written by somebody else and insert gags into them, thus creating vehicles for his 'ad-lib' brand of humor. Writer Melville Shavelson said the weak, vain, cowardly character created for him was really based to a large extent on the man himself. 'Hope is not a comedian', grouched Groucho Marx. 'He just translates what others write for him'.

Although remaining married to his wife Dolores, he was a habitual philanderer all his life. She knew all about his affairs. After all, he was away from home an average of 250 days and nights a year. The only one of his romances that really bothered her was the lengthy relationship he enjoyed with actress Marilyn Maxwell.

'The most self-centered person I have ever known', said his manager Elliott Kozak who was especially critical of the comedian's lack of affection for Dolores. 'I never saw him go to her and give her a peck on the cheek, and I was with him for twenty-five years'.

Rock! Rock! Rock! (1956)

Tuesday Weld (1943 -)

Known relationships:

Barrymore, John Drew
Beymer, Richard
Burr, Raymond
De Rola, Stash
Fabian
Finney, Albert
Hamilton, George
Hopper, Dennis
Ireland, John
Lockwood, Gary
Mankiewicz, Tom
McKay, Gardner
Mineo, Sal
O'Neal, Ryan
Pacino, Al
Presley, Elvis
Sands, Tommy
Sharif, Omar
Sinatra, Frank
Stamp, Terence
Steinberg, David
Wayne, Patrick

Married:

Dudley Moore & 2 others

Weld's early years were pretty rough. She suffered a nervous breakdown at nine, was a seasoned drinker at ten and botched a suicide attempt at twelve. A year later she made this movie and immediately caught the public's eye.

She was soon carrying her sexy screen persona into her private life, as her teenage years and twenties were spent in wild drugs parties, and sex flings with many lovers. Her affair with Sinatra allegedly began when she was fourteen and he was forty-four! Two years later she and the much older John Ireland even discussed marriage. She would eventually wed British comedian Dudley Moore, but it didn't last.

Rocky (1976)

Sylvester Stallone's droopy eye and speech impediment are the result of a doctor misusing a pair of forceps during his birth in a charity hospital. Sly wrote *Rocky* in just four days and the film itself took only a month to shoot. 'I'm astounded that it takes some people 18 years to write something', said the suddenly brilliant writer, 'like that guy who wrote *Madame Bovary*. It was a lousy book, and it made a lousy movie'. Perhaps someone should explain to him that writing *something* and something exceptional are two different things. After refusing a flat $300,000 for the rights to *Rocky* he accepted $75,000 plus a percentage of the profits, along with a guarantee he would play the lead himself.

Six years earlier he appeared in a porno flick entitled *A Party at Kitty & Studs*. Once he became the hottest property in Hollywood, the film was retitled *The Italian Stallion*, and became a much sought after film for private parties, renting out at $10,000 a showing before pirate copies began to circulate.

Brigitte Nielson was determined to meet Stallone, so she deserted her husband and family in Europe and went to America to fulfil that aim. She met him, married him and milked him for $6 million when they eventually divorced. In 1997, Brigitte was said to have accepted a million dollars from a member of the Saudi Royal family to take part in a twelve-hour sex marathon.

Romancing the Stone (1984)

Stuntwoman Jeannie Epper was awarded the 'Most Spectacular Stunt of the Year' trophy after doubling for Kathleen Turner in the mud-sliding sequence. Disaster almost struck the crew during location shoots in Mexico, when heavy rains caused part of the mountainside to collapse a meagre five minutes after seventy crew and actors had completed the bus crash sequence. The slide completely engulfed the area in which they were working.

The movie is based upon a story written in her spare time by waitress Diane Thomas. After several rejections, she finally managed to sell it to Michael Douglas's company for $250,000 in 1979. Five years later it became a huge hit. In the interim, Stephen Spielberg hired her as a writer on the strength of that one story. When Douglas struck problems with the script of the sequel *Jewel of the Nile*, Thomas was brought in to work on it for him. In appreciation he gave her a brand new white Porsche. As the final touches were being put to the film in post-production, she was killed in a car crash while driving the very same Porsche.

Roman Holiday (1953)

After Gregory Peck had worked with the then unknown Audrey Hepburn for just two weeks, he insisted she be given equal billing with him, even though his contract stipulated he receive solitary top billing in all his films. When his agent reminded him that nobody had heard of her, he replied, 'they will hear of her. This picture's about Audrey Hepburn. I'm just holding her while she does her pirouettes'. He was certain she would win the Oscar for her role and she duly did. A classy guy was Greg Peck.

Eddie Albert plays Peck's photographer buddy. During the Second World War he was a bona fide hero, although he never liked to talk about it. While in command of an assault craft during the bloody Tarawa landings, Eddie rescued 150 wounded Marines while under heavy machine-gun fire on the first day and was cited for 'outstanding performance of duty'.

Another actor, Louis Hayward, won a Bronze Star on Tarawa, also for bravery. Albert would later become well known to TV viewers in the popular series *Green Acres*.

Romeo & Juliet (1936)

Norma Shearer (1902-1983)

Known relationships:

Bartholomew, Freddie
Bell, Monta
Bogart, Humphrey
Brown, Johnny Mack
Cody, Lew
Conway, Jack
Fairbanks Jr, Douglas
Fleming, Victor
Gable, Clark
Gilbert, John
Haines, William
Hawks, Howard
Hughes, Howard
Kennedy, John F
McGregor, Malcolm
Meredith, Burgess
Montgomery, George
Nagel, Conrad
Niven, David
Pickford, Jack
Raft, George
Rooney, Mickey
Selznick, David O
Stewart, James

Married:

Irving Thalberg & 1 other

Shearer was born in Montreal, Canada but moved with her family to New York where she attempted to gain work with the Ziegfeld follies as a dancer. Ziegfeld himself rejected her, telling the young girl to her face that she was 'a dog'.

At 5'3", stumpy-legged, a cast in her eye and bad teeth she was certainly no beauty. Later in her film career these problems would be corrected or camouflaged. The turn in her eye was the biggest drawback. People who spoke to her said they often could not tell if she was looking at them or not. Clever cameramen, shooting from flattering angles, would solve that. Her teeth were capped and she wore long dresses to conceal her unattractive legs.

When she agreed to marry MGM boss Irving Thalberg, he laid down certain conditions. Because of his frail health they were not to indulge in passionate sex. Norma must remain subdued. She must also agree to his mother living with them, and she must accept Judaism. She complained after his death that he never once told her he loved her, although he demonstrated his affection in other ways.

Thalberg was always perceived by LB Mayer to be a constant threat to his dominance at MGM. Despite their strong working relationship, Mayer was not saddened by the young executive's early death. Eddie Mannix remembered his boss smiling and murmuring, as they drove away from the funeral, 'God is good to me'.

Norma's marriage saw her career blossom overnight. Amid complaints from Crawford and others, she invariably had first refusal on the best roles available, a situation that continued until her husband's death. *Romeo & Juliet* provides a classic example of this. She was thirty-six years old when Irving chose her to play the teenager, Juliet. Consequently, an older actor was needed to play Romeo, so the forty-four year-old Leslie Howard got lumbered with it. Shakespeare must have spun like a top in his grave!

Although she seems to have remained faithful throughout her marriage, Norma cut a swathe through the movie fraternity once she became a free agent. Mickey Rooney, who was just nineteen at the time, wrote of her seducing him over a number of months. He especially recalled the much older actress servicing him', on her knees', in her dressing room, while still dressed in her regal costumes, in between takes on *Marie Antoinette.* Eventually everybody got to know about Norma and Mickey, including Mayer. He called the two stars in and ordered them to cease their rutting at once, or else! 'You're Andy Hardy!' he yelled at Rooney. 'You're the United States! You're a symbol! Behave yourself!'

Her next conquest was the young Jimmy Stewart. He soon became embarrassed by the constant media attention to their affair, as well as her penchant for spoiling him with expensive gifts, one of which was a gold cigarette case studded with diamonds. After six weeks he terminated their relationship.

The openly gay William Haines was a very close friend of hers, and some sources claim the relationship had a physical side to it as well. Despite her considerable efforts, she never managed to trap Tyrone Power who found her far too aggressive for his liking.

In 1940, she met George Raft at a party. Mutual attraction was immediate and they were in bed together a few hours later. In August they sailed on the *Normandie* for Europe and were briefly engaged, but George was unable to afford the divorce conditions imposed by his current wife. Shearer was rich enough to have settled things, but she was too proud and too tight with her money, so that affair also came to a screeching halt.

Clark Gable considered her a tease because she never wore underwear beneath her form-fitting gowns. 'She's flaunting it', he complained. 'She must be one hot lay if she can behave like that with the camera turning. She kisses like a whore in heat'. Lillian Hellman simply found her boring and quite stupid: 'A face un-clouded by thought', she said.

Shearer lived until 1988. By then she was in an old people's home, her hair snow white. She was scarcely capable of a lucid thought. At eighty-three she attempted to jump from the top floor of the building. Her final years saw this little, old lady sadly wandering the corridors of the home, asking the same question of everyone she met, 'Are you Irving?'

Romeo Must Die (2000)

In 1994, recording artist Aaliyah briefly married singer/songwriter Robert Kelly, the man who activated her career. The union was annulled when it was revealed that Aaliyah was only fifteen years old. Sadly, a year after making *Romeo Must Die*, she was killed when a private plane in which she was a passenger crashed on take-off in the Bahamas. The overloaded craft plummeted into Marsh Harbor, Abaco Island. She was twenty-two and had just signed to make four more films.

Romper Stomper (1992)

Russell Crowe's co-star, twenty-three year-old Daniel Pollock, was a long-time sufferer from drug addiction. In the same year as the film was released he committed suicide by throwing himself under a train.

Rope (1948)

This tale of two young friends who kill, simply for the thrill of it, is based on the Leopold and Loeb murder in the 1920s, a subject covered in another film *Compulsion*. Unable to openly depict the killers' homosexuality on screen, Hitchcock insinuates it throughout. Interestingly, both young actors who play the killers (Farley Granger and John Dall) were themselves bisexuals but, of course, the public was unaware of this. Dall is probably best remembered for this film and his portrayal of the disgraced Commander of the Garrison of Rome in *Spartacus*.

Rose, The (1979)

As a presenter at the 1981 Oscars, Bette Midler brought the house down when she solemnly announced that, even though she had been overlooked in 1979 for *The Rose*, 'my heart is as big as the sky and I have a mind that retains absolutely nothing. This is the Oscars. We must be dignified. We must rise to the occasion'. Then, with both hands she extravagantly hoisted up her considerable bosom as the place erupted.

Ruthless People (1986)

Early in 1970, the then unknown Bette Midler was regularly performing at a gay bathhouse called the New York Continental Baths. The equally unknown Barry Manilow was the house pianist. In those early days Bette was willing to do almost anything outrageous onstage to gain attention and publicity. This included 'mooning' an audience in Massachusetts, and flashing her breasts onstage in St Louis. When she went to collect her Hasty Pudding Award at Harvard University in 1976, she swung open her slit dress, and showed her bare derriere to the gathered academics and guests. Only Bette could get away with it and still having them eating out of the palm of her hand.

Ryan's Daughter (1970)

The papers were full of Sarah Miles' supposed affair with Robert Mitchum on the set of this picture. The two stars did spend a *lot* of time in his caravan, but Miles denied any intimacy. When Mitchum told reporters she was a secret 'urine therapy addict', (in other words, she drank her own urine), she quite candidly owned up to the fact.

The dyslexic actress was born illegitimate. She lost her virginity to actor James Fox when he was a Royal Guardsman at Buckingham Palace. He was away in Kenya doing National Service when she decided on a backyard abortion, choosing not to inform him of her condition.

Saboteur (1942)

Celebrated wit, Dorothy Parker, makes her only screen appearance in this Hitchcock film. She is seen in a car with the director as he makes his customary 'quickie' appearance. It was Parker who, when told President Truman had died, drily asked, 'How could they tell?'

Sabrina (1954)

Marjorie Bennett plays Margaret the cook in this. She and her sister Enid were very popular silent stars from the small town of York in Western Australia. Enid played Maid Marian opposite Douglas Fairbanks in the silent classic *Robin Hood*, and was married to director Fred Niblo who directed the 1925 version of *Ben-Hur*. When Enid became homesick he suggested she ask Marjorie to join her in Hollywood to keep her company. Before long, Marjorie was also in the movies and enjoyed a long career that included playing Miss Lark in Julie Andrews' *Mary Poppins,* and Victor Buono's mother in *Whatever Happened to Baby Jane?*

Sailor Beware (1951)

If you look closely, during the boxing scene, you can spot nineteen year-old James Dean in a bit part in this film. Dean, incidentally, was a protégé of Clifton Webb, who claimed his *first* protégé was none other than Rudolph Valentino back in the twenties.

Saint, The (1997)

Aussie director Phillip Noyce turned down Russell Crowe and George Clooney, who were both keen to play Simon Templar, and opted for the troublesome Val Kilmer instead. The studio did not want Clooney because executives considered him to be, 'one of a thousand pretty faces that's been hanging around the Hollywood Hills for years going nowhere'.

Salome (1918)

For years Theda Bara was billed as the wickedest woman in the world, yet there is not a shred of scandal attached to her name. In fact, her only marriage lasted forty-four years until her death.

She was born in Cincinnati, Ohio, but the studio publicity machine soon turned her beginnings into something more befitting a screen 'vampire' by proclaiming she was born in Egypt 'in the shadow of the Sphinx'. Her name was also an anagram of 'Arab Death', they said. Actually, Theda was a contraction of her real first name 'Theodosia', and Bara was the family name of her Swiss maternal grandmother.

Of course, that was far too dull for Fox Studios. They touted her as the daughter of a French painter and an Arab princess who had eloped to a Saharan oasis where Theda was conceived. During World War One, when Belgium was being over-run by the Germans, Fox conveniently discovered that she also had a few pints of Belgian blood coursing through her veins. At the height of her fame even the New York Times saw fit to run a 600 word article, minutely describing a dream she supposedly had in which it was foretold a woman would bring about an end to World War One.

Because of her stupendous movie success, the entire family changed their names from Goodman to Bara. To keep the charade going, she would give interviews to an eager press, telling them she had been re-incarnated four times, and that one of her previous lives was as the original daughter of Seti, the Egyptian High Priest of the Pharaohs. Studio PR soon released a 'scoop' stating that a recently discovered Egyptian tomb had disclosed hieroglyphics prophesying the coming of Theda!

While making Cleopatra then, it came as no surprise when the actress announced she was, lo and behold, the re-incarnation of the Queen of the Nile as well. 'It is not a mere theory of mine', she told reporters. 'I have positive knowledge that such is the case. I live Cleopatra. I breathe Cleopatra. I am Cleopatra!' To reinforce the claim, she would conduct interviews in a room permeated with the aroma of burning incense, as she casually stroked a serpent (non-poisonous, of course). The public lapped all this twaddle up.

Her three-year contract, signed in 1916, forbade her going out in daylight hours, and insisted she be heavily veiled in public. The curtains were always to be drawn on her limousine. Although women's groups all over the country protested about her immoral vampire roles, it was mostly females who went to see her films.

'Kiss me, my fool', a line from her first hit film, became a popular phrase in the pre-twenties. When she pleaded for more sympathetic roles and was given them, the public stayed away in droves, forcing her to return to the man-eating parts by which she was always identified.

One day, by simply handling a hat in a New York City store, she inadvertently touched off a riot. Women fought each other to get to the hat and feel it themselves, hoping to acquire some of the reputed 'power' Theda presumably had over men. By the same token, women would kick her photograph as they entered theatres where her films were playing. But they still went in and paid to watch her. On one occasion, a woman on a New York street called police simply because Theda stopped and spoke to her child.

In 1919, she demanded (and got) the title role of the sweet Irish colleen in Kathleen Mavourneen. Hibernian Societies everywhere suffered mass apoplexy. A *Jewess* playing the symbol of Irish womanhood was all a bit much for them. They went on a rampage, stoning theatres and disrupting performances with stink bombs.

When her contract expired in the same year, she held out for a rise from $4,000 to $5,000 a week, plus the right to choose her own stories. The studio, aware 'the vamp' was a fad of the past, refused to renew her contract, and her film career was over. Only three of her movies survive to this day. A pity, because she truly was a phenomenon in her time.

Salome (1923)

Although the credits list Charles Bryant as the director, this film was actually directed by his wife, Alla Nazimova, probably the most notorious lesbian queen in Hollywood history. She chose to employ only gay people in the cast and crew, a 'first' that is unique in the annals of mainstream moviemaking.

Samson and Delilah (1949)

Victor Mature (1913-1999)

Known relationships:

Barrymore, Diana
Blanchard, Mari
Brooke, Phyllis
Caldwell, Cleatus
Cobb, Buff
Darvi, Bella
Faye, Alice
Field, Virginia
Grable, Betty
Haver, June
Hayworth, Rita
Hill, Virginia
Hutton, Betty
Lake, Veronica
Landis, Carole
Methot, Mayo
Paget, Debra
Sharpe, Karen
Shay, Mildred
Shirley, Anne
St Cyr, Lili
Steele, Karen

Stewart, Elaine
Taylor, Elizabeth
Tierney, Gene
Turner, Lana
Williams, Esther

Married:

5 times to non-actors

Twenty-three year-old Angela Lansbury plays a *blonde* Philistine and the *older* sister to thirty-five year old Hedy Lamarr's Delilah. Mr. Universe of 1947, Steve Reeves, tested for the role of Samson but his acting skills were considered to be microscopic. Douglas Fairbanks Junior was considered as well. Director Cecil B DeMille even approached Cary Grant to play the muscleman to end all musclemen! Now *that* would have been something to see. DeMille's ultimate choice was Victor Mature, a man who greatly aggravated the director with his unwillingness to participate in *any* strenuous action stuff. All of that was handled by Vic's double.

Despite being built like a block of flats, Mature was reputed to be the biggest sissy in Hollywood. He was literally afraid of *everything*. He was frightened of fire, horses, swords and insects, just to name a few. While making *The Robe* he was required to wield a club, but adamantly refused to do so because it frightened him. The wardrobe department came up with one made out of a painted balloon, but he was still unsure of his safety. 'What if the balloon bursts?' he timidly asked. Even he admitted: 'I wouldn't walk up a wet step'.

Michael Wilding walked in on his wife Elizabeth Taylor and Mature in bed making love one day. Scarcely a he-man himself, Wilding left at once and ran off to confide in his good friend Stewart Granger. Granger was made of sterner stuff and confronted Mature a few days later, ordered him to apologize 'on his knees' to Wilding, or suffer the consequences. Mature, who was even afraid of Wilding, did so, on his knees as instructed.

He and Oleg Cassini converted the former's yacht the *Bar Bill* into a coast guard vessel and spent the entire war 'patrolling' off the Catalina coast, whenever they felt inclined to do so. It was a whole lot safer than active service overseas. One of his lovers was Virginia Hill who would later become 'Bugsy' Siegel's girlfriend.

Vic had no illusions about his ability as a thespian, often remarking to interviewers that he was never an actor, 'and I've got 64 pictures to prove it', he proudly added.

Sanders of the River (1935)

Singer Paul Robeson, and a non-actor named Jomo Kenyatta, play West African chieftains in this. Kenyatta would later achieve worldwide notoriety, accused by the British (almost certainly unjustly) of leading the Mau Mau in its bloody campaign to dislodge British settlers from his homeland. Later still, he would become Kenya's first president and be knighted by the Queen of England.

Sands of Iwo Jima (1949)

Sands of Iwo Jima was the biggest box-office hit Republic Studios ever had. The three surviving Marine veterans who raised the *first* flag on Mount Suribachi have small parts here. There were actually two flag raisings, the second one being staged for the cameras and posterity.

Forrest Tucker plays the GI who causes the deaths of his buddies when he stops off for a cup of coffee, instead of rushing desperately needed ammunition back to the front line. Other than being a fine actor, Tucker laid claim to being the most generously endowed actor in Hollywood, although Milton Berle's admirers often dispute that.

During a touring production of *The Music Man* he realized his reputation had preceded him, so he called all the male dancers into his dressing room and dropped his trousers in front of them. 'I know all the whispering behind my back', he said, 'so let's get it out in the open right now, so you can concentrate on your work'. As usual, everybody was mightily impressed and the whispering ceased. Lovers of the sixties TV comedy *F Troop* (produced, incidentally by Mel Brooks) will remember him as Sergeant O'Rourke.

San Francisco (1936)

Nelson Eddy's buddy Clark Gable could not abide Jeanette MacDonald. He hated making *San Francisco* with her and only did the picture because he wanted to play the character Blackie in the film. For her part, Jeanette complained that he stunk of garlic and booze in their love scenes. Gable's friends said he only ever truly disliked two actresses in Hollywood – MacDonald and Greer Garson. He preferred down-to-earth blousy women like Lombard, Crawford and Blondell.

MacDonald began as a dancer in New York. When opportunities dried up she tried her hand as an escort to well-heeled gentlemen, made some money and had several abortions in the process. In 1929 she moved to Hollywood and continued as an escort earning $100 a night accompanying influential men about town. Please, feel free to substitute the word 'prostitute' for 'escort' whenever you feel like it.

She soon worked out how to give her limited singing and acting gifts a boost. She let L B Mayer seduce her whenever he wanted to. And he wanted to a *lot*. Director Robert Mamoulian said of her, 'Jeanette was the easiest lay in Hollywood'.

Joan Blondell said she was 'a conservative priss, who in real life had several lovers. John Cassavetes was particularly scathing. 'Actresses like Jeanette MacDonald and Grace Kelly pretended they were Madonnas but were real sluts', he said. 'And now you have a slut named Madonna!'

When Jeanette met Nelson Eddy the couple fell in love almost immediately. Eddy, unaware of her past, held off seducing her believing she was still a virgin. When he eventually learned the truth he angrily beat and then ravaged her. Evidently, this only served to draw her to him and they became intimate on a regular basis. Although they remained lovers on and off for the rest of their lives, his violent mood swings and obsessive jealousy always made her wary of marrying him – even if she could. When they became a highly successful singing duo in a series of quite diabolical musicals, Mayer forbade any thought of her getting a divorce and marrying her lover. Fans still took a dim view of adulterous stars as LB well knew.

She spontaneously married gay actor Gene Raymond following one of her spats with Eddy, a decision both she and Nelson forever rued. Jeanette's mother knew about Raymond *before* the wedding, but kept the knowledge from her daughter because she intensely disliked Eddy. On the honeymoon cruise Jeanette soon found out for herself when Gene began sleeping with Mary Pickford's husband Buddy Rogers. The new Mrs. Raymond cut the honeymoon short by six weeks and returned to Hollywood.

Before long the songbirds were intimate again, until another argument saw a blind drunk Eddy rush off to Las Vegas and marry an acquaintance named Ann Franklin. Returning to Los Angeles on the train, he could not even remember the wedding. Both MacDonald and Eddy tried, albeit half-heartedly, to get divorces but their spouses threatened to expose the details of their affair if they pursued the matter in court. Consequently, both unions endured for the rest of their lives, while the two mixed up lovers continued to sleep together in between feuds. Over the decades Jeanette would miscarry three and possibly four pregnancies to Eddy.

In 1952, following two suicide attempts, she was placed in a sanitarium by her husband and underwent a series of shock treatments. She died in 1965. Eddy suffered a fatal heart attack on stage while touring in Australia two years later. At his funeral his widow leaned across to Raymond and drily commented, 'Now they can sing together forever'.

Saratoga Trunk (1945)

Gary Cooper and Ingrid Bergman had a torrid affair when making this picture together. 'Ingrid loved me more than any woman in my life loved me', recalled Cooper. 'The day after the picture ended, I couldn't get her on the phone'.

Save the Tiger (1973)

Jack Gilford's career was almost wrecked by the HUAC in the 1950s. When asked by the committee if he believed in the overthrow of the United States by force and violence, he quietly replied, 'No, just gently'. Two decades later he won himself an Oscar nomination for *Save the Tiger*.

Scalp Hunters, The (1968)

During this picture, set in the 1880s, Ossie Davis points to the sky and mentions something about 'Jupiter moving in on Pluto'. Pluto was not discovered until 1930. Oops!

Scaramouche (1952)

In the scene in the gypsy's wagon when Eleanor Parker wallops Stewart Granger across the face, you can see her stifle a laugh. The slap was much harder than he expected and she spontaneously started to react to the genuine look of surprise on his face.

Stewart Granger's real name was James Stewart, so he had to act under a stage name since Jimmy Stewart already had first dibs. Granger risked all by leaping to the defense of Michael Wilding after his friend was accused in print by Hedda Hopper of being gay. In a phone call that reverberated around Hollywood, he gave the columnist a verbal lashing that has since become legendary.

'I think you're a monumental bitch', he roared, 'How bloody dare you accuse a friend of mine of being queer, you raddled, dried up, frustrated old cunt!' *Nobody* spoke to Hedda that way and everyone expected her to destroy his career, which she tried hard to do, but without success.

Actually, Hedda was not far off the mark with her accusation. Wilding was certainly bisexual. Had she lived until the eighties, she would have also learned that Granger, too, had once strayed from the heterosexual straight and narrow with, of all people, his good buddy Wilding!

According to Granger, the two friends were intimate one evening in London during an air raid at the height of the Blitz. 'People would say we were both queers, and that isn't so', he said. 'It was just the kind of thing that happened during the war'. Well, not to *everybody*, Stewy!

Despite marriages to Norma Shearer's daughter and Alan Ladd's stepdaughter, Richard Anderson's career never progressed beyond playing minor roles such as Granger's best friend in this. He is now probably best remembered for his role as Goldman in the TV series *The Six Million Dollar Man*.

Scared Stiff (1953)

Confidential Magazine hinted in the 1950s that Lizabeth Scott was a lesbian who hired call girls for sex. Their investigators found her name (they claimed) in the accounts book of a lesbian brothel, along with those of George Raft and George Jessel. She sued the magazine, but lost the case, despite being defended by the redoubtable Gerry Geisler. It was one of his few defeats.

In an interview with Sidney Skilsky, Lizabeth admitted she always wore men's colognes and men's pajamas and detested frilly women's dresses. On a jaunt to Europe she made a beeline for Paris and a woman named Frede, the most notorious lesbian queen in the country. She spent time at Frede's nightclub, one that catered exclusively to the 'twilight set'. Feel free to draw your own conclusions. Incidentally, I always thought she was terrific, especially that husky voice.

Schindler's List (1993)

Schindler's List brought forth the following response from the chief censor in Malaysia: 'The story reflects the privilege and virtues of a certain race only. The theme of the film is to reveal the brutality and cruelty of the Nazi soldiers to the

Jews. It seems, the illustration is propaganda with the purpose of asking for sympathy, as well as to tarnish the other race'. With this as its premise, the Malaysian government insisted on cuts; fifteen minutes of screen time be made. Steven Spielberg responded by withdrawing from Malaysian distribution, not only *Schindler's List,* but every other Amblin Entertainment production past and present.

The real Oscar Schindler never received a Golden Nazi Party badge, so he could scarcely have sold it to save more Jews. Anyway, Nazi Party badges were nearly always made from gold-plated brass.

When they liquidated the Krakow ghetto on March 13, 1943 a small Jewish boy named Roman Polanski escaped that day. Spielberg asked him to direct the film, but he understandably did not wish to relive the experience.

Seabiscuit (2004)

No fewer than ten different horses played the legendary Seabiscuit in this film. Five were used for the racing sequences and another five were utilized in the 'special interest' segments that showed the horse sleeping, being feisty, or whatever.

Searchers, The (1956)

It was John Wayne's uttering of the line 'that'll be the day', several times in this film, that inspired the Buddy Holly hit song of that name. If *The Searchers* is not the best western ever made, then it must run a close second to whatever is. The Academy, in its infinite wisdom, chose not to recognize it, however, and it was not even *nominated* for Best Picture, the statuette ultimately going to the pedestrian (and so *boring) Around the World in 80 Days*.

John Wayne was never better, yet he too went un-nominated, *that* Oscar going to Yul Brynner (inexplicably) for *The King And I*. Even the superb cinematography was overlooked. *The King and I* won in that category as well. In fact, *The Searchers* failed to gain a single nomination, much less an Oscar.

For some reason, the Academy has generally been reluctant to recognize westerns and comedies come Oscar time. I guess that makes Lee Marvin's win for *Cat Ballou* the greatest upset in history, a Best Actor Oscar for a player in a western comedy.

The writers err when they have Ethan Edwards give a medal to his niece, a decoration awarded him by the Confederate government during the Civil War, he tells her. The Confederacy never issued medals at any time throughout the conflict.

Harry Carey Senior was a long-time friend of John Wayne and John Ford. In the final scene, where Wayne is silhouetted in the doorway of the homestead, he adopts a pose peculiar to Carey, that of his left hand grasping his right forearm. Carey had died some eight years before and the stance was adopted as a tribute to their friend by the director and his leading man. In the scene, Wayne is looking back into the hut at the homesteader's wife, played by Olive Golden. She was the real life widow of Harry Carey.

Carey's career had been going up and down for some time back in the 1920s, when he was astonished to receive an invitation to be a pallbearer at MGM whiz kid Irving Thalberg's funeral. He had never even met the man. From then on, opportunities and roles improved dramatically. Apparently, Thalberg's secretary intended the invitation for Irving's old and dearest friend, Carey Wilson, but sent it to Harry by mistake. His son Harry Carey Junior plays the young cowhand who suicides by single-handedly attacking the Comanche camp.

Natalie Wood's younger sister, Lana, plays her as a little girl here. A couple of decades later, a voluptuous Lana (36-24-35) would portray Plenty O'Toole in the Bond film *Diamonds Are Forever*. Natalie, by comparison, never measured up quite as well - (32-22-34).

Ward Bond and Wayne were both playing football for the University of Southern California when director John Ford selected them to appear in an Annapolis film entitled *Salute*. The three men became firm friends, working together in several films over the ensuing decades. They were about as right wing as it gets, outspoken and vituperative in their opposition to anything and anyone they considered 'un-American'.

Best remembered for his role as Festus in TV's *Gunsmoke,* Ken Curtis got his start in John Ford westerns. Ford's daughter Barbara married him, hoping to gain acceptance with her father. He was one of her Dad's favorites and regularly sang at his gatherings. When the marriage collapsed, his chauffeur had to break into Barbara's place to rescue her from an alcoholic coma.

Send Me No Flowers (1964)

Paul Lynde hilariously plays the manager of a cemetery in this Hudson/Day comedy. A flaming homosexual, he drowned in his Beverly Hills pool at the age of fifty-six. The coroner said his heart was the equivalent of that of an eighty-eight year-old man when he died.

Sense & Sensibility (1995)

Emma Thompson and Greg Wise were lovers when they made this picture together. She took up with him after she and husband Kenneth Branagh split. Branagh went off with Helena Bonham-Carter. Wise plays the part of Willoughby, the man who jilts Kate Winslett's character. Bit actor Richard Lumsden married Emma's sister Sophie during the shoot. He plays the role of Hugh Grant's brother Robert Ferrars.

As soon as his commitment to the picture was concluded, Hugh Grant hopped on a plane for Los Angeles to promote his up-coming movie *Nine Months*. Once there, he found himself under arrest for consorting with a prostitute, winding up on front pages all over the world. The cast of *Sense & Sensibility* back in England found the whole thing hilarious.

Serenade (1956)

The overbearingly vain Mario Lanza once followed an obese, unattractive maid into an adjoining room at his hotel and seduced her. He later explained to friends that such an unappealing woman deserved to have sex with a famous, attractive man at least once in her life.

There has always been speculation surrounding Lanza's death in Italy in 1959. Just a few days before his sudden demise at a clinic, he brazenly refused a request from gangster Charles 'Lucky' Luciano to perform at a benefit for him. Luciano's henchmen warned the singer not to show the mobster disrespect but he ignored them.

On October 7, Lanza was found in a coma with an empty IV tube pumping nothing but air into his veins. He never recovered. Many people believe a nurse at the clinic may have interfered with his medication, although the official cause of death was listed as a coronary thrombosis, brought on through embarking on a crash diet. Despite the suspicious circumstances, no autopsy or investigation was conducted. Robert Alda (the father of TV star Alan Alda) and Rossano Brazzi were pallbearers at his funeral.

Sergeant York (1941)

Gary Cooper was forty-one and Joan Leslie just sixteen when they portrayed York and his sweetheart in this film.

Although this was an Oscar winning vehicle for Cooper, it also featured triple Oscar winner Walter Brennan, who made a career out of playing toothless, limping sidekicks to the biggest stars. An accident in 1932 knocked his teeth out and helped to create the persona he adopted for his character roles. Apparently, the limp he carried for the latter part of his career was faked. He felt it fitted his character. He and Ruth Welles were childhood sweethearts and stayed married for fifty-four years.

7th Heaven (1927)

Janet Gaynor was one of the biggest stars of the late 1920s and early 1930, but came out of retirement, in 1957, to play Pat Boone's mother in *Bernadine*. The lovely Gaynor teamed with Charles Farrell in several successful films and won an Oscar for *Seventh Heaven* in 1927-8. It has often been said, however, that the diminutive actress was 'more of a man' than her co-star.

Standing just five feet tall, she was the long-time 'husband' in a gay relationship with singer Mary Martin, the mother of Larry Hagman of *Dallas* fame. Gaynor was encouraged to wed gay costume designer Adrian in 1939 for the sake of appearances. Another of her earlier lovers was actress Helen Hayes, but the love of her life was a minor player, Margaret Lindsay. Gaynor, Martin, and Hayes were involved in a car crash in 1982, with Janet suffering severe injuries to which she succumbed two years later. Martin passed away in 1990, Hayes three years later.

Charles Farrell was bi-sexual, a secret the studio went to great lengths to successfully conceal from the public. Like so many others, he entered into a lavender arrangement when he wed actress Virginia Valli. The couple moved to Palm Springs in 1941 as a 'twilight tandem' (a term used to describe a marriage in which both parties were gay) and helped establish that city's gay community.

Seven Year Itch, The (1955)

The famous scene, in which Marilyn's skirt billows upwards as she stands over a New York subway grating, was staged for publicity and proved to be the final blow to her marriage to baseball great Joe DiMaggio. He fumed as he witnessed the crowd's response to take after take. Marilyn's knickers were sheer enough for one bystander to exclaim, 'Jesus, I thought she was a real blonde'.

She quickly changed to a more opaque brand but the damage had been done. Joe took out his frustration on her that night, and the following morning she appeared on set badly bruised. Photos and shots were restricted to those of her legs only. Ironically, only the first shot of her and Tom Ewell walking along Lexington Avenue was ultimately used. The shots of her dress billowing were done later on a sound stage in Hollywood.

Sextette (1978)

When she made *Sextette* in 1978, Mae West was in her mid-eighties, quite deaf and a little blind. To build up her height for the film she wore high platform shoes. A prop man had to lie on the floor, stretch his arms around her feet and literally turn her to whichever camera she was supposed to be facing. She was too deaf and senile to take direction.

It evidently did not bother her or the writers that the eighty-five year old Mae's character beds thirty-three year old Timothy Dalton's character in the script. Not surprisingly, the picture bombed.

Sgt. Bilko (1996)

Phil Silvers played the original Bilko on television. That is his real life daughter, Catherine Silvers, who appears here as the bespectacled Pentagon auditor. A young Chris Rock portrays the other auditor.

The very funny Phil Hartman plays Major Thorn in this Steve Martin comedy, but is best remembered as a featured voice on the TV series *The Simpsons*, and as a regular on *Saturday Night Live*. His emotionally disturbed wife Brynn, apparently jealous of his success and her failure to hit it big in show business, shot him to death in 1998 while he slept. She then turned the gun on herself. Hartman was forty-nine when he died from 'multiple gunshot wounds to the head and neck'.

Shampoo (1975)

The notorious under the table fellatio scene in *Shampoo*, featuring Julie Christie and Warren Beatty, was supposedly inspired by a real life incident at Ciro's nightclub. Patrons there reportedly witnessed Paulette Goddard disappear under the table while dining with her lover, Anatole Litvak.

Other sources argue that it was Litvak who did the disappearing.

Beatty's character is loosely based on real life Hollywood hairdresser Jay Sebring, the same Jay Sebring who was butchered by the Manson Gang along with Sharon Tate and other unfortunates.

Shane (1953)

The original intention was to cast Montgomery Clift as Shane; William Holden as Joe Starrett and Katharine Hepburn as Marian Starrett, but each one dropped out of contention. Director George Stevens even made pre-shoot notes that Clift would need to be 'muscled up' for the bare-chested stump-chopping scene.

The reason for the Teton Mountains towering over every scene was because all outside shots, even close-ups involving dialogue, were taken with a telephoto lens to bring the peaks closer. The result is quite breathtaking.

When 'Stonewall' is shot by Wilson in the muddy street outside the saloon, wires attached to Elisha Cooke Junior jerk him backwards as the shot is fired. This was the first time such a reaction to a gunshot was ever used in a mainstream movie. Actually, the whole concept is flawed. Since every action, according to the laws of physics, has an equal and opposite reaction, Wilson should also have been propelled backwards by the recoil, but he was not.

Stevens wanted Palance to dismount and mount his horse 'like a cat'. The dismount at Starrett's homestead was done very slowly and deliberately, but the remount was too difficult, until they simply reversed the film of the dismount to get the effect Stevens wanted.

Her co-stars on *Shane* recalled Jean Arthur spending most of her idle time on the set with the litter of pigs used in the film. She had an eccentric affection for animals and drove out to the location site at midnight on occasion to check on the well-being of the horses, cows and dogs used in the picture. Brandon de Wilde, who plays Van Heflin's son, was killed in a car accident near Denver in 1972 at the age of twenty-nine.

Jean's first marriage in 1928 to Julian Ancker lasted just *a single day* before it was annulled. He died a few years later from sunstroke while out fishing. Although a lesbian, Arthur had an affair with producer David O Selznick in the late twenties. She and gay singer Mary Martin were life-long friends, and almost certainly lovers.

Jean was also a chronic sufferer from stage fright, a victim of her own insecurities. 'You can't get her in front of the cameras without her crying, whining, vomiting and all that shit', complained director Frank Capra. '...then when she finishes the scene she runs back to the dressing room and hides'.

Her extreme shyness was often mistaken for aloofness. The first time she heard her voice on a soundtrack she screamed 'foghorn!' and ran sobbing from the studio. After her acting career dried up she taught drama at the all- female Vasser College.

Although he only appears for twenty minutes on the screen and speaks just eighteen lines, Jack Palance earned an Oscar nomination for his portrayal of the evil gunfighter named Wilson. Born in 1920 to Ukranian parents, he was a boxer in his teens winning eighteen of his first twenty bouts, before injury forced him out of the ring.

When the acting bug bit him, he went to Chicago and snared the job of understudy to Anthony Quinn's Stanley Kowalski in *A Streetcar Named Desire*. Unluckily for Jack, Quinn never missed a performance, so he never got to replace him. He did, however, replace Brando when he became ill while playing the same role in New York City. His screen career took off from there.

Quick draw expert Ron Red Eagle showed Jack how to draw his gun quickly, and suggested he laugh at the same time, a sinister touch that made his character appear even more deadly. Having come direct from the New York stage, he had never handled a six-gun before. Neither had he ever ridden a horse.

Elisha Cooke Jr. plays the feisty confederate veteran gunned down by Wilson. When not acting he led a solitary life, in a cabin in the High Sierras, fishing for golden trout. A courier would deliver scripts to him there or advise him of acting opportunities. If something took his fancy he would come down out of the mountains, fulfil his obligations on the picture, and then return to his fishing.

Sheik, The (1921)

Rudolph Valentino's heavy lidded, sexy look was due to a deadened nerve that caused one eye to droop. Former co-star Nita Naldi commented years later on his poor eyesight as well. 'We were blind as bats. Poor Rudy groped his way through many a love scene, and I mean really groped'.

In 1919 he married the bisexual actress Jean Acker, a union apparently orchestrated by the woman's lesbian lover Alla Nazimova. His bride locked him out of the bedroom on their wedding night and the marriage was never consummated.

A few years later, he fell for another of Nazimova's 'girls', Natasha Rambova. She was actually Winifred Shaughnessy of Utah, and the stepdaughter of cosmetics tycoon Richard Hudnut. The couple wed before Valentino's divorce from Acker had been finalized, so he was briefly jailed for bigamy until the studio pulled a few strings. This union too was never consummated since Rambova had as little sexual interest in men as Rudy had in women.

Shortly before his death, he was also involved with *another* bisexual, Pola Negri. It was a full *two weeks* before his body was laid to rest following his unexpected death. It was displayed in Los Angeles first, and then transported to New York for another lying in state. Hundreds of thousands of people queued to gaze upon his remains. Miss Negri put on a fainting, swooning screaming performance at each one.

She Loves Me Not (1934)

Early in his career at Paramount, Bing Crosby hated having his protruding ears stuck back with spirit glue or adhesive tape. During the making of *She Loves Me Not* he at last rebelled and refused to return to the set until the studio agreed to stop the practice. Consequently, in some of the scenes his ears are streamlined, while in others they stick out as nature intended.

Sheriff of Fractured Jaw, The (1959)

In this picture, Jayne Mansfield mimes her songs to Connie Francis's voice. Kenneth More, her co-star, referred to the big-busted blonde as 'Miss United Dairies'. Eight years after making this film she was killed when her car collided with a truck near New Orleans. Reports of her being decapitated in the crash were completely incorrect. A passing motorist noticed her blonde wig lying in the road and the story spread from there. Her fiancée also died at the scene.

Mansfield played her movie star image to the hilt. Her home, car, and even her pet poodles, were all colored *pink*. She even bathed in pink champagne once for a photo shoot. A one-night stand with Elvis Presley was rewarded with a gift from him of a pink motorcycle. The first time she attempted to dye one of her poodles it did not survive the process. For publicity purposes she agreed to lead a tiger down Sunset Boulevard on a pink ribbon!

Excited patrons at the Copacabana, in Rio in 1959, ripped the top of her dress off, stripping her to the waist, as she danced an impromptu shimmy. Michael Caine wrote of the time he saw her dress come apart while she was again dancing at a disco. The entire crowd stopped and gaped as she simply stepped out of it, draped it over her arm, and casually walked, completely naked and utterly unconcerned, from the floor. Like many sex symbols she rarely wore bras or knickers.

Eddie Fisher described her as 'a nasty drunk' who reveled in instigating attention-drawing brawls, so that her husband, Mickey Hargitay, would have to wade in and salvage her honor. 'She had about as much honor as she had talent', noted Fisher. She was one of the few celebrities who offered him sex and get a negative response – or so he said.

Joan Collins recalled finding her in her trailer one day, naked but for a bra, with one leg nonchalantly cocked up on a chair, while her make-up man lathered and shaved her pubic hairs into a heart shape. It was to be a surprise for her husband!

In a way, she was responsible for Dick Cavett getting started on television. Jayne was making her twelfth appearance on *The Jack Paar Show* when Cavitt applied for a position as a writer for the program. Paar told him to come up with a new and interesting introduction for the exceedingly voluptuous actress if he wanted get the job. Cavitt was hired after he came up with, 'And now, here they are, Jayne Mansfield'.

Shining, The (1980)

In order to get the appropriate reaction from Jack Nicholson in the scene where a rotting hag steps out of the bathtub in room 237, director Stanley Kubrick had him study graphic photographs of car accident victims as the camera focused on his face.

After shooting completed, Jack enjoyed the London nightlife for a while. It was there he met the former First Lady of Canada, Margaret Trudeau, and shared what she referred to as 'a mad episode...in the back of a Daimler'. Later, at a Hollywood party, he took her into the men's room where she stripped and sat on a toilet seat, hoisted her legs in the air to avoid being seen by any men entering the room, and had him service her again.

Ship of Fools (1965)

It was on the set of this film that Lee Marvin met an extra named Michelle Triola. The couple were together for over a decade, until he called it quits and Michelle filed history's first ever 'palimony' suit against him in 1979. Chasing $3.6 million she lost the case, yet was awarded $104,000 by the judge, which she also lost following an appeal. In 1981, she was convicted of shoplifting 'two bras and two sweaters' from a department store.

Showboat (1951)

Kathryn Grayson was reputed to have the biggest breasts in Hollywood. "With her they didn't need 3D', commented her co-star in *Showboat*, Ava Gardner. She was also a lady who solved her own problems. While making *The Toast of New Orleans* with Mario Lanza, she understandably took umbrage to her arduous co-star's habit of poking his tongue down her throat during their love scenes. After he repeatedly ignored her protests, she wore a pair of brass knuckles onto the set and punched him in the groin when he tried it again. Problem solved.

Sincerely Yours (1955)

This was the flamboyant pianist Liberace's singular chance at movie stardom and he blew it. In the picture he receives his one and only screen kiss from Dorothy Malone. To nobody's surprise the chemistry between the sultry Malone and the gay Liberace did not exactly steam up the cameras or the screen. The movie bombed.

Throughout his life he steadfastly denied his homosexuality, even after Rock Hudson revealed that the two men had a brief affair when Rock was just starting out. 'Just a few weeks', was how Rock described the liaison.

From the time he was first seduced at sixteen (by a pro footballer), the popular pianist enjoyed scores of male lovers, usually muscular blond young men, many of whom accompanied him on tour as part of his troupe.

In 1959, he sued the London *Daily Mirror* over allegations pertaining to his homosexuality. On the stand he was asked if he had 'ever indulged in homosexual practices', to which he responded, 'No sir, never in my life. I am against the practice because it offends convention and it offends society'. His perjury won him the case and the largest settlement for libel (in Britain) to that date, but it infuriated the gay community who had expected him to 'out' himself. After his death from AIDS in 1987, the same newspaper ran a light-hearted article asking for its money back.

Since You Went Away (1944)

It may have just been coincidence but four reputed lesbian/bisexual actresses appear in this picture. Claudette Colbert plays the lead, Hattie McDaniel is her maid, Agnes Moorehead portrays the interfering friend of the family and Alla Nazimova is cast as the refugee woman who befriends Colbert at the factory. Gay actor Monty Woolley and reputed bi-sexual Keenan Wynn also feature.

Colbert was extremely unlucky to get beaten by Ingrid Bergman in *Gaslight* for the Best Actress Oscar. Tearjerker or not, this movie is beautifully crafted and holds up well today, due in no small part to her superb portrayal of the war-time mother who holds the family together after dad trots off to kill people. *Everybody* is good in this terrific picture. The screenplay too is absolutely brilliant so, of course, it wasn't even nominated!

Agnes Moorehead's portrayal of the busybody, hypocrite friend of the family was a highlight of the film. A closeted lesbian, she was once described by gay comedian Paul Lynde as 'classy as hell, but one of the all-time Hollywood dykes'.

Television audiences no doubt remember her as Samantha's mother Endora in *Bewitched*.

One of Alla Nazimova's lovers was Edith Luckett, the mother of Nancy Davis who, as Ronald Reagan's wife, would later become America's First Lady. Nazimova was Nancy's godmother. Another Nazimova intimate was the first female director to amount to anything in Hollywood, Dorothy Arzner.

Emma Goldman was yet another, and notorious in Hollywood for running a massage parlor that specialized in 'vulvular massage to orgasm', a so-called remedy for stress, post-menstrual depression and other maladies. The treatment was legally practiced right up until the 1920s and 1930s.

Alla's orgies at the Garden of Allah were legendary. The gorgeous Barbara la Marr, who once stated that 'lovers are like roses. Best by the dozen', put a sign outside her bungalow that read 'Come one – Come all'. *Since You Went Away* was Alla's last film. She died in 1945.

Robert Walker is probably best remembered for his portrayal of the doomed young soldier who falls in love with Jennifer Jones. He and Jones were still real life husband and wife when this picture was made, although she was involved with David O Selznick at the time and would later marry him.

Female fans loved Walker's 'little boy lost', quizzical look. They were unaware it was brought about by his poor eyesight and an inability to focus properly. In 1951, he suddenly died at the age of thirty-two. A doctor gave him a shot of Sodium Amytal to calm him during one of his violent moments, but the actor had some sort of reaction to it and passed away shortly afterwards.

Jennifer Jones 'needed to be told every thought that went through her head', said character actress Jean Anderson. 'She was terribly starry and nervous'. She was probably the most insecure and fragile actress ever to make it to the top of the pile in Hollywood. Paralyzed with shyness, she even developed a nervous tic of the head because of it, and was forever calling her husband, Selznick, for reassurance and support.

Interestingly, Charlton Heston singled her beauty out for special praise. 'The one actress I thought really stunning was Jennifer Jones', he once told an interviewer. 'She's the only actress I've ever worked with who worked without makeup. She was a rather *skittish* girl, but stunning'.

Guy Madison made his movie debut in this film playing an American sailor on leave, which was what he was at the time in real life, having secured a seven-day pass to shoot his scenes. He instantly struck a chord with young fans, who fired in over 4,000 fan letters in one week to set his career in motion. His marriage to Gail Russell was a rocky one, not helped by her affair with Mia Farrow's father, director John Farrow.

Monty Woolley plays Colonel Smollett. Before becoming an actor he was a lecturer at Yale University and taught the writer Thornton Wilder. It was at Yale as a student that he became intimately involved with a classmate, songwriter Cole Porter. He and Porter often cruised about together in search of gay pick-ups. In 1936, at the age of forty-eight, he gave up his academic career for the movie business.

Singin' in the Rain (1952)

In the scene where Debbie Reynolds stands behind the curtain and provides the voice for Jean Hagen, the voice you hear is actually Miss Hagen's! Ironically, Debbie's voice was not considered classy enough.

Her son Todd was named after Mike Todd, the best friend of her husband Eddy Fisher. Although Debbie was Matron of Honor at Liz Taylor and Mike's Mexican wedding, she was not a close friend of the bride. In fact, according to Fisher, Liz and Todd barely tolerated her. She just happened to be there because he was the 'American' best man. Comedian Cantinflas was the 'Mexican' best man.

When Fisher left Debbie for Taylor, Debbie was depicted by the press as the heartbroken, deserted mother. Actually, the marriage was already on its last legs, and she was not upset at all. MGM publicity people convinced her to play the role of victim for all she was worth. They even arranged a TV interview, which showed Debbie with a diaper pinned to her shoulder and baby Carrie in her arms. After it was shown there was scarcely a dry eye left in America.

Her career received a welcome boost from the mountains of publicity and public sympathy. In fact, her annual earnings jumped from under $75,000 to nearly a million that year. 'We were never happier than we have been in the last year', she sadly told an interviewer. 'While Eddie was in New York he called me every day'. Taylor and Fisher burst out laughing when they saw the interview on TV. The highpoint (or lowpoint, depending on whose side you're on) came with a magazine photo of Debbie, the kids (and a dog) appearing on news- stands, captioned: 'Can't Daddy be with us all the time?'

'Debbie Reynolds was indeed the girl next door', said Fisher in a 1999 interview. 'But only if you lived next door to a self-centered, totally driven, insecure, untruthful phony'. When asked about Liz Taylor, he responded, 'Sexually she was every man's dream; she had the face of an angel and the morals of a truck driver'.

As for Debbie, he confided, 'sex with Debbie was about as exciting as a December afternoon in London'. In his biography he wrote, 'I don't think Debbie ever really enjoyed having sex with me. She was just not a sensual person'. He would not be drawn on unfounded rumors about her sexual proclivities, not even after her son, Todd Fisher, stated that she and Agnes Moorehead had been lovers for over a decade, ever since they met on the set of *How the West Was Won.*

In 1964, Debbie and Liz accidentally met aboard the QE2 en route to France. 'Well, isn't this the silliest', gushed Liz. 'It's just totally ridiculous', piped Debbie, who was with her new and wealthy husband. Liz had already dumped Fisher. 'Just look how you lucked out, and how I lucked out', exclaimed Liz over a glass of Dom Perignon. 'Who the hell cares about Eddie?" Who, indeed, cares about any of them?

Six Days, Seven Nights (1998)

In a TV interview with Oprah Winfrey, Anne Heche described how she fell in love with Ellen DeGeneres the moment she saw her at a party, curiously adding, 'I was not gay before I met her. I never thought about it'. She claims she suffered from mental illness for the first thirty-one years of her life, because her Baptist minister father had sexually abused her. He died in 1983 from AIDS.

Smokey & the Bandit (1977)

Burt Reynolds (1936 -)

Known relationships:

Arnaz, Lucie
Barbeau, Adrienne
Basinger, Kim
Brennan, Colleen
Day, Doris
Dunaway, Faye
Edelman, Kate
Evert, Chris
Field, Sally
Little, Tawny
Luft, Lorna
Mayama, Miko
Miles, Sarah
Nelson, Lori
Noel, Chris
Rauch, Gig
Seals, Pam

Shore, Dinah
Stevens, Inger
Taylor, Elizabeth
Van Doren, Mamie
Wynette, Tammy

Married:

Judy Carne
Loni Anderson

Burt Reynolds and his co-star Sally Field fell in love on the set of 'Smokey' and were together for five years. Burt also became involved with tennis champion Chris Evert for a while. In the early 1970s he and talk show hostess Dinah Shore had a lengthy relationship, even though she was nearly twenty years his senior.

His grandmother was a Cherokee Indian. At the age of nineteen he flat-lined after a car crash and was lucky to be revived in the nick of time. In 1972 he became the first nude male centerfold to appear in a major magazine. Helen Gurley Brown, the editor of *Cosmopolitan,* met him on a TV chat show and talked him into it.

Snow White & the 7 Dwarfs (1937)

Dancer Marge Champion, who was then married to animator Art Babbitt, was the model used for Snow White. Adriana Caselotti provided Snow White's voice after winning out over 150 other young hopefuls, including the then unknown Deanna Durbin.

Each dwarf was drawn as a completely separate identity that walked, talked, looked and reacted in his own peculiar way. For example, Doc was the tallest and wore spectacles. Dopey was the shortest and the only one without a beard. Grumpy's hat pointed down and his beard was scruffy. Sleepy had stooped shoulders and the longest, biggest beard. Bashful had no neck and pigeon toes. Even the reaction time for each one varied. Happy would usually react first if, say, Doc spoke. Sleepy would react slower than the others. Originally, there were eleven dwarfs created by Disney animators for the film. The four that did not make the final cut were Dirty, Awful, Deafy and Biggo Ego

It took six months just to complete the goldmine sequence. Since each dwarf was a different height and even marched differently (Dopey marched *out of step* with the others as well), the painstaking chore of drawing them receding into the distance, for instance, seemed to take forever to accomplish. Disney's animators learned so much in the years creating this film, that Walt would have preferred to scrap the whole movie and start again by the time it was completed, but that was financially out of the question. His second feature *Pinocchio,* made two years later, was technically far superior.

The Observer described *Snow White & the Seven Dwarfs* as having 'all the roughness and error of a first try'. The studios refused to nominate it for Best Film for fear it would establish a precedent for cartoons.

Disney projects were the subject of close scrutiny by the Censorship Board. In his early days, for example, Walt was instructed that in all future cartoons featuring Clarabelle

Cow, he must show her wearing a dress covering her udders because they were deemed 'extremely provocative'. In 1935 Mickey Mouse was banned in Romania because he was considered to be too frightening for children.

For a similar reason LB Mayer refused to sign Walt as an aspiring young cartoonist for MGM in 1928. He was convinced pregnant women would be terrified by a ten foot high mouse on the screen. By the mid-thirties, no doubt to Mayer's chagrin, Mickey Mouse was receiving more fan mail than any other star in Hollywood.

Alfred Hitchcock once quipped, 'Disney has the best casting. If he doesn't like an actor he just tears him up'.

'Girls bored me', Walt admitted one day. 'They still do. I love Mickey Mouse more than any woman I've ever known'. Not everyone, however, was such a fan of Mickey. When King George V was asked which film he would like to watch while convalescing, he answered, 'anything except that damned mouse!'

Disney always insisted on a 'one big happy family' atmosphere at his studio. Everyone, even lowly paid office boys and girls, was expected to call him Walt. He liked his employees to eat at the studio commissary, so he could table hop and discuss work while they dined. Veterans on his staff tended to dine away from the commissary, just to get a break from work and work talk.

Walt Disney *was not* frozen in death for future regeneration as is popularly believed. He was cremated and lies interred in Forrest Lawn Cemetery.

Somebody Up There Likes Me (1956)

Pretty Pier Angeli was the twin sister of actress Marisa Pavan. They are probably the only Hollywood stars born in Sardinia. Pier had a passionate affair with James Dean shortly before his early death. Her mother detested him and forced her into marriage with singer Vic Damone, but the union barely lasted four years. Damone later wed black actress Diahann Carroll.

'Love died in a Porsche', Angeli said when asked about her moment with Dean. She never got over his death, ending up in sexploitation pictures in Italy. Ultimately, she took her own life with barbiturates at the age of forty.

Some Like it Hot (1959)

Marilyn Monroe's contract guaranteed all her films were to be shot in color. Tony Curtis and Jack Lemmon looked almost *green* when they were shot in color in their female make-up, so she relented and agreed to let Billy Wilder shoot the picture in black and white.

'She has breasts like granite and a brain like Swiss cheese, full of holes', said Billy of his exasperating star during the shoot. 'Extracting a performance from her is like pulling teeth'. But he was the first to admit she captured the camera like no other. Fans may be surprised to learn she spent hours practicing how to 'lower' her smile in order to camouflage her excessively high gum-line.

Early in the production she point blank refused to continue. 'I'm not going back into that film until you re-shoot my opening', she told Wilder. 'When Marilyn Monroe comes into a room, nobody's going to be looking at fucking Tony Curtis doing Joan Crawford, they're going to be looking at Marilyn Monroe'. The shot was changed to show her walking provocatively along a railway platform.

It was the Marx Bros who perfected timing for 'talkie' comedy films. Before then, up to 30% of gags were missed by audiences, because they were still laughing at a previous joke and missed the lead-up line into the next. Groucho & Co timed the length of audience response to a joke and then inserted some non-descript action, such as lighting a cigarette or folding a newspaper, until the audience quietened down enough to hear the set-up for the next gag. Wilder utilized this procedure brilliantly in a scene from *Some Like it Hot* where he had Lemmon shaking a maracas in between gags in one scene.

Curtis qualified his oft-quoted comment, 'kissing Marilyn was like kissing Hitler', by adding, 'It wasn't *that* bad. But you can see through the line. There was this woman, beautifully endowed, treating all men like shit. Why did I have to take that?'

In fairness to Marilyn, her marriage to Arthur Miller was on the skids, and she was three months pregnant. Morning sickness, depression and shaking off the effects of the pills she needed to get to sleep each night, made it difficult for her to make it to the set early in the morning. Curtis understandably hated sitting around made up as a woman, waiting for her to show each day, so occasionally his frustration bubbled over. When the costume fitter laughingly mentioned he had a more shapely rear than his co-star, Monroe unbuttoned her blouse and displayed her bosom. 'He hasn't got tits like these', she countered.

Joe E Brown plays the millionaire who wants to marry Lemmon. He died a few weeks after filming finished. His extra-large mouth was his trademark, so his contracts forbade him to cover it by growing a moustache.

Beverly Wills, the daughter of comedienne Joan Davis, plays Dolores. She looked set for a promising career in comedy but it all ended before she turned thirty. In 1963, she fell asleep while smoking a cigarette and was burnt to death. Her grandmother and two young sons also perished in the inferno.

Growing up in New York's Hell's Kitchen, seven year-old George Raft befriended a recently arrived immigrant boy named Owney Madden. A decade later, Raft was perfecting his craft as a pickpocket, and Madden was in prison for murder. On his release, the two men began working for mobster Dutch Schultz and soon became pals with gunman Bugsy Siegel. Raft often drove getaway cars for Siegel and others.

George's ears naturally stuck out as prominently as Bing Crosby's. An operation was performed to cut a muscle behind each ear, enabling them to fall back against his head. When once asked who she thought was the best lover in Hollywood, Carole Lombard replied, 'George Raft...or did you just mean on the screen?' In his declining years he fronted for organized crime as a greeter/host at their casinos, signing autographs and dancing with the wives of high rollers at joints like the Colony Club in London. He died in 1980.

Something's Got to Give (1962)

Fox was making this picture and *Cleopatra* at the same time. Faced with massive over costs on the Liz Taylor blockbuster, and unable or unwilling to halt production on it, the studio looked for a desperately needed cash influx to avoid going under. Executives chose to save their careers by canning *Something's Got to Give*, and blaming its cancellation on Marilyn Monroe's numerous absences from the set. There is no doubt her unprofessionalism was costing the studio money, but it was a pittance compared to what was transpiring in Italy on *Cleopatra*. The studio was in the hole for a fortune with *Cleopatra,* yet could not possibly close it down even if it wanted to, without going bankrupt. So Marilyn (briefly) became the scapegoat for the company's woes.

Her co-star Dean Martin exercised his contractual rights and refused to work with her replacement, Lee Remick. It had to be Marilyn or nobody. 20th Century Fox promptly sued him for $500,000. This created a snowball effect in lawsuits. Dean's stance caused co-star Cyd Charisse to sue him for $14,000 in lost earnings, Fox sued Marilyn for $750,000, and then hit Martin for $3,339,000. He counter-sued to the tune of $6,885,000.

When the smoke finally cleared, Marilyn was reinstated (for a great deal more money) and production was all set to resume. And then, suddenly, she was dead, and the picture was shut down once and for all. In 1963, it was retitled as *Move Over Darling*, and shot with Doris Day, James Garner and Polly Bergen in the leads.

How did Marilyn die? There are three options to choose from. Either she overdosed accidentally, or she committed suicide, or she was murdered. Those who favor the first option cite her history of drug and alcohol abuse, arguing she went to the well once too often and paid the ultimate price. Those who support the suicide theory say her private and professional problems finally became unbearable. Murder theorists say she was the victim of a conspiracy aimed at silencing her before she could go public over her involvement with the Kennedys and cause political mayhem.

In her last year Marilyn descended more and more into random promiscuity. She was sexually active with one of the workmen remodeling her home, and was known to have invited a taxi-driver inside one evening for a brief interlude. Another time, a District Attorney's Office investigator stumbled across her having sex in a darkened corridor at a Hollywood party. It is also believed she was being used by the CIA to coerce foreign dignitaries for the purposes of blackmail, among them President Sukarno of Indonesia.

JFK would continue to have girlfriends in the time he had left to enjoy them. The last of these was Mary Meyer, who made LSD and marijuana available to the President and was still with him until the time of his assassination. She announced plans in 1964 to publish a book on their relationship. Before that could happen, however, she was shot to death gangland style with two bullets to her head while out walking in Georgetown. The book died with her.

Reporter Dorothy Killgallen was the first to write of the Kennedys' involvement with Marilyn. Not long after JFK's killing she too was dead. The official cause of death for the nosy reporter was 'accidental overdose', but many people remain unconvinced of this. Like Marilyn before her and Mary Meyer after her, Killgallen died just before things began hotting up for the Kennedys. Coincidence? Perhaps.

Sylvia Chase of ABC-TV compiled seven hours of raw footage in 1985, in which witness after witness confirmed Bobby Kennedy's presence at Marilyn's on the day she died. By the time her documentary was ready to go to air, the head of ABC-TV's news and sports section Roone Arledge had cut it down to six minutes! There was nothing left of any interest to anybody. Arledge was a close friend of Bobby's widow Ethel Kennedy. In that same year Dr. Thomas Noguchi was asked the question on Los Angeles ABC-TV, 'was Marilyn murdered?' Twenty-three years after he bungled the chance to answer it, he thought for a moment, then said, 'could be'.

Marilyn died on August 4, 1962 in Brentwood, California. On November 22, 1963 it was JFK's turn in Dallas. Bobby followed in Los Angeles on June 5, 1968. Judith Exner-Campbell told an interviewer shortly before she died, 'Marilyn was killed'. She had maintained her silence for twenty years, she said, out of fear for her life.

Only twenty-four people were permitted to attend Marilyn's funeral services. Sinatra, Sammy Davis Junior and the Lawfords were refused entry by Joe DiMaggio who took charge of proceedings. He also expressly left orders that 'none of those damn Kennedys' be admitted. He had nothing to fear there. They had never *heard* of Marilyn Monroe.

In 1965 DiMaggio and other baseball greats were lined up at Yankee Stadium to honor superstar Mickey Mantle. When Robert Kennedy walked down the line shaking hands with the players, Joe pointedly stepped back to avoid doing so. For twenty years after Marilyn's death the forlorn baseball player sent two-dozen red roses three times a week to her crypt. In 1982 he abruptly ceased without explaining why. One of her former lovers, Robert Slatzer, has sent white roses ever since with a covenant that will continue the practice after his death.

At the time of her death Marilyn had just $5,000 in her bank account. The residuals from her latest films had not yet been deposited. A Mexican surgeon later bought her home for five times its market value. The rhinestone-studded gown she wore the night she serenaded JFK was auctioned at Christie's in 1999, going for a record price of $1,300,000!

Those who consider her to be over-rated should take a look at the surviving footage from *Something's Got to Give*.

Shot just weeks before her death, it contains close-ups of her chatting with a couple of child actors at the pool. The sheer beauty and vulnerability in her face puts her in a class all her own. She was never more beautiful on screen than in this footage. There have been scads of gorgeous women in the cinema over the years, but there has only ever been one Marilyn.

Song of Old Wyoming (1945)

Lash LaRue starred as the Cheyenne Kid in this. He probably holds the Hollywood record for trips down the aisle – an impressive ten times! His later years were quite a mixture. After being arrested for stealing candy from a baby (true), he wrote scripts for porno films and then did a complete switch and became an evangelist!

Son of Ali Baba (1952)

Suzan Cabot often provided the decoration in 1950s second features such as *Tomahawk, Flame of Araby*, and this Tony Curtis sword and sandal flick. In 1959, she hit the news, involving herself in a twelve-month romance with King Hussein of Jordan. She made the news again in 1986, (but for the last time) when her twenty-two year old dwarf son bludgeoned her to death in her run-down mansion. She was fifty-nine.

Son of Captain Blood, The (1962)

Sean Flynn was the son of swashbuckler Errol Flynn. When the boy was twelve years old, his sex mad father took him to a brothel as a birthday present!

Eight years after making this less than memorable film, Sean disappeared near the South Vietnam-Cambodian border, while working as a cameraman for *Life* magazine during the Vietnam War. He and a free-lance cameraman named Dana Stone left a village one morning and headed off to a Viet Cong road-block to take some pictures. They were never seen again. His mother, Lili Damita, kept his apartment ready and his clothes regularly laundered for the next decade, refusing to believe her son would never return.

Son of Lassie (1945)

'Lassie was a vicious bastard', recalled Peter Lawford. What appeared on the screen to be true love between man and his best friend, was achieved by sticking raw meat under the actor's arms and down his shirt. It was even rubbed on his face. A male dog named Pal played Lassie *and* the pup, Laddie. While Lawford went without a dressing room on the set, Pal enjoyed a two-bedroom suite provided by the studio. Then again, of the two, the dog was by far the better actor.

Son of the Sheik (1926)

When asked at her wedding what she and husband Rod La Rocque planned to name their first child, Vilma Banky inadvertently let slip the hold the studio had over their lives when she answered, 'I don't know, you'll have to ask Mr. Goldwyn'.

The couple had planned an elopement, but Goldwyn vetoed that idea and insisted on a wedding catering for 600 guests! While shooting love scenes with Ronald Colman in the silent picture *The Dark Angel* in 1925, the non-English speaking Banky spoke in her native Hungarian while Englishman Colman chattered away about cricket!

Sons of the Pioneers (1942)

In 1926, the fourteen year-old Dale Evans gave birth to a son whom she passed off as her younger brother for many years. She wrote many songs, including her husband Roy Rogers' signature tune *Happy Trails*, and the religious hit, *The Bible Tells Me So*. They had no luck in their family life. Their only child died of Down syndrome at the age of two. Of their four adopted children, one was killed in a Church bus accident, and then the following year another choked to death.

Sound of Music, The (1965)

In Munich, the virtual birthplace of Nazism, this picture was cut short, ending with the wedding of Maria and the Baron. Their escape from the Nazis was considered too touchy an issue for the locals.

In Korea, the movie was considered to be too long, so they took out all the songs! Over 200 children auditioned for the parts of the Von Trapp children. Among those rejected were

Richard Dreyfuss, Lesley Anne Down, Mia Farrow, Kurt Russell and Kim Darby.

South Pacific (1958)

Rossano Brazzi is said to have had 200 lovers in his life. His second wife forgave his many infidelities explaining, 'Rossano is timid and does not like having to say no to a woman.'

During her brief romance with Brazzi, Marilyn Monroe would park outside his home waiting for him. 'My wife would notice her waiting out there, so I would have to act as if I didn't know what Marilyn wanted, parked out there in the middle of nowhere', he said.

When Louella Parsons asked his wife why she put up with his many affairs, the lady replied, 'You know, I married Rossano when he was only nineteen years old, so if he didn't go to bed with someone else since then, how would he know that I am so good?'

Spartacus (1960)

When Stanley Kubrick decided to add the homosexual bathing scene featuring Sir Laurence Olivier and Tony Curtis to his director's cut of *Spartacus,* he needed a voice-over for the deceased Olivier. Larry's widow, Joan Plowright, suggested Anthony Hopkins. He often mimicked her husband at parties with great effect. It is virtually impossible to tell the difference when listening to the finished article.

Kirk Douglas, in effect, ended the Hollywood blacklist when he insisted Dalton Trumbo be listed under his own name as having written the screenplay. Until then Trumbo, like the rest of the banned Hollywood Ten, could only work under a pseudonym. Kubrick and Douglas fell out over the issue but Kirk had his way. It should be noted that Kirk got Trumbo for a fraction of what it would have cost him had the man not been black-listed.

It almost defies belief that John Wayne's mind-numbing, silly flag-waver, *The Alamo*, was nominated for Best Picture this year and *Spartacus* was not. Neither, for that matter, was *Psycho* or *Inherit the Wind*. The Academy Awards really are a bit of a joke.

Spartacus contains numerous historical errors. For example, the real Spartacus was not 'the son and grandson of slaves' at all. He was a Thracian prisoner of war and quite possibly of noble birth. Julius Caesar and Gracchus had nothing whatsoever to do with his moment in history. Neither was Crassus ever dictator of Rome. The position of Prefect of Rome given to both Caesar and Glaberus in the picture was a title not yet existent at the time of the slave revolt. Also, Spartacus was not crucified with his followers. It was assumed he died in the fighting, although his body was never found and identified.

Crixus the Gaul (played by John Ireland in the picture) broke away from Spartacus following a disagreement and took with him 20,000 of his countrymen. His army defeated a Roman force sent against them, but then started celebrating their victory too soon. The Romans counter-attacked that same evening and slaughtered the lot, Crixus included.

Spartacus was not nearly as forgiving or as civilized as the film would have us believe. Following the defeat of Crixus he staged a spectacle in which 300 captured Romans fought in pairs to the death. Later, in retaliation for Crassus' refusal to negotiate his proposed escape to Sicily, he ordered the crucifixion of a captured legionary to be carried out within sight of the Roman army.

Although the movie tells us the slaves were tricked into staying in Italy when Silesian pirates reneged on their offer of a fleet of ships to evacuate them to safety, this also is untrue. When Spartacus proposed they cross the Alps to freedom, his men voted against it, preferring to remain in Italy and continue plundering the countryside.

Although the ambitious Crassus defeated him at Calabria (near modern day Salerno), it was the equally ambitious Pompey who received the bulk of the credit. He managed to round up 5,000 runaways who had fled the battle with Crassus, and took them to Rome where he was lauded for putting down the revolt. An incensed Crassus ordered the crucifixions more or less out of frustration and anger. The crucified slaves were placed at intervals of forty yards along *via Appia* and were never cut down. For years after the revolt their rotting carcasses reminded everyone of the awful power of Rome.

Kirk Douglas (1916 -)

Known relationships:

Angeli, Pier
Bardot, Brigitte
Crawford, Joan
Darnell, Linda
Dietrich, Marlene
Diggins, Peggy
Ferraday, Lisa
Greer, Jane
Hayworth, Rita
Kelly, Betsy
Keyes, Evelyn
Knight, Patricia
Knox, Mona
Koscina, Sylva
Maxwell, Marilyn
Moore, Terry
Neal, Patricia
Pall, Gloria
Sothern, Ann
Stanwyck, Barbara
Threatt, Elizabeth
Tierney, Gene
Turner, Lana

Married:

Diana Dill & one other.

Kirk Douglas served aboard a US Navy patrol boat in the Second World War and was injured when the crew accidentally depth charged its own vessel! He was eventually discharged with amoebic dysentery.

Burt Lancaster once spoke at a tribute to him: 'I'm here to speak about his wit, his charm, his warmth, his talent...at last, a real acting job'. The two men were strong friends. Others were less impressed by either of them. Writer Sheilah

Graham described Douglas as, 'boastful, egotistical, resentful of criticism, if anyone dare give it'. Doris Day said of him: 'Kirk never makes much of an effort toward anyone else. He's pretty much wrapped up in himself'. For the record, he didn't like her either, describing America's 'girl next door' as 'just about the remotest person I know.

Sir Laurence Olivier (1907-1989)

Known relationships with women:

Bloom, Claire
Fonteyn, Margot
Landi, Elissa
Miles, Sarah
Tutin, Dorothy
Winters, Shelley

Known relationships with men:

Ainley, Henry
Brando, Marlon
Coward, Noel
Kaye, Danny
Payn, Graham
Tynan, Kenneth

Married:

Jill Esmond
Vivien Leigh
Joan Plowright

Dame Peggy Ashcroft recalled, 'of course I knew Danny Kaye and Laurence Olivier were having a long-term affair. So did all of London. So did their wives. Why is America always the last to know?' Olivier actually described his homosexual exploits (including his romance with Kaye) in his autobiography, but his last wife Joan Plowright persuaded him to remove those passages to avoid embarrassing the family.

In 1979, he received a Special Oscar for his life's work in the movies. His acceptance speech ranks as probably the most affected, posturing speech in Academy Awards history. It went thus:

'Mr. President and Governors of the Academy, committee members, Fellows, my very noble and approved good masters, my friends, my fellow students...in the great wealth, the great firmament of your nation's generosities, this particular choice may perhaps be found by future generations as a trifle eccentric but the mere fact of it, the prodigal, pure, human kindness of it must be seen as a beautiful star in that firmament which shines upon me at this moment, dazzling me a little, but filling me with warmth and extraordinary elation, the euphoria that happens to so many of us at the first breath of the majestic glow of the new tomorrow. From the top of this moment, I thank you for this great gift, which lends me such a very splendid part in this glorious occasion. Thank you.'

Larry could not order breakfast without delivering an oration.

Howard Hughes of RKO became obsessed with Jean Simmons (as indeed he was with any full-breasted beauty he spied), and was determined to bed her. He bought out her Rank contract, took her to Hollywood, and harassed her until she and her husband Stewart Granger actually considered luring him to their house and murdering him - or so Granger wrote in his memoirs. Common sense prevailed instead, and they wound up suing him to get Jean out of her RKO contract. Hughes hated her with a passion from that day onwards.

The shooting of *Spartacus* went on forever it seemed. When one of Peter Ustinov's children was asked what his father did for a living, the boy thought for a moment and replied, '*Spartacus*'.

Charles McGraw portrays the head trainer at Ustinov's gladiator school. A much respected character actor, he had the misfortune to fall through a glass shower door in 1980 with fatal consequences. Watch him closely during his fight with Spartacus in the galley. He takes a tremendous whack to the mouth on the rim of a soup cauldron as Spartacus attempts to drown him in it, but does not break character. A real pro.

John Gavin plays Julius Caesar. He certainly doesn't look Mexican but he was born in Chihuahua, Mexico, the same town as Anthony Quinn. He was a college major in the economic history of Latin America and later an expert in the field. From 1981-6 President Reagan rewarded his expertise by making him the US Ambassador to Mexico.

Spice World (1997)

Rock singer Gary Glitter had a cameo in this film, but it was cut at the last moment after he was arrested and charged with possession of child pornography. He had sent his computer to a repair shop and the technicians there noticed the offensive material on the hard drive, so they notified police.

Stalag 17 (1953)

The uncredited soldier who sings at the Christmas party is Ross Bagdasarian. Three years later he would become internationally known as David Seville. He and his 'Chipmunks' would have a smash novelty hit tune with 'Witchdoctor' that would sweep the world.

Stand by Me (1986)

River Phoenix's mother once (a trifle exaggeratedly) described him in an interview as 'the savior of mankind.' Sadly, he could not even save himself. In 1993 he collapsed outside Johnny Depp's Viper Club after ingesting a half a dozen substances that, together, proved lethal. As he convulsed on the sidewalk, his girlfriend Samantha Mathis and brother Joaquin argued with the doorman. His sister meanwhile jumped on him and tried to stop the seizures, but without success. Eventually, Joaquin called '911'. 'I'm thinking he had Valium or something', he suggested. Well, he did. The problem was it was mixed with cocaine, heroin, ephedrine and marijuana. He died in the street before help could arrive.

Star! (1968)

Robert Reed, the actor who portrayed architect Paul Brady in the extraordinarily popular TV series *The Brady Bunch*, makes one of his rare big screen appearances in this. The cast of the TV show was astonished to learn after his death that he was a closely closeted homosexual. Reed died from colon lymphoma but was also infected with the AIDS virus.

Star 80 (1983)

This film depicts the tragic story of beautiful *Playboy* centerfold Dorothy Stratten, who was murdered by her insanely jealous husband and mentor, a small-time hustler named Paul Snider. After she told him their affair was over, he managed to lure the twenty-two year old to his apartment where he blew her head off with a shotgun.

He then sodomized her corpse before turning the gun on himself. Dorothy was involved in a hot romance with director Peter Bogdanovich before her death. Years later, he wed her younger sister Louise Hoogstraten, who would go to great lengths, cosmetically, in an endeavor to emulate her sister's great physical beauty. The murdered girl's film appearances were unmemorable; the 1981 Bogdanovich vehicle, *They All Laughed*, being the best of them.

Star Trek: The Motion Picture (1979)

Nichelle Nichols played Lt. Uhura, both in the TV series and in the movies. She was outraged to learn that, of all the major characters in the TV series, she was the only one not under contract and still being paid on a weekly basis. She also discovered that the studio, concerned she might act on her popularity and insist on more money, had withheld all her fan mail from her.

Her son Thomas was one of the 'Heaven's Gate' cult members who suicided in Rancho Santa Fe in 1997. In a 1968 episode of *Star Trek* entitled 'Plato's Stepchildren', she and William Shatner shared the first ever inter-racial kiss on American television. They were soon deeply involved off-screen as well.

James Doohan, who plays engineer Scotty, was a fighter pilot in the Royal Canadian Air Force in World War Two. Cited for 'performance above and beyond the call of duty', he flew numerous sweeps deep into enemy-held territory, during one of which he lost the middle finger of his right hand to enemy fire.

Star Wars (1977)

When George Lucas first wrote the script, Luke Skywalker was to be named Luke Starkiller and Han Solo was to be a green alien with gills. It is commonly known that Anthony Daniels plays C3PO, but many fans are unaware R2D2 is also played by an actor. Kenny Baker, a three feet five inch midget, is concealed inside the metallic casing of the little droid.

The breathing sounds made by Darth Vader were achieved by placing a tiny microphone inside a regulator in a scuba tank. In the second film of the series, *The Empire Strikes Back*, Yoda is a puppet controlled by Frank Oz.

Lucas went to the first showing of *Star Wars* when it was initially released in Japan, shortly after it burst on the scene in America to rave reviews. Whereas American audiences stood and applauded at the end of the film, the Japanese remained silent. He immediately assumed they hated it, until he was informed that complete silence was a sign of the utmost respect from a Japanese audience.

St Elmo's Fire (1985)

In 1988, Rob Lowe participated in a sex romp in a hotel room with two young women, one of whom was only sixteen years old. A seven-minute video he took of proceedings was stolen by the girl and later found by her mother. She promptly sued the actor for a million dollars! The issue was settled out of court for an undisclosed sum, but Lowe was very fortunate not to go to prison for carnal knowledge of a minor. It is believed the video has netted over a million dollars since then in black market sales.

Stormy Weather (1943)

When she signed with MGM in 1942, Lena Horne became the first black female to obtain a long- term contract with a major studio. During World War Two she was the number one pin-up for black GIs. That is not altogether surprising, considering they were not officially permitted to have pin-ups of *white* women in their billets under any circumstances.

On bond selling tours she was barred from staying with the white performers at their hotels, and had to find alternative accommodation herself. On USO tours she was required to perform for white troops *first,* and then the black GIs.

One morning at Fort Riley, Kansas, she arrived at a black mess tent and was told to put on a show for German POWs. Only *then* could she entertain black troops. Horne disgustedly stormed off the stage, went to the back of the tent and performed for the black soldiers seated there. Such outspoken defense of her blackness alienated her studio and the USO. Consequently, when touring the southern states, she had to find her own financial backing. For the southern market, all sequences in which she appeared in films were deleted to placate redneck audiences.

Even though she was only the second ever headliner in the history of the Flamingo Casino in Vegas, Horne could not enter the hotel premises except to perform. The equally great Billie Holiday was singing with Artie Shaw's orchestra when she encountered the same problem. Shaw temporarily solved it by painting a red dot on her forehead and passing her off as an Indian at the reception desk.

Story of G I Joe, The (1945)

This picture, which was based on a story by war correspondent Ernie Pyle, launched Robert Mitchum's career. Over one hundred real US Army soldiers served as extras in it. On its completion, they were all returned to the war and to the invasion of the Japanese island of Okinawa. Most did not survive. As for Pyle, he was killed by a sniper a little later and never saw his story on the screen. Burgess Meredith portrays him here.

Shortly after the film came out, Mitchum was arrested following a domestic disturbance that quickly ballooned into a brawl between the actor and two police officers. Sentenced to six months or the option of joining the services, he most reluctantly chose the latter. 'When they took me away, I still had the porch rail under my fingernails', he joked.

He smoked marijuana for years prior to his arrest in 1949, even growing his own supply at one time. The man, seemingly, was well ahead of his time. He and starlet Lila Leeds, along with two others, were busted in a set-up raid on a cottage in Los Angeles. Leeds' tilt as an actress, such as it was, ended abruptly, and Mitchum received a suspended sentence, plus ninety days on a Prison Farm. If anything, the publicity bolstered his career.

Sunset Boulevard (1950)

Originally, the opening scene was shot in a morgue, with the deceased William Holden discussing his death with other corpses. The preview audience did not respond favorably to it, probably because of its length, so the briefer swimming pool shot of him floating face down was used instead.

Because Erich von Stroheim never learned to drive a motor vehicle, the old Isotta Fraschini in which he 'drives' the two main actors to Paramount Studios was pulled along on ropes. He merely sat behind the wheel and pretended to steer.

Gloria Swanson was first signed in 1913 as a 'guaranteed extra' at $13.25 a week. 'I was more excited about a bigger event in my life', she confided later. 'I had just been kissed by a boy wearing an orange tie, and I was sure I was going to have a baby'.

When she married actor Wallace Beery she was nineteen and still a virgin. After he assaulted her on their wedding night, she crawled into the bathroom and stayed there until morning, endeavoring to stop her ravaged body from bleeding. In her own words she was, 'brutalized in pitch blackness by a man who whispered filth in my ear while he ripped me almost in two'.

Within weeks she was pregnant to him. Suffering from stomach cramps, she took 'medicine' supplied by Beery that was toxic and resulted in a miscarriage. He did not want a child, she claimed. Commenting upon her later marriages, Beery bragged to reporters, 'damned if she didn't keep on getting married. I got her into an awful habit'. In March 1923 one of those later husbands sued for divorce, claiming she had committed adultery with no fewer than fourteen different men during their marriage.

By 1926 she was being paid the phenomenal salary of $900,000 a year and drove about in a leopard upholstered Lancia. Her home featured a black marbled bathroom with a gold bathtub. Upon meeting another future husband, the Marquis de la Coudraye, she dashed off a two- word telegram to her beau, Marshall Neilan, that read, 'Forget me!' He cabled back a *one*-word answer, 'Forgotten!'

When eleven-year old John F Kennedy caught his father and her having sex aboard their yacht, the sight so distressed the boy that he leapt overboard. Joe had to dive in and rescue him. Speaking of Joe Kennedy, it was he who arranged for Eunice Pringle to scream rape against Alexander Pantages in 1930. Kennedy wanted control of Pantages' sixty cinemas, so he bribed the girl to accuse the old man of assaulting her. Alexander was initially sentenced to fifty years in prison, but the conviction was later overturned. Miss Pringle confessed to the set-up on her deathbed years later.

Louella Parsons and Hedda Hopper wrote gossip columns syndicated nationwide for three decades. At the peak of their power they could destroy an actor's career with a single line, and there was not a soul in Hollywood who did not recognize the fact.

Louella was a devout Catholic. An illuminated Virgin Mary, standing ten feet tall, was enshrined in her backyard. She was also a hypocrite who went to great lengths to expunge any record of her early life, in particular her two divorces.

Her first husband left her when she caught him *en flagrante* with his secretary. Louella claimed he died on a troop transport returning from World War One. He didn't. Marriage number two collapsed because of her affair with the married union leader Peter Brady. She erased that husband from her memoirs altogether.

Her third trip down the aisle was to a drunken gynecologist who treated many of the Hollywood stars. It was from him that she obtained many of her 'scoops' regarding pregnancies, abortions and bouts of venereal disease, information she held over several big stars as leverage in exchange for juicy stories about their peers.

She made no bones about telling anyone who would listen that her hero was Italian dictator Benito Mussolini. By the time Parsons died in 1966 she was in a home, decrepit, powerless and all but mute. When told of the demise of her archrival Hedda, she managed to mumble the word 'good', and never uttered another word for the remaining six years of her life.

Sun Valley Serenade (1941)

Sonja Henie finished third in the figure-skating event at the 1924 Olympics representing Norway. In three subsequent games she won gold in each figure skating event. For a time she was the biggest movie star in the world, appearing in scores of films usually involving ice-skating, a sport in which she had no peers.

Norwegians were appalled when she shouted 'Heil, Hitler' and gave the German leader a Nazi salute as she finished her program in the 1936 games in Berlin. 'I was honoring Germany, not the Nazis', she angrily explained. 'I don't even know what a Nazi is'. Hitler later entertained her several times at his Bavarian retreat.

Milton Sperling, the screenwriter on one of her pictures, said of her, 'among other things, this guileless, simple girl was one of the most voracious, sexy broads in town. On the set she was an utter shrew who treated the crew like dirt and was generally detested by nearly everyone'. When Darryl Zanuck chastised her for conducting an open affair with a film crewmember, she retorted, 'it is the irresistible lure of making love to a star that has him under my spell'.

Although extremely rich, she invariably stripped every hotel room in which she stayed of linen, silverware, towels, bath mats, thermos bottles and even toilet paper. During the Second World War the government of her native Norway asked if she would contribute some of her vast wealth to the defense of her country. 'No', was her one-word response.

Superman, the Movie (1978)

One of the first people considered to play Superman in this movie was boxing champion Mohammed Ali! After much discussion it was agreed a black Superman would alienate the fans of the comics too much, so the idea was dropped. Steve McQueen, Paul Newman and Robert Redford all refused an offer of $4 million each to play the Man of Steel. Even Nick Nolte was asked.

Marlon Brando received $290,000 *per day* for just twelve days work, a total of $2,225,000 for his part the film. He was, in fact, the first actor to receive $1 million for a single movie role, even though his performance took up just ten minutes of screen time. Not content with that, he then sued the producers for a percentage of the gross.

Margot Kidder, who plays Lois Lane, was once wed to actor John Heard. It lasted six days. Heard is now best known for playing Macaulay Culkin's father in the *Home Alone* films.

When Gene Hickman was asked by an interviewer why he had agreed to play the villain, he replied, 'You mean, besides the two million dollars?' Hackman joined the US Marine Corps at sixteen in 1947. A motorcycle accident broke both his legs and made him ineligible for re-enlistment when he got out of the hospital. His unit went to Korea without him and suffered 90% casualties during the heavy fighting there.

As a young actor Christopher Reeve was induced into joining the Scientology sect. He recalled being 'audited' by an official using the E Meter, a kind of crude polygraph. With increasing skepticism, he fed into it a totally fabricated story of his life based on a Greek myth. It went completely undetected by his auditor and he left the sect soon afterwards.

Had he been a big star at the time, he speculated, and revealed his private life in detail as required, escape might well have been impossible without jeopardizing his career. In 1995 he was paralyzed from the neck down after being thrown from a horse during a jumping competition. He died in 2004.

Support Your Local Sheriff (1969)

The Canadian born Joan Hackett, who plays James Garner's love interest here, was a cigar-smoking lesbian who died from cancer at the age of fifty. She was actor Anthony Perkins first heterosexual affair. When asked her opinion of him she responded with a one-word answer – 'nuts'.

Swarm, The (1978)

The bees used in this woeful film were real. Made in the days before computer generation, it was necessary to first store them in a refrigerated railway wagon to make them slow and drowsy. Then a group of expert women gently squeezed each bee and snipped off its stinger.

Sweet Smell of Success (1957)

Burt Lancaster's role as J.

J. Hunsecker was based on the life style of columnist Walter Winchell. Not only was Winchell the undisputed king of the New York columnists, he was also obsessed with his daughter Walda, much as Hunsecker is with his sister in the movie.

Winchell had table 25 reserved for him every day at the Stork Club. In the movie Hunsecker has a table permanently reserved for him at the 21 Club. So powerful and influential was Winchell, that, during the Second World War, he travelled to Washington once a week, dressed in the uniform of a Commander in the United States Naval Reserve, and delivered in person to President Roosevelt all the latest gossip that was too hot to print.

When he died fourteen years after this film's release, nobody attended his funeral that was not paid to be there. He was not a very likeable man. He once explained his method for success. 'Pick the most famous person you can find and attack him'.

Swiss Family Robinson (1960)

Janet Munro plays Roberta in this Disney film. It is probable that her acute alcohol problem in her thirties led to her early death (at 38) from chronic ischemic heart disease. She married actor Ian Hendry in the late sixties and both became seasoned drinkers.

His career struck a major snag when he lost the lead in *Get Carter* after Michael Caine surprised director Mike Hodges by showing interest in the role. A disgruntled Hendry was reduced to playing Caine's nemesis in the picture, and was very jealous of the Cockney superstar throughout the production.

Tommy Kirk, the gay actor who plays the middle brother, drifted out of the business in the late sixties after making *Track of Thunder* with Ray Stricklyn (also gay). Kirk's homosexuality became common knowledge and nervous studios simply stopped using him.

James MacArthur was the adopted son of screen legend Helen Hayes. In 1967, the thirty year-old married actor fell head over heels for TV bit part actress, eighteen year-old Melody Patterson. She played Wrangler Jane in the western spoof series *F Troop*, and lied about her age to get the role in. In fact, seven episodes were shot before it was learned she was only fifteen years old. Not that age much worried her anyway. At sixteen she was involved with a thirty-two year old Warner's producer until MacArthur came along. The two stayed together until the end of the seventies, then went their separate ways.

Take Me Out to the Ball Game (1949)

Busby Berkeley was a 'ladies man' with a fondness for the occasional guy as well. He was also a neurotic alcoholic who killed three people while driving his roadster during a drunken binge in Los Angeles on September 8, 1935. Full of remorse afterwards, he slashed his wrists and throat but survived. MGM's fixer Howard Strickling, as he did many times for many stars, 'handled' the problem.

Berkeley liked to sexually humiliate young actresses and dancers auditioning for him. He would start by asking them to lift their skirts and 'Show me your legs'. When they did so he would then suggest, 'Well, I need to see more than that'. Once the girl was standing, humiliated and degraded, with her dress held above her *head*, he would let her know she already had the job from the beginning; that the 'dress thing' was his idea of a joke.

Taming of the Shrew, The (1929)

Mary Pickford began at Biograph earning $40 a week in 1909. In 1910, she moved to IMP for $175 a week. A year later, she was pulling in $275 at Majestic, and the year after that jumped up to $500 a week working for Zukor's Famous Players. Impressive as these pay rises appear, they were chicken feed compared to the money she would make in the war years.

When she signed with the newly merged Famous Players-Lasky Company, the terms of her contract were extraordinary. First off, she received $40,000 for the month layoff period while negotiations were being finalized. Then she agreed to $10,000 *a week,* as well as a $300,000 bonus for signing. Furthermore, she was guaranteed 50% of the net profits of any pictures made under the contract. At least two sources claim that *her mother* was given $150,000 for goodwill as well! It was possible for the studio to pay her these unprecedented amounts and still make a handsome profit because her movies made a fortune.

The public was kept in the dark about her drinking problem, a weakness inherited from her early days in Hollywood. Her first husband, Owen Moore, was a drunk and set Mary on the road to alcoholism. For much of her adult life she consumed a quart of whiskey a day. Her imbibing had much to do with the failure of her union with Douglas Fairbanks. He was a snobbish, puritanical, tea-totaller, who could not handle his wife's drinking any more than she could. 'In his private life Douglas had always faced a situation in the only way he knew how, by running away from it', Mary said, thus placing the blame squarely on his shoulders.

Mary's brother Jack was once married to 'the world's most beautiful girl', actress Olive Thomas. She died in mysterious circumstances in 1920 when she was just twenty-two, after ingesting dichloride of mercury (a common treatment in those days for syphilis). It was said she mistook it for sleeping pills, even though a clearly marked bottle of the latter was found near her body. The poisoning left her speechless, blind and in agony before sending her into a coma from which she failed to recover.

Her husband had infected her with syphilis months before she died. The presence of a recently written will, naming him as sole beneficiary to a large insurance policy, had people talking and wondering about his possible role in her death. Any fears of skullduggery were quickly quashed. The powers that be had no intention of letting a scandal damage his famous sister's reputation. So, there was no real inquiry, and Olive officially went to her grave as the unfortunate victim off an accident.

Jack Pickford was an infamous rake who fell to his death from a window, in 1933, after quarrelling with a man whose identity has never been revealed. The official verdict was 'suicide'. It, too, was arrived at very quickly, before any investigation could sully the Pickford family name.

The beautiful Olive embarked upon her life of promiscuity and immorality at the ripe old age of ten, at which time she posed for pornographic photographs with her older, grown brothers. At *twelve* she wed a twenty-six year old miner. He delighted in showing her naked form to his drunken friends, and having her demonstrate her considerable sexual skills for them. At fourteen, she took off for New York and the casting couch of impresario Flo Ziegfeld. Then came stardom, Jack Pickford, and a squalid early death.

Tap Roots (1948)

The Production Code people informed director George Marshall he must adequately prove Susan Hayward's character does not indulge in any sexual activity when she stays the night with one of the male characters, or else the film could not be released. George solved the problem by having the man in the scene sit in a chair, holding a cup of coffee in his hand just before turning in for the night. He then cut to him waking up in the same chair next morning, with the cup *still in his hand.*

At least two of Hayward's co-stars went on the record with their opinions of her. 'Anything I had to say about Susan Hayward you couldn't print', was the comment from Robert Preston. Robert Cummings described her as 'distant, non-talkative and no sense of humor.' Even her agent Benny Milford conceded that off-stage she was a total bitch. 'This is not a very nice girl', he remarked.

On her deathbed she barred all non-family visitors with the single exception of Katharine Hepburn. One day, however, a mysterious woman dressed in black arrived, unannounced, at the house and was quickly admitted. It was

Greta Garbo. The extraordinary thing about her visit was that the two women had never been friends. In fact, nobody could remember them having ever met before. Hayward's death was a terrible one. Suffering from more than twenty brain tumors, she had no control over her bowels and was in constant agony. She died from a massive seizure during which she bit off her own tongue.

Tarzan Movies (1932-42)

The line, 'Me Tarzan, you Jane', was not spoken in the first movie, nor does it feature in Edgar Rice Burroughs' 1914 novel. In fact, in the novel, Tarzan and Jane only communicate by writing notes to each other. Evidently, Burroughs was happy for his Ape man to *write*, but not to enunciate.

Maureen O'Sullivan plays Jane in ten of these pictures, beginning with *Tarzan, The Ape Man* in 1932 and ending with *Tarzan's New York Adventure* in 1942. 'Cheetah, the chimp, bit me whenever he could', she said. 'The Tarzan apes were all homosexual, eager to wrap their paws around Johnny Weissmuller's thighs. They were jealous of me and loathed me', she claimed. O'Sullivan, by the way, was the mother of actress Mia Farrow.

Weissmuller was actually born in Rumania, not in Pennsylvania, as he asserted when queried about his eligibility to swim for the United States at the Olympics! He came into movies via his great Olympic swimming record of five gold medals at the 1924 and 1928 Games (plus a bronze in water polo). Over his career he held sixty-seven world records.

While being paid $500 a week to model BVD underwear, his picture was noticed by a Hollywood scout in search of the new Tarzan. His nose was badly misshapen and broken prior to his movie career, but plastic surgery soon fixed that, and he instantly fell in love with himself.

He had a particularly nasty habit of offering to show what he called 'my magnificent equipment' to his leading ladies. O'Sullivan was asked by Esther Williams if he had tried his ritual on her, and if so what did she do? 'I let him show me', she replied. Esther was not so obliging. She had no time for the man.

In 1959, while golfing in Cuba, Weissmuller was suddenly surrounded by a group of armed Castro guerrillas. Thrusting out his chest, he let fly with his famous call, much to the men's delight. 'Tarzan! Tarzan!' they yelled and gathered around him asking for autographs. We still hear Weissmuller's call in Tarzan movies today. It was created using electronics combined with playing his shout backwards.

Lex Barker made five films as Tarzan and he was pretty good too. Two of his marriages were to actresses Arlene Dahl and Lana Turner. And they were *not* so good. The second of these ended when Lana discovered he had been masturbating in front of her daughter, Cheryl, and forcing her into full on sex by the time she was ten! When doctors confirmed the assaults, Lana produced a gun and gave him twenty minutes to pack and get out.

After he dropped dead in the street from a heart attack in 1973, she was asked for a comment. 'What took him so long?' she answered. Barker, for the record, denied the accusations until his dying day.

Taxi Driver (1976)

In 1989, Robert De Niro described how he prepared for his role in this picture. 'I got this image of Travis as a crab', he said. 'To prepare for that, I swam around underwater and looked at the sea life. I've used a cat, a wolf, a rabbit, a snake and an owl. Certain animals give you certain feelings'. A crab? The 'Method'. Sheesh!

According to John Hinkley, the man who attempted to assassinate President Reagan, his obsession with Jodie Foster, following her performance in *Taxi Driver*, led him to commit an act he believed would impress her. He had never even met the girl, although there appears to be evidence he stalked her during the time she was attending university.

Teacher's Pet (1958)

Mamie Van Doren (1931 -)

Known relationships:

Aragon, Art
Beatty, Warren
Belinsky, Bo
Carson, Johnny

Chandler, Jeff
Cochran, Steve
Curtis, Tony
Dempsey, Jack
Evans, Robert
Fischetti, Charlie
Fisher, Eddie
Gable, Clark
Grant, Johnny
Hamilton, George
Harvey, Laurence
Hilton Jr, Conrad
Hudson, Rock
Hughes, Howard
Jones, Tom
Kissinger, Henry
McHugh, Jimmy
McQueen, Steve
Montand, Yves
Namath, Joe
Palance, Jack
Reynolds, Burt
Rivers, Johnny
Rojo, Gustavo
Webb, Jack

Married:

Ray Anthony & 4 others

Mamie was married and divorced at fifteen and into a steamy affair with the boxer Jack Dempsey at sixteen. Eddie Fisher had an entirely physical affair with her two years after that. 'The casting couch did exist', admitted Mamie, 'and I did occasionally find myself on it. Many of us who made a career out of the movies did. Many, many more than want to admit it!'

Diana Dors recalled Mamie's trailer being 'in constant motion as she accommodated her lovers on the set'. She even managed to get a rise out of Rock Hudson in 1953 (or so she claimed) on the kitchen floor at his mother's home. The bout ended 'prematurely' as she recalled.

Ten Commandments, The (1956)

It could never happen today, but in 1955 director Cecil B DeMille recruited ten thousand *Arabs* from around Cairo to portray the Israelites during the Exodus. And because labor laws prevented children from working more than four hours a day on a film set, he used a dozen or so midgets from *The Court Jester* production to portray some of them in the Exodus sequence. The parting of the Red Sea was done with a miniature model made of mounds of gelatin, over which water was filmed cascading. The film was then reverse-printed.

When Adolph Zukor complained to him about the rising cost of the production, DeMille asked, 'what do you want me to do? Stop shooting now and release it as *The Five Commandments*?' At his peak he was the best-known director in the world. Surprisingly, he was never once even *nominated* for a Best Director Oscar throughout his very long career. Today, his films seem woefully dated so, perhaps, that is why.

On the set he was quite tyrannical, an attitude he deliberately adopted to curb any petulant or stand-over ideas some of his stars might bring with them. Even his family found him a handful at times. 'He had all the patience God gave him', said one family member, 'because he never used any of it'.

He readily admitted there existed no archeological evidence to confirm any of the events depicted in the Five Books of Moses, or even if the man himself ever existed. After consulting archeologists and historians, he opted to place Moses in the 13th century BC with the pharaoh Rameses as his protagonist. But it was all a matter of educated guesswork.

In the 1920s, CB and his wife, Constance, adopted Katherine Lester, a little girl whose father had been killed in the war, and whose mother had died of tuberculosis. In 1937, Katherine would marry actor Anthony Quinn.

DeMille's lover, Jeanie MacPherson, wrote large portions of the scripts (with him) of several of his pictures. Their romance lasted for years. Constance DeMille's doctors advised against her having more children so she tacitly approved of the affair.

Throughout much of his career CB employed a 'chair boy' whose job it was to carry a seat about in the footsteps of the director wherever he went on the set. If DeMille needed to sit for a moment the chair had better be there. It always was.

'CB had a foot fetish' claimed actress Paulette Goddard. 'I know. I drove him mad with my feet and actually used my bare feet to get better roles out of him'. Angela Lansbury too recalled, 'he cast you by your feet, not your profile. If you had good feet you were in'. Costume designer Edith Head advised her to walk around barefoot in his office one day. 'He'd just like to make sure', she said.

Yvonne De Carlo (1922-2007)

Known relationships:

Brady, Scott
Cabre, Mario
Cameron, Rod
Cochran, Steve
Curtis, Tony
Duff, Howard
Flynn, Errol
Gable, Clark
Hartford, Huntington
Hayden, Sterling
Hines, Jerome
Hudson, Rock
Hughes, Howard
Khan, Prince Aly
Lancaster, Burt
MacGregor, Lee
Mahoney, Jock
Matthau, Walter
Meredith, Burgess
Milland, Ray
Pahlavi, Shah Reza
Quinn, Anthony
Reed, Philip
Shaw, Artie
Skelton, Red
Stack, Robert
Stewart, James
Taylor, Robert
Thompson, Carlos
Vallee, Rudy
Wagner, Robert

Wilder, Billy

Married:

Robert Morgan

She had one of the most tarnished reputations of all the actresses in Hollywood in her day. According to Tony Curtis, possibly a tad harshly, 'everyone in town has had Yvonne De Carlo'.

In her early days in the movie capital, however, she strove hard to make it without recourse to casting couches and the like. She initially lost her chance to dance at the Earl Carroll Theatre because she refused to expose her breasts to Mr. Carroll, a prerequisite for any girl wishing to work for him. After a year dancing in girlie shows at another establishment, she ventured back to him, showed him her quite spectacular bosom and was hired on the spot.

She recalled wanting Sterling Hayden to take her virginity, but he didn't make a bold enough attempt, so she surrendered it to a casual acquaintance instead. There were no such problems with Burt Lancaster. They had sex on a mink coat under an oleander bush in her backyard.

Terminator 2: Judgment Day (1991)

Linda Hamilton was married to James Cameron who directed this film, *Titanic* and many other successful pictures. She left him after learning of his affair with Suzy Amis (she played Lizzy Calvert) during the filming of *Titanic*. Torn between his love for both women, Cameron went back to Linda and they married. Eight months later it was over and he moved back with Suzy. The settlement with Linda reputedly cost him $50 million. Linda is still reputed to be bisexual.

Terms of Endearment (1983)

Most of Debra Winger's off-camera time was allegedly spent in Jack Nicholson's trailer. While she and Jack were hitting it off, her already strained relationship with Shirley MacLaine worsened. When Shirley accused her of being unable to hit her marks, Winger walked to a spot on the floor, bent over, lifted her skirt and loudly broke wind. 'How's *that* for a mark?' she asked.

Tess (1979)

Nastassja Kinski met and fell in love with director Roman Polanski when she was fifteen and he twenty-five years her senior, which seems to be about par for the course for him – the sleaze bag. She openly admitted to a tendency to fall passionately in love with all her directors, albeit briefly. When she gave birth to a son in 1984, a German magazine listed the names of *eight* different men as the possible father. An Egyptian producer was ultimately proven to be the unlucky winner and the couple married that same year.

That Forsyte Woman (1949)

Everybody connected with this film expected the reserved Greer Garson and the outrageous Errol Flynn to clash when they were brought together. But it did not happen. Errol strode onto the set on day one of shooting, 'goosed 'her, and greeted her with a resounding, 'Hi ya, Red!' She thought it was hilarious.

Both were pranksters and she soon got even, arranging for the door handles of her carriage in the film to be electrically charged to give him a boot when he touched them. He retaliated by hiding in her walk-in wardrobe (naked but for a top hat) and springing out when she opened the door.

During production Errol's wife Nora Eddington filed for divorce, having recently fallen for crooner Dick Haymes. He in turn filed for a divorce from his wife, actress Joanne Dru. Not to be outdone Miss Dru became engaged to actor John Ireland at the same time. 'It's a classic case of all change partners and dance', Flynn told reporters.

Thelma & Louise (1991)

When this movie was shot Geena Davis was engaged to marry Christopher McDonald, the actor who plays her chauvinist husband in the picture. Before becoming an actress, Geena worked as a live costume dummy in a dress shop window. She is a member of Mensa and considered to be in the top 2% of the most intelligent people on the planet. In 1999, she made the final thirty-two in trials to choose the US Olympic Archery Team. At the ripe old age of forty-eight she gave birth to twins.

Marco St. John is the actor who portrays the revolting truck driver whose rig is blown to pieces by the girls. 'Funnily enough', recalled director Ridley Scott, 'that guy went off and played Hamlet in Philadelphia a month after doing our movie. He wasn't anything like the trucker he played in *Thelma & Louise'*. St. John kept telling Scott, 'after this, I'll never get a date with another woman!'

Brad Pitt's career kicked off in this film after he beat George Clooney for the role of JD.

They Died With Their Boots On (1941)

Many of Colonel Custer's men despised him. During the Battle of the Washita he abandoned a small detachment of soldiers under Major Joel Elliott, on the premise that he was unwilling to risk further losses by going back for them. The frozen bodies of the group were retrieved weeks later. Major Frederick Benteen, an officer three times brevetted for valor, publicly criticized his abandonment of Elliott and his men. Benteen's hatred of his commanding officer would continue for the rest of his life and bring on a drinking problem in his final years.

Custer also ruthlessly executed deserters. There was, nevertheless, no questioning his courage. During the Civil War, while leading numerous cavalry charges, he had no fewer than twenty-three horses shot out from under him.

His brother Tom, who also died at the Little Big Horn, was a hero of the Civil War as well, winning *two* Medals of Honor. German immigrant, Charles Windolph, was in Major Reno's command and won the Medal of Honor for his conduct at the Little Big Horn, yet was virtually forgotten in the furor surrounding the fate of Custer and his men. He retired from the army in 1883. When he died in 1950 he was the last survivor of the fight. Incidentally, nearly half the men killed with Custer were not American by birth. Irish, German and English migrants made up 45% of his command.

The historical inaccuracies in this picture are legion. First of all, we see Libbie meet Custer at West Point where her 'uncle' Phil Sheridan is the Commandant of the Academy. They actually met in Monroe. As for 'uncle' Phil, well, he was not even remotely related to her, nor was he at West Point at the time either, in *any* capacity. In fact, he was an obscure lieutenant at a fort on the Oregon frontier.

Next, we see Custer elevated to the rank of General through a paperwork bungle. As if that is likely to happen in the real world. The Union Army was running short of commissioned officers, so he was properly appointed to lead one of the many new cavalry brigades.

The film then moves forward to about 1875, where we find Libbie dragging her husband out of his alcoholic haze by securing for him a commission with the Seventh Cavalry (courtesy of good old 'uncle' Phil, of course). Another fabrication. Custer's drinking problem ceased during the Civil War (in 1862), a full *fourteen years* before he took over the Seventh. As for Captain Butler teaching him the tune *Garry Owen*, that too is a myth. Butler was a sergeant, not a captain, and the *Garry Owen* was a popular tune of the time.

Now we get to the really reprehensible stuff. The film's claim that Custer was a champion of Indian rights must have sent a lot of deceased Sioux, Cheyenne and Arapaho rotating in their graves. He was a confirmed Indian *hater* whose troops butchered entire families whenever and wherever they got the chance. Their attacks on peaceful villages on the Washita and Rosebud rivers are well documented.

Next we find him capturing the Sioux war chief Crazy Horse, then magnanimously releasing him after giving his solemn vow that he will do all in his power to keep the white gold seekers out of the Black Hills. As far as we know, Custer and Crazy Horse never met, unless it was momentarily on the Little Big Horn battlefield, and even *that* is unlikely given the numbers of combatants present. As for keeping out the prospectors, well, it was Custer who led the expedition into the Black Hills in search of gold in the first place, with orders from the government to precipitate a gold rush if he possibly could. And that he did. He most certainly did not care a whit about the Sioux and their sacred claims to the area. Nor did he have any qualms at all about violating the treaty guaranteeing the region to them.

Nobody knows if he was the last man standing when his command was wiped out on June 25, 1876, but the recollections of several Sioux veterans of the battle suggest he was not. According to Sioux accounts, the aforementioned Sergeant Butler was probably the last to fall, remembered by them because he sported a monocle. Nobody really knows for sure.

After Custer is killed, Libbie shows 'uncle' Phil a letter written by her beloved before he rode off to his fate. In it he *implores* the President to care for the Sioux and observe the treaties. Of all the liberties taken in the film this has to be the most nauseous. Custer wrote no such letter, nor would he have done under *any* circumstances.

Sheridan's final words to Libbie, 'Come my dear, your soldier has won his last fight after all', refer to our hero's supposed request to save the noble Redman. Even if Sheridan had been involved, (and he wasn't), he of all people would have been the last to champion the Sioux cause on Capitol Hill. It was, after all, the same Phil Sheridan who is remembered for his infamous remark, 'the only good Indian is a dead Indian', or words to that effect.

As a publicity stunt, director Raoul Walsh was made an Honorary Brother of the Sioux Nation and given the name Thunder Hawk. Hoping to recruit real Sioux Indians for his film he advertised in the newspapers for them, but received only fourteen responses. He was compelled to use Filipinos instead. Perhaps, somebody slipped them a copy of the script. Most likely they simply knew what to expect from a Hollywood western.

One of the extras in *They Died With Their Boots On* was a young woman named Peggy Satterlee. Fourteen months later she would achieve brief notoriety as one of two 'under-aged' girls who accused Errol Flynn of statutory rape. Actually, she was at least eighteen and probably twenty-one at the time of the alleged assault. Her acquaintance with the truth throughout the trial was a fleeting one at best, and the jury recognized this.

During the trial it was revealed that she lived in an apartment paid for by a forty-three year-old man. Under cross-examination she even admitted, much to the jury's disgust, that she and her male friend once visited a mortuary where they pranced about pulling sheets off corpses and pressing their faces against the naked bodies! Peggy was not the world's greatest witness, and the jury had little difficulty finding in favor of the defendant.

William Mead was an intimate of Flynn's. He was killed making this picture when his horse stumbled and he was impaled on his own sabre. Flynn was deeply saddened by his friend's death and, against the wishes of Mead's family, convinced Walsh to leave the few feet of film featuring Mead in the released cut.

They Shoot Horses, Don't They? (1969)

Gig Young was once married to Elizabeth Montgomery who played Samantha in the *Bewitched* TV series. His career hit rock bottom in 1974 when he had to be replaced in *Blazing Saddles* because of his drug problem. In 1978, three weeks after the sixty-four year-old actor wed thirty-one year-old Kim Schmidt, he and his new bride were found dead in their apartment. Young had taken his .38 Smith & Wesson revolver into the bedroom, shot his wife through the head, placed the barrel in his mouth and pulled the trigger.

Acquaintances suggested he might have snapped over his wife's taunts about his inability to satisfy her in bed.

They Were Expendable (1945)

Hundreds of dramas related directly to the war were churned out in Hollywood between Pearl Harbor and VJ Day. *Three hundred* of these were made in 1942 alone! The list of credits at the end of this 1945 flag-waver is interesting, in that director John Ford included the wartime service rankings alongside the names of cast and crew. He is believed to have insisted on this to belittle the star John Wayne. Ford was most upset with Wayne because of his successful maneuvering to keep himself out of the forces.

Ward Bond was a great friend of Wayne's and appeared in this film with him. Bond was an out and out Fascist and anti-Semitic. Frank Sinatra, for one, detested him. After visiting the presumed resting place of Adolf Hitler during the fifties, Frank delighted in sending him a photograph of himself urinating on the spot near the bunker where the Fuhrer was thought to have been buried at the time. Unlike Wayne, Bond was genuinely exempted from service in the war because of his epilepsy.

For a time Robert Montgomery was an adviser to President Dwight Eisenhower, in much the same way as Peter Lawford briefly advised President Kennedy. Both actors offered tips to their respective presidents on how best to perform before the cameras. It was, for instance, Lawford's technical know-how that enabled Kennedy to come across as cool and sincere (as opposed to Nixon's sweaty and uncomfortable persona) when the two presidential candidates debated on national TV prior to the 1960 elections.

Montgomery was a Lieutenant Commander in PT boats following Pearl Harbor, seeing action at Guadalcanal and in the Marshall Islands. He was also a deck officer on a destroyer at Normandy and was awarded the Bronze Star at Cherbourg. Elizabeth Montgomery was his daughter.

They Won't Forget (1937)

This was Lana Turner's first screen appearance. The sixteen year-old (she may even have been fifteen) played the small role of a young girl who is murdered early in the story. Although she was only in the picture for the first twelve minutes, Lana brought a wild reaction from the preview audience as she sashayed down the street in tight skirt and sweater, to the strains of an upbeat version of 'Dixie'. The 'Sweater Girl' had arrived.

High school classmates at that time recalled her classic beauty. She was 'absolutely ravishing', they said, five feet three, voluptuous, with perfect features, big blue eyes and creamy, dimpled skin. Lana herself was more than happy with the looks God had given her. She had a habit, schoolmates said, of hugging herself and laughing in sheer ecstasy over her appearance.

Thirteen Women (1932)

This was Peg Entwhistle's only film and it was not very good. The twenty-four year old London born starlet became despondent when she lost her RKO contract following its release, so she climbed fifty feet up an electrician's ladder on the thirteenth letter of the 'Hollywoodland' sign and threw herself from its top. Her body was found a few days later. At her apartment, unbeknown to the dead girl, was a letter from the Beverly Hills Playhouse, asking her to play the lead in an upcoming production. Ironically, it was a story about a young woman who commits suicide.

This is the Army (1943)

Irving Berlin could neither read nor write music, and could only play the piano in the key of F-Sharp Major. He had a special lever built into his piano that enabled him to transpose into any key he desired. When a melody was ready, he would play it ten or twenty times to his musical secretary, adjusting the tune as he went until he was happy with it. She would then write it down.

Those Magnificent Men in Their Flying Machines (1965)

Stuart Whitman was nearly forty when he won the lead opposite twenty-three year-old Sarah Miles in this. Although he never reached the top bracket of leading men, he still managed to accumulate $100 million during his career, mostly from shrewd investments in securities, real estate, cattle and thoroughbred horses.

Singer Matt Monro (*From Russia with Love, Born Free*) said comedian Tony Hancock attempted to seduce him in 1962. Monro laid him out with a single punch. The bisexual comedian frequented gay bars in Soho and was reputed to be a violent husband when drunk.

While touring in Australia he committed suicide with an overdose of amylo-barbitone tablets, washed down with copious quantities of vodka. At the time he was involved with Joan le Mesurier, the wife of one of his best friends, actor John le Mesurier of *Dad's Army* fame.

After being unceremoniously dumped in 1989, after twenty years starring in his Thames Television comedy show, Benny Hill lost interest in everything and was dead inside three years. Greatly depressed, he began to drink and eat to excess. When doctors advised him to have a heart bypass operation, he declined to do so out of fear. When neighbors complained about an unpleasant odor issuing from his flat, an old friend Dennis Kirkland peered through the window and found the sixty-eight year-old Benny slumped on a sofa. He had been dead for two days.

Despite popular belief to the contrary he was not homosexual, although he had little interest in bedding women. Stefanie Marrian, who gained fleeting recognition as the *Sun's* 1976 Page 3 Girl, said she masturbated him on a regular basis. 'I hated the sight of his naked body, but he loved me wanking him', she charmingly added. 'I always kept my knickers on, and he would never touch me'. Model Cherie

Gilham also claims to have administered 'sympathy blowjobs' whenever the comedian seemed upset.

Terry-Thomas inserted the hyphen in his name to match the gap in his teeth. Parkinson 's disease ended his career in the mid-seventies, and medical costs would drain away every penny he had accumulated in a highly successful decade or so in both British and American films.

Reduced to living in the bleakest of conditions in a London flat, he was rediscovered by the media in April 1989. A surge of public sympathy resulted in a Terry-Thomas Benefit Concert staged at the Theatre Royal Drury Lane. It generated in excess of seventy-five thousand pounds for the much-loved funny man, due mainly to an impromptu appearance by the then extremely popular performer Phil Collins. The money enabled the ailing comic to move into a nursing home, but he died four months later at the age of seventy-eight.

Three Coins in the Fountain (1954)

Maggie McNamara was a beautiful and promising actress who features here, having won an Oscar nomination for *The Moon Is Blue* in 1953. Plagued by mental illness for most of her life, she killed herself in 1978.

Jean Peters' career was cut short when she married billionaire Howard Hughes. Audie Murphy used to brag to his friends that he 'laid her nine times in one night' when they were going together.

Three Men and a Baby (1987)

In the scene where Celeste Holm comes to the bachelors' apartment, a small boy can be seen standing in the background of the living room. He has nothing to do with the storyline. When the camera follows Holm as she walks through the apartment, a shotgun can also be spotted resting against a wall. This, too, has no relevance to the story. When audiences first noticed these images, rumors spread that the apartment in which the sequence was shot had once been the scene of a domestic killing, and that the little boy had been murdered with a shotgun. That story has since been completely refuted, but the presence of the boy and the gun are yet to be satisfactorily explained.

Leonard Nimoy (Mr. Spock from TV's *Star Trek*) directed this successful comedy. The directing job was a condition he insisted upon before he would agree to participate in the Star Trek series of films about to be made.

Tillie and Gus (1933)

This was the first film to pit W C Fields against Baby LeRoy. Contrary to the popular story, Fields did not spike the child's orange juice with gin. Actually, he quite liked the boy and had him written into several scripts against studio wishes. Although it was said he hated infants, Fields designated $800,000 in his will for distribution to a home for orphaned children.

While being sponsored by Lucky Strike cigarettes he took delight in mentioning his 'son' Chester at every opportunity.

Chesterfields was one of Lucky Strike's biggest competitors. Mae West recalled hearing the alcoholic Fields exclaim one day, 'Somebody has stolen the cork out of my lunch'. When once asked what he had against drinking water, he retorted, 'fish fuck in it!' The line has developed a life of its own since then, but Fields is believed to be its originator.

During World War Two he deposited money in a bank in Hitler's Germany, 'just in case the little bastard wins', he told friends. Even though he distrusted banks, he held accounts in over 700 of them in countries scattered around the globe. Many were under aliases. After his death only thirty were tracked down. 'I am free of all prejudices', he once said. 'I hate everybody equally'. Ironically, he died on Christmas Day 1946, the day of the year he especially despised.

Both LeRoy and his mother were too young to sign contracts, so the boy's grandfather handled him. Leroy's career began at the age of one and lasted for five movies.

Tillie's Punctured Romance (1914)

A tiny child seen clinging to Marie Dressler's skirts in this picture is actually the future comedy king Milton Berle.

Charlie Chaplin was once involved in a real life murder mystery that happened aboard newspaper magnate Randolph Hearst's yacht the *Oneida*. The dead man was Thomas Ince, a producer known in the industry as 'the father of the western'.

Ince, Hearst and his mistress Marion Davies, Chaplin, Louella Parsons, bandleader Paul Whiteman's wife Margaret Livingstone, actress Aileen Pringle and six others was aboard the *Oneida* one evening when it is believed Hearst shot Ince by mistake, believing him to be Chaplin.

Hearst had long suspected the rampant Charlie of having an affair with his mistress Miss Davies (which was true) and mistook the unfortunate producer for the comedian in the darkness. It was Ince's misfortune to bear a strong resemblance to Chaplin. The *Los Angeles Times* on November 21, 1924 ran the following front-page headline: 'Movie Producer Shot On Hearst Yacht'. It was withdrawn the same afternoon, without any explanation, after Hearst brought pressure to bear on the editor.

At least three people said they saw Ince taken ashore from the *Oneida*. One of them was Chaplin's secretary, a man named Kono, who saw him carried from the yacht 'bleeding from a head wound'.

The only person to ever be interviewed about the death, however, was a good friend of Hearst's, Dr Daniel Goodman, who vowed there were no suspicious circumstances. San Diego DA Chester Kempley interrogated him briefly, learning that he was a Hearst employee and Production Head at the mogul's Cosmopolitan Pictures. To nobody's surprise, Goodman categorically denied anything untoward had occurred. None of the guests on board the yacht were ever officially questioned!

Ince died at his home on the following Wednesday and his funeral held two days after that. He was then cremated before an autopsy could be performed. The official cause of death was registered as 'a heart attack brought on by acute indigestion'. It was also initially reported (in the Hearst papers) that death had taken place while Ince was visiting Hearst at his ranch, but too many people had seen him board the yacht, so that tall tale was quietly withdrawn.

As for the yacht, well, no logs, records or photos pertaining to the cruise ever surfaced. No two stories from those aboard ever sounded the same, but it mattered little because authorities were not too interested in the truth anyway. It was not very wise to publicly challenge Hearst on *any* issue, much less this particular one. Those not frightened off were reputedly bought off with substantial bribes.

Although he was a good friend of the dead man, Hearst did not attend Ince's funeral. He did, however, financially back his widow, Elinor, in a couple of highly profitable business ventures. Each of the people aboard the yacht on that day *reputedly* received a 'present' from Hearst of a million dollars. Louella Parsons' minor column was suddenly syndicated America-wide and her career blossomed. Mrs. Ince would die a wealthy woman, although several sources mistakenly stated she died destitute, reduced to driving a taxi in New York City. That has since proven to be a fallacy.

Toast of New York, The (1937)

'The nicest thing I can say about Frances Farmer', said director William Wyler, 'is that she is unbearable'. Not exactly the biggest wrap anyone has ever received, but she really was a handful at the peak of her short career.

Her troubles began on October 19, 1942 when she was pulled over by a traffic cop while on her way to a party at Deanna Durbin's home. She was travelling in a blackout zone with her lights on. Unable to produce her license, she turned nasty and was arrested, charged and fined.

Later that year she received a six months probationary sentence for drunk driving and using foul language to the arresting policeman. A short time after that incident she broke her hairdresser's jaw in a fight and then, following a drunken brawl in a bar, was observed running topless down Sunset Boulevard. Again she was charged.

Her next arrest, for parole violation this time, saw her dragged naked and screaming through the lobby of the Knickerbocker Hotel in Hollywood. In the ensuing struggle she punched a policewoman and knocked another officer to the ground. When the judge sentenced her to jail for those offences an enraged Frances threw an inkwell at him! Her own mother signed the papers to have her committed to an insane asylum. The old girl had her own mental issues, blaming her daughter's erratic behavior on 'world communism'!

Frances spent the next decade in an asylum, where she was strait jacketed and subjected to electric shock treatment and ice baths. She may also have been given a frontal lobotomy by the notorious quack, 'Doctor' Walter Freeman. Although he never held any type of certificate in surgery, Freeman boasted of having performed nearly 3,500 lobotomies in his lifetime. His method was barbaric to say the least. He would induce unconsciousness by administering electric shocks, before driving a spike via a tear duct one and a half inches into the patient's skull.

There were also stories of staff at the asylum secretly taking money from men in exchange for letting them, 'fuck a movie star', as they so crassly put it. When Frances was finally released, it was discovered that her disorder could have been successfully treated all those years before by dieting or administering mild medication. When she was first stopped and arrested for speeding a decade before, she had been on the verge of a nervous breakdown. Had she been diagnosed correctly when her troubles first began and given proper help, she need never have been committed to an institution at all.

From 1936 to 1942 she was married to actor Leif Erickson who was the star of the TV series *High Chaparral* during the sixties. Many years after her ordeal, she appeared regularly on TV talk shows. Frances died from cancer in 1970.

To Catch a Thief (1955)

It may be apocryphal, but when Alfred Hitchcock celebrated his birthday during the making of *To Catch a Thief*, his secretary announced to the cast and crew, 'Would you all come into the other room, please, and have a piece of Mr. Hitchcake's cock?' The scene in which Jesse Royce Landis stubs out a cigarette in her fried egg was an in-joke from the director. He loathed eggs.

The young French actress, Brigitte Auber, plays Danielle Foussard. Screenwriter John Michael Hayes recalled, 'She had a casual way of wearing a blouse, which exposed her bosom frequently. And Hitch, of course, was delighted'.

After announcing his retirement in 1953, Cary Grant and his wife Betsy Drake toured the world for several months before settling down in Palm Springs. His penchant for Hitchcock scripts, however, brought him out of retirement to make this film.

He was also swayed by the opportunity to act with Grace Kelly. As his wife feared, Cary took one look at Kelly and was a goner. Twenty-five year-old Grace was engaged to fashion designer Oleg Cassini at the time, so her attraction to the fifty year-old actor had to be restrained. Nevertheless, the chemistry on screen between the two stars was enough for her future husband Prince Rainier to ban the film from ever being shown in Monaco. Interestingly, it is the only one of her movies thus banned.

The scene where she drives Cary in her sports car at breakneck speed along the cliffs near Monaco was shot in a studio with a backdrop of the Three Corniches along the Cote d'Azur, the very stretch of road that would claim her life in a crash in 1982. Neither actor was actually in Monaco.

Off-screen Grace always wore spectacles because she was very near-sighted. While some say she probably suffered a mild stroke that caused her car to miss the hair-pin bend the day she was killed, others speculate she may have been arguing with her rebellious daughter Stephanie and took her eyes off the road for a moment. Stephanie probably remembers, but she has never said.

To Have and Have Not (1944)

A very young Andy Williams was hired to dub Lauren Bacall's singing voice, but it turned out to be unnecessary and, ultimately, she did her own vocals. Her sultry debut in *To Have and Have Not* established her as an instant star, but she trembled so badly from nerves that her first scenes had to be shot several times. In desperation, to keep her head from uncontrollably shaking, she tucked her chin into her chest and simply uplifted her eyes to speak. 'The Look', as it was called, was born in just that way.

Humphrey Bogart fell in love with her on the set, despite the big difference in their ages. To put that in perspective, it is interesting to note that by the time she graduated from high school he had already been married and divorced three times!

When the forty-six year-old Bogey wed the nineteen year-old Bacall both bride and groom wept copiously throughout the ceremony. At his funeral she placed a golden whistle in the urn containing his ashes. It was engraved 'If you want anything, just whistle', her famous line from *To Have and Have Not*.

To Hell and Back (1955)

When Universal decided to put Audie Murphy's wartime experiences on the screen in *To Hell and Back,* it proved to be the studio's biggest grossing film of all time. It would hold that honor until *Jaws* came along in 1975. Murphy's lifelong friend in real life was Charles Drake, the actor who portrays his buddy in the movie.

Murphy was a genuine hero of the Second World War, earning twenty-seven medals, including the Medal of Honor, before he was twenty-one years old. The most highly decorated American soldier of the entire conflict, he was wounded in action three times and credited with *personally* killing 240 Germans while fighting in the Ardenne.

Not surprisingly, he suffered from what we now call post-traumatic stress disorder when he returned to civilian life. He always kept a loaded revolver under his pillow. Once, during an argument with his wife he pushed the barrel of the gun into her mouth. He claimed his hatred for his father spurred him on during the war. 'Every time I shot one of the enemy I pretended I was killing my dad', he said.

As he got older he experienced huge drink and drug problems that resulted in numerous run-ins with the law, usually for drink driving or for brawling in public places. The police always let him go because of his heroic war record. An inveterate gambler, he had ties with organized crime in New Orleans. In 1970 was acquitted of killing a man in a bar fight.

His movie career was successful without being overly significant. Good friend Doug McClure reckoned the pint-sized actor 'seduced more girls than any man I ever knew, with the possible exception of Errol Flynn'. It may surprise you to learn that Audie wrote the country & western hit *Shutters and Boards*. He died in an air crash in 1969 at the age of forty-six and is buried in Arlington National Cemetery, Virginia.

Tom Jones (1963)

While making *Tom Jones,* Dame Edith Evans (once reputed to have been Winston Churchill's lover, by the way) asked director Tony Richardson, 'I don't look 70, do I? Now be honest'. Richardson replied, 'No, love, you don't. Not any more'.

Top Gun (1986)

The whole concept of fighter pilots competing against each other at fighter school was concocted by the writers. No such policy exists in the US Navy, nor is it likely to.

In 1982, Kelly McGillis was brutally raped in her apartment by two men who had broken in. She told police her two assailants, 'took turns with me ...they did vile and horrible things'. Both men were soon apprehended. One of them, a fifteen year-old, was sentenced to just three years for rape and sodomy. The older man, inexplicably, walked free.

At an end of week pool party during production of *Top Gun*, McGillis turned up with a lesbian girlfriend, much to the astonishment of some cast members. After a few drinks, the actress stripped naked in front of everyone (including several fighter pilots involved with the technical side of things) and dived into the pool.

Twenty-two year-old Val Kilmer and thirty-six year-old Cher lived together for a month in 1982. 'We went to a play, and then he never went home', recalled Cher. 'We stayed together for a month, and we didn't even kiss', she added. Then he suddenly walked out. 'That was very painful and it took me a long time to get over it'. And they never even *kissed*?

Track of Thunder (1968)

Brenda Benet was a promising young actress whose career was hampered by her marriage to actor Bill Bixby, the star of TV's *My Favorite Martian, The Incredible Hulk*, and *The Courtship of Eddie's Father*. Their union was not always a happy one and ended in divorce. Shortly after the couple parted their child died, a tragedy Benet was unable to handle. She ended her own life a little later at the age of thirty-seven.

Treasure Island (1950)

This Disney classic, his first ever all live-action feature, stars Robert Newton as Long John Silver and Bobby Driscoll as Jim Hawkins. The Ohio Censorship Board tried to have the film banned because, 'it would encourage children to piracy'. The delightful child actor Bobby Driscoll, who was also in *Song of the South,* met a tragic end in real life. He began shooting heroin into his arm at seventeen when his film career, like that of many child actors, dried up as he reached adolescence. By the age of thirty-one, after serving time in Chino Penitentiary, he was dead. His badly decayed body was found by some children playing in an abandoned tenement building in New York. Buried in a pauper's grave, he was only identified through dental records over a year later.

Trip to Bountiful, The (1985)

The name Geraldine Page is not one that readily springs to mind when average movie-goers discuss great actors, yet when this lady finally won an Oscar for this picture she received a standing ovation from *everybody* including the other nominees. *The Trip to Bountiful*, you see, was her *eighth* time at bat and her only home run. Presenter F. Murray Abraham, on opening the envelope said, 'Oh, I consider this woman the greatest actress in the English language'. Remarkably, her eight nominations came from a career tally of just twenty-five films.

Trouble With Harry, The (1955)

The child actor playing Arnie Rogers is Jerry Mathers. Two years later he became a household name playing the title role in the hit TV series, *Leave it to Beaver.*

This was Shirley MacLaine's movie debut. When she audaciously improvised at the first script- reading, director Alfred Hitchcock was unusually impressed. 'My darling', he told her, 'you have the guts of a bank robber'.

Truth About Cats & Dogs, The (1996)

Janeane Garofalo, who co-stars here with Uma Thurman, gave her views on homosexuality in an interview. 'When you have a gay parade on Christopher Street in New York, with naked men and women on a float cheering, 'We're here, We're queer'; that's what makes my heart swell. Not the flag, but a gay, naked man or woman burning the flag. I get choked up with pride'. 'I enjoy watching lesbians', she said in another interview. 'Who doesn't want to see good-looking girls making out?' Well, not *everybody*.

True Grit (1969)

John Wayne quipped on receiving his Oscar for this film: 'If I'd known what I know now, I'd have put a patch over my eye thirty-five years ago'. He then flew back to Old Tucson to complete shooting *Rio Lobo*. When he arrived on the set the following morning the entire crew, including his horse, were sporting Rooster Cogburn eye patches.

Twilight Zone – the Movie (1982)

In July 1982, an accident happened on the set of *Twilight Zone – The Movie* that resulted in the deaths of two small children and actor Vic Morrow. While shooting a sequence at

2.20am, with Morrow carrying the children across a creek in a Vietnam War scene, a helicopter crashed into the trio killing them instantly.

Director John Landis and others were charged with manslaughter. In 1987 they were acquitted, but fined for illegally hiring non-professionals. The two children, six year-old Renee Shin-Yi Chen and seven year-old My-Ca Dinh Lee, were not licensed actors as the law demanded, and had been recruited, off the cuff, to do the scene because no dialogue was involved.

Apparently, the helicopter was hovering twenty or so feet above the trio when two explosions caused the pilot to lose control. It crashed directly onto the little girl crushing her instantly. The rotors decapitated the boy and Morrow. Crewmembers retrieved Morrow's torso and laid it on the bank. The severed heads were placed in a plastic rubbish bag.

Morrow's daughter Jennifer Jason-Leigh was left just $78.18 in his will. The remaining $600,000 went to her older sister Carrie Anne. Jennifer had alienated her father when she changed her name to avoid being known as 'Vic Morrow's daughter', the ultimate insult in his eyes.

Two-Faced Woman (1941)

This was Greta Garbo's final film, although she is overshadowed by the performance from Constance Bennett. A huge star by 1939, Bennett was earning $30,000 a week from Warners and a further $3,000 a week from Pathe

Films. Even then she was not content, insisting RKO pay the weekly tax on her salary. 'I must have $30,000 clear', she said.

The value of a dollar then can be gauged by what she paid her staff. Constance employed five people – a cook, a chauffeur, a secretary and two maids. Their *annual* wage bill came to just $6,000, an average of about $23 a week each. Bennett, incidentally, was already a millionaire *before* she started in movies.

Constance owned a Rolls Royce and another car in Paris, keeping them in storage at a cost of just $10 a year. She annually took a ten-week holiday in Europe, and owned a villa in Biarritz that a full-time caretaker looked after for $40 a month. From 1941-6 she was married to actor Gilbert Roland, and once told a reporter he was a wonderful husband, 'but in one room of the house only'.

Unconquered (1947)

Paulette Goddard was a 5'4" green-eyed beauty, a woman who gained fame and fortune by marrying Charlie Chaplin, and by her innate talent for acquiring wealth (especially gifts of jewelry, from her legion of male admirers. She had female lovers as well, among them notorious lesbians Anita Loos and Constance Collier.

'Never, ever sleep with a man until he gives you a pure white stone of at least ten carats', she once told Marlene Dietrich, not that Marlene needed any telling. Goddard was probably the role model for Loralei Lee in Anita's best-seller *How to Marry a Millionaire.*

As a young girl, Paulette would stand on street corners and proposition attractive looking men. 'If you give me a quarter, I'll let you look under my skirt', was her standard opening offer. Things generally progressed from there. At fifteen she wed 32 year-old playwright Edgar James, then left him four years later, walking away with a cool $375,000 settlement.

One of her first Hollywood conquests was billionaire Howard Hughes. 'He never kisses on the lips', she confided to friends. He also services 'five or six women daily', she added.

She and Dietrich *may* have been lovers at one time, according to some sources, but there is little doubt that Marlene thoroughly detested Goddard for most of her life. Maybe they had a falling out. Who knows? For decades Marlene disdainfully referred to her as *'The Goddard'.*

Even outside the movie industry Paulette seduced men and women from many walks of life. Apart from Miss Loos, other authors such as John Steinbeck, Aldous Huxley and H G Wells, all experienced intimate sojourns with her. Erich Remarque, author of *All Quiet on the Western Front,* actually married her. Sexually, he was a *very* busy man in the movie capital, so it is a wonder he even found time to do so.

Other intimates of Goddard's included shipping mogul Aristotle Onassis, US Army General Alexander Haig, politician Harry Hopkins, composer George Gershwin, and artist Diego Rivera. She even bedded Jack Warner's wife, Ann, a well-known lesbian in the community. Paulette's list of bedmates from the *male* acting lists is too long to mention here, but it included most of the big names of the day. Charlie Chaplin and Burgess Meredith became two of her four husbands.

One evening in 1940, patrons at Ciro's Restaurant were taken aback when her intoxicated escort, Anatole Litvak, took out her breasts and began kissing them passionately as they sat at a ringside table. The management quickly moved the couple to the rear of the dining area, only to see Litvak disappear under the table and bury his head between her legs. Paulette's giggling and moaning left nobody in doubt of what he was doing. It was the talk of the town for months.

As she began to age, Paulette's insatiable appetite for sex with young lovers only increased. Gardner McKay, the star of TV's *Adventures in Paradise*, was accosted by her when she guested on the show. 'Paulette would start first thing in the morning', he recalled. 'She said whatever came into her mind, usually something about fucking, and moved her hands freely whenever I came too close to her. She seemed to be about seventy...if there can be dirty old men, there can be dirty old women too. Paulette was indeed ahead of her time.' Actually, she was 49 when she appeared in that series in 1959.

Throughout her final years Paulette took to consuming large amounts of vodka straight from the bottle. Her secretary (a woman) was appalled to see the once glamorous star urinating in the back seat of her chauffeur-driven limousine, rather than stopping to find a bathroom. A life-long exhibitionist, Paulette would take her underwear off in the car in front of driver and secretary, 'because she loved to flaunt her private parts'.

In those last, lonely years, Goddard attempted suicide five times. She eventually died from emphysema in 1990, clutching in her hands the Sotheby's catalogue that listed her jewelry for auction. She left behind $20 million plus her jewels, one of the most famous collections in the world. Paulette left more than $20 million to the New York University to be used for scholarships.

Underwater (1955)

For the premiere of *Underwater* in 1955, its producer Howard Hughes came up with a really dumb idea. He invited 150 critics and journalists to view the thing from specially constructed benches *at the bottom of a Florida lake!* Supplied with breathing apparatus, his guests labored through the presentation, unable to hear much of the dialogue because of all the gurgling and glopping sounds.

But the evening wasn't a total waste. The picture's star Jane Russell was late arriving, so the then unknown Jayne Mansfield took advantage of her tardiness in true Hollywood fashion. She began parading around for photographers in the skimpiest of bathing costumes, the top of which 'accidentally' came off altogether when she dived into the pool. The resultant shots of her feebly trying to re-attach her bra, and cover her enormous orbs at the same time, made the front pages across America. With hours she had a seven-year contract with Warner Bros. studio. The movie, incidentally, flopped.

Untouchables, The (1987)

In real life Eliot Ness and Al Capone never met, so you can chalk up the confrontation on the stairs at Al's hotel as a figment of the screenwriter's imagination. When big Al was finally incarcerated it was mainly due to the efforts of the Internal Revenue Service (IRS), although confiscated cash and accounts books taken by the Untouchables in various raids were used in court against him.

His successor, Frank Nitti 'The Enforcer', was harassed by Ness and his men, but he most certainly was *not* hurled off the top of the court building by Eliot, as depicted in this movie. In 1943, despondent over the likelihood of spending an extended time in prison for tax evasion, he blew his own brains out.

Eighty-eight year-old Al Wolff was hired by the producers to give actor Kevin Costner detailed information about Ness, his mannerisms, habits etc. Wolff was one of the original Untouchables. Incredibly, it was not until the movie's producers came calling that his family became aware of this. Costner had a lesson in humility one day on the set. A young woman behind the crowd barricade kept trying to catch his eye all day, so at the end of the day's filming he sauntered over and asked if he could help her. 'Could you get me Sean Connery's autograph?' she answered.

For his portrayal of Capone, Robert De Niro tracked down the actual tailor who had made all of the gangster's underwear back in the roaring twenties, and then had him make the exact same silk underpants for him to wear in the picture. It was one of De Niro's ways of 'getting into character'.

Of all the performers taking part in *The Untouchables*, none got their money easier than Englishman Bob Hoskins. He was given $260,000 to be De Niro's stand-in, just in case the man became ill and could not continue in the role. He was not called upon.

In 1959 the Desilu Studios, owned by Desi Arnaz and Lucille Ball, released the first episode of their new TV series, *The Untouchables*, starring Robert Stack as Eliot Ness. It immediately came under fire from Italian-Americans (including members of the *Cosa Nostra*), the so-called American branch of the Mafia. Sonny Capone, a childhood friend of Arnaz, sued the studio for portraying his father 'in a bad light'! The judge ruled against him, declaring it was inconceivable to portray America's most notorious mobster in any *other* kind of light. Frank Sinatra, probably kowtowing to his Mob pals, moved his production company off the Desilu lot in protest.

Mobster Sam Giancana went one better, ordering Aladena Fratianno, known in mob circles as 'Jimmy the Weasel', to murder Arnaz. Fortunately, wiser heads prevailed and the hit was cancelled. It is interesting to note that while all this was going on, Giancano's long-time girlfriend Phyllis McGuire (of the singing group the McGuire Sisters), was one of Lucille Ball's closest friends.

New York columnist and radio personality Walter Winchell was paid $25,000 an episode to narrate the series. He was entirely Desi's choice because Lucy detested him. During the witch-hunts of the early fifties he had publicly named her as a card-carrying communist. Technically, he was correct, because she had joined the party in 1936, but only to make her dominating grandfather happy. His accusations nearly ended her career.

U. S. Marshals (1998)

One of the stars of this 1998 thriller is Robert Downey Jr, who was allowed out of prison for five weeks to complete his acting obligations, then promptly re-incarcerated to complete his sentence for drug abuse and disorderly conduct. Part of the flower child generation, his parents smoked pot with him when he was a little boy. They said he looked cute getting high! The bi-sexual actor has had a long-running battle with drugs for most of his life.

In 1996, he was arrested for drunk driving and possession of heroin, crack and cocaine, and for carrying a .357 Magnum revolver. On another occasion he was apprehended while stark naked in his car, tossing imaginary rodents out of the window. In the same year, a woman rang 911 to report that a complete stranger (Downey) was unconscious in her eleven year-old son's bed! Following his third drug-related offence inside a month he was jailed in Malibu, then released on condition he attend rehab and stay off illegal substances. He soon violated parole and was busted yet again for drugs. This time he was given a three-year prison sentence.

Valley of the Dolls (1967)

Authoress Jacqueline Susann based the character Helen Lawson in *Valley Of The Dolls* on her lesbian lover Ethel Merman. Susann herself has a small part as a reporter in the film. Richard Dreyfuss also has a tiny role in a backstage sequence, a full decade before he hit it big in *The Goodbye Girl*. Patty Duke's character is loosely based on Judy Garland, while Sharon Tate's is supposed to be a depiction of Carole Landis.

Susann was once asked what she thought of author Philip Roth, who wrote that over-rated tribute to masturbation *Portnoy's Complaint*. 'I like him', she replied, 'but I wouldn't want to shake hands with him'.

While visiting her husband's office one day, she noticed a letter on his desk from a female fan. 'It read: 'Dear Mr. Mansfield, I am Sally May, and I would do anything to be on your show, and when I say anything, I mean anything'. Jackie sat down and quickly typed out a reply. 'Dear Sally May, I have read your letter to Mr. Mansfield. I am Mrs. Mansfield and I do everything for Mr. Mansfield, and when I say everything, I mean everything'.

Virginia City (1940)

Character actor Victor Kilian plays Abraham Lincoln in this film. In 1979 at the age of eighty-eight he was murdered by burglars in his Hollywood apartment.

When Miriam Hopkins decided to adopt a child she sent a friend to Chicago to pick one out for her! The moment her adopted son turned six years of age, she enlightened him on the wonders and pitfalls of sex!

Her long-running feud with Bette Davis can be summed up by Bette's comment to the press when told of Miriam's demise. 'God has been good. He has taken her from us', she said, and meant every word of it.

Wake up and Dream (1934)

Although he only appeared in a couple of films, Russ Columbo was very big for a few years on the music scene in the early thirties, singing and playing with many of the top acts including Bing Crosby. At the height of his romance with Carole Lombard he died in a bizarre accident.

While visiting portrait photographer Lansing Brown Junior in his home in 1934, the two men were examining the latter's Civil War gun collection when one of the old pieces accidentally discharged after Brown struck a match on it. The bullet ricocheted off a nearby table and hit Columbo in the left eye. The wound proved fatal and he was dead at the age of twenty-six.

In a further bizarre twist, it was decided by friends and family to keep his death a secret from his ailing mother. Concerned that the shock might be too much for the old girl, they told her Russ and Lombard had married and moved to Europe to further his career. Letters and telegrams were concocted and read to the old lady *for the next ten years* until her death in 1944. 'Tell Russ how happy and proud he has made me', she asked loved ones shortly before she died.

Lombard said years later that Columbo (not Gable) was the love of her life. When she died in an air crash in 1942 she was buried near Russ, as she had requested, in Forest Lawn Memorial Park.

War and Peace (1956)

Darryl F Zanuck rarely read books. Instead, he ordered his writers to deliver to him synopses of books he considered might be turned into movies. Producer David Brown recalled being instructed to provide him with a *one page* synopsis of *War and Peace* within twenty-four hours.

War of the Worlds (2005)

The stars of the 1953 version, Gene Barry and Ann Robinson, appear right at the end of this one as Tom Cruise's in-laws. The scene where an alien places its 'hand' on Dakota Fanning's shoulder was a redo of the same (less scary) scene in Steven Spielberg's earlier movie *ET, the Extra-terrestrial*.

Because no living creature on Earth walks on three legs, Spielberg made the alien machines tripods, a decision that enabled his special effects people to give them a menacing, sinister mobility unlike anything we are used to seeing. Very clever.

Waterloo Bridge (1940)

Vivien Leigh suffered from a mental disorder that escalated as she aged. She swore like a sailor most of her life anyway, but that even got worse in her later years. In the end, friends feared for her safety, as her behavior grew more and more erratic. They became especially concerned when she began picking up complete strangers in the street and accompanying them to hotel rooms for casual sex.

One of her many lovers in those later years was Peter Wyngarde, the mustached star of TV's *Jason King* and *Department S*. He was a homosexual whose career evaporated after he went to court charged with performing an indecent act on a man in a public toilet block.

Her affair with Peter Finch on the set of *Elephant Walk* probably happened because of a nervous breakdown, brought on by the discovery that her husband Sir Laurence Olivier and comedian Danny Kaye were lovers.

Finch and his wife returned home early from an engagement one evening to find Vivien in the act of smothering their daughter with a pillow! Her mental issues had clearly reached very dangerous levels. She even invented a bizarre party game she called 'How to Murder an Infant', in which players were required to think up horrendous methods of dispatching babies! We know now that she was bipolar and suffering from manic depression.

Tuberculosis claimed her at 53 in 1967. Despite her iconic status as an extraordinary film star, it is surprising to learn that she only made nineteen movies in her entire life.

Way Down East (1920)

While making *Way Down East* in 1920 for DW Griffith, Lillian Gish's life was in real danger when she was required to step across ice floes in one sequence. Scorning the use of a double, she completed the scene during which any slip would have hurled her into the icy torrent. Another featured female in the film, Clarine Seymour, actually died from exposure during the shoot.

Westerner, The (1940)

For about a decade, until the rules were changed in 1946, all Guild Members were eligible to vote for nominations as well as for the ultimate winners of Academy Awards. Most members were extras and they often voted 'in block'. They, therefore, exerted a huge influence over the results.

Walter Brennan began as an extra and benefited from this. He chalked up three Oscars from his first three tries (*Come And Get It* in 1936, *Kentucky* in 1938 and this film in 1940). From 1946 onwards, however, only Academy Members could vote for the actual awards, a rule change that saw the numbers drop from 9,000 to 1,610. It is generally believed it was the 'extras vote' that gained a Best Song Oscar for the trite *Sweet Leilani* over Gershwin's classic *They Can't Take That Away From Me* in 1937.

West of Cimarron (1942)

West of Cimarron incurred the censor's wrath because it contained thirteen killings. The producers were consequently ordered to reduce the body count to 'seven or eight'; but were allowed to make up the balance with 'a series of serious woundings!'

West Side Story (1961)

At the age of fourteen Natalie Wood lost her virginity to actor Nick Adams. According to Adams, her mother asked him to show her daughter 'the ways of the world' because she trusted him more than she did the other men hanging around her daughter.

Natalie's brief affair with James Dean was consummated in his tiny Porsche Spider on Mulholland Drive high above the Hollywood lights. At seventeen she also had an affair with the gay Raymond Burr, who was in his late thirties when they made *A Cry in the Night* together in 1955.

Her mother, Maria Gurdin, was considered to be the 'pushiest' stage mother in Hollywood history, and that *includes* Brooke Shields' mother. Mrs. Gurdin brought fifteen year-old Natalie to Frank Sinatra's home with the expressed object of furthering her career. Natalie was soon Frank's mistress, and remained so on an occasional basis for several years.

'I never saw what was so great about Natalie', said a not overly gallant Steve McQueen. 'She was short and lousy in bed'. Some sources claim her quest for meaningful relationships may have led her into the beds of several lesbian women over the years. She even had limited success with the homosexual Tab Hunter. It is interesting to note that she was only fifteen years old when she was sleeping with forty-four year-old director Nicholas Ray, as well as her co-stars in *Rebel Without A Cause,* namely Dennis Hopper, Nick Adams and James Dean.

Her mysterious drowning has never been fully explained. What is known is that she died shortly after her husband Robert Wagner and their guest Christopher Walken had an argument about her alleged affair with Walken. When her body was found floating in the water at 7.44am, there were bruises on her cheek, arms and hands, while the dinghy she supposedly used to leave the yacht was found floating about 200 meters away. In it were four life jackets. A woman on a nearby boat said she heard a woman cry for help and a man respond. A verdict of accidental death was returned.

Rita Moreno remembered being in tears as she left the podium clutching the Oscar she won for *West Side Story* at the 1962 Academy Awards. Suddenly, Joan Crawford threw her arms about the young actress and literally dragged her off to her nearby dressing room. 'There, there', whispered Crawford, 'I'll take care of you'.

Moreno was required at a media interview, but Joan kept her until they were photographed together. Only then did she let her go. A week later Rita received a thank you note from Crawford. It read: "Dear Rita, it was so thoughtful of you on your night of triumph to take the time to stop by my dressing room'. Until that night at the Oscars she had never even *met* Crawford before.

Depressed over the end of her nine-year relationship with Marlon Brando, and frustrated by her inability to gain substantial roles following her Oscar for this film, Moreno downed a quantity of pills and came within an inch of dying in a hospital emergency room. To her credit she bounced back to become the first performer *ever* to add a Grammy, a Tony and an Emmy to her Oscar. She was later seen regularly on TV's *The Rockford Files* with James Garner.

When Harry Met Sally...(1989)

Director Rob Reiner gave his mother a bit part in what turned out to be the most talked about movie scene in a decade. When Meg Ryan fakes an orgasm in the crowded Katz's Delicatessen in New York City, it is Estelle Reiner who drily says to the waiter, 'I'll have what she's having'.

Where the Boys Are (1963)

Until the Beatles came along, the only single to ever reach number one in the USA, Britain, France and Australia was Connie Francis's 1957 recording of *Who's Sorry Now?* Her next 12 records all made it to the top as well. From 1957- 67 she sold 90 million singles and had seven million-selling albums, while also finding time to make five awful movies for

MGM, including this one. She appeared a record 22 times on the Ed Sullivan Show.

In 1974, she was raped in a Howard Johnson Motel on Long Island. Four years later, her younger brother was shot to death in front of his New Jersey home soon after being convicted for bank fraud.

Wild in the Country (1961)

That is Christina Crawford playing Gary Lockwood's daughter here. She is the real life daughter of Joan Crawford and the writer of *Mommie Dearest*, the best-selling biography in which she effectively harpooned her own mother. Opinions remain divided on just how much of the book is true.

Wings (1927)

Two years before she starred in *Wings,* Clara Bow was the highest paid star in the world, collecting a staggering $35,000 a week! She drove about in a red Kissell convertible, owned seven Chow dogs (all colored auburn to match her own hair coloring) and was dubbed 'the It Girl' by the media.

The oft-cited story that she had sex with an entire football team one night is simply untrue. She did, however, play a game of touch football with a group of USC footballers that included a young Marion Morrison, before he became John Wayne. And everybody did play naked. It would be fair to say, however, that Clara was certainly no saint, but then saints were few and far between in Tinsel Town in that decade – or any other for that matter. It is also true she seduced most of the young actors she met on the set of her biggest film, *It*.

Clara and Gary Cooper were lovers for some years. She recklessly told Hedda Hopper he was, 'hung like a horse and could go all night', so, of course, Hedda told everyone. Clara was engaged to both Gilbert Roland and Victor Fleming before she met Coops. Another of her lovers known for his sexual prowess was song and dance man Harry Richman. She sent him a picture of herself captioned, 'to my gorgeous lover, Harry. I'll trade all my 'it' for all your 'that'.

Her childhood was the stuff of nightmares. Born dirt poor in New York City, she had the 'mother from Hell', a deranged woman who twice attempted to kill her with a butcher's knife. Her father was no better, sexually assaulting her when she was a teenager. Both her mother and grandmother died in asylums. Her father was plagued with mental problems and often mistook his daughter for his wife (and vice-versa), which may or may not explain the assaults.

When columnist Whitney Bolton asked her, 'Miss Bow, when you add it all up, what is *it*?' She paused to think for a moment, and then answered, 'I ain't real sure'. Poor Clara had beauty, but was as thick as a plank. The 'Brooklyn Bonfire', as she was sometimes called, was mortally afraid of the introduction of sound into the movie industry. When a fire broke out on the lot one day, she ran from the building screaming, 'Christ, I hope it was the sound stages!'

Paramount, aware of the importance of her image, offered her a $500,000 bonus if she could remain scandal-free for the tenure of her contract. She never collected. Her regular trips to the Hollywood VD Clinic, plus several abortions in Mexico, attest to the reasons why.

Her final years were spent in total obscurity. Each December, towards the end of her life, she would send Hedda Hopper pathetic Christmas cards, on which she would write: 'Do you remember me?' She died in 1965.

Winslow Boy, The (1999)

Neil North, the actor who plays the First Lord of the Admiralty here, is the same Neil North who played the role of the accused boy in the 1948 version.

Wizard of Oz, The (1939)

The yellow brick road was made of painted soft cork to cushion the Scarecrow's dancing falls.

Toto was a pet Cairn terrier bitch named Terry, belonging to director Mervyn LeRoy's son Warner. Born in 1932, Terry (Toto) lived until 1945. He and Judy Garland were the lowest paid featured performers in the picture.

Judy was sixteen when she played twelve year-old Dorothy, and only chosen because LB Mayer was unable to procure Shirley Temple. For the first two weeks of production she wore a blonde wig, before it was decided to make her a brunette. Jean Harlow's death in 1937 put paid to an MGM - Fox deal that would have seen Shirley playing Dorothy.

Frank Morgan played five parts in the picture, including that of the Wizard. He got the job because W C Fields turned it down. Morgan's drunkenness and Garland's fits of giggling often delayed production. Edna May Oliver was originally cast as the Wicked Witch.

The dwarfs who played the Munchkins also caused several delays in production because of their raucous and sometimes drunken behavior. They also considered the sixteen year-old Garland to be a woman, and were forever pinching her bottom and propositioning her. Leo Singer of Singer's Midgets was contracted to supply the bulk of the 124 midgets employed on the movie. MGM paid him $100 a day for each one hired. He gave $50 to each of his performers and pocketed the rest.

Because she had a weight problem, Judy was fed Benzedrine tablets to keep her thin enough for the role. She was also prescribed uppers and downers to help her handle the workload. When her giggling fits caused several re-takes, director Victor Fleming resorted to slapping Judy's face to keep her mind on the job. Her breasts were too developed for those of the twelve year-old Dorothy, so they were tightly bound each time she went before the cameras. Studio executives would discuss them in her presence, how they were sprouting or pointing in different directions and why they would require taping down.

Judy possessed undeniable talents, but she was a bit of a 'plain Jane'. MGM decided to spare no expense in transforming their 'ugly duckling', if not into a swan, then at worst into a better looking duck. They capped her teeth, restructured her nose and crammed her into corsets to disguise her thick waist. Pills and massages were then administered to reshape her torso (Mayer called her 'my little hunchback', quite often to her face). Little wonder she had self-esteem issues throughout much of her career. Little wonder, too, that her dependence upon pills grew into an obsession that would later claim her life.

Although she only received $500 a week for *The Wizard of Oz,* Judy's salary jumped to $2,000 a week inside twelve months. Throughout her first decade at MGM she earned a half a million dollars, although she never personally signed a contract during that period. Her domineering mother handled such things.

Consequently, she never saw any of the money because Mum spent nearly all of it. She would later get even with her mother by denying her visiting rights to her granddaughter Liza. Mrs. Gumm lived out her final days barely making ends meet, working in a factory until her death in the company car park from a heart attack in 1953.

Dorothy's ruby slippers, or at least *one* of the six pairs she wore in the film, were auctioned at Christies in 2000 for $666,000, the buyer believing he had purchased *the* pair. In 1956, *The Wizard of Oz* became the first feature film to be released in its entirety to prime time television. It cost about

$2,777,000 to make. By the end of the twentieth century it had raked in over $300 million.

Clara Blandick played Aunty Em. She took her own life, in 1962, when in her eighties and unable to contend with the pain of her arthritis any longer. On that day she had her hair done at a beauty parlor, donned a royal blue bathrobe, swallowed a quantity of pills and then tied a plastic bag over her head to make sure she would not survive the attempt. She left behind a suicide note that read: 'I am now about to make the great adventure. I cannot endure this agonizing pain any longer. It is all over my body. Neither can I face the impending blindness. I pray the Lord my soul to keep. Amen'.

Buddy Ebsen was all set to play the Tinman, but had a severe reaction to the paint when it was applied to his face. It caused him to be hospitalized, so he relinquished the role. When LB Mayer was told, he replaced him with Jack Haley; then saw to it that Ebsen did not gain any decent roles in the industry for the next eight years. Many years later, Jack Haley Junior would marry Judy's daughter Liza Minnelli.

Margaret Hamilton, who played the Wicked Witch of the West, was just thirty-six years old when she made *The Wizard Of Oz*. She made more than fifty movies over a long career, although most people remember her only in this. In her later years she appeared as the kindly Cora in a series of Maxwell House coffee advertisements.

Billie Burke played Glinda, the Blue Fairy. From 1914 until his death in 1932, she was married to impresario

Florenz Ziegfeld, the biggest producer on Broadway for over a decade. Rather than call out, or worse still *walk* all the way to the front of the theatre, he used to send *telegrams* from the back of the auditorium to his actors on the stage!

Victor Fleming, the director of such films as *Gone with the Wind, The Wizard of Oz* and *Joan of Arc,* was a former chauffeur and racing car driver who began in the film business as Walter Wanger's assistant cameraman, covering the 1918 Versailles Peace Conference. Fleming was dragged off 'Oz' before filming was completed and ordered to the set of *GWTW* to replace the sacked George Cukor. Consequently, the scene most identified with the film, Garland's singing of 'Over the Rainbow', was not shot by him, but by his replacement King Vidor.

Judy Garland (1922-1969)

Known relationships with women:

 Asher, Betty
 Crawford, Joan
 Dietrich, Marlene
 Hepburn, Katharine
 Merman, Ethel
 Thompson, Kay

Known relationships with men:

 Bautzer, Greg
 Begelman, David
 Bogarde, Dirk
 Brynner, Yul
 Drake, Tom
 Fisher, Eddie
 Ford, Glenn
 Kennedy, John F

Khan, Prince Aly
Lanza, Mario
Lawford, Peter
Lear, Norman
Levant, Oscar
Mankiewicz, Joseph
Mason, James
Mercer, Johnny
Power, Tyrone
Remar, David
Rubirosa, Porfirio
Shaw, Artie
Sinatra, Frank
Stack, Robert
Tracy, Spencer
Walker, Robert
Welles, Orson

Married:

David Rose
Vincente Minnelli
Sid Luft & 2 others

Judy Garland was just four feet eleven and a half inches tall and had a curvature of the spine that caused her to hunch slightly. Throughout her years at MGM she always felt out of place among all the beautiful starlets like Lana Turner and Elizabeth Taylor that milled about her.

She was signed by MGM under unusual circumstances. After seeing her and Deanna Durbin sing, Mayer told an underling, 'hire the flat one'. He was referring to Durbin, who occasionally sang flat. The man thought he said 'hire the *fat* one', so he signed Garland to a contract.

Mayer insisted his young actresses sit on his knee during interviews to receive his 'fatherly' advice, and Judy Garland was no exception. He was known to fondle her breasts as they talked, and invite other executives to do likewise if they wished. In her early days at MGM she accepted such treatment as part and parcel of the movie business. Little wonder she sought comfort in the arms of her press secretary Betty Asher and other women. In time, she developed a tough exterior, as evidenced by her later bawdy sense of humor and her use of language more befitting a truck driver than a lady.

Her last real attempt at a comeback happened in 1963-4, when she signed a lucrative deal for a variety show on CBS television, one that promised her $24 million over the next few years. CBS executives stupidly slotted her show opposite the phenomenally successful *Bonanza* and it folded after twenty-six episodes.

CBS vice-president Hunt Stromberg Junior left an orchid and a card in her trailer after the final show. It read, 'You were just great. Thanks a lot. You're through'. In a way that insensitive note summed up the way she was viewed by the entertainment industry's powerbrokers. To them she was a commodity, nothing more, nothing less.

Wolf Man, The (1941)

Eight years after playing the old fortune-teller Maleya in this film, Maria Ouspenskaya died from burns when a fire consumed her Los Angeles apartment.

Women in Love (1969)

Oliver Reed and Alan Bates created a mainstream movie 'first' when they wrestled naked in the mud in this picture. Both men were reluctant to do the scene because each wondered if he could 'measure up' to the other. So they adjourned to a toilet block and compared 'equipment'. Satisfied they were of similar size, they went ahead with the scene.

Women, The (1939)

This film brought together on the same set, Joan Crawford, Rosalind Russell, Norma Shearer and Paulette Goddard and resulted in a monumental clash of egos. Goddard said Russell 'was good in it because she really was just a nasty bitch', and that, 'Shearer looked good because she had all her close-ups redone ten times'. Executives complained of one or more of the stars driving around the parking lot each day, intent on being the last one on the set. None could bear the thought of waiting on a co-star to make her appearance. Delays cost a fortune.

Upon observing some of the early rushes, Russell insisted on being billed above the title alongside Shearer and Crawford. When the studio refused, she feigned an illness and went home, where she stayed for the next four days. Production came to a standstill. Eventually, she was informed her demands had been met, so could she possibly return to the set. 'Hm. I'll take a stab at it', she magnanimously replied.

The Women was an all-female affair, except for the director George Cukor. All 135 speaking parts went to women, every animal in the picture was a female, every painting or art object was the work of a woman. Even every book in the set library was written by a female author. Yet, for all this obsessing with things feminine, ninety percent of the dialogue is about men!

The renowned costume designer known simply as Adrian helped shape the careers of numerous actresses by designing dresses and gowns that disguised their shortcomings. For example, he raised the waistlines on Norma Shearer's dresses to make her short legs seem longer, and extended the shoulders to make her hips appear narrower.

For Crawford he exaggerated her shoulders, and to suggest more femininity and minimize her aggressive stride, he put frills on her. He also made her wear extra-large brimmed hats to complement her wide mouth.

He quit films when ordered to create 'ordinary' clothes for Greta Garbo in her final film *Two-Faced Woman*. Adrian, whose real name was Adolph Greenburg, was a homosexual who counted among his lovers Francis Taylor, the father of Elizabeth Taylor. In 1959 he committed suicide.

Eight years after *The Women,* Rosalind Russell was considered a certainty to win an Oscar for her performance in *Mourning Becomes Electra.* Every poll in the country had her streets ahead of the opposition. On Oscar night she was virtually out of her seat in anticipation of victory when Loretta Young's name was called out instead. Continuing to her feet, she had little option but to lead the applause. Ironically, she was one of the actresses that turned down Young's award-winning role in *The Farmer's Daughter*. Russell's sleazy agent Fred Brissom was known by wags around Hollywood as 'The Lizard of Roz'.

Working Girl (1988)

Melanie Griffith met Don Johnson when she was fourteen and he was thirty-two. At the time he was her mother's co-star in *The Harrad Experiment*. Melanie and Don were living together before her sixteenth birthday. She married him when she turned eighteen, but they divorced four months later. Then they re-married. Then they re-divorced. Her cocaine habit began in her early teens and lasted for thirteen years.

Producer Don Simpson told of meeting her before she became a star. He said he was attending the Deauville Film Festival when she knocked on his hotel door one evening. 'It was Melanie Griffith, totally nude! She was only nineteen then – her body, you could bounce quarters of it. So I went to her room and partied till the sun came up. I mean, thank you God'.

Wrath of God, The (1972)

This was Rita Hayworth's final film. By then she was mentally sliding downhill at an alarming rate. Robert Mitchum, who secured the role for her, was deeply shocked by her deterioration. She could not remember a single line of script, nor was she capable of reading the 'idiot cards'.

Many of her scenes were shot from *behind* and her dialogue dubbed by another actress later. She was drunk nearly all the time and loudly abusive of everyone, especially any young women on the set. She was actually in the first stages of Alzheimer's, the illness that would kill her in 1987, not that any of this stopped Frank Langella from bedding her for several weeks before tiring of her and moving on.

Wuthering Heights (1939)

Prop man Irving Sindler was disappointed at not receiving a mention in the credits, so he contrived to ensure his work on the film would not go un-noticed. If you look closely at the scene shot in a cemetery, you will notice a gravestone prominently featured and bearing the inscription, 'I. Sindler - a good man".

Year of Living Dangerously, The (1983)

Method actor Sigourney Weaver stars opposite Mel Gibson, who was compelled to wear built up shoes for their scenes together because she is six feet tall. She took her Christian stage name, incidentally, from that of a minor character in *The Great Gatsby*.

Young Guns (1988)

William S Bonney, better known as Billy the Kid, is positively credited with just four solo killings in his brief life, although he had a hand in several more. The legend that he killed twenty-one men in his twenty-one years is false. Whether or not he was left or right handed is still a mystery. The only known photograph of him shows his gun on the left side, but some experts argue that the negative has been reversed.

Pat Garrett, the part-time lawman and killer of Billy the Kid, set up several ambushes to get his man. They resulted in at least three hapless innocents being gunned down in error because they vaguely resembled the outlaw. Finally, in Fort Sumner, New Mexico, Garrett waited in a darkened room for his unarmed prey and shot him dead without warning. Twenty or so years later, in 1908, Garrett was himself ignominiously shot dead from ambush as he stepped from a buggy to urinate in the road.

Between 1866 and 1900, about 20,000 people were shot to death on the American frontier. In 1877, the state adjutant of Texas posted descriptions of 5,000 known outlaws in the Rio Grande district alone! As a matter of interest, in the old west more cowboys died by drowning than from gunshot wounds, Indian attacks or stampedes. That was because very few of them could swim. On cattle drives they crossed scores of rivers and streams, and if a man got into trouble in the water there were few swimmers able to go to his rescue.

Young Lions, The (1958)

What must the odds be of the same German (Marlon Brando) who has a brief fling with Barbara Rush's character in Bavaria in 1938, getting shot by her American fiancée (Dean Martin) in a chance combat encounter seven years later? Writers really do expect audiences to swallow some tall tales.

Young Winston (1972)

For a movie supposedly intent upon historical accuracy and authenticity, the scene where a reporter questions Lady Churchill about her husband's rumored venereal disease is an inexplicable lapse. Even the lowliest of tabloids in the England of the 1890s would *never* have sent a reporter to grill the wife of a Cabinet Minister (and a peer of the realm to boot) about her husband's syphilis problem.

Zabriskie Point (1970)

Mark Frechette, the star of the 1970 flop *Zabriskie Point,* soon found his career foundering because of his drug addiction. In 1973, desperately in need of funds to support his habit, he and two others attempted to rob a bank. One of his accomplices was shot dead during the raid, while Frechette was captured and sentenced to the penitentiary for 6-15 years.

After being molested several times by persons unknown, he was found dead in the gymnasium in 1975, a 160 pound weight wedged across his throat. It has never been determined if his death at twenty-seven was a murder, an accident or suicide.

Zulu (1964)

The 2,000 Zulu extras in this had no concept of what acting was supposed to be. It was not until director Stanley Baker showed them an old Gene Autry western that they finally understood what they were expected to do. Each man wore his own personal battle attire in the movie. In the final scene, every warrior held out a piece of wood attached to two extra Zulu shields, each adorned by a fake head-dress, to give the impression of 6,000 combatants lining the hills.

Michael Caine went to London to audition for the role of the cockney soldier Private Hook, but was told he was too late. The part had already gone to Anthony Booth. As an afterthought, the producer asked him if he could do an aristocratic accent for the role of Lt. Bromhead, a much bigger part. This he was able to do, so at the age of thirty-one he was at last on his way to stardom.

It was not all plain sailing on Zulu, all the same. The early rushes of his scenes were awful and, if not for the intervention of Stanley Baker, he would most probably have been replaced. Caine spoke fifty-two lines in a shoot that lasted sixteen weeks, and received four thousand pounds for his performance. The movie grossed twelve million pounds. For a long time after he achieved celebrity status for his aristocratic pose as Bromhead, people he met for the first time were astonished to find he spoke with a broad Cockney accent.

South African born Nigel Green, who impresses as Color-Sergeant Bourne, died from an accidental overdose of sleeping pills in 1972 at the age of forty-eight.

Zulu made Baker a very wealthy man. He chose to move to Spain, play golf, and enjoy his money, rather than fully realize his potential as an actor. Diagnosed with cancer in 1976, he returned to Britain for treatment where he was unexpectedly knighted for his services to the British film industry. Some say the knighthood was bestowed because it was common knowledge he was dying. He passed away three months short of his fiftieth birthday.

Appendix

Suicides – Proven or Probable

ADAMS, Nick **Drugs** 'Rebel Without A Cause'

ADAMS, Stanley **Shot** 'North By Northwest'

ALEXANDER, Ross **Shot** 'Captain Blood'

ANGELI, Pier **Pills** 'Somebody Up There Likes Me'

ARMENDARIZ, Pedro **Shot** 'From Russia With Love'

BAGGETT, Lynne **Pills** 'D.O.A.'

BARRY, Don 'Red' **Shot** 'Red Ryder' Series

BATES, Barbara **Pills** 'All About Eve'

BECKETT, Scotty **Pills** 'King's Row'

BENNETT, Jill **Pills** 'Julius Caesar'

BLANDICK, Clara **Pills** 'The Wizard Of Oz'

BOYER, Charles **Pills** '**Gas**light'

BRANDIS, Jonathon **Pills** 'Never Ending Story 2'

CAPUCINE **Leapt to her death** 'North To Alaska'

CHEUNG, Leslie **Leapt to his death** 'Farewell My Concubine'

DALBERT, Suzanne **Pills** 'My Favorite Spy'

DANDRIDGE, Dorothy **Pills** 'Carmen Jones'

DARVI, Bella **Gas** 'The Egyptian'

DAVIS, Georgia **Shot** 'The Harvey Girls'

DUEL, Peter **Shot** 'Cannon For Cordoba'

ENTWHISTLE, Peg **Leapt to her death** 'Thirteen Women'

FOX, Sidney **Pills** 'Murders In The Rue Morgue'

GOODLIFFE, Michael **Leapt to his death** 'A Night To Remember'

HALL, Jon **Shot** 'The Hurricane'

HANCOCK, Tony **Pills** 'The Wrong Box'

HARRON, Robert **Shot** 'Intolerance'

HARTMAN, Elizabeth **Pills** 'A Patch Of Blue'

HARVEY, Rodney **Drugs** 'My Own Private Idaho'

HEMINGWAY, Margaux **Pills** 'Lipstick'

HUTCHENCE, Michael **Hanged** 'Frankenstein Unbound'

KEITH, Brian **Shot** 'Krakatoa – East Of Java'

LADD, Alan **Pills** 'Shane'

LANDIS, Carole **Pills** 'Four Jills In A Jeep'

Hollywood Warts 'N' All

LAWRENCE, Florence **Poison** 'Intolerance'

LEWIS, Ronald **Pills** 'Billy Budd'

McNAMARA, Maggie **Pills** 'Three Coins In The Fountain'

MORRIS, Chester **Pills** 'The Great White Hope'

MUNSON, Ona **Pills** 'Gone With The Wind'

O'NEAL, Peggy **Pills** 'Song Of The Open Road'

PELLICER, Pina **Pills** 'The One-Eyed Jacks'

PLATO, Dana **Pills** 'California Suite'

RAPPAPORT, David **Shot** 'Time Bandits'

RAWLINS, Judith **Pills** 'G I Blues'

ROBERTS, Rachel **Poison** 'Picnic At Hanging Rock'

SALMI, Albert **Pills** 'The Unforgiven'

SANDERS, George **Pills** 'All About Eve'

SCALA, Gia **Pills** 'The Guns Of Navarone'

SEBERG, Jean **Pills** 'Paint Your Wagon'

SLEZAK, Walter **Shot** 'Lifeboat'

SLOANE, Everett **Pills** 'Citizen Kane'

STEVENS, Inger **Pills** 'House Of Cards'

STRADNER, Rose **Pills** 'The Keys Of The Kingdom'

SULLAVAN, Margaret **Pills** 'The Mortal Storm'

THOMPSON, Carlos **Shot** 'Valley Of The Kings'

TWELVETREES, Helen **Pills** 'Times Square Lady'

VELEZ, Lupe **Pills** 'Mexican Spitfire'

VILLECHAIZE, Herve **Shot** 'The Man With The Golden Gun'

WEAVER, Doodles **Shot** 'Gentlemen Prefer Blondes'

WESSON, Dick **Shot** 'Calamity Jane'

WHITE, Carol **Drugs** 'The Fixer'

WILLIAMS, Kenneth **Pills** 'Carry On Cleo'

WILLIAMS, Pat **Pills** 'Sound Off'

WITHERS, Grant **Pills** 'My Darling Clementine'

WOODBURY, Doreen **Pills** 'The Shadow On The Window'

YOUNG, Gig **Shot** 'They Shoot Horses Don't They'

Hollywood Warts 'N' All

Accidental Deaths

AALIYAH *Air Crash* 'Romeo Must Die'

AAMES, Angela *Diet Pills* 'Bachelor Party'

ADRIAN, Iris *Earthquake* 'The Paleface'

BANNEN, Ian *Car Crash* 'The Flight Of The Phoenix'

BARRYMORE, Diana *Pills* 'Eagle Squadron'

BELUSHI, John *Drugs* 'The Blues Brothers'

CASSIDY, Jack *Fire* 'The Eiger Sanction'

CHANDLER, Jeff *Operation* 'Broken Arrow'

COLUMBO, Russ *Shot* 'Wake Up And Dream'

DARNELL, Linda *Fire* 'Forever Amber'

De WILDE, Brandon *Car Crash* 'Shane'

DEAN, James *Car Crash* 'Giant'

DELL, Dorothy *Car Crash* 'Little Miss Marker'

DENVER, John *Air Crash* 'Oh God!'

DICKSON, Gloria *Fire* 'They Won't Forget'

DORLEAC, Francoise *Car Crash* 'Genghis Kahn'

DRISCOLL, Bobby *Drugs* 'Song Of The South'

FREDERICK, Lynne *Choked to death* 'Schizo'

GARLAND, Judy **Drugs** 'The Wizard Of Oz'

GREEN, Nigel **Drugs** 'Zulu'

HAZEL, Hy **Choked** 'Anastasia'

HEXUM, Jon-Erik **Shot** 'The Bear'

HOLDEN, William **Bled to death** 'Sunset Boulevard'

HOWARD, Leslie **(casualty of war) Air Crash** 'Gone With The Wind'

JENNINGS, Claudia **Car Crash** 'The Man Who Fell To Earth'

JONES, Buck **Fire** 'Red Ryder' Series

KELLY, Grace **Car Crash** 'High Society'

KILBRIDE, Percy **Car Crash** 'Ma & Pa Kettle' series

KINNEAR, Roy **Fall from horse** 'Juggernaut'

KOVACS, Ernie **Car Crash** 'North To Alaska'

LEE, Belinda **Car Crash** 'The Belles Of St Trinians'

LEE, Brandon **Shot** 'The Crow'

LLEWELYN, Desmond **Car Crash** 'Thunderball'

LOMBARD, Carole **Air Crash** 'My Man Godfrey'

LOVELACE, Linda **Car Crash** 'Deep Throat'

LYNDE, Paul **Drowned** 'Send Me No Flowers'

MAHONEY, Jock **Car Crash** 'Tarzan's Three Challenges'

MANSFIELD, Jayne **Car Crash** 'The Sheriff Of Fractured Jaw'

MANTZ, Paul **Air Crash** 'The Flight Of The Phoenix'

MARTIN, Dean Paul **Air Crash** 'Backfire'

McGRAW, Charles **Bled to death** 'Spartacus'

McQUEEN, Butterfly **Fire** 'Gone With The Wind'

MEAD, William **Impaled in a fall** 'They Died With Their Boots On'

MIX, Tom **Car Crash** 'Riders Of The Purple Sage'

MORROW, Vic **Decapitated** 'Blackboard Jungle'

MUNDIN, Herbert **Car Crash** 'The Adventures Of Robin Hood'

MUNRO, Janet **Choked to death** 'Swiss Family Robinson'

MURPHY, Audie **Air Crash** 'To Hell And Back'

NELSON, Ricky **Aircraft Fire** 'Rio Bravo'

OUSPENSKAYA, Maria **Fire** 'The Wolf Man'

PHOENIX, River **Drugs** 'Stand By Me'

PRESLEY, Elvis **Pills** 'Love Me Tender'

ROBIN, Dany **Fire** 'Topaz'

THORBURN, June **Air Crash** 'The Cruel Sea'

TODD, Mike **Air Crash** 'Around The World In 80 Days'

TYLER, Judy **Car Crash** 'Jailhouse Rock'

URE, Mary **Choked to death** 'Where Eagles Dare'

WAYNE, Carol **Drowned** 'Heartbreakers'

WILLS, Beverly **Fire** 'Some Like It Hot'

WOOD, Natalie **Drowned** 'Rebel Without A Cause'

Murders – Proven or Probable

BARSI, Judith **Shot** 'Jaws-The Revenge'

BERENSON, Berry **Terrorist attack** 'Remember My Name'

CABOT, Susan **Beaten to death** 'Son Of Ali Baba'

COLBY, Barbara **Shot** 'California Split'

CRANE, Bob **Beaten to death** 'Auto Focus'

DEKKER, Albert **Asphyxiated?** 'Beau Geste'

DUNNE, Dominique **Strangled** 'Poltergeist'

EVANS, Barry **Beaten to death** 'Here We Go Round T. Mulb. Bush'

HARTMAN, Phil **Shot** 'Sgt. Bilko'

KUPCINET, Karyn **Strangled** 'The Ladies' Man'

LANZA, Mario **Assassinated?** 'Serenade'

MAXWELL, Jenny **Shot** 'Blue Hawaii'

MINEO, Sal **Stabbed** 'Rebel Without A Cause'

MITCHELL, Carolyn **Shot** 'The Cry Baby Killer'

MONROE, Marilyn **Assassinated?** 'All About Eve'

NGOR, Haing S **Shot** 'The Killing Fields'

NOVARRO, Ramon **Suffocated** 'Ben-Hur'

REEVES, George **Shot** 'From Here To Eternity'

SHAKIR, Tupac **Shot** 'Nothing But Trouble'

SMITH, Jay R **Shot** 'Our Gang' series

STAHL, Jennifer **Shot** 'Firehouse'

STRATTEN, Dorothy **Shot** 'They All Laughed'

SWITZER, Carl 'Alfalfa' **Shot** 'Our Gang' series

TATE, Sharon **Stabbed** 'Valley Of The Dolls'

TAYLOR, William Desmond **Shot** 'Anne Of Green Gables'

TODD, Thelma **Asphyxiated?** 'Horse Feathers'

The Author's Favorite 50 Movies of all Time

1 CASABLANCA Humphrey Bogart

2 THE GODFATHER PT 2 Robert de Niro

3 L A CONFIDENTIAL Russell Crowe

4 SINCE YOU WENT AWAY Claudette Colbert

5 DOUBLE INDEMNITY Barbara Stanwyck

6 LOVE ACTUALLY Hugh Grant

7 MIDNIGHT RUN Robert de Niro

8 PULP FICTION Samuel L Jackson

9 SHANE Alan Ladd

10 SENSE AND SENSIBILITY Emma Thompson

11 THE SEARCHERS John Wayne

12 CHICAGO Renee Zellweger

13 LAWRENCE OF ARABIA Peter O'Toole

14 MY COUSIN VINNY Joe Pesci

15 FROM HERE TO ETERNITY Burt Lancaster

16 SUPPORT YOUR LOCAL SHERIFF James Garner

17 HEAVEN KNOWS, MR ALLISON Robert Mitchum

18 PIRATES OF THE CARIBBEAN Johnny Depp

19 TWELVE O'CLOCK HIGH Gregory Peck

Selected Bibliography

Adler, Bill, 1987, Sinatra: The Man and the Myth, Signet, New York.

Agee, James, 1964, Agee on Film: Reviews and Comments, Beacon, New York.

Amburn, Ellis, 2000, The Most Beautiful Woman In The World, HarperCollins, New York.

Amburn, Ellis, 2002, Warren Beatty: The Sexiest Man Alive, Harper Entertainment, New York.

Anger, Kenneth, 1975, Hollywood Babylon, Straight Arrow, San Francisco.

Anger, Kenneth, 1984, Hollywood Babylon 11, Random Century, GB.

Arce, Hector, 1979, The Secret Life of Tyrone Power, William Morrow, New York.

Austin, John, 1994, Hollywood's Babylon Women, Shopolsky, New York.

Austin, John, 1994, Hollywood's Greatest Mysteries, Shopolsky, New York.

Bacon, James, 1976, Hollywood Is A Four Letter Town, Henry Regnery Company, Chicago.

Bacon, James, 1977, Made In Hollywood, Contemporary Books, Chicago.

Baxter, John. 1976. The Hollywood Exiles, Taplinger Publishing Company, New York.

Beauchamp, Cari & Behar, Henri, 1992, Hollywood On The Riviera, William Morrow & Co, New York.

Berg, A. Scott, 1989, Goldwyn: A Biography, Alfred A Knopf, New York.

Bergan, Ronald, 1992, The Life And Times Of The Marx Brothers, The Green Wood Publishing Coy, London.

Bergan, Ronald, 1986, The United Artists Story, Crown, New York.

Bergan, Ronald & Karney, Robyn, 1986, Movie Mastermind, Shuckburgh Reynolds, Hong Kong.

Billman, Larry, 1993, Betty Grable: A Bio-Bibliography, Greenwood, Westport, Conn.

Birchard, Robert S, 2004, Cecil B DeMille's Hollywood, The University Press of Kentucky.

Birtles, Jasmine, 2004, Chick Wit, Carlton Publishing Co, London.

Black, Shirley Temple, 1988, Child Star, Warner, New York.

Boland, Michaela and Bodey, Michael, 2004, Aussiewood, Allen & Unwin, Crow's Nest, NSW.

Bradford, Sarah, 1984, Princess Grace, Stein & Day, New York.

Brady, Frank, 1989, Citizen Welles, Charles Scibner's Sons, New York.

Bragg, Melvin. 1988. Richard Burton: A Life, Little, Brown, Boston.

Braun, Eric, 2002, Frightening the Horses: Gay Icons of the Cinema, Reynolds & Hearn Ltd, Richmond, Surrey.

Bret, David, 2000, Satan's Angel, Robson Books, London.

Brian, Denis, 1972, Tallulah, Darling: A Biography of Tallulah Bankhead, MacMillan, New York.

Brody, Louise, MacPherson, Don, & Welch, Julie, 1989, Stars Of The Screen, Conran Octopus, London.

Brown, Peter H, 1986, Reluctant Goddess, St. Martin's Press, New York.

Brown, Peter Harry & Patty Barham, 1992, Marilyn: The Last Take, Dutton, New York.

Brown, Peter Harry and Pat H. Broeske. 1996. Howard Hughes: The Untold Story, Dutton, New York.

Brynner, Rock. 1989. Yul: The Man Who Would Be King, Simon & Schuster, New York.

Buck, Pearl S. 1970. The Kennedy Women, Cowles, New York.

Buskin, Richard. 2001. Blonde Heart, Billboard Books, New York.

Cader, Michael, ed. 1994, 'Saturday Night Live': The First Twenty Years, Houghton Mifflin, Boston.

Callan, Michael Feeney, 2003, Richard Harris, Sex, Death & The Movies, Robson Books, London.

Cameron-Wilson, James & Speed, Maurice F, 1995, Film Review 1995-6, Virgin Books, London.

Cameron-Wilson, James, 1999, Film Review- 1999-2000, Reynolds & Hearn, Richmond, Surrey.

Cameron-Wilson, James, 2001, Film Review 2001-2002, Reynolds & Hearn, Richmond, Surrey.

Capell, Frank A. 1966. The Strange Death of Marilyn Monroe, Herald of Freedom.

Capra, Frank. 1971. The Name Above The Title, MacMillan Company, New York.

Carey, Gary, 1981, All The Stars In Heaven, E.

P. Dutton, New York.

Carter, Graydon & Friend, David, 2000, Vanity Fair's Hollywood, Thames & Hudson, London.

Cawthorne, Nigel, 1997, Sex Lives of the Hollywood Goddesses, Prism, London.

Cawthorne, Nigel, 1987, Sex Lives of Hollywood Idols, Prism, London.

Cher, as told to Jeff Coplon, 1998, The First Time, Simon & Schuster, New York.

Clinch, Minty, 1985, Burt Lancaster, Stein & Day, New York.

Cohen, Daniel & Susan, 1986, History of the Oscars, Bison Books, London.

Collier, Peter, 1990, The Fondas: A Hollywood Dynasty, Putnam, New York.

Collins, Bill, 1987, Bill Collins Presents The Golden Years Of Hollywood, Sun Books, South Melbourne.

Collins, Joan, 1984, Past Imperfect, Simon & Schuster, New, York.

Considine, Shaun, 1989, Bette and Joan: The Divine Feud, E. P. Dutton, New York.

Crane, Cheryl & Jahr, Cliff, 1988, Detour: A Hollywood Story, Arbor House, New York.

Crawford, Christina, 1978, Mommie Dearest, William Morrow, New York.

Crimp, Susan and Burstein, Patricia, 1988, Hollywood Sisters: Jackie & Joan Collins, Robson Books, London.

Cunningham, Ernest, 1998, The Ultimate Marilyn, Renaissance, Los Angeles.

Curtis, Tony and Barry, Paris. 1993. Tony Curtis: The Autobiography, William Morrow, New York.

Da, Lottie and Alexander, Jan. 1989, Bad Girls of the Silver Screen, Carroll & Graf, New York.

Davidson, Bill. 1990. Jane Fonda: An Intimate Biography, Dutton, New York.

Deacon, Richard. 1980. A History Of British Secret Service.

De Gregorio, George. 1981. Joe DiMaggio: An Informal Biography. Stein and Day, New York.

Dewey, Donald. 1997. James Stewart, Turner, Atlanta.

Dick, Bernard, 1997, City of Dreams: The Making and Remaking of Universal Pictures, University Press of Kentucky, Lexington, Kentucky.

Donnelley, Paul, 2003, Fade To Black, Omnibus Press.

Donnelley, Paul, 2003, Julia Roberts Confidential, Virgin Books, London.

Dougan, Andy, 2001, Michael Douglas: Out Of The Shadows, Robson Books, London.

Douglas, Edward, 2004, Jack: The Great Seducer, Harper Collins, New York

Douglas, Kirk. 1997. Climbing the Mountain: My Search for Meaning, Simon & Schuster, New York.

Douglas, Kirk, 1988, The Ragman's Son: An Autobiography, Simon and Schuster, New York.

Eames, John Douglas, 1975, The MGM Story, Crown, New York.

Eames, John Douglas, 1985, The Paramount Story, Crown, New York.

Edelman, Ray, and Kupferberg, Audrey F. 1996. Angela Lansbury: A Life on Stage and Screen, Carol Publishing Group, New York.

Edmonds, Andy, 1993, Bugsy's Baby: The Secret Life of Mob Queen Virginia Hill, Birch Lane, New York.

Edwards, Anne, 1977, Vivien Leigh, Simon & Schuster, New York.

Eels, George, 1973, Hedda and Louella, Warner Books, New York.

Eels, George, 1985, Robert Mitchum, Jove, New York.

Ehrenstein, David, 1998, Open Secret: Gay Hollywood, William Morrow & Co.

Eliot, Marc, 2004, Cary Grant – A Biography, Random House, New York.

Elley, Derek, edited by, 1999, Variety Movie Guide, Penguin Putnam Inc, New York.

Englund, Steven, 1984, Grace of Monaco, Doubleday, New York.

Epstein, Edward Z & Morella, Joe, 1991, Mia: The Life of Mia Farrow, Dell, New York.

Ewbank, Tim & Stafford, Hildred, 2001, Russell Crowe the Biography, Carlton Books, London.

Fairbanks, Jr., Douglas. 1988, The Salad Days, Doubleday, Garden City, New York.

Farber, Stephen, and Green, Mark, 1984, Hollywood Dynasties, Putnam, New York.

Fido, Martin. 1993. The Chronicle Of Crime, Carlton Books Ltd, London.

Finler, Joel W, 1988, The Hollywood Story, Crown, New York.

Fisher, Eddie, 1999, Been There, Done That, Thomas Dunne Books, New York.

Fleiss, Heidi, 2003, Panderings, Hour Entertainment, Los Angeles.

Fleming, E.

J. 2000, Hollywood Death and Scandal Sites, McFarland, Jefferson, N.

C.

Fleming, E.

J., 2004, The Fixers: Eddie Mannix, Howard Strickling & the MGM Publicity Machine, Kindle Edition.

Flynn, Errol, 1959, My Wicked, Wicked Ways, Putnam, New York.

Fontaine, Joan, 1978, No Bed Of Roses, William Morrow, New York.

Fornatale, Peter T, and Scatoni Frank R, 1999, Say Anything, Penguin Books, Middlesex.

Frank, Gerold. 1975. Judy, Harper & Row, New York.

Frank, Gerold, 1960, Zsa Zsa Gabor, World, Cleveland.

Freedland, Michael, 1983, The Warner Brothers, St. Martin's Press, New York.

Gabor, Zsa Zsa, with Wendy Leigh, 1991, One Lifetime Is Not Enough, Delacorte, New York.

Gardner, Ava, 1990, Ava: My Story, Bantam, New York.

Gehman, Richard, 1961, Sinatra and His Rat Pack, Belmont, New York.

Gentry, Curt. 1991. J. Edgar Hoover: The Man and the Secrets, Norton, New York.

Giancana, Sam and Giancana, Chuck. 1992. Double Cross: The Explosive Inside Story of the Mobster who

Controlled America, Warner Books, New York.

Gingold, Hermione, 1988, How To Grow Old Disgracefully, Cox & Wyman Ltd, Reading, Berks.

Giroux, Robert, 1990, A Deed of Death: The Story Behind the Unsolved Murder of Hollywood Director William Desmond Taylor, Knopf, New York.

Glatt, John, 1995, Lost in Hollywood: The Fast Times and Short Life of River Phoenix, Primus, New York.

Golden, Eve, 1991, Platinum Girl: The life and Legends of Jean Harlow, Abbeville, New York.

Goodall, Nigel, 1998, Winona Ryder, Blake, London.

Goodman, Ezra, 1961, The Fifty Year Decline and Fall of Hollywood, Simon & Schuster, New York.

Govoni, Albert, 1971, Cary Grant: An Unauthorized Biography, Henry Regnery, Chicago.

Granger, Stewart. 1981. Sparks Fly Upward, Putnam, New York.

Grant, Richard E. 1996. With Nails: The Film Diaries of Richard E. Grant, Picador, New York.

Graysmith, Robert, 1994, The Murder of Bob Crane, Berkley, New York.

Gregory, Adela and Speriglio, Milo. 1993. Crypt 33: The Saga of Marilyn Monroe – The Final Word, Birch Lane Press, New York.

Guiles, Fred Lawrence. 1982, Jane Fonda, Doubleday, Garden City, New York.

Guiles, Fred Lawrence1995. Joan Crawford: The Last Word, Birch Lane Press, New York.

Guiles, Fred Lawrence. 1984. Legend: The Life and Death of Marilyn Monroe, Stein and Day, New York.

Guiles, Fred Lawrence, 1980, Tyrone Power: The Last Idol, Berkley, New York.

Gussaw, Mel. 1971, Don't Say Yes Until I Finish Talking: A Biography of Daryl F. Zanuck, Doubleday, Garden City, New York.

Hadleigh, Boze, 1996, Hollywood Gays, Barricade Books, New York.

Halliwell, Leslie & Walker, John (ed), 2001, Halliwell's Film & Video Guide 2002, Harper Collins.

Harris, Warren G, 1974, Gable and Lombard, Simon & Schuster, New York.

Harris, Warren G, 1991, Lucy & Desi, Simon & Schuster, New York.

Harris, Warren G, 1988, Natalie & RJ: Hollywood's Star-Crossed Lovers, Berkley, New York.

Haspiel, James. 1991. Marilyn: The Ultimate Look at the Legend, Henry Holt, New York.

Haver, Ronald. 1980, David O. Selznick's Hollywood. Alfred A. Knopf, New York.

Head, Edith and Calistro, Paddy. 1983, Edith Head's Hollywood, E.

P. Dutton, New York.

Herman, Gary, 1982, Rock 'n' Roll Babylon, Plexus Publishing, London.

Heymann, C. David, 1995, Liz: An Intimate Biography of Elizabeth Taylor, Citadel/Carol, Secaucus, N.

J.

Higham, Charles, 1981, Bette: The Life of Bette Davis, MacMillan, New York.

Higham, Charles, 1980, Errol Flynn : The Untold Story, Doubleday.

Higham, Charles, 1977, Marlene: The Life of Marlene Dietrich, W.

W. Norton, New York.

Higham, Charles. ----. Olivia & Joan, New English Library, London.

Higham, Charles, 1984, Sisters: The Story of Olivia De Havilland and Joan Fontaine, Putnam, New York.

Hirschorn, Clive, 1979, The Warner Bros. Story, Crown, New York.

Holden, Anthony. 1993. Behind the Oscar, Simon & Schuster, New York.

Holden, Anthony, 1994, The Oscars, Little Brown & Company, Great Britain.

Hopkins, Jerry, 1981, Elvis: The Final Years, Playboy, New York.

Horan, James D., and Sann, Paul. 1954, Pictorial History of the Wild West, Crown, New York.

Hoskyns, Barney, 1996, Waiting For The Sun, Viking, Great Britain.

Hudson, Rock and Davidson, Sara. 1986, Rock Hudson: His Story, William Morrow, New York.

Jacobson, Laurie & Wanamaker, Marc, 1994, Hollywood Haunted: A Ghostly Tour of Filmland, Angel City Press, Santa Monica, Calif.

Jennings, Dean, 1992, We Only Kill Each Other, Pocket, New York.

Jewell, Derek. 1985. Frank Sinatra, Little, Brown & Company, Boston.

Jewell, Richard B., and Vernon Harbin. 1982. The RKO Story, Octopus Books, London.

Kaminsky, Stuart, 1980, Coop: The Life and Legend of Gary Cooper, St. Martin's Press, New York.

Kashner, Sam & MacNair, Jennifer, 2002, The Bad and the Beautiful: Hollywood in the Fifties, W W Norton & Co, New York.

Katcherm, George A, 1991, Eighty Silent Film Stars, McFarland, Jefferson, N.

C.

Katz, Ephraim, 1994, The Film Encyclopedia. 2nd ed, Harper Collins, New York.

Kelley, Kitty, 1981, Elizabeth Taylor: The Last Star, Simon and Schuster, New York.

Kelley, Kitty, 1986, His Way: The Unauthorized Biography of Frank Sinatra, Bantam, New York.

Kening, Dan et al, 1994, Too Young To Die, Signet, New York.

Kiernan, Thomas, 1980, The Roman Polanski Story, Delilah/Grove, New York.

Koppes, Clayton R, & Black, Gregory D, Hollywood Goes To War, Free Press, New York.

Kotsilibas-Davis, James and Loy, Myrna, 1987, Myrna Loy, Alfred A. Knopf, New York.

Lacey, Robert, 1994, Grace, Putnam, New York.

LaBrasca, Bob. 1988. Marilyn, Bantam, New York.

Ladowsky, Ellen, 1999, Julia Roberts, People Profiles, New York.

Lamarr, Hedy, 1966, Ecstasy and Me: My Life as a Woman, Bartholomew House, New York.

Lambert, Gavin, 1990, Norma Shearer, Knopf, New York.

Langella, Frank, 2015, Dropped Names: Famous Men and Women as I Knew Them, Harper, New York.

Laufe, Abe. 1969. Broadway's Greatest Musicals, Funk & Wagnalls, New Jersey.

Lawford, Patricia Seaton, with Ted Schwarz, 1988. The Peter Lawford Story, Carroll & Graf, New York.

Leff, Leonard J & Simmons, Jerold L, 2001, The Dame In The Kimono, University Press of Kentucky.

Levin, Martin, 1970, Hollywood & The Great Fan Magazines, Arbor House, New York.

Levy, Shawn, 1998, Rat Pack Confidential, Doubleday, New York.

Lewis, Jon E. 1996, The Mammoth Book of the West, Robinson, London.

Lewis, Judy, 1994, Uncommon Knowledge, Pocket Books, New York.

Love, Andrea, 1988, The Ultimate Celebrity Love Secrets & Scandals Book, Siena/Carlton, Bristol.

MacLaine, Shirley. 1995. My Lucky Stars: A Hollywood Memoir, Bantam, New York.

Madsen, Axel, 1994, Stanwyck, Harper-Collins, New York.

Madsen, Axel, 1996, The Sewing Circle: Hollywood's Greatest Secret, Robson, GB.

Mailer, Norman. 1967. Marilyn, Galahad Books, New York.

Maltin, Leonard (ed.), 2003, Leonard Maltin's 2004 Movie & Video Guide, Signet, USA.

Martin, Deana, 2004, Memories Are Made Of This, Harmony Books, New York.

Marx, Arthur, 1976, Goldwyn, Norton, New York.

Maxford, Howard, 2002, The A – Z of Hitchcock, B.

T. Batsford, London.

McGilligan, Patrick, 1991, George Cukor: A Double Life, Faber & Faber, London.

McLellan, Diana, 2000, The Girls: Sappho Goes To Hollywood, Weekly/St. Martin's, New York.

Meyers, Jeffrey, 2001, Gary Cooper: American Hero, Cooper Square Press, New York.

Morella, Joe and Epstein, Edward Z. 1985. Jane Wyman, Delacorte Press, New York.

Morley, Sheridan, 1988, Elixabeth Taylor, Pavilion Books, London.

Mosley, Leonard. 1984, Zanuck: The Rise and Fall of Hollywood's Last Tycoon, Little, Brown, Boston.

Munn, Michael, 1987, The Hollywood Murder Casebook, St. Martin's Press, New York.

Munn, Michael, 1991, Hollywood Rogues, Robson, GB.

Nash, J. Robert. 1992, World Encyclopedia of Organized Crime, Headline Book Publishing, London.

Naughton, John & Smith, Adam, 1998, Movies A Crash Course, Simon & Schuster, London.

Nickson, Chris. 1997. Emma: The Many Faces of Emma Thompson, Taylor Publishing Company, Dallas, Texas.

Niven, David, 1975, Bring On The Empty Horses, Hamish Hamilton, GB.

Noguchi, Thomas T., with Joseph DiMona. 1983. Coroner, Simon & Schuster, New York.

Norman, Barry, 1979, The Hollywood Greats, Hodder & Stoughton, GB.

O'Hara, Maureen with Nicoletti, John, 2004, 'Tis Herself, Simon & Schuster, New York.

Olson, James S., and Randy Roberts. 1995. John Wayne: American, Free Press, New York.

Osborne, Robert, 1989, 60 Years of the Oscar; The Official History of the Academy Awards, Abbeville Press, New York.

Otash, Fred. 1976. Investigation Hollywood, Regnery, Washington, D. C.

Paris, Barry. 1989, Louise Brooks, Alfred A. Knopf, New York.

Parish, James Robert, 2002, Hollywood Bad Boys, Contemporary Books, Chicago.

Parish, James Robert, 2002, Hollywood Divas, Contemporary Books, Chicago.

Parish, James Robert, 2001, The Hollywood Book of Death, Contemporary Books, Chicago.

Parish, Robert James, 2004, The Hollywood Book of Scandals, Contemporary Books, Chicago.

Parish, James Robert, 1974, The RKO Girls, Rainbow Books, New Jersey.

Parish, James Robert & Don. E. Stanke, 1975, The Glamour Girls, Arlington House, New Rochelle, N.

Y.

Parish, James Robert & Ronald L. Bowers, 1973, The MGM Stock Company: The Golden Era, Arlington House, New York.

Peary, Danny edited by, 1978, Close-Ups, The Movie Star Book, Workman Publishing Company Inc.

Peary, Danny, 1989, Cult Movies Three, Sidgwick & Jackson, London.

Pepitone, Lena and William Stadiem. 1979. Marilyn Monroe: Confidential, Simon & Schuster, New York.

Petzke, Ingo, 2004, Phillip Noyce: Backroads To Hollywood, MacMillan, Sydney, Australia.

Quinlan, David, 2000, Quinlan's Film Stars, Batsford, GB.

Quinlan, David, 1985, Quinlan's Illustrated Directory of Film Character Actors, B.

T. Batsford Ltd, London.

Quinlan, David, 1997, The Film Lover's Companion, Citadel Press, Secaucus, N.

J.

Quinn, Anthony, 1995, One Man Tango, Headline Book Publishing, Great Britain.

Quirk, Lawrence J. 1990, Fasten Your Seatbelts: The Passionate Life of Bette Davis, William Morrow, New York.

Rapf, Maurice, 1999, Back Lot, The Scarecrow Press Inc., London.

Reed, Rex. 1968. Do You Sleep in the Nude?New American Library, New York.

Rees, Nigel, 2000, Cassell's Movie Quotations, Cassell & Co, London.

Reid, Ed. 1972, The Mistress and the Mafia: The Virginia Hill Story, Bantam, New York.

Rhode, Eric, 1976, A History of the Cinema, Hill & Wang, New York.

Robb, Brian J. 1996. Johnny Depp: A Modern Rebel, Plexus Publishing, London.

Roberts, Randy and James Olson, 1995, John Wayne: American, Free Press, New York.

Robertson, Patrick, 2001, Film Facts, Aurum Press Ltd, London.

Rosten, Norman. 1973. Marilyn: An Untold Story, Signet, New York.

Rubin, Steven Jay, 1995, The Complete James Bond Movie Encyclopedia, Contemporary Books Inc.

Russo, Vito. 1987, The Celluloid Closet: Homosexuality in the Movies, Harper & Row, New York.

Sanello, Frank, 2000, Julia Roberts, Mainstream, Edinburgh, Scotland.

Sauter, Michael, 1995, The Worst Movies of All Time, Carol Publishing Group, Secaucus, NJ.

Sennett, Ted. 1986. Great Movie Directors, Harry N. Abrams, New York.

Server, Lee. 2001. Robert Mitchum: Baby I Don't Care, Picador, New York.

Shepherd, Donald, and Slatzer, Robert. 1985, Duke: The Life and Times of John Wayne, Doubleday, Garden City, New York.

Shiach, Don, 1995, The Movies, Anness Publishing Ltd, London.

Shindler, Colin. 1979. Hollywood Goes To War, Routledge and Kegan Paul, London.

Shipman, David. 1993, Judy Garland, Hyperion, New York.

Shipman, David, 1970, The Great Movie Stars: The Golden Years, Crown, New York.

Shulman, Irving. 1964. Harlow: An Intimate Biography, Bernard Geis Associates, New York.

Siegel, Scott & Barbara Siegel, 1994, American Film Comedy, Prentice Hall, New York.

Siegel, Scott & Barbara Siegel, 1990, The Encyclopedia of Hollywood, Facts On File, New York.

Slatzer, Robert F, 1992, The Marilyn Files, Shapolsky, New York.

Smith, Ronald L, 1992, Who's Who In Comedy, Facts on File, New York.

Spada, James, 1988, Grace: The Secret Life of a Princess, Dell, New York.

Spada, James, 1991, Peter Lawford: The Man Who Kept The Secrets, Bantam Books.

Speriglio, Milo. 1986. The Marilyn Conspiracy, Pocket Books, New York.

Steele, Joseph Henry, 1959, Ingrid Bergman, David McKay, New York.

Stenn, David, 2000, Bombshell: The Life and Death of Jean Harlow, Lightning Bug, Raleigh, N. C.

Strodder, Chris, 2000, Swingin'Chicks of the 60's, Sedco Publishing Co, San Raphael, California.

Summers, Anthony, 1980, Conspiracy, McGraw-Hill, New York.

Summers, Anthony, 1985, Goddess: The Secret Lives of Marilyn Monroe, MacMillan, New York.

Swanson, Gloria, 1980, Swanson on Swanson, Random House, New York.

Swindell, Larry. 1969. Spencer Tracy...A Biography, New American Library, New York.

Taraborrelli, J, 1987, Cher, St. Martin's Press, New York.

Temple Black, Shirley, 1988, Child Star, McGraw-Hill, New York.

Thomas, Bob, 1958, King Cohn: The Life and Times of Harry Cohn, Bantam, New York.

Thomas, Bob, 1983, Golden Boy: The Untold Story of William Holden, Berkley, New York.

Tomkies, Mike, 1972, The Robert Mitchum Story: 'It Sure Beats Working', Regnery, Chicago.

Torme, Mel, 1988, It Wasn't All Velvet, Zebra/Kensington, New York.

Turner, Lana. 1982, Lana: The Lady, The Legend, The Truth, E.

P. Dutton, New York.

Upton, Julian, 2004, Fallen Stars, Headpress/Critical Vision, Manchester, UK.

Ustinov, Peter. 1977. Dear Me, Heinemann, New Hampshire.

Wallace, Amy, Irving & Sylvia, Wallechinsky, David, 1993, The Secret Sex Lives Of Famous People, Chancellor Press.

Wallace, Irving; David Wallechinsky; Amy Wallace; and Sylvia Wallace, 1980, The Book of Lists 2, Morrow, New York.

Wallis, Hal, and Higham, Charles. 1980, Starmaker: The Autobiography of Hal Wallis, MacMillan, New York.

Walker, Alexander. 1990, Elizabeth: The Life of Elizabeth Taylor, Grove Weidenfeld, New York.

Walker, John, ed, 1999, Halliwell's Who's Who in the Movies. 13th ed. Harper Collins, London.

Wansell, Geoffrey. 1984. Haunted Idol: The Story of the Real Cary Grant, William Morrow, New York.

Ward, Geoffrey C. 1996. The West: An Illustrated History, The Orion Publishing Group, London.

Wayne, Jane Ellen. 1990, Ava's Men, St. Martin;s Press, New York.

Wayne, Jane Ellen, 1988, Cooper's Women, Hale, London.

Wayne, Jane Ellen, 1988, Crawford's Men, Prentice-Hall, New York.

Wayne, Jane Ellen, 1987, Gable's Women, Prentice-Hall, New York.

Wayne, Jane Ellen, 1981, Grace Kelly's Men, St. Martin's Press, New York.

White, David, 1984, Australian Movies To The World, Fontana Australia, Sydney.

Wiley, Mason and Bona Damien, 1988, Inside Oscar, Ballantine Books, New York.

Wiley, Mason and Bona, Damien. 1986. Inside Oscar: The Unofficial History of the Academy Awards, Ballantine, New York.

Williams, Esther & Diehl, Digby, 1999, The Million Dollar Mermaid, Simon & Schuster, New York.

Wilson, Earl, 1976, Sinatra: An Unauthorized Biography, MacMillan, New York.

Winters, Shelley. 1980. Shelley: Also Known As Shirley, Morrow, New York.

Winters, Shelley, 1990, Shelley 11: The Middle of My Century, Pocket, New York.

Young, Jordan R. 1975, Reel Characters, Moonstar Press, Beverly Hills.

Note: It has not always been possible to trace every copyright source. I would be glad to hear from any unacknowledged copyright holders.

Alan Royle

About The Author

Alan Royle was born in Fremantle, Western Australia in 1947. After working as a Labour Allocator on the Fremantle waterfront for many years he retired in 1997, then attended Murdoch University in 2001 where he earned four 'Outstanding Achievement Awards en route to a Bachelor of Arts in History before earning Honors with his thesis on the British Army in the Nineteenth Century.

From 2004 until 2014 he taught history units At Murdoch University, including 'Hollywood and History', as well as foundation and academic writing courses at Murdoch, Edith Cowan University and with the Open University of Australia (OUA). In 2012 OUA selected him as one of only four tutors nation-wide to be awarded the bi-annual Excellence Award in Melbourne.

He is now retired and living in Fremantle with his wife.

19193005R00450

Printed in Poland
by Amazon Fulfillment
Poland Sp. z o.o., Wrocław